Shrimad Bhagavad Gita

Shrimad Bhagavad Gita

Commentary by
Subhash C Kashyap

Vitasta

Published by
Renu Kaul Verma
Vitasta Publishing Pvt Ltd
4348/4C, Ansari Road, Daryaganj
New Delhi-110 002
info@vitastapublishing.com

ISBN 978-81-19670-78-9
© Subhash C Kashyap
First Edition 2024

MRP ₹ 495

All Rights Reserved.
No part of this publication may be reproduced, stored in a retrieval system, or transmitted in any form, or by any means—electronic, mechanical, photocopying, recording or otherwise—without the prior permission of the publisher.

Cover Design by Somesh Kumar Mishra
Printed by Chaman Enterprises, New Delhi

CONTENTS

Preface · vii
Introduction · xi
Gist of Cantos · xix

First Canto: Vishad-Yoga · 1
Second Canto: Sankhya-Yoga · 24
Third Canto: Karama-Yoga · 59
Fourth Canto: Gyana-Karma-Sanyasa Yoga · 79
Fifth Canto: Nishkam Karma-Sanyasa Yoga · 99
Sixth Canto: Dhyana-Yoga · 113
Seventh Canto: Gyana-Vigyana Yoga · 137
Eighth Canto: Akshar-Brahma Yoga · 150
Ninth Canto: Rajvidya-Rajguhya Yoga · 164
Tenth Canto: Vibhuti Yoga · 180
Eleventh Canto: Vishwaroop Darshan · 198
Twelfth Canto: Bhakti Yoga · 226

Thirteenth Canto:	Brahma-Vidya	235
Fourteenth Canto:	Gunatriya-Vibhag Yoga	250
Fifteenth Canto:	Puroshottam Yoga	263
Sixteenth Canto:	Devasursampad Vibhag Yoga	273
Seventeenth Canto:	Shraddhatraya-Vibhag-Yoga	284
Eighteenth Canto:	Moksha-Sanyasa Yoga	297

PREFACE

A humble student of Sanskrit in my pathshala and school days, I have no presumptions of being a Sanskrit scholar. Honestly, I am far from being anywhere near. Again, although, I took my Master's and Doctorate degrees in Philosophy and for some time taught postgraduate classes at the university, I have no credible credentials in Indian Philosophy either. My professional life made me more a lifelong student and practitioner of Law, Constitutional Studies, and Political Science.

I was attracted to Gita from my childhood days. As a 13-14 year-old at school, in my 9th and 10th classes (1942-44), I was a regular subscriber of *Prabuddha Bharata* and enjoyed reading several other publications of the Advaita Ashrama. I was very fascinated and influenced by the thinking of Swami Vivekananda. Later, while in the 11th and 12th classes at Meerut College (now CCS University), I was initiated by my Sanskrit teacher into the philosophy of Shrimad Bhagavad Gita. In fact, the crucial first three chapters were part of the compulsory curriculum for passing the Board Examination in Sanskrit. More significantly, my fascination for understanding the message of the Gita led me to reading all the sundry material that I could lay my hands on. Also, at that young age of 15-16 years, I organised a group of interested students and teachers under the aegis of an informal body we called the "Gita Parishad". We met fairly regularly once a week and discussed the teachings of Gita and its relevance in our daily lives. Whenever possible, visiting scholars, leaders and saints were invited to address us and clear our doubts and queries. When in 1946, I moved to the University of Allahabad, I carried the idea of the Gita Parishad along. We had opportunities of interacting with some of the most distinguished scholars and professors who also enjoyed meeting with our strange group of young seekers of the celestial knowledge. The Gita Parishad continued to function for a couple of years but somehow could not be sustained for long thereafter. I mention all this only to submit that my interest in trying to understand the teachings of Gita was ignited more than eighty years ago and has continued ever since.

During my long writing career, I can brag about having over a hundred published works – big and small including some multi-volume studies – and more than a thousand research papers and articles published in India and abroad. But, all these have been mainly in the area of Political Science, Constitution, Law and allied fields. I had however resolved that the last book from my pen would be a simple commentary on the Gita in Hindi and English. While beginning the 88th year of my life on earth, I felt that the time had come to take up this last writing venture. I am very happy that now while entering the 94th year of my life, I am able to say that I have finalised the manuscript of the work in both English & Hindi. I must admit that this has been the most satisfying part of my life's journey.

The Bhagavad Gita is probably among the most widely circulated books, one which has been translated repeatedly in almost all languages of the world and on which the largest number of commentaries have been written by some of the most distinguished scholars, saints and publicmen. It's teachings have impacted the lives of millions in India and in different and distant parts of the world. Some of the most eminent men in India and abroad felt their lives transformed by the philosophy propounded in the Gita. Some of the names that immediately come to mind include Lokmanya Balgangadhar Tilak, Swami Vivekananda, Sri Aurobindo, Vir Savarkar, Mahatma Gandhi, Edwin Arnold, Emerson, Thoreau, Walt Whitman, Carlyle, Albert Einstein, Will Durant, Oppenheimer, Aldous Huxley, Wilhelm von Humboldt, Arthur Isenberg and others.

When the father of the Atom Bomb, Oppenheimer witnessed its first detonation at Hiroshima on 16 July 1945, he remembered the Gita. Einstein "made the Gita as the main source of his inspiration and guidance for the purpose of scientific investigation and formation of his theories". Gita made Gandhi experience smiles "in the midst of overwhelming tragedies".

Beginning with Adi Shankaracharya, some of the most erudite scholars, intellectual giants, and the greatest of saints have written on the Gita or presented commentaries thereon. I respectfully acknowledge my debt to all the learned authors whose works I had occasion to read and which helped shape my views. I have benefitted and unhesitatingly borrowed from several treatises and other works like those of Tilak, Sri Aurobindo, Mahatma Gandhi, Swami Vivekananda, Paramhansa Yogananda, Swami Prabhupada, Swami Ranganathananda, Dr Radhakrishnan, Swami Swarupananda, Swami Vireshwarananda, Jaidayal Goenka, Swami Chinmayananda, Swami Gambhirananda and many others. A question may be legitimately asked about the justification for foisting on the readers yet another commentary on the Gita. I have no hesitation in admitting that I started writing it purely for self satisfaction and for crystalising in my own mind on how I have understood and tried to live or failed to live the practical philosophy of a happy life propounded by the Gita. Also, I view it as a part of my continuing endeavour to keep educating myself and remaining on a voyage of discovering and better understanding the sublime message of the Gita. I invite all my potential readers to join me on this voyage and find their own thrills. For me, the exercise has not always been easy or simple. There were occasions when for days together I had to grapple with the problem of understanding the essence of a verse and interpreting it in easily understandable language.

With due deference and apologies, I would like to submit that sometimes the text of a verse in original may appear simple and easy to comprehend before reading the learned commentators. May be at times some of them tend to read too much of spiritual or philosophical meaning and metaphysical depth or scholarly erudition in the text of every verse thereby making its explanation far more terse and complex for the ordinary readers. With the best of efforts, at times, it becomes difficult to relate the interpretation to the words in the original text. Also, the thought content has to be separated from the story content. Not every verse can be expected to contain the same sublime profundity of thought.

The format adopted by me is to first give the original text of the verse in Sanskrit followed by an analysis of its contents, meaning of each word and each part of the verse and then finally offer an integral view of the verse as a whole. At the end, after completing the commentary on each verse of the 18 cantos, somewhat subjective gists of each of the cantos have been added.

I have been intrigued by the use of some words to mean different things. Sometimes in the same verse a word is used more than once in different connotations. Depending on the context, the same word assumes somewhat different shades of meaning. In the matter of interpretation generally, the perspective is mine and I own full responsibility for any inadvertent error or inaccuracy in the understanding of words or ideas. Sometimes what I have said may not be literally true or strictly grammatically correct. I should acknowledge my tendency to twist and turn the meaning of words to buttress my views and tally with my basic perspective.

I am beholden to the distinguished publishers for joining me in this quest for understanding the message of Shrimad Bhagavad Gita and carrying it to a wide readership hopefully helping everyone of them to lead a happier, successful and more meaningful life.

I shall welcome any comments or suggestions for improvement from the esteemed readers.

New Delhi
10 May 2022, Subhash C Kashyap
sckashyap@gmail.com

INTRODUCTION

Shrimad Bhagavad Gita was not conceived as a separate or independent work. It was an integral part of one of the greatest epics of all times, the Mahabharata consisting of some ninety thousand to one lakh verses. The author was the legendary saint Krishna DvapayanVyasa, popularly known as Ved Vyasa. He was also the Grandfather of the five Pandava and the hundred Kaurava brothers who constituted the two warring camps in the larger Kuru family. The Great War - Mahabharata - lasted 18 days. Perhaps, it was symbolic that the epic Mahabharata was also divided into 18 Parts or Parvas which were further sub-divided into chapters. Again, it is the 18 Chapters (25 to 42) consisting of 700 verses in the Sixth Part titled Bhisma Parva that constitute what we know as Shrimad Bhagavad Gita or just Gita. It was the great saint Adi Shankaracharya who for the first time took out from the Mahabharta these 18 chapters or cantos with their 700 verses and gave them a separate and independent identity as a highly revered work containing presumably the deepest metaphysical thoughts and the quintessence of the Vedas and the Upanishads. As a crowning glory of his erudite commentaries on the Upanishads, Shankaracharya also produced an excellent commentary on the Gita. However, while the Upanishads were conceived and given shape in the quiet and peaceful ambience of the Ashramas of the Rishis in the sublime Himalayan heights, Shrimad Bhagavad Gita was said to have been born on the battlefield in the midst of intense activity with two large armies facing each other. What better example of practical Vedanta than Lord Krishna expounding at length the profoundest philosophy of life in the midst of intense activity of battle-ready warriors on both sides of the field. The most substantial part of the Gita is a discourse between Lord Krishna and Arjuna with the Lord asking Arjuna to fight and do his duty selflessly knowing fully well that the results are not in his hands.

The story content in the Gita flows from and is a part of the main narrative of the Mahabharata. It is simple and well-known. King Shantanu got infatuated with Satyavati, the daughter of a fishermen chief. Bhishma, Shantanu's son from his earlier wife Ganga, took a vow of celibacy to remain a life-long bachelor in order to assure Satyavati that only her progeny would succeed to the throne. Satyavati as a maiden happened to be the foster mother of a son from Rishi Parashar and this son was no other than Ved Vyasa himself, the author of Mahabharata. Married to Shantanu, Satyavati gave birth to two sons, Chitrangada and Vichitravirya. The former died young and the latter got the throne. The two wives of Vichitravirya, after his death, gave birth to two sons, Dhritarashtra and Pandu. Dhritarashtra, born blind, married Gandhari and begot a hundred sons, eldest being Duryodhana. Pandu married Kunti and Madri and gave birth to the five Pandavas. Although the five Pandavas and the hundred Kauravas were all scions of Kuru and belonged to the same dynasty, we find that practically throughout the epic Mahabharata, the sons of Dhritarashtra are known as Kauravas and the sons of Pandu as Pandavas.

Because the elder of the two sons of King Vichitravirya, Dhritarashtra was blind, Pandu ascended the throne. But, Pandu often remained away from the capital, engrossed in fighting battles to expand the frontiers of the kingdom, for most of the time, Dhritarashtra virtually functioned as the King. Following the early death of Pandu, his five young sons also came under the care of Dhritarashtra. The eldest among the 105 brothers was Yudhistara but Dhritarashtra was anxious to see his son Duryodhana succeed him. Duryodhana himself tried various evil plots to harm and even kill the Pandavas.

Lord Krishna, the spiritual master and ruler of Dwarka who was also a close relation as the nephew of mother Kunti, stood as a close advisor and protector of the Pandavas.

After losing everything including his four brothers in a sinister gambling match, Yudhistara staked wife Draupadi also and lost. Draupadi was dragged to the open court and humiliated. Ugly attempt was made to publicly strip her naked. Her honour was saved by Lord Krishna coming to her rescue. The Pandavas had to undertake twelve years of exile and stay away in jungles and one year of living incognito. Even after their return, Duryodhana refused to share the kingdom with the Pandavas. Lord Krishna himself tried his best to act as a messenger of peace to resolve the conflict through negotiation, accomodation and reconciliation but in reply to the willingness of Pandavas to settle for bare five villages only, Duryodhana retorted that he was not prepared to concede even a needle size land. War remained the only option.

Finally, the day arrived when the scions of the large Kuru dynasty, their close relatives, Kings, Princes, renowned warriors and large armies from all parts of the country gathered on the large Kurukshetra (meaning the land of the Kuru clan or the land of action) battlefield. All on the two sides were combat ready. And, it was here that the episode of Shri Bhagavad Gita opened with Dhritarashtra asking Sanjay about what was happening on the battle ground. Sanjay was the charioteer and close aide of the blind King Dhritarashtra who was anxious to be kept informed contemporaneously and concurrently of what was happening on the battlefield. Ved Vyasa had, therefore, bestowed on Sanjay special powers to keep viewing from a distance the happenings on the battlefield and simultaneously report them to King Dhritarashtra.

Before we start trying to interpret one by one the 700 verses of the Gita spread over its 18 cantos, a popular misconception needs to be cleared: King Dhritarashtra, Sanjaya, Arjuna, Duryodhana, Shri Krishna and others are all different characters in the Mahabharata and several of them find mention in the Gita. The author of the entire epic is believed to be Rishi Vyasa. While the historicity of Mahabharata cannot be doubted – the great battle did take place at Kurukshetra and Krishna did advise Arjuna – there is every danger of the many benign illusions created by the great author being misconstrued. Ved Vyasa's Mahabharata is unquestionably one of the greatest literary creations based on historical events but it is not history. Often, we tend to feel as if Lord Krishna himself is expounding at length the profound philosophies of Sankhya, Karma Yoga, Bhakti Yoga, Gyana Yoga etc while trying to persuade Arjuna to perform his duty and fight. Obviously, it is not conceivable that the extensive discourse could actually take place on the battlefield with the huge armies on the two sides waiting patiently for hours while the discourse continued. The great saint and creative genius that he was, Vyasa was building his elaborate philosophical edifice on the foundations of what Lord Krishna was believed to have said to Arjuna on the battlefield. The author of Gita is not Krishna but Ved Vyasa. Incidentally, 'Krishna' was also part of the first name of Ved Vyasa - Krishna Dvapayan. It is important to remember that it is Rishi Vyasa who gives words and ideas to the characters of the Mahabharata and it is he who speaks through Krishna, Arjuna, Sanjay, Dhritarashtra and others or the other way round *i.e.* the characters are made to speak through and in the language of Ved Vyasa.

Shrimad Bhagavad Gita is not a book of any religion or theology. The myth of identifying it as a book of Hinduism was the creation of the British colonial masters during the Company rule. Gita has been universally known for epitomising the highest and the most profound philosophical insights. It presents a complete philosophy of life, a holistic vision of the universe and a comprehensive and all inclusive world view. It's message has the potential to transform our lives to be more meaningful and make us happier beings. Gita is a treatise on human relationships, ethics and moral conduct, life skills and science and spirituality. Through skill development and raising of ourselves to super-conscious levels, Gita expects our transcendence to a knowledge state and collective or supreme consciousness levels.

Also, Gita has been variously described as a unique spiritual and intellectual discourse, an independent treatise on life and death and after-death, a message for humanity from God incarnate, Lord Krishna, a sublime course in yoga and it's facets of Karma (dutiful selfless action), Bhakti (worship of the Supreme) and Gyan (knowledge of the Ultimate), the way to win the perennial psychological struggle in the minds of men - the Mahabharata within - between the forces of evil and righteousness, good and evil, justice and injustice, with each person fighting his own battle of Kurukshetra for Dharma or Rule of Law. Gita may be seen as the best summation and gist or the end of the Vedas (Vedanta) and the quintessence of the Upanishads. The supreme contribution of Gita to our thought and life is the confluence, harmonisation, fusion or integration of the Gyan Yoga, Bhakti Yoga and Karma Yoga - of knowledge, devotion and action - of desireless action founded on the knowledge of Brahaman and devotion to God. The three are really not very different. Knowledge or Gyan of the philosophy of non-dualism and the devotional prayer and Bhakti of the believer in a personal God with the inevitable action or Karma without attachment to results, all meet in selfless action with the knowledge and realisation that whatever you call it - light, energy, Brahman, Atman, Spirit, Self, Consciousness or God - the ultimate reality is one and the same. It pervades all existence and knowledge and is the supreme reality within all that is sentient or insentient.

That Gita extols war and violence is an unfortunate perception. Perhaps, it would be best to view Bhagavad Gita as a stern warning against all the evil forces of violence and an invocation for lasting peace. Every possible effort is made by the Pandavas and by Lord Krishna himself to broker peace. But when it becomes a question of Justice, Lord Krishna himself exhorts Arjuna to stand up and fight for Dharma, (11-34) and what is right. Gita may be seen as a clarion call to learn from the sad experience of Mahabharata and avoid armed conflicts which result in massive destruction on all sides. Actually, as is well-known, Gita begins with Arjuna being grief-stricken, overtaken by doubts and despondency, remorse and delusion. He has to be persuaded by Krishna to remember his dharma and duty to fight for truth and a just cause.

What is necessary for us is to apply the wisdom of the Gita to various aspects of daily life. Teachings of Gita are for universal application and available to all those who are willing to be benefitted. Above all, Gita may be seen as the most practical philosophy for leading a fruitful and happy life. Our life is a long, arduous and an unending journey. Happiness in life comes through struggle, pain and suffering and requires constant action, service, sacrifice and selflessly ones duty without seeking results or desire for fruits or rewards of action and without expectation of any returns for sacrifices made or services rendered. The fight for justice against injustice and for good against evil is important but it should not be for any reward (5-3, 4&5). The source of much of our sorrow can be traced to our attachment to returns and expectation of rewards. Fulfillment and joy comes from doing ones duty, serving others and sacrificing for others. Doing good as a duty towards someone, and not for returns, is bound to bring real happiness. To take a simple example: parents love their children and do their duty towards them. This gives them happiness. But, if they do it expecting returns, things may be different. In many cases, desire for mundane personal gains in return may lead to disappointment and sorrow. The prime source of unhappiness is selfishness and desires. Looked at from another angle, the hard fact is that action in performance of our duty is largely in our control but not the results thereof. We have no authority to demand results.

karmanyevadhikarste ma phaleshukadachana

(for doing your duty, you certainly have every authority but you never have any control over the results of your action) (2-47), (5-2, 3&6-1&2).

Gita teaches us not to be torn between the opposites of pleasure and sorrow, gain and loss, good and evil, life and death, success and failure. Accepting these as coexisting realities and maintaining ones equilibrium is the highest form of yoga.

sukhe dukhe samay kritva labha labhau jaya jayo

(treating pleasure and sorrow, profit and loss and victory and defeat as the same (2(38)).

When one is inspired by some great purpose beyond selfish interests, all thoughts break their barriers, all limitations are off and (to use Patanjali's concept) consciousness expands in all directions, nothing remains unachievable. Gita crystallises the principles of secularism on the firm foundations of Vedanta philosophy. It teaches us that the ultimate reality is One. It pervades the entire universe and is identical with it. The same One is present in every one of us.

What appear to be many are actually the One only. The One God is everything, in everything, in everyone, everywhere. When we look upon all as God or the Self comes to encompass all, there can be no question of discrimination between man and man. All are equal and equally divine. The divine in one sees the same divine in all others. This realisation is the surest foundation for the essential unity of all mankind. The ultimate goal is the realisation and the manifestation of the Supreme Self, Param Atman or the Divine within (Param-Atma-Chaitanya).

Speaking through the central character, Lord Krishna, Maharishi Ved Vyas propounds his concepts of Gyan Yoga and ultimate metaphysical reality. Gita accepts the duality of Purusha and Prakriti, mind and matter, soul and body, unmanifest and manifest of sankhya philosophy propounded by Kapil Muni and other ancient sages, but adds that there is also the Supreme Self or the Param Atma or Purushottaama, Supreme Self or Soul.

Thousands of years ago, our ancestors asked the questions: "Who am I? Why am I here? What is the purpose of life?" The simple answer the Rishis found was that I am not the body, the senses nor the mind. I am the divine Self, Atman, Brahaman or Consciousness present in all beings. The ultimate reality is One and the realised soul sees this One in all living beings and all living beings in the Self. Gita asks us "to perform without any desire for fruits". Happiness comes from action. The realised souls live simple lives in ordinary minds and bodies. Their distinction comes from their dedication to a life of ceaseless action, deriving joy from the struggle in the cause of performing their duties and rendering selfless service. The end (purpose) of Vedas (Vedanta) and the essence of Upanishads is encapsulated in Gita's philosophy of desireless action or its invocation to do ones duty with pleasure and without looking for any rewards.

The progress made in the history of human civilisation during the recent centuries has revolutionised the means of physical comforts, material amenities and sensory enjoyments. But, the quantum of happiness has suffered a decline. There has been a tremendous erosion in values. Endless pursuit of success, power, money and sensory pleasures at any cost have become the supreme motivations in life and to achieve these we are willing to compromise all our basic values. We have become slaves to our ever insatiable desire or sheer greed. Rich and poor, the affluent and the deprived, all are unhappy. Today, all of us are standing at the crossroads of doubt and despondency waiting for our Krishna to appear and tell us where to go and what to do. Unfulfilled desires and expectations of rewards for our actions become the causes of our pain and grief. All human beings pine for satisfaction and happiness. Even the non-believers - atheists - believe in seeking happiness which is not the absence of sorrow or the feeling of pleasure. It is going beyond the two, transcendence of pleasure and sorrow. According to the teachings of Gita, real happiness does not come merely from sensory pleasures. It comes from within, from the joy of giving, helping others, selfless service and sacrifice, and from following certain basic values in life. Above all, what constitutes the essence of the teachings of the Gita is commitment to perennial action in performance of ones duty without seeking any rewards or returns thereof. We must not ever desert the battlefield of life and must fight on. The path is not very difficult. Kurukshetra is our field of action. One soon begins to enjoy selfless action for real happiness, here and now, on this earth. Shapes change. Life never dies. The journey continues.

GIST OF CANTOS

Somewhat subjective, the very quintessential take-home gist of each of the 18 cantos of Shrimad Bhagavad Gita for me, is as follows:

Canto 1
The huge armies of Pandava and Kaurava cousins are facing each other on the battlefield of Kurukshetra. Seeing on either side close relatives - grandfathers, fathers-in-laws, uncles, brothers, brothers-in-laws, sons, grandsons, gurus, and friends - Arjuna is overtaken by feelings of intense grief and remorse. "How can we be happy by killing our own people ?" he asks Lord Krishna, gives up his bow and arrows and takes a back seat.

Canto 2
Lord Krishna considers it to be unmanly and unbecoming for a brave hero like Arjuna to become a slave to such petty weakness on the battlefield. Completely overpowered by confusion, Arjuna surrenders completely. "I am your disciple", he says and begs Lord Krishna to tell him what is good for him to do. Krishna responds by asking Arjuna not to be concerned about those who do not deserve to be mourned. The wise do not grieve for the past or the future. The Atman (Self or Soul) is eternal, immutable and indestructible, it dwells in each one of us, it never dies, it is only the body that perishes. All the bodies that we see are subject to an end, as we discard old and worn out clothes and put on new one. The Atman in the same way drops old and worn out body and adopts a new one, the Atman is never born nor ever dies and can neither be killed nor can it kill anyone. There is nothing higher than to fight for ones principles and for performing ones duties.

Anyone who is born is sure to die and everyone who dies is bound to be born again. Knowing all this, Krishna asks Arjuna, "not to grieve and to arise and fight". Krishna warns his disciple that if he does not fight to discharge his duty, he shall lose honour which is worse than death, incur sin, people will utter unspeakable bad words about him and question his ability to fight.

Krishna proceeds to propound the profoundest life philosophy of performance of ones duty without attachment to fruits of action. Action is within our powers but results thereof are not in our control. We must, therefore, always continue to discharge our duties without bothering about fruits thereof. When a person gets over sensory desires, transcends the dualities of physical nature and attains equanimity in the face of pleasure and pain (joy and sorrow), profit and loss, victory and defeat, good and evil, light and darkness, life and death, etc he can be said to have got established in the state of pure Atman (supreme self (soul) consciousness). Yoga is the skill of doing ones job well, of performing ones responsibilities with efficiency and without attachment to any fruits of action. Mind has to become tranquil and steady so that the Self learns to remain satisfied in itself. True happiness that comes from the Self is different from and far superior to all sensory pleasures. One who is free from fear, anger and attachment to results of action is a truly realised soul. With a mind fixed and stabilised in the knowledge of the ultimate, one can be said to have attained the stage of yoga and of divine bliss. This is the highest yoga of equanimity (Samatva Yoga). As guided by wisdom (buddhi), it may also be called the Yoga of Wisdom or Knowledge (Buddhi Yoga or Sankhya Yoga).

Canto 3

Arjuna is again confused and finds contradictions in Krishna's formulation of the philosophy of unattached action and seeming superiority of yoga of knowledge. "Tell me one definite way", he asks. Krishna replies by reinforcing his earlier arguments and clarifies that actually there are two alternative paths of reaching the Supreme, of getting salvation or becoming one with the ultimate soul consciousness - one is through the meditative path of knowledge (Gyana Yoga) and the other is through the philosophy of action and performance of ones duties without looking for any rewards (Karma Yoga), but the two are not exclusive. "Whichever path you choose, action is essential", one should discipline the senses and perform his bounden duties as action without attachment is definitely far superior. But, it should also not be forgotten that all action has its source in creative consciousness coming from the supreme, imperishable Brahman and the ultimate goal of action without any attachment is also communion with the Supreme Self (Soul) Consciousness. Once that stage is reached, there remains no action or duty to be performed. Thus, there is no contradiction and the two paths of knowledge and action - of Gyana Yoga and Karma Yoga - merge.

Those who are regarded by the people as their icons and role models have to be specially careful to set a good example by their conduct of performing their duties through selfless action. What they do is bound to be followed by others.

Canto 4

Lord Krishna says that when virtue wanes and vice prevails, to protect the virtuous and punish the wicked and to establish righteous conduct (Dharma), He descends on earth from time to time. In whatever way one worships Him, He responds accordingly, whichever path men may follow, it converges on the path to Him. In other words, every path is divine, equally valid and leads to Him alone. The four-fold caste division of society is based on the nature of work done by each (i.e. it was not intended to be based on birth). Everyone should perform ones own duties. We need to understand what is meant by duty or unattached action. Ultimately, all action concludes in the knowledge of the Supreme (Brahman). In this universe there is nothing that is not Brahman. The one who realises the supreme truth of unattached action and of oneness with the One has reached the ultimate destination of union with the Supreme Self (Soul) Consciousness. It can also be understood as the individual soul (Self) merging in the collectivity of soul consciousness or as a river meeting the ocean.

Canto 5

Renouncing all action or taking complete Sanyasa and pursuing Karma Yoga or action without desiring its fruits, both the paths are good but between the two, it is better to remain dedicated to selfless action, because renunciation also requires action. Actually, all the three paths of Knowledge (Sankhya or Gyana), Renunciation (Sanyasa) and Selfless Action (Karma Yoga) are not very different. Anyone who sincerely follows either path gets to enjoy the benefits of all and reaches the ultimate aim of self realisation and union with Supreme Self (Soul) Consciousness. A true Yogi is one who has conquered his self, has achieved full control over the senses, has a pure soul and seeing his self in all beings, is dedicated to selfless action. Those who have realised self consciousness stand emancipated and feel one with the same Self in all others. This is the ultimate stage for the embodied individual soul joining the Supreme Soul Consciousness. One who has reached the Supreme, enjoys bliss within the Self, his mind remains steady and undisturbed with pleasure or pain, gain or loss, success or failure etc. Equipped with the knowledge of the Supreme, the happiness that he gets by meditating on it is eternal and not subject to diminution or decay. Endowed with inner light, bliss and happiness, he has become one with Supreme Soul Consciousness and a true Yogi.

Canto 6

Krishna keeps iterating again and again his central teaching of the superiority of Karma Yoga meaning action in the performance of ones duty without any attachment to results thereof or interest in objects of sensory gratification. A Yogi is better than the learned (gyani) and the one who renounces the world. In fact, a true Karma Yogi is also a true sanyasi i.e. one who is committed to a life of renunciation. The ultimate aim of both is to reach the Supreme Self. The Yogi sees all living beings in the Self and treats them equally. Also, the Self lives in all living beings. When by practising yoga, the mind is fully controlled, a state of tranquility is reached and the Self is satisfied that it sees only the Self in the Self. This is the state of the union of the individual soul with the Supreme Soul Consciousness. The Yogi, realising the oneness of all life rises above all dualities and knows that the same Supreme Soul Consciousness pervades all beings or all are one and the same.

Canto 7
Krishna explains to Arjuna how to reach Him (the Supreme) or, in other words, how to achieve self-realisation. Whatever exists comes out of the ocean of the Supreme Soul or self-consciousness and merges in the same. This is the source of all the fragrance on earth, brightness in fire, intellect in intelligence and radiance of the powerful. This is what holds all beings together. The Supreme is immutable and beyond all qualities (gunas). Knowing that everything is ultimately the same Supreme, the wise (gyani) take shelter in its worship. "In whatever form anyone worships me, I definitely strengthen his faith in that very form" says Lord Krishna making the point that all paths lead to the same. The ultimate transcendental reality is that of Supreme Soul (Self) Consciousness and selfless action.

Canto 8
Arjuna asks Krishna to explain to him the concepts of the Supreme (Brahman), the Soul/Self (Atman), consciousness etc. Krishna says that the Supreme is indestructible and dwells in every individual as the universal Self/Soul Consciousness. Yoga seeks to realise the union between the Self in our individual beings and the supreme universal Self. Krishna goes on to speak about rules for sitting in yogic meditation, importance of the divine syllable "Om", best time for departure from the world etc.

Canto 9
Personifying in Himself the One Supreme, Lord Krishna proceeds to share with Arjuna the way to be relieved of the cycle of life and death and attain Moksha or ultimate salvation. Nature creates all the animate and inanimate beings and the world keeps revolving the cycle of creation and annihilation. Only unhealthy minds put their faith and hope in all sorts of gods, ghosts, spirits, demons and devils. Those with great souls and divine nature take shelter in the Supreme

Immutable One and worship Him only as the origin of all that exists and as the master of the universe. Those engaged in selfless yogic action and faithful discharge of their duties without desiring any returns are the dearest to the Lord. Even a wicked person who takes refuge in Him will soon turn righteous and the individual soul will become one with Supreme Soul Consciousness.

Canto 10
Krishna again says that as the Supreme Lord of the universe, He is the origin and master of all that exists and the various qualities of mind, body, life and soul also are born of Him alone. He is the Supreme Soul (Self) situated in the hearts of all living beings and is their beginning, their middle and their end. His attributes are endless. He is consciousness.

Canto 11
After hearing Krishna's discourse on spiritual science, Arjuna's delusion stands fully dispelled and he realises that his Self and Krishna's Self are the same and one with the Supreme Self. Arjuna says: "O my Supreme Lord! I wish to see you in your divine form". Lord Krishna shows to Arjuna His cosmic (universal) form. It is a miraculous vision of many mouths, many eyes, body decorated with many celestial ornaments and raised weapons. The Lord is wearing celestial garlands and dresses with many divine perfumes smeared all over the body. Mouths opening on all sides and emitting blazing fire, make it the most wonderful sight of the Eternal. Even the luminosity of a thousand suns would be no match to the effulgence of the cosmic (universal) form of the Lord (the Supreme Self). Arjuna sees at one place in the body of the One, the God of gods (the cosmic self) and the entire universe. Arjuna says, he is seeing the Lord in infinite forms, boundless from all sides, with unlimited number of arms, bellies, mouths and sun and moon as His eyes, with a crown, a mace and a disc, glowing from all sides with lot of radiance, very much like burning fire and immeasurably bright sunshine all around making it difficult for anyone to look towards the Lord. Groups of gods are seen entering into the cosmic

body. Some of them have folded hands and appear frightened. Hosts of great sages and realised souls are seen worshipping the Lord with excellent hymns. Arjuna also sees all the greats on the side of Kauravas and many warriors on his side rushing into the mouths of the cosmic body made fearful by the terrible teeth. As the rivers rush towards the ocean or as the moths enter the blazing fire with full force only to die, all the warring kings of the world are entering the blazing cosmic mouth. Krishna flags the point that the warriors on the opposite side would not last even if Arjuna and his army do not kill them. They, in fact, already stand slain and he is only an instrument. Therefore, Krishna in his universal form exhorts Arjuna to proceed to destroy them all. He adds: "Do not be disturbed, just fight. You will conquer all the enemies". Arjuna is thrilled but awe-stricken, he begs Krishna to return to His normal form.

Canto 12
After upholding the validity of all the paths - of selfless action (performance of ones duties without desiring any rewards), higher knowledge, meditation and renunciation - and asserting that there is no conflict between them, none of them is exclusive or stand-alone, in fact, they often merge, Krishna proceeds to tell Arjuna how the path of worship and devotion is better and easier for reaching the Supreme. If those who have controlled their senses, renounced all fruits of action and are engaged in the service of other beings, worship the Lord with single-minded devotion, they can certainly realise Him. Knowledge is better than practice, meditation is superior to knowledge and action without attachment to fruits is the most highly valued. A true Yogi and devotee dear to the Lord should not be offensive or have ill-will towards anyone, should be friendly and compassionate to all, free from false ego always forgiving and contented, self-controlled, independent, free, unattached, pure, competent, strong-willed, of settled mind and intelligence, free from joy, envy, fear, sorrow and anxiety, equipoised and same in pleasure and pain.

Canto 13

Krishna says that the yoga of oneness or non-dualism and search for the knowledge of the Self leads one to the state of bliss in the Supreme Soul (Brahaman) that covers all, creates, sustains and destroys all. Though one and indivisible, it seems to stand as if divided in all living beings. Some see the Supreme Soul within their individual embodied self consciousness through meditation, some experience it through Sankhya Yoga, others reach the Supreme Self by following the path of Karma Yoga meaning selfless action or performance of duty without attachment to its fruits only he sees the imperishable Supreme Self equally present in all living beings.

When one sees thus, he achieves the stage of Supreme Self (Soul) Consciousness (Brahaman, the Supreme or the Absolute).

Canto 14

Krishna goes on to describe three natural qualities (gunas) or modes of Sattva, Rajas and Tamas (righteousness/goodness, passion and evil/ignorance) which keep the Supreme Soul (Param Atman) in the confines of the body. Goodness is attached to happiness and knowledge. Passion is born of the desire for sensory gratification, attachment to material objects acquired and action with desire for its fruits. Evil coming from ignorance leads to delusion, idleness and madness. The three gunas keep the embodied Soul in bondage.

At a time, anyone of the three may dominate the other two. When sensory openings bring knowledge, goodness dominates. When rajo guna dominates, greed, longing, unrest and result-oriented activity grow. When mode of ignorance becomes predominant, darkness, idleness (avoidance of duty) and delusion arise. When one rises above these three modes, only then he can be freed from birth, death, old age and sorrows, reach the Supreme, remain the same in sorrow and pleasure, condemnation and praise, endearing and disagreeable, honour and dishonour.

Canto 15

Krishna further explains to Arjuna the nature of the Supreme. One who is free from false pride and delusion, has achieved control over sensory desires and stays the same in the face of opposites like pleasure and pain, can hope to reach unfazed the ultimate objective of the union with the Supreme Self. The individual soul is not outside or different from the Supreme Self (Soul). It is limited only by being embodied. While the body perishes, the soul is imperishable. As distinguished from individual embodied souls, Supreme Soul may be seen as the principle of the all-embracing collectivity of pure soul consciousness or the One Supreme Self Consciousness or Param Atma Chatanya .

Canto 16
Krishna says that there are two kinds of living beings in the world - the divine (noble) and the demonic (evil-minded). The qualities of the two are described in depth. For example, fearlessness, purity of heart, getting established in yoga and knowledge, charity, ontology over the senses, sacrifice, study of spiritual works, penance and simplicity etc. happen to be the attributes of those of divine nature. Ostentation, arrogance, self-conceit, anger, rudeness etc. are some of the attributes of those of demonic nature. One who disregards scriptures and remains engaged in acts of lust can neither attain perfection nor happiness and can never reach the supreme destination of union of the embodied Self with the Supreme Self.

Canto 17
Krishna explains that faith happens to be of three kinds depending on the nature of the embodied. It may be in goodness (sattvika), in passion (rajasika) or in ignorance (tamasika). The food that we eat is also of these three kinds according to the likes of persons in three categories. For example, food that is cold, foul-smelling, stale, tasteless or filthy is dear only to those in the quality of ignorance (of tamasika nature). Also, any offerings made in sacrifice, donations given in charity, penance practised or good deeds done without faith are all meaningless both here in this life and also after death.

Canto 18

Responding to the day's last query by Arjuna, Krishna clarifies the concepts of renunciation and sacrifice: renunciation of all action performed with a desire for material fruits is sanyasa (renunciation of worldly life) and action to abandon the results thereof is tyaga (sacrifice). One should never give up acts involving sacrifice, charity and penance because these purify minds. It is best to continue to perform ones duties. Since no embodied self can completely renounce all action, anyone who renounces the fruits of action is called a renouncer.

Krishna describes three kinds of happiness: one, what looks like poison in the beginning but ultimately results in nectar is an example of goodness (sattvika) born of the understanding that concerns itself with the satisfaction of the Self. Two, the happiness that comes from the coming together of the senses with sensory objects and which at the beginning seems to be like nectar but at the end works like poison, is considered to be in the mode of passion (rajasika). Three, that happiness which at the beginning as also at the end is self-deluding and is born of sleep, laziness and illusion, is said to be of the quality of ignorance (tamasika). Each person performing his own duty can attain the highest realisation/as performing ones duty with defects is better than other's duty well-done. Krishna warns Arjuna: "If depending on your self-conceit, you think you will not fight, this resolve will fail as your nature will compel you to fight. You will feel helpless and will have to do even that what you do not desire (you will have to fight whether you like it or not)". At the end, Arjuna's delusion is destroyed, his doubts are dispelled and he agrees to go ahead and fight the righteous war. Sanjaya who reported the whole discourse concludes by saying:

> "Where there is the master of yoga, Lord Krishna and the holder of Gandiva, Arjuna, there is surety of prosperity, victory, happiness and firmness of policy."

First Canto

VISHAD-YOGA
Yoga of Grief

(1)

धृतराष्ट्र उवाच
धर्मक्षेत्रे कुरुक्षेत्रे समवेता युयुत्सवः।
मामकाः पाण्डवाश्चैव किमकुर्वत संजय॥१-१॥

*Dhritashtra uvacha
dharmakshetre kurukshetre samaveta yuyutsavah,
mamakah pandavashchaiva kimakurvata sanjaya (1.1)*

Dhritarashtra | uvacha : said/spoke/asked | Dharmakshetre : on the field of dharma - the land of eternal (natural) law | Kurukshetre : at the place named after the Great King Kuru/the field of action | samveta : gathered/assembled together/arrayed | yuyutsavah : eager to fight | mamakah : mine | Pandava : Pandu's sons | cha : and | aiva : also | kim : what | kurvat : did/do | Sanjaya | Dhritarashtra asks Sanjaya

O Sanjaya! what did my and Pandu's sons assembled at Kurukshetra, on the field of dharma, eager to fight, do?

The huge armies of the five Pandava and 100 Kaurava cousins are assembled on the field of Kurukshetra. They are facing each other and are eagerly awaiting orders to begin the fight. (The Kaurava King, Dhritarashtra is blind and is staying at the palace at Hastinapur, far away from the scene of the battle. But, he is anxious to remain informed of what is happening on the battlefield. Rishi Ved Vyasa has bestowed on Sanjaya, the charioteer and chief aide of Dhritarashtra, special powers to see and listen from a distance and act as a transmitter and live reporter to the King). At the very beginning of Shrimad Bhagavad Gita, in the first verse, Dhritarashtra is asking Sanjaya to tell him about what his sons and Pandu's sons are doing on the battlefield. Rishi Ved Vyasa, the creator of the great epic Mahabharata of which Gita is an integral part, calls the battlefield dharmakshetra as he wishes to underline his conviction that the battle is between the forces of good and evil, truth and untruth, justice and injustice. It is for establishing Dharma, which is the eternal law of nature or, in modern terminology, the Rule of Law.

(2)
संजय उवाच
दृष्ट्वा तु पाण्डवानीकं व्यूढं दुर्योधनस्तदा।
आचार्यमुपसंगम्य राजा वचनमब्रवीत्॥१-२॥

Sanjaya uvacha
drishtva tu pandavanikam vyudham duryodhanastada
acharyamupasangamya raja vachanamabravit (1.2)

Sanjaya | uvach : said | drishtva : having seen | tu : but/and | Pandavanikam : the armed forces of Pandavas | vyudham : in battle array/in military formation | Duryodhanastada : then (after) acharyam | Guru Dronacharyaupsangamya : going near raja : kingvachnam : wordsabravit : /spoke | Sanjaya : said

O King! Having seen (the strength of) the armed forces of the Pandavas in battle array, Duryodhana (the eldest son of Dhritarashtra and claimant to the throne) went near the acharya (Guru Dronacharya) and spoke the (following) words :

(3)
पश्यैतां पाण्डुपुत्राणामाचार्य महतीं चमूम्।
व्यूढां द्रुपदपुत्रेण तव शिष्येण धीमता॥१-३॥

pashyaitam panduputranam acharya mahatim chamum
vyudham drupadputrena tava shishyena dhimata (1.3)

pashya : see | etam : this | Panduputranam : of Pandu's sons/Pandavas | Acharya : Guru Dronacharya | mahatim : large | chamum : army | vyudham : in battle array/arranged in battle formation | Drupadputren : son of Drupada | tav : your | shishyen : disciple | dhimata : bright /wise

O my Guru! see this large army of the sons of Pandu, arranged in battle formation by your bright disciple, son of Drupada.

King Drupada was the father of Draupadi, who was married to the Pandavas. There was a history of sharp differences between Guru Dronacharya and King Drupada. Drupad's son, Dhrastadyuman is a military strategist. He has put the Pandava army in battle formation. Duryodhana wants Dronacharya to have a look at what has been done for the Pandavas by his disciple, Dhrastadyuman.

(4)

अत्र शूरा महेष्वासा भीमार्जुनसमा युधि
युयुधानो विराटश्च द्रुपदश्च महारथः॥१-४॥

*atra shura maheshvasa bhimarjuna sama yudhi
yuyudhano viratascha drupadashcha maharathah (1.4)*

atra : here | shura : brave warriors | maheshvasa : with mighty bows | Bhima-Arjuna : Bhima and Arjuna | sama : like /equal | yudhi : in the matter of fighting | Yuyudhano : Virata | cha : and | Drupadah | cha : and | maharathah : great warriors

Here (on the battlefield, on the side of Pandavas), there were several brave bowmen and great warriors like Yuyudhana, Virata and Drupada who, in the matter of fighting, were equal to Bhima and Arjuna.
It seems that Duryodhana wanted to impress on Dronacharya that the Pandava side not only had distinguished heroes like Bhima and Arjuna but there were many others who were equally good fighters.

(5)

धृष्टकेतुश्चेकितानः काशिराजश्च वीर्यवान् ।
पुरुजित्कुन्तिभोजश्च शैब्यश्च नरपुङ्गवः ॥१.५॥

*dhrishtaketush chekitanah kashirajashcha viryavan
purujit kuntibhojascha shaibyashcha narapungavah (1.5)*

Dhrishtaketush | Chekitanah | Kashiraja | cha : and /also | viryavan : powerful | Purujit | Kuntibhoja | cha : and /also | Shaibyash | cha : and /also | nara-pungavah : eminent human beings /icons of society

Other very powerful warriors present on the side of Pandavas are Dhrashtakeu, Chekitana and Kashiraja, also eminent human beings (icons of society) like Purujit, Kuntibhoja and Shaibya

(6)
युधामन्युश्च विक्रान्त उत्तमौजाश्च वीर्यवान् ।
सौभद्रो द्रौपदेयाश्च सर्व एव महारथाः ॥१-६॥

yudhamanyushcha vikranta uttamoujashcha viryavan
saubhadro drapadeyashcha sarva eva maharathah (1.6)

Yudhamanu | cha : and | vikranta : brave | Uttamauja | cha : and | viryavan : powerful /strong | Saubhadro | Draupdeyash | cha : and | sarva : all | aiva : surely | maharathah : great warriors

(Also present on the side of Pandavas are) mighty Yudhamanu and powerful Uttamauja and brave son of Subhadra (Abhimanyu) and the sons of Draupadi, all surely great warriors (fighters from chariots).

(7)
अस्माकं तु विशिष्ठा ये तान्निबोध द्विजोत्तम ।
नायका मम सैन्यस्य संज्ञार्थं तान्ब्रवीमि ते ॥१-७॥

asmakam tu vishishtha ye tannibodha dwijottama
nayaka mama sainyasya sanjnartham tanbravimi te (1.7)

asmakam : our /on our side | tu : also /but | vishishtha : specially powerful/ distinguished | ye : who | tan : them | nibodh : for information | dwijottama : o! the best of Brahmins /the most eminent of the learned | nayaka : generals | mama : my | te : to you | sanyasya : of the army | sanjnartham : for information | tan : to you | bravimi : I am speaking | te : to you

O the most eminent of the learned (the best of the Brahmins, Guru Dronacharya)! I tell you that on my side also, there are especially talented generals to lead the armed forces. After drawing the attention of Guru Dronacharya to the military formation and distinguished warriors on the side of Pandavas, Duryodhana turns towards his own side to assure the Acharya that the Kaurava army is also not without eminent generals.

(8)

भवान्भीष्मश्च कर्णश्च कृपश्च समितिंजयः ।
अश्वत्थामा विकर्णश्च सौमदत्तिस्तथैव च ॥१-८॥

bhavanbhishmashcha karanashcha kripashcha samitinjayah
ashvatthama vikarnashcha saumdattis tathaiva cha (1.8)

bhavan : yourself | Bhishma | cha : and | Karan | cha : and | Kripa | cha : and | samitimjayah : one who always wins in war | Ashvatthama | Vikarna | cha : and | Saumadatti | Jayadratha

Continuing, Duryodhana addresses Guru Dronacharya, thus: Apart from your own distinguished self, we have several outstanding persons like Bhishma (Pitamaha, grandfather of all the Pandavas and Kauravas), Karna (foster brother of the five Pandavas and eldest son of Kunti, born before her marriage with Pandu), Kripacharya (brother-in-law of Dronacharya), Ashwatthama (son of Dronacharya), Vikarna (one of the Kaurava brothers), Saumdatti (son of Saumdatta, also known as Bhurishrava) and Jayadratha (brother-in-law of the Kauravas married to the only sister of the 100 Kaurava brothers), all eminent warriors known to be invariable winners in all battles.
(Some texts do not mention the name of Jayadratha here and instead put the words 'tathaiva cha'. Obviously, addition of the name Jayadratha seems to add meaning and so makes more sense).

(9)

अन्ये च बहवः शूरा मदर्थे त्यक्तजीविताः ।
नानाशस्त्रप्रहरणाः सर्वे युद्धविशारदाः ॥१-९॥

anye cha bahavah shura madarthe tyaktajivitah
nanashastrapraharanah sarve yuddha-visharadah (1.9)

anye : others | cha : and | bahavah : several | shura : brave warriors | madarthe : for my sake | tyaktjivithah : prepared to sacrifice their lives | nana : many | shastrapraharnah : well-versed in using weapons | sarve : all | yudhavisharadah : highly talented in warfare matters

And, there are several other brave warriors who are ready to sacrifice their lives for my (Duryodhana's) sake and many who are well-versed in using weapons. All of them are highly talented in matters of war.

(10)
अपर्याप्तं तदस्माकं बलं भीष्माभिरक्षितम् ।
पर्याप्तं त्विदमेतेषां बलं भीमाभिरक्षितम् ॥१-१०॥

aparyaptam tadasmakam balam bhishmabhirakshitam
paryaptam tvidmetesham balam bhimabhirakshitam (1.10)

aparyaptam : inadequate / some commentators, however, translate it as immense or unlimited | tat : that | asmakam : our | balam : strength, power | Bhishma | abhirakshitam : protected by | paryaptam : adequate /some commentators have translated this word as limited | tu : but /however | idam : this | itesam : of these | balam : strength, power | Bhima | abhirakshitam : under the protection of

Protected by Bhishma, our strength is inadequate but under the protection of Bhima their's is adequate.
This implies that Duryodhana is trying to impress upon Guru Dronacharya the inadequacies or weaknesses on his side, but if the word 'aparyapatam' is translated to mean 'unlimited' and the word 'paryapatam' is to mean 'limited', as some commentators have done, the meaning of this verse is reversed to mean that Duryodhana is sure of the superiority of his army commanded by the great Bhishma and the opposite army of the Pandavas under Bhima being inferior.

(11)
अयनेषु च सर्वेषु यथाभागमवस्थिताः ।
भीष्ममेवाभिरक्षन्तु भवन्तः सर्व एव हि ॥१-११॥

ayaneshu cha sarveshu yathabhagamavasthitah
bhishmamevabhirakshantu bhavantah sarva eva hi (1.11)

ayaneshu : at special points on the battlefield | cha : and | sarveshu : all | yathabhagam : as in different parts | avasthita : situated /stationed | Bhishmam : of Bhishma | aiva : surely | abhirakshantu : protect | bhavantah : all of you | sarva : all | aiva hi : certainly

(Addressing all the warriors on his side of the battlefield, Duryodhana says:) All of you stationed at special points in different parts must certainly protect (give full support to) Bhishma Pitamaha (the commander of the armed forces on the Kaurava side).

(12)
तस्य संजनयन्हर्षं कुरुवृद्धः पितामहः ।
सिंहनादं विनद्योच्चैः शङ्खं दध्मौ प्रतापवान् ॥१-१२॥

*tasya sanjanayan harsham kuruvriddhah pitamahah
simhanadam vinadyochchaih shankham dadhmau pratapavan (1.12)*

tasya : his | sanjanayan : generating | harsham : joy | Kuruvradhah pitamaha : the most elderly, grandfather of the Kuru dynasty/Pitamaha Bhishma | singhanadam : lion like roar | vinadya : raise sound | uchchaih : on a high pitch | sankham : conch shell | dadhmau : blew | pratapavan : valiant

The grand old man of the Kuru dynasty, the valiant Bhishma Pitamaha blows the conch on a high pitch, making a loud sound resembling a lion's roar and thereby generating joy in the heart of Duryodhana.

(13)
ततः शङ्खाश्च भेर्यश्च पणवानकगोमुखाः ।
सहसैवाभ्यहन्यन्त स शब्दस्तुमुलोऽभवत् ॥१-१३॥

*tatah shankhashcha bheryashcha panavanakagomukhah
sahasaivabhyahanyanta sa shabdastumuloabhavat (1.13)*

tata : then/thereafter | sankha : conch shells | cha : and | bherya : large drums /nagare | cha : and | panavanaka : small drums and kettle drums / dhol, mridangam etc. music | instruments | gomukhah : cow horns | sahasa : suddenly | aiva : surely | abhyahanyant : sounded | sa : that | shabda : word/ sound | tumula : tumultuous/very loud/terrific | abhavat : happened

(After Bhishma blows his conch, thereby announcing the beginning of the battle), all of a sudden, several large and small musical instruments (conch shells, drums - big and small, bugles, cymbals, trumpets, cow horns etc.) make a tumultuous sound.

(14)
ततः श्वेतैर्हयैर्युक्ते महति स्यन्दने स्थितौ ।
माधवः पाण्डवश्चैव दिव्यौ शङ्खौ प्रदध्मतुः ॥१-१४॥

*tatah shvetairhayairyukte mahati syandane sthitau
madhavah pandavashchaiva divayou shankhau pradadhamatuh (1.14)*

tata : then/thereupon | shvetai : white | hayai : horses | yukte : yoked | mahati : large | syandane : charriot | Madhava : Krishna /charioteer of Arjuna, believed to be the reincarnation of God Vishnu | Pandava : Pandu's son Arjuna | cha : and | divyau : divine, celestial | aiva : surely, also | shankhau : conch shells | pradadhamatuh : sounded/blew

Thereupon, Lord Krishna and Arjuna mount on the large charriot driven by white horses also blow their divine conch shells.

(15)
पाञ्चजन्यं हृषीकेशो देवदत्तं धनञ्जयः ।
पौण्ड्रं दध्मौ महाशङ्खं भीमकर्मा वृकोदरः ॥१-१५॥

*panchajanyam hrishikesho devaduttam dhananjayah
paundrum dadhmau mahashankham bhimakarma vrikodarah (1.15)*

Panchajanyam : the name of the special conch shell of Lord Krishna | Hrishikesho : another name for Lord Krishna | Devaduttam : the name of the conch shell of Arjuna | Dhananjayah : another name of Arjuna meaning winner of wealth | Paundrum : the name of the conch shell of Bhima | dadhmau : blew | maha : large | shankham : conch shell | bhimakarma : one doing great deeds i.e. Bhima | vriakodarah : one with a big stomach/a big eater i.e. Bhima

Lord Krishna blows his conch shell Panchajanyam, Arjuna blows his conch shell Devaduttam and the voracious eater and doer of great deeds Bhima blows his large conch shell named Paundrum.

(16)
अनन्तविजयं राजा कुन्तीपुत्रो युधिष्ठिरः ।
नकुलः सहदेवश्च सुघोषमणिपुष्पकौ ॥१-१६॥

anantavijayam raja kuntiputro yudhishthirah
nakulah sahadevashcha sughosha manipushpakau (1.16)

Ananatavijayam : meaning one that is eternally victorious, the conch shell of | Yudhishtirah | raja : king | Kuntiputro : son of Kunti, Yudhishtirah/ Nakulah/Sahadeva | cha : and | Sughosha : the name given to the conch shell of Nakula | Manipushpakau : the conch shell of Sahadeva

King Yudhishtira, son of Kunti, blows his conch shell Ananatavijayam, Nakula blows his conch shell Sughosha and Sahadeva blows his Manipushpaka.

(17)
काश्यश्च परमेष्वासः शिखण्डी च महारथः ।
धृष्टद्युम्नो विराटश्च सात्यकिश्चापराजितः ॥१-१७॥

kashyashcha parmeshvasah shikhandi cha maharathah
dhrishtadyumno viratascha satyakischaparajitah (1.17)

Kashya : the king of Kashi /Kashi Naresh | cha : and | parmeshvasah : the eminent archer, one with an excellent bow, Shikhandi | cha : and | Maharathah : great warrior | Dhristadyumna | Virata : King Virata | cha : and | Satyaki | aparajitah : invincible

The eminent archer, the king of Kashi (Kashi Naresh) and the great warrior, Shikhandi, Dhristadyumna, Virata and invincible Satyiki

(18)
द्रुपदो द्रौपदेयाश्च सर्वशः पृथिवीपते ।
सौभद्रश्च महाबाहुः शङ्खान्दध्मुः पृथक्पृथक् ॥१-१८॥

drupado draupadeyashcha sarvashah prithvipate
saubhadrashcha mahabahuh shankhandadhmuh prithak prithak (1.18)

Drupada : King of Panchal | Draupadeya : sons of Draupadi | cha : and | sarvashah : all | prithvipate : master of the earth/King | Saubhadra : son of Subhadra (Abhimanu) | cha : and/also | mahabahuh : one with long (powerful) arms | sankhandadhmuh : blew horns | prithak prithak : separately

King Drupada, sons of Draupadi and O! King, all others including Abhimanu, blow horns separately, one by one.

(19)
स घोषो धार्तराष्ट्राणां हृदयानि व्यदारयत् ।
नभश्च पृथिवीं चैव तुमुलो व्यनुनादयन् ॥१-१९॥

sa ghosho dhartarashtranam hridayani vyadarayat
nabhashcha prithivim chaiva tumulo abhyanunadayan (1.19)

sa : that | ghosha : strong sound | Dhritarashtranam : in the Dhritarashtra camp | hirdayani : hearts | vyadarayat : pierced/shattered | nabha : sky/heaven | cha : and | prithivim : the earth | chaiv : and also | tumul : fierce/terrific | vyanunadayan : reverberating/echoing

That terrific sound reverberating all over the earth and heaven shatters the hearts of those in the Dhritarashtra camp.

(20)
अथ व्यवस्थितान्दृष्ट्वा धार्तराष्ट्रान्कपिध्वजः ।
प्रवृत्ते शस्त्रसंपाते धनुरुद्यम्य पाण्डवः ।
हृषीकेशं तदा वाक्यमिदमाह महीपते ॥१-२०॥

atha vyavasthitan drishtva dhartarashtran kapidhwajah
pravritte shastrasampate dhanurudyamya pandavah
hrishikesham tada vakyam idam aha mahipate (1.20)

atha : then | vyavasthitan : standing battle ready/ in military array | dristava : seeing | Dhritarashtran : those related to Dhritarashtra | kapidhwajah : with the monkey (Hanuman) emblem on the flag | pravratte : about to strike/begin shooting | shastrasampate : raising the bow and releasing the arrow | dhanu : bow | u dyamya : raising | Pandavah : son of Pandu, here refers to

Arjuna | Hrishikesha : Lord Krishna | tada : thereupon | vakyam : sentence | idam : this | aha : said | mahipate : O! King

O! King, thereupon, Arjuna said to Lord Krishna
At this time, seeing the forces in the Dhritarashtra camp, Arjuna, whose flag has an Hanuman emblem raises his bow and is prepared to shoot his arrow.

(21)
अर्जुन उवाच
सेनयोरुभयोर्मध्ये रथं स्थापय मेऽच्युत ॥१-२१॥
Arjuna uvacha
senayor ubhayor madhye ratham sthapaya meachyuta (1.21)

senayor : of armies | ubhayo : both | madhye : in the middle | ratham : charriot | sthapaya : station | me : me | Achut : Lord Krishna:

O! Lord Krishna, please take my chariot and station me in the middle of the two armies,

(22)
यावदेतान्निरिक्षेऽहं योद्धुकामानवस्थितान् ।
कैर्मया सह योद्धव्यमस्मिन् रणसमुद्यमे ॥१-२२॥
yavadetan niriksheham yoddhukaman avasthitan
kairmaya saha yoddhavyam asmin ranasamudyame (1.22)

yavad : as long as/until | etan : these | nirikshe : seeing carefully | aham : I | yoddhukaman : eager to fight | avasthitan : stationed | kai : whose | maya : me | saha : with/together | youddhavyam : having to fight | asmin : this | ransamudyame : in war like business, attempt at conflict

until I am able to carefully see these battle-hungry people firmly stationed in the field on the opposite side with whom I have to fight in this war.

(23)

योत्स्यमानानवेक्षेऽहं य एतेऽत्र समागताः ।
धार्तराष्ट्रस्य दुर्बुद्धेर्युद्धे प्रियचिकीर्षवः ॥१-२३॥

*yotsyamanan aveksheham ya eteatra samagatah
dhartarashtrasya durbuddher yuddhe priyachikirshavah (1.23)*

yotsyamanan : those going to fight | avekshe : shall (like to) see | aham : I | ya : that | ete : these | atra : here | samagatah : arrived | Dhritarashtrasya : son of Dhritarashtra meaning Duryodhana | durbudhe : evil-minded | yudhe: in war | priyachikirshavah : well-wishers

I shall like to see all those who, wishing to please the evil-minded Duryodhana, have arrived here on the battlefield with a desire to fight for him.

(24)

संजय उवाच
एवमुक्तो हृषीकेशो गुडाकेशेन भारत ।
सेनयोरुभयोर्मध्ये स्थापयित्वा रथोत्तमम् ॥१-२४॥

*Sanjaya uvacha
evamukto hrishikeso gudakeshan bharata
senayor ubhayor madhye sthapayitva rathottamam (1.24)*

Sanjaya | uvacha : said | aivam : thus | ukta : told/spoken to | Hrishikesha : another name for Lord Krishna meaning one who has control over the senses | | Gudakesha : a name for Arjuna meaning one who has conquered sleep | Bharata : descendant of King Bharat, Dhritarashtra | senaya : of the armies | ubhaya : both sides | madhye : in the middle | sthapayitva : stationing | rathotamam : excellent charriot

Sanjaya said: 'O king!' Having been so spoken to by Arjuna, Lord Krishna drives the excellent chariot to the middle and stations it between the armies of both sides.

(25)
भीष्मद्रोणप्रमुखतः सर्वेषां च महीक्षिताम् ।
उवाच पार्थ पश्यैतान्समवेतान्कुरूनिति ॥१-२५॥

bhishma dronapramukhtah sarvesham cha mahikshitam
uvacha partha pashyaitan samavetan kuruniti (1.25)

Bhishma : Bhishma Pitamaha, the grand old man | Drona : Guru Dronacharya, the common teacher of all the Pandavas and Kauravas | pramukhtah : in front of/ in the presence of | sarvesham : all | cha : and | mahikshitam : lords of the earth /kings and chiefs from different parts of the world | uvacha : said | Partha : Arjuna | pashya : look | etan : all these | samvetan : gathered | Kurun : descendants of Kuru, the Kauravas | iti : thus

Thus, in front of Bhishma Pitamaha, Guru Dronacharya and all the lords of the earth (kings and chiefs from different parts of the world present on the battlefield), Lord Krishna asks Arjuna to look at all the Kauravas gathered on the battlefield.

(26)
तत्रापश्यत्स्थितान्पार्थः पितृ नथ पितामहान् ।
आचार्यान्मातुलान्भ्रातृ न्पुत्रान्पौत्रान्सखींस्तथा ॥१-२६॥

tatrapashyat sthitan parthah pitrin atha pitamahan
acharyan matulan bhratrin putran pautran sakhims tatha (1.26)

tatra : there | apashyat : saw | sthitan : present | Parthah : Arjun | pitrnatha : fathers | pitamahan : grandfathers | acharyan : teachers | matulan : maternal uncles | bhratrin : brothers | outran : sons | pautran : grandsons | sakhim : friends | tatha : also | and

Arjuna realises that those present (on the battlefield) include fathers, grandfathers, teachers, maternal uncles, brothers, sons, grandsons and friends.

(27)

श्वशुरान्सुहृदश्चैव सेनयोरुभयोरपि ।
तान्समीक्ष्य स कौन्तेयः सर्वान्बन्धूनवस्थितान् ॥१-२७॥

shvasuran suhridash chaiva senayor ubhayor api
tansamikshya sa kounteyah sarvan bandhun avasthitan (1.27)

shvasuran : fathers-in-law | suhridash : well-wishers | cha : and | eva : surely | senayo : of the armies | ubhaya : on both sides | api : also | tan : them | samikshya : on seeing | sa : he | Konteyah : son of Kunti, Arjuna | sarvan : all | bandhun : relatives | avasthitan : situated, standing

Seeing all those present on the battlefield, Arjuna realises that there are fathers-in-laws, well-wishers and other relatives on both sides.

(28)

कृपया परयाविष्टो विषीदन्निदमब्रवीत् ।
अर्जुन उवाच
दृष्ट्वेमं स्वजनं कृष्ण युयुत्सुं समुपस्थितम् ॥१-२८॥

kripaya parayavishto vishidann idam abravit
Arjun uvacha
drestvemam svajanam krishna yuyutsum samupasthitam (1.28)

krapaya : compassion | paraya : of a high order | avishta : overtaken | vishidan : grieving | idam : thus | abravit : spoke | drestve : seeing | imam : these | svajanam : close relatives/kinsmen | Krishna : Lord Krishna | yuyutsum : in a fighting mood/battle array | samupasthitam : present

Overtaken by compassion of a high order and grief stricken, Arjun spoke thus.
Arjuna said: O Krishna, I am seeing all these close relatives present here in a fighting mood.

(29)

सीदन्ति मम गात्राणि मुखं च परिशुष्यति ।
वेपथुश्च शरीरे मे रोमहर्षश्च जायते ॥१-२९॥

sidanti mama gatrani mukham cha parishushyati

vepathush cha sharire me roma harshash cha jayate (1.29)

sidanti : getting cold/ trembling/ quivering | mama : my | gatrani : limbs of my body | mukham : mouth | cha : and | parishushyati : is drying up | vepathu : trembling | cha : and | shrire : on the body | me : may | roma-harsh : hair standing on end | cha : and | jayate : is happening/ taking place

I feel limbs of my whole body are having quivers, my mouth is drying up and my hair are standing on ends.

(30)
गाण्डीवं संस्रते हस्तात्त्वक्चैव परिदह्यते ।
न च शक्नोम्यवस्थातुं भ्रमतीव च मे मनः ॥ १-३० ॥
gandivam sramsate hastat tvak chaiva paridahyate
na cha shaknomy avasthatum bhramativa cha me manah (1.30)

Gandivam : Arjuna's bow named Gandiva | sransate : is slipping | hastat : from the hands | tvak : skin | cha : and | aiva : for sure | paridahyate : is on fire/ is burning | na : not | cha : also | shaknomi : I can | avasthatum : remain standing | bhramativa : is almost getting confused | cha : also | me : my | manah : mind

My Gandiva is slipping from my hands and my skin is burning. Also, I cannot remain standing anymore. My mind is also much confused.

(31)
निमित्तानि च पश्यामि विपरीतानि केशव ।
न च श्रेयोऽनुपश्यामि हत्वा स्वजनमाहवे ॥ १-३१ ॥
nimittani cha pashyami viparitani keshava
na cha shreyo nupashyami hatva svajanam ahave (1.31)

nimittani : causes/forebodings | cha : also | pashyami : I see | vipritani : adverse things | Keshava : Lord Krishna | na : nor | cha : also/and | shreya : good | nupashyami : foresee | hatva : by killing/ slaying | swajanam : close relatives/ kinsmen | ahave : in the fight

O Krishna! What I see are forebodings of something adverse happening. Also, I do not see any good in slaying my close relatives in the fight.

(32)
न काङ्क्षे विजयं कृष्ण न च राज्यं सुखानि च ।
किं नो राज्येन गोविन्द किं भोगैर्जीवितेन वा ॥१-३२॥

*na kankshe vijayam krishna na cha rajyam sukhani cha
kim no rajyena govinda kim bhogair jivitena va (1.32)*

na : nor/ not | kankshe : seek/desire | vijayam : victory/ win | Krishna : O My Lord! Krishna | na : nor | cha : also | rajyam : kingdom | sukhani : pleasures | cha : also | kim : what | no : our | rajyena : from kingdom | Govinda : Lord Krishna | kim : what | bhogair : enjoy | jivitena : from life/living

O My Lord! I do not seek victory, nor do I desire the pleasures of the kingdom, what (satisfaction can we derive from) our kingdom, Krishna, and how can we have any joy in living (when all our kinsmen are killed).

(33)
येषामर्थे काङ्क्षितं नो राज्यं भोगाः सुखानि च ।
त इमेऽवस्थिता युद्धे प्राणांस्त्यक्त्वा धनानि च ॥१-३३॥

*yeshamarthe kankshitam no rajyam bhogah sukhani cha
ta imeavasthita yuddhe pranams tyaktva dhanani cha (1.33)*

yesham : for whom | arthe : benefit/pleasure | kankshitam : desire | no : we | rajyam : kingdom | bhogah : joys | sukhani : pleasures | cha : also | te : they | ime : these | avasthita : situated/standing | yuddhe : in the battle | pranams : lives | tyaktwa : giving up | dhanani : wealth

(Victory in war makes no sense) when those for whom the pleasures of the kingdom and joys of life are desired themselves stand arrayed in battle giving up all their wealth and lives.

(34)

आचार्याः पितरः पुत्रास्तथैव च पितामहाः ।
मातुलाः श्वशुराः पौत्राः श्यालाः संबन्धिनस्तथा ॥१-३४॥

acharyah pitarah putras tathaiva cha pitamahah
matulah shvashurah pautrah shyalah sambandhinas tatha (1.34)

acharyah : teachers | pitarah : fathers | putra : sons | tatha : and | eva : surely | cha : also | pitamahah : grandfathers | matulah : maternal uncles | shvashurah : fathers-in-law | pautrah : grandsons | shyalah : brothers-in-law | sambandhinas : relatives | tatha : and/as well as

(Present on the battlefield are) teachers, fathers, sons and surely also grandfathers, maternal uncles, fathers-in-law, grandsons, brothers-in-law as well as other near ones.

(35)

एतान्न हन्तुमिच्छामि घ्नतोऽपि मधुसूदन ।
अपि त्रैलोक्यराज्यस्यहेतोः किं नु महीकृते ॥१-३५॥

etanna hantumichchhami ghnatoapi madhusudana
api trailokya rajyasya hetoh kim nu mahikrite (1.35)

etan : all these | na : not | hantum : to kill | ichchhami : I wish | ghnata : being killed | api : even if | Madhusudana : Lord Krishna | api : even if | trailokya : of three worlds | rajyasya : for the kingdom | hetoh : for the purpose of | kim : what | nu : to say | mahikrite : for the sake of the earth

O Lord Krishna! I do not wish to kill all these even if I myself get killed. I shall not do it even in return for the kingdom of the three worlds what to say for the sake of the earth.

(36)

निहत्य धार्तराष्ट्रान्नः का प्रीतिः स्याज्जनार्दन ।
पापमेवाश्रयेदस्मान्हत्वैतानाततायिनः ॥१-३६॥

nihatya dhritarashtrannah ka pritih syaj janardana
papamevashreyedasman hatvaitan atatayinah (1.36)

nihatya : by killing | Dhritarashtran : sons of Dhritarashtra, Kauravas | na : our | ka : what | priti : pleasure | syat : will be | Janardana : Lord Krishna | papam : vice/sin | eva : surely | ashrayed : fall upon/overtake | asman : us | hatwa : by killing | etan : these | atatayinah : perpetrators of crime

O Lord! what pleasure can we derive from killing the sons of King Dhritarashtra (Kauravas)? On the other hand, by our killing of these perpetrators of crime, sin will surely fall upon us.

(37)
तस्मान्नार्हा वयं हन्तुं धार्तराष्ट्रान्स्वबान्धवान् ।
स्वजनं हि कथं हत्वा सुखिनः स्याम माधव ॥१-३७॥
tasmannarha vayam hantum dhartarashtran sabandhavan
svajanam hi katham hatva sukhinah shyama madhava (1.37)

tasmat : therefore | narha : undeserving/not qualified | vayam : we | hantum : to kill | dhartarashtran : sons of dhartarashtra, the Kauravas | sa : with | bandhavan : brothers/kinsmen | svajanam : own people/relatives | hi : certainly | katham : how | hatva : by killing | sukhinah : happy | shyama : become | madhava : O Lord Krishna

Therefore, we are not qualified to kill the sons of Dhartarashtra (the Kauravas) alongwith our other kinsmen. O Madhava (Krishna)! Certainly how can we be happy by killing our own people?

(38)
यद्यप्येते न पश्यन्ति लोभोपहतचेतसः ।
कुलक्षयकृतं दोषं मित्रद्रोहे च पातकम् ॥१-३८॥
yadapyete na pashyanti lobhopahata chetasah
kula kshaya kritam dosham mitradrohe cha patakam (1.38)

yadapyete : even if/although | na : not | pashyanti : see | lobho : greed | pahata : overtaken | chetasah : hearts | kula kshaya : destruction of the family | kritam : causing/bringing about | dosham : shortcoming/fault/wrong | mitradrohe : acting against friends | cha : also | and | patakam : sin

Although these people (the Kauravas) have been so overtaken by greed that they see no sin and nothing wrong in destroying their family and causing hurt to friends, (we cannot be like them).

(39)
कथं न ज्ञेयमस्माभिः पापादस्मान्निवर्तितुम् ।
कुलक्षयकृतं दोषं प्रपश्यद्भिर्जनार्दन ॥ १-३९॥

*katham na jneyam asmabhih papad asman nivartitum
kulakshaya kritam dosham prapashyadbhir janardana (1.39)*

katham : why | na : not | jneyam : know | asmabhihh : we also | papad : from sins | asman : these | nivartitum : to escape from | kulakshaya : destruction of family | kritam : done | dosham : crime | prapashyadbhir : those who can see i.e. those who know | Janardana : Lord Krishna

O Janardana (Lord Krishna)! Why should we also, who know that it is a crime to cause the destruction of our own family, indulge in this sin?

(40)
कुलक्षये प्रणश्यन्ति कुलधर्माः सनातनाः ।
धर्मे नष्टे कुलं कृत्स्नमधर्मोऽभिभवत्युत ॥ १-४०॥

*kulakshaye pranashyanti kuladharmah sanatanah
dharme nashte kulam kritsnam adharmo bhibhavaty uta (1.40)*

kula : family/dynasty | kshaye : destruction | pranashyanti : gets destroyed | kuladharmah : family culture/traditions/values of the family | sanatanah : eternal | dharme : religion | naste : on destruction | kulum : family | kritsnam : whole | adharma : vice/irreligion/unrighteousness | abhibhavati : happens/ spreads widely/permeates | uta : it is said

If the family is destroyed, it's Dharma eternal culture (values and traditions) also perishes. On the demise of Dharma, it is said unrighteousness permeates the whole society.

(41)

अधर्माभिभवात्कृष्ण प्रदुष्यन्ति कुलस्त्रियः ।
स्त्रीषु दुष्टासु वार्ष्णेय जायते वर्णसंकरः ॥१-४१॥

adharmabhibhavat Krishna pradushyanti kulastriyah
strishu dushtasu varshneya jayate varnasankarah (1.41)

adharma : irreligion/unrighteousness, vice | abhibhavat : happens/becomes dominant/prevails | Krishna : Lord Krishna | pradushyanti : gets polluted/corrupted | kulastriyah : family women | strishu : of womanhood | dushtasu : become polluted | Varshneya : Lord Krishna | jayate : is born/ comes into being | varnasankarah : illegitimate progeny

When virtue vanes and vice prevails, O Lord Krishna! Family women get corrupted, womanhood becomes polluted and that gives birth to illegitimate progeny.

(42)

संकरो नरकायैव कुलघ्नानां कुलस्य च ।
पतन्ति पितरो ह्येषां लुप्तपिण्डोदकक्रियाः ॥१-४२॥

sankaro narakayaiva kulaghnanam kulasya cha
patanti pitaro hyesham lupta pindodaka kriyah (1.42)

sankaro : out of wedlock children/ illegitimate progeny | narakayaiva : like hell | kulaghnanam : destroyers of their families/family values | kulasya : of the family | cha : also | patanti : fall | pitara : forefathers | hy : surely | esham : those/their | lupta : disappear | pindo : food offerings to the dead elders | daka : water | kriyah : rites

The prevalence of out of wedlock children leads to a hellish life both for the families concerned as also for the destroyers of family values. Those forefathers also fall who are deprived of the rites of food and water offerings as homage from their children.

(43)
दोषैरेतैः कुलघ्नानां वर्णसंकरकारकैः ।
उत्साद्यन्ते जातिधर्माः कुलधर्माश्च शाश्वताः ॥१-४३॥

doshairetaih kulaghnanam varna sankara karakaih
utsadyante jatidharmah kuldharmash cha shashvatah (1.43)

doshair : shortcoming/fault/defect/sin/evil deed | etai : these | kulaghnanam : destroyers of families | varnasankara : the out of wedlock born children | karakaih: causing | utsadyante : are destroyed | jatidharmah : values of the clan/caste | kuldharma : family values | cha : also | shashvatah : eternal

The sins of these destroyers of families cause the phenomenon of out of wedlock children and this in turn results in the destruction of eternal values of the family and the clan.

(44)
उत्सन्नकुलधर्माणां मनुष्याणां जनार्दन ।
नरकेऽनियतं वासो भवतीत्यनुशुश्रुम ॥१-४४॥

utsanna kuladharmanam manushyanam janardana
narake niyatam vaso bhavatityanushushrum (1.44)

utsanna : ruin/spoil | kuladharmanam : family values and traditions | manushyanam : of the human beings | Janardana : Lord Krishna | narake : in hell | niyatam : for unlimited period | vaso : stay | bhavati : happens | iti : thus | anushushruma : it is so heard

O Lord Krishna! As the old saying goes, those human beings whose family values and traditions get ruined are doomed to reside in hell for unlimited period.

(45)
अहो बत महत्पापं कर्तुं व्यवसिता वयम् ।
यद्राज्यसुखलोभेन हन्तुं स्वजनमुद्यताः ॥१-४५॥

aho bata mahatpapam kartum vyavasita vayam
yadrajyasukhalobhena hantum svajanamudyatah (1.45)

aho : alas | bata : how sad | mahat : great | papam : sin | kartum : to do | vyavasita : ready | vayam : we | yat : which/what | rajya : kingdom | sukh : pleasures | lobhena : by greed | hantum : to kill | svajanam : own relatives/kinsmen | udyatah : became ready

Alas, how sad it is that motivated by the greed of enjoying kingly pleasures, we are prepared to commit the great sin of killing our own kinsmen.

(46)
यदि मामप्रतीकारमशस्त्रं शस्त्रपाणयः ।
धार्तराष्ट्रा रणे हन्युस्तन्मे क्षेमतरं भवेत् ॥१-४६॥

yadi mam apratikaram ashastram shastrapanayah
dhartarashtra rane hanyustanme kshemataram bhavet (1.46)

yadi : if | mam : my/me | apratikaram : without resistance/not prepared to react | ashastram : unprepared/unarmed | shastrapanayah : with weapons in hand | Dhritrasthtra : sons of dhartarashtra, Kauravas | rane : in the battle | hanyus : kill | tan : that | me : for me | kshemataram : better | bhavet : would happen

If the sons of dhartarashtra with weapons in their hands kill me in the battle even when I am unarmed and not prepared to react, it would be better for me.

(47)
संजय उवाच
एवमुक्त्वार्जुनः संख्ये रथोपस्थ उपाविशत् ।
विसृज्य सशरं चापं शोकसंविग्नमानसः ॥१-४७॥

Sanjaya uvacha
evamuktvarjunah sankhye rathopastha upavishat
visriajya sasharam chapam shoka samvigna manasah (1.47)

Sanjaya : charioteer and chief aide of king Dhritarashtra | uvacha : said | evam : thus | uktva : after speaking | Arjuna | sankhye : on the battlefield |

ratha : chariot | upastha : back side | upavishat : sat down | visriajya : leaving aside | sasharam : with arrows | chapam : the bow /his Gandiva | shoka : sorrow, lament | samvigna : in despondency/distress/grief | manasah : in the mind

Sanjaya said: Thus speaking on the battlefield, Arjuna sat down on the back seat of the chariot, leaving his bow and arrows aside and with his mind overtaken by sorrow and distress.

Thus ends the first Canto titled 'Yoga of Grief'.

Second Canto

SANKHYA-YOGA
Yoga of Knowledge

(1)

संजय उवाच
तं तथा कृपयाविष्टमश्रुपूर्णाकुलेक्षणम्।
विषीदन्तमिदं वाक्यमुवाच मधुसूदनः॥२-१॥

*Sanjaya uvacha
tam tatha kripayavishtamashru purnakulekshanam
vishidantamidam vakyam uvacha madhusudanah (2-1)*

Sanjaya : the charioteer and chief aide of Dhritarashtra | uvacha : said | tam : to him (Arjuna) | tatha : thus | kripaya : compassion | avishtam : overtaken by | ashru : tears | purnakul : full of | ekshanam : eyes | vishidantam : grieving | idam : this | vakyam : sentence | uvacha : spoke | Madhusudanah : Krishna

Sanjaya said : Thus finding Arjuna overtaken by compassion and full of tears in his eyes, Lord Krishna spoke to him these words :

(2)

श्रीभगवानुवाच
कुतस्त्वा कश्मलमिदं विषमे समुपस्थितम्।
अनार्यजुष्टमस्वर्ग्यमकीर्तिकरमर्जुन॥२-२॥

*Shribhagavan uvacha :
kutastva kashmalamidam vishame samupasthitam
anarya justamasvargyam akirti karamarjuna (2.2)*

Shribhagvan : Lord Krishna | uvacha : said | kutas : from where | tva : on you | kashmalam : dirt/dirty stuff | idam : this | vishame : at this critical time | samupasthitam : come | anarya : not befitting an aryan (gentleman, civilised person, goodman, noble) | jushtam : practised by | asvargyam : disqualifying one for achieving heaven after death | akirtikaram : bringing bad name/ causing disrepute | Arjuna : O Arjuna

Lord Krishna said: O Arjuna! at this critical time, from where did all this dirt come to you? It is not befitting a noble person or one aspiring for heaven after death. It shall bring only bad name.

(3)
क्लैब्यं मा स्म गमः पार्थ नैतत्त्वय्युपपद्यते ।
क्षुद्रं हृदयदौर्बल्यं त्यक्त्वोत्तिष्ठ परन्तप ॥२-३॥

*klaibyam ma sma gamah partha naitat tvayyupapadyate
kshudram hridaya-dourbalyam tyaktvottishtha parantapa (2.3)*

klaibyam : weakness/unmanliness | ma sma gamah : do not go to (surrender to) | Partha : another name for Arjuna derived from his being the son of Pratha (Kanti) who was Krishna's aunt (sister of his father Vasudeva) | na : not | etat : this | tyayi upapadyate : becoming of you/befitting you | kshudram : petty | hridayadourbalyam : weakness of the heart | tyaktva : give up | uttishtha : get up | parantapa : scorcher of enemies/brave hero

O Partha! Do not surrender to unmanliness. It is not becoming of you. O scorcher of enemies, brave hero, give up all petty weakness of heart and get up, arise, stand up.

(4)
अर्जुन उवाच
कथं भीष्ममहं संख्ये द्रोणं च मधुसूदन ।
इषुभिः प्रति योत्स्यामि पूजार्हावरिसूदन ॥२-४॥

*Arjuna uvacha :
katham bhishmam aham sankhye dronam cha madhusudana
ishubhih pratiyotsyami pujarhauari sudana (2.4)*

Arjunauvacha : Arjuna said : | katham : how | Bhishmam : Bhishma Pitamaha | aham : I | Sankhye : in the battle | Dronam : Guru Dronacharya | cha : and | Madhusudana : Lord Krishna | ishubhih : with arrows | prati : against | yotsyami : shall fight | pujarhauri : worthy of worship | sudana : Lord Krishna (destroyer of enemies)

Arjuna said: O Lord Krishna, destroyer of enemies! How shall I fight with arrows in the battle against Pitamaha Bhishma and Guru Dronacharya who are both worthy of worship.

(5)

गुरूनहत्वा हि महानुभावान् श्रेयो भोक्तुं भैक्ष्यमपीह लोके ।
हत्वार्थकामांस्तु गुरूनिहैव भुञ्जीय भोगान् रुधिरप्रदिग्धान् ॥२-५॥

gurunahatva hi mahanubhavan shreyo bhoktum bhaikshyamapiha loke
hatvarthakamamstu gurunihaiva bhunjiya bhogan rudhirapradigdhan (2.5)

gurun : teachers/elders | ahatva : not killing | hi : surely/because | mahanubhavan : distinguished personalities/respected elders | shreyo : better | bhoktum : to enjoy | bhaikshyam : by begging alms | api : even | iha : this | loke : in this world | hatva : killing | artha : wealth | kaman : desire of | tu : but | gurun : teachers/elders | iha : this | eva : surely | bhunjiya : enjoy | bhogan : articles of enjoyment | rudhira : blood | pradigdhan : tainted with

It would surely be much better for me to live in this world by begging alms but not kill my respected elders and teachers (distinguished personalities). If by killing them I am able to fulfil my desires and even enjoy wealth and such other pleasures, it would all be stained with blood.

(6)

न चैतद्विद्मः कतरन्नो गरीयो यद्वा जयेम यदि वा नो जयेयुः ।
यानेव हत्वा न जिजीविषाम- स्तेऽवस्थिताः प्रमुखे धार्तराष्ट्राः ॥२-६॥

na chaitadvidmah katarnno gariyo yadva jayema yadi va no jayeyuh
yaneva hatva na jijivishams teavasthitah pramukhe dhartarashtrah (2.6)

na : not | cha : also | etat : this | vidmah : know | katarat : which (of the two) | nah : us | gariya : good/desirable | yat va : whether/or | jayema : we shall win | yadi : if | va : or | nah : us | jayeyuh : they win | yan : who | eva : surely | hatva : killing | na : not | jijivishama : wanting to live | te : they | avasthitah : situated/standing | pramukhe : in front | Dhartarashtrah: sons of Dhritarashtra

Also, we do not know what is more desirable for us, whether we win or they win. Certainly, we do not wish to live by killing the Kauravas (sons of Dhritarashtra) standing in front.

(7)

कार्पण्यदोषोपहतस्वभावः पृच्छामि त्वां धर्मसम्मूढचेताः ।
यच्छ्रेयः स्यान्निश्चितं ब्रूहि तन्मे शिष्यस्तेऽहं शाधि मां त्वां प्रपन्नम् ॥२-७॥

karpanya doshopahata svabhavah
prichhami tvam dharma sammudha chetah
yach chhreyah syannishchitam bruhi tanme
shishyasteham shadhi mam tvam prapannam (2.7)

karpanya : miserliness (in use of mind)/cowardice/sense of self pity | dosha : weakness/defect | upahata : affected/overtaken/afflicted/overwhelmed | svabhavah : nature/character | prichhami : I am asking you/I beg of you to please tell me | tvam : you | dharma : sense of duty/right conduct | sammudha : puzzled/confused/upset/bewildered | chetah : intelligence/at heart | yat : what | shreyah : good/right | syat : is/may be | nishchitam : definitely | bruhi : speak | tat : that | me : to me | shishya : disciple/pupil | te : your | aham : I/self | shadhi : instruct/order | mam : me | tvam : to you | prapannam : surrendered

Because of the weakness of miserly use of mind, my nature is completely overpowered by confusion in regard to the sense of my duty. I beg of you to please tell me definitely what is good for me to do. I am your disciple. I surrender to you completely. Please instruct me.

(8)

न हि प्रपश्यामि ममापनुद्याद् यच्छोकमुच्छोषणमिन्द्रियाणाम् ।
अवाप्य भूमावसपत्नमृद्धं राज्यं सुराणामपि चाधिपत्यम् ॥२-८॥

na hi prapashyami mamapanudyad
yachchhokam uchoshanam indriayanam
avapya bhumav asapatnamraddham
rajyam suranamapi chadhipatyam (2.8)

na : not | hi : certainly/definitely/surely | prapashyami : I am seeing/visualize | mama : my | apanudyad : can remove | yat : which | sokam : sorrow/grief |

uchoshanam : drying up | indriayanam : senses | avapya : getting, acquiring | bhumav : on earth | asapatnam : unrivalled/without any opposition | raddham : affluent/prosperous/rich | rajyam : kingdom | suranam : gods | api : even | cha : also/and | adhipatyam : dominance/supremacy

I am definitely not able to visualise any way out of the grief which is stilling my senses (I cannot hope to get rid of this grief) even if I acquire a rich kingdom without any enemies and with supreme powers like those enjoyed by gods in heaven.

(9)

संजय उवाच
एवमुक्त्वा हृषीकेशं गुडाकेशः परन्तप ।
न योत्स्य इति गोविन्दमुक्त्वा तूष्णीं बभूव ह ॥२-९॥

Sanjaya uvacha
evamuktva hrishikesham gudakeshah parantapa
na yotsya iti govindam uktva tushnim babhoova ha (2.9)

Sanjaya | uvacha : said/spoke thus : | evam : this/thus | uktva : having said/spoken | Hrishikesham : to Lord Krishna/to one who has mastered his senses | Gudakeshah : Arjuna, one who has conquered sleep | parantapa : of whom enemies are afraid | na : not | yotsya : fight | iti : this/thus | Govindam : to Lord Krishna | uktva : having said/spoken | tushnim : silent | babhoova : became | ha : surely

Sanjaya said : Having so spoken, Arjuna known as one who had conquered sleep, said to Lord Krishna: "O Govinda! I shall not fight" and thereafter he became completely silent.

(10)

तमुवाच हृषीकेशः प्रहसन्निव भारत ।
सेनयोरुभयोर्मध्ये विषीदन्तमिदं वचः ॥२-१०॥

tamuvacha hrishikeshah prahasanniva bharata
senayorubhayor madhye vishidantam idam vachah (2.10)

tam : to him | uvacha : said | Hrishikeshah : Lord Krishna | prahasan :

smiling | iva : as if | Bharata : O! Bharata (descendent of King Bharat), King Dhritarashtra | senayo : armies | ubhayo : both sides | madhye : in the midst | vishidantam : grieving | idam : this, these | uvachah : said

O King Dhritarashtra, descendent of Bharat! Lord Krishna standing between the two armies, with a smile, said these words to the grieving Arjuna.

(11)
श्रीभगवानुवाच
अशोच्यान्वशोचस्त्वं प्रज्ञावादांश्च भाषसे ।
गतासूनगतासूंश्च नानुशोचन्ति पण्डिताः ॥२-११॥

Shribhagwan uvacha :
ashochyan anvashochas tvam pragya vadanshcha bhashase
gatasun agatasunscha nanushochanti panditah (2.11)

Shribhagwan : Lord Krishna | uvacha : said | ashochyan : those unworthy of attention/not deserving any thought | anvashochas : worrying | tvam : you | pragyavadan : like intellectuals | cha : also/and | bhashase : talk/speak | gatasun : gone/past/dead | agatasun : not gone/alive/living | cha : and | na : not | anushochanti : think about/lament | panditah : the wise

Lord Krishna said: you are unnecessarily feeling concerned about those who do not deserve to be mourned, you talk like intellectuals, the really wise do not grieve either for what is gone or for what is to come, neither for the past nor for the future.

(12)
न त्वेवाहं जातु नासं न त्वं नेमे जनाधिपाः ।
न चैव न भविष्यामः सर्वे वयमतः परम् ॥२-१२॥

na tvevaham jatu nasam na tvam neme janadhipah
na chaiva na bhavishyamah sarve vayamatah param (2.12)

na : not | tu : so | eva : surely | aham : I | jatu : at any period of time | na : not | asam : existed | na : not | tvam : you | na : not | ime : these | janadhipah : rulers/kings | na : not | cha : also/and | eva : surely | na : not | bhavishyamah

: will happen | sarve : all | vayam : we | atah : here | param : after

It is not so that I did not exist at any time earlier or that you and all these rulers never existed before. Also, quite definitely, it is not as if we shall all not be there hereafter. All of us as individual souls are eternal, have always been there and shall always live.

(13)
देहिनोऽस्मिन्यथा देहे कौमारं यौवनं जरा ।
तथा देहान्तरप्राप्तिर्धीरस्तत्र न मुह्यति ॥२-१३॥

dehinoasminyatha dehe kaumaram yauvanam jara
tatha dehantara praptir dhiras tatra na muhyati (2.13)

dehin : embodied soul/self | asmin : this | yatha : as | dehe : in the body | kaumaram : childhood/boyhood | yauvanam : youth/young age | jara : old age | tatha : in the same way/and | dehantara : after change of body | prapti : receipt/achievement | dhir : person with patience/serious minded/sober | tatra : there | na : not | muhyati : gets deceived/deluded

Every self while in a body passes through different stages of childhood, youth and old age and similarly receives another body but a wise one does not get deceived thereby.

(14)
मात्रास्पर्शास्तु कौन्तेय शीतोष्णसुखदुःखदाः ।
आगमापायिनोऽनित्यास्तांस्तितिक्षस्व भारत ॥२-१४॥

matrasparshastu kounteya shitoshna sukha duhkha dah
agamapayino nityas tans titikshasva bharata (2.14)

matra : objects of the senses | sparsha : touch | tu : only | Kounteya : son of mother Kunti, Arjuna | shit : cold/winter | ushna : summer | sukha : pleasure | duhkha : pain | dah : giving | agama : appear | apayina : disappearing | anitya : transient/non-permanent | tan : them | titikshasva : try to tolerate | Bharata : descendent of King Bharata

O son of Kunti! Transient pleasure and pain that come from contact with senses appear and disappear with the change of seasons of winter and summer. O descendent of Bharata! One has to try to show tolerance and not get disturbed.

(15)
यं हि न व्यथयन्त्येते पुरुषं पुरुषर्षभ ।
समदुःखसुखं धीरं सोऽमृतत्वाय कल्पते ॥२-१५॥

yam hi na vyathayantyete purusham purusharshabha
samadukhasukham dhiram so mritatvaya kalpate (2.15)

yam : whom | hi : surely | na : not | vyathayanti : distressed | ete : these | purusham : person | purusharshabha : best of persons | sama : same/ maintaining equanimity | dukha : sorrow | sukha : pleasure | dhiram : patience | sa : he | mritatvaya : for immortality | kalpate : entitled/eligible

O Best of persons! Only one who is not distressed by all these and who can maintain equanimity in the face of pleasure and pain - happiness and sorrow - can aspire for or is entitled to immortality (ultimate liberation from the cycle of birth and death).

(16)
नासतो विद्यते भावो नाभावो विद्यते सतः ।
उभयोरपि दृष्टोऽन्तस्त्वनयोस्तत्त्वदर्शिभिः ॥२-१६॥

nasato vidyate bhavo nabhavo vidyate satah
ubhayorapi drishtoanta stvanayos tattva darshibhih (2.16)

na : not | asta : what does not exist/what is not/non-being/unreal/changing | vidyate : appears/is seen/is known | bhava : existence | na : not | abhava : non-existence | vidyate : is known/seems | satah : truth/the supreme being/ the real/eternal/unchanging | ubhayo : of both | api : also | drishta : seen/ observed | anta : the end | tu : truly/indeed | anyo : of those/of the others | tattva : truth/essence | darshibhih : the seers

The seers who know the truth have studied the essence of both, the real and the unreal, and concluded that what is unreal does not exist and what is real is eternally there. The material body is unreal and perishes, the spirit, soul or the self is real and continues for ever.

(17)
अविनाशि तु तद्विद्धि येन सर्वमिदं ततम् ।
विनाशमव्ययस्यास्य न कश्चित्कर्तुमर्हति ॥२-१७॥

avinashi tu tadviddhi yena sarvamidam tatam
vinasham avyayasyasya na kaschit kartum arhati (2.17)

avinashi : indestructible/imperishable | tu : but, truly, indeed | tat : that | viddhi : know | yena : by whom | sarvam : all/the whole universe | idam : this | tatam : pervading | vinasham : destruction | avyayasya : of what is indestructible/imperishable | asya : it's | na : not | kaschit : anyone | kartum : to do | arhati : is qualified/competent

It needs to be known that that which pervades this entire material world (or the human body) is imperishable and no one can ever destroy this indestructible realty (the soul).

(18)
अन्तवन्त इमे देहा नित्यस्योक्ताः शरीरिणः ।
अनाशिनोऽप्रमेयस्य तस्माद्युध्यस्व भारत ॥२-१८॥

antavanta ime deha nityasyoktah sharirinah
anashino prameyasya tasmad yudhyasva bharata (2.18)

antavanta : that which is perishable/ having an end | ime : these | deha : material bodies | nityasya : eternal | uktah : said to be | sharirinah : the soul in the body | anashina : indestructible | apremeyasya : immeasurable/illimitable | tasmat : therefore | yudhyasva : fight | Bharata : descendent of king Bharata

O descendent of the great king Bharata! All these bodies that you see are subject to an end, are perishable, but the soul within them is illimitable, eternal and indestructible and therefore, fight.

(19)

य एनं वेत्ति हन्तारं यश्चैनं मन्यते हतम् ।
उभौ तौ न विजानीतो नायं हन्ति न हन्यते ॥२-१९॥

ya enam vetti hantaram yashchainam manyate hatam
ubhau tau na vijanito nayam hanti na hanyate (2.19)

ya : who | enam : this | vetti : knows | hantaram : the killer | ya : who | cha : also/and | enam : this | manyate : believes/thinks | hatam : killed | ubhau : both | tau : they | na : not | vijanita : have known | na : not | ayam : this | hanti : kills | na : neither | ayam : this | hanti : kills | na : nor | hanyate : is killed

Anyone who thinks that the soul (atman) is the killer or that it gets killed are mistaken. The soul neither kills nor is ever killed.

(20)

न जायते म्रियते वा कदाचि-न्नायं भूत्वा भविता वा न भूयः ।
अजो नित्यः शाश्वतोऽयं पुराणो न हन्यते हन्यमाने शरीरे ॥२-२०॥

na jayate mriyate va kadachin
nayam bhutva bhavita va na bhuyah
ajo nityah shashvato yam purano
na hanyate hanyamane sharire (2.20)

na : neither | jayate : is born | mriyate : dies | va : either/or | kadachit : at anytime | na : never | ayam : this | bhutva : having been | bhavita : will come to be | va : or | na : not | bhuyah : coming to be | aja : not born | nityah : eternal | shashvata : ever lasting/permanent | ayam : this | purana : old | na : never | hanyate : is killed | hanyamane : on the killing of | sarire : body

The Atman (the soul) is neither born at anytime nor does it ever die. It is not as if it was not there, is not there or will not again be there. The soul is never born, it is eternal, everlasting and never gets killed even when the body is killed.

(21)

वेदाविनाशिनं नित्यं य एनमजमव्ययम् ।
कथं स पुरुषः पार्थ कं घातयति हन्ति कम् ॥२-२१॥

*vedavinashinam nityam ya enamajamavyayam
katham sa purushah partha kam ghatayati hanti kam (2.21)*

veda : knows | avinashinam : imperishable | nityam : eternal | ya : who | enam : this | ajam : not born | avyayam : immutable | katham : how | sa : he | purushah : person | Partha : Arjuna | kam : whom | ghatayati : causes to kill | hanti : kills | kam : whom

O Partha (Arjuna)! One who knows this that the Atman (soul) is unborn, immutable, imperishable and eternal, how can such a person kill anyone or cause anyone to kill?

(22)

वासांसि जीर्णानि यथा विहाय नवानि गृह्णाति नरोऽपराणि ।
तथा शरीराणि विहाय जीर्णान्यन्यानि संयाति नवानि देही ॥२-२२॥

*vasansi jirnani yatha vihaya navani grihnati naroaparani
tatha sharirani vihaya jirnanyanyani sanyati navani dehi (2.22)*

vasansi : clothes/garments | jirnani : worn out | yatha : as | vihaya : discarding | navani : new | grihnati : accepts | nara : man | aparani : others | tatha : in the same way | sharirani : bodies | vihaya : giving up | jirnani : worn out | anyani : another | sanyati : accepts | navani : new | dehi : the soul in the body

As a person discards old and worn out clothes and puts on new ones, In the same way, the Atman (soul) drops old and worn out body and adopts a new one.

(23)

नैनं छिन्दन्ति शस्त्राणि नैनं दहति पावकः ।
न चैनं क्लेदयन्त्यापो न शोषयति मारुतः ॥२-२३॥

*nainam chhindanti shastrani nainam dahati pavakah
na chainam kledayantyapo na shoshayati marutah (2.23)*

na : not | enam : this (Atman, soul) | chhindanti : cut | shastrani : weapons | na : not | enam : this | dahati : burns | pavakah : fire | na : not | cha : and/also | enam : this | kledayanti : wets | apa : water | na : not | shoshayati : dries | marutah : wind

No weapons can cut this Atman (soul), fire cannot burn it, water does not wet it and wind cannot dry it.

(24)
अच्छेद्योऽयमदाह्योऽयमक्लेद्योऽशोष्य एव च ।
नित्यः सर्वगतः स्थाणुरचलोऽयं सनातनः ॥२-२४॥

achchhedyo yam adahyo yam akledyo shoshya eva cha
nityah sarvagatah sthanur achalo yam sanatanah (2.24)

achedya : cannot be broken/pierced | ayam : this | adahya : that cannot be burned | ayam : this | akledya : that never gets wet | asosya : not able to dry | eva : surely | cha : also/and | nityah : permanent/everlasting | sarvagatah : all pervading | sthanur : unchangeable/immutable/stable | achalah : immovable | ayam : this | sanatanah : eternal

This Atman (soul) cannot be broken, it cannot be burned, it neither ever gets wet nor does it dry. It is surely everlasting, all pervading, immutable, immovable and eternal.

(25)
अव्यक्तोऽयमचिन्त्योऽयमविकार्योऽयमुच्यते ।
तस्मादेवं विदित्वैनं नानुशोचितुमर्हसि ॥२-२५॥

avyakto yam achintyo yam avikaryo yam uchyate
tasmadevam viditvainam nanushochitum arhasi (2.25).

avyakta : unmanifest/invisible/unspoken/unexpressed | ayam : this Atman (soul) | achintya : inconceivable/unthinkable/incomprehensible | ayam : this | avikarya : incorruptible/unchangeable | ayam : this | uchyate : is so said | tasmat : thereby/therefore | evam : thus/in this way | viditva : knowing it | enam : this | na : not | anushochitam : to grieve/lament | arhasi : deserve

The Atman (soul) is unmanifest, it cannot be seen and is incomprehensible. It is said to be unchangable. Knowing all this, Arjuna! You do not deserve to grieve.

(26)
अथ चैनं नित्यजातं नित्यं वा मन्यसे मृतम् ।
तथापि त्वं महाबाहो नैवं शोचितुमर्हसि ॥२-२६॥

atha chainam nityajatam nityam va manyase mritam
tathapi tvam mahabaho naivam shochitumarhasi (2.26)

atha : if | cha : also/and | nityajatam : always being born | nityam : always | va : either/and | manyase : believe/think | mritam : dead/dying | tathapi : even then | tvam : you | mahabaho : one with big/strong arms | na : not | shochitum : to think/to grieve about/mourn/lament | arhasi : deserve

O strong-armed one, Arjuna! If you think that the Atman (soul) is always in the process of being born and forever dying, even then you have no reason to lament.

(27)
जातस्य हि ध्रुवो मृत्युर्ध्रुवं जन्म मृतस्य च ।
तस्मादपरिहार्येऽर्थे न त्वं शोचितुमर्हसि ॥२-२७॥

jatasya hi dhruvo mrityur dhruvam janma mritasya cha
tasmad apariharye rthe na tvam shochitum arhasi (2.27)

jatasya : anyone who is born | hi : because | dhruvam : sure | janma : birth | mritasya : of the dead | cha : also/and | tasmat : for this reason also/therefore | apariharye : that which is inevitable/unavoidable | arthe : for this | na : not | tvam : you | shochitum : to grieve | arhasi : deserve

Anyone who is born is sure to die and everyone who dies is bound to be born again. Therefore, from this angle also, you should not grieve.

(28)
अव्यक्तादीनि भूतानि व्यक्तमध्यानि भारत ।
अव्यक्तनिधनान्येव तत्र का परिदेवना ॥२-२८॥

avyaktadini bhutani vyaktamadhyani bharata
avyakta nidhananyeva tatra ka paridevana (2.28)

avyaktadini : unmanifest in the beginning i.e. before birth | bhutani : all living beings | vyakta : manifest | madhyani : in the middle | Bharata : descendent of king Bharata, Arjuna | avyakta : unmanifest | nidhanany : after death | eva : again/this way | tatra : there/in that situation | ka : what | peridevana : grieving

O descendent of king Bharata, Arjuna! All living beings are unmanifest (not visible) before their birth, they become manifest in the middle and again at the end, after death, they become unmanifest. Therefore, in this situation, where is the need to grieve?

(29)
आश्चर्यवत्पश्यति कश्चिदेन- माश्चर्यवद्वदति तथैव चान्यः ।
आश्चर्यवच्चैनमन्यः शृणोति श्रुत्वाप्येनं वेद न चैव कश्चित् ॥२-२९॥

ashcharyavat pashyati kashchidenan
mashcharyavad vadanti tathaiva chanyah
ascharyavach chainam anyah shrinoti
shrutvapyenam veda na chaiva kashchit (2.29)

ashcharyavat : with surprise/amazement/wonder/ bewilderment | pasyati : sees, witnesses | kaschit : someone | enam : this | ashcharyavat : with wonder | vadati : speaks | tatha : thus, and | eva : surely | cha : and, also | anyah : another | ashcharyavat : with amazement | cha : also, and | enam : this | anyah : another | shrinoti : hears | shrutva : on hearing | api : even, also | enam : this | veda : knows | na : not | cha : and, also | eva : surely | kashchit : someone

Some people look at it with bewilderment, some speak about it with a sense of wonder and some hear of it with amazement but there are some who even after hearing about it do not surely get to really know it.

(30)
देही नित्यमवध्योऽयं देहे सर्वस्य भारत ।
तस्मात्सर्वाणि भूतानि न त्वं शोचितुमर्हसि ॥२-३०॥

dehi nityamavadhyo yam dehe sarvasya bharata
tasmat sarvani bhutani na tvam shochitum arhasi (2.30)

dehi : Atman (soul) | nityam : everlasting/always/eternal | avadhya : one who cannot be killed | ayam : this | dehe : in bodies | sarvasya : of all | Bharata : Arjuna | tasmat : therefore | sarvani : all | bhutani : living | na : not | tvam : you | shochitum : to grieve | arhasi : deserve

O Arjuna! Atman (soul) is eternal. It dwells in all our bodies. It can never be killed. Therefore you do not need to grieve for anyone.

(31)
स्वधर्ममपि चावेक्ष्य न विकम्पितुमर्हसि ।
धर्म्याद्धि युद्धाच्छ्रेयोऽन्यत्क्षत्रियस्य न विद्यते ॥२-३१॥

swadharmam api chavekshya na vikampitum arhasi
dharmyaddhi yuddhach chhreyonyat kshatriyasya na vidyate (2.31)

svadharmam : ones own duty/principles | api : also | cha : and | avekshya : considering | na : not | vikampitum : tremble/be afraid | arhasi : deserve | dharmyat : for ones principles | hi : surely | yuddhat : as against fighting | shreya : better/more righteous | anyat : any other | kshatriyasya : of the warrior class | na : not | vidyate : does not seem to be

Considering the matter from the angle of following ones principles or performing ones ordained duties also, you need not be upset as for one from the warrior class there does not seem to be any duty higher than to fight for ones principles.

(32)
यदृच्छया चोपपन्नं स्वर्गद्वारमपावृतम् ।
सुखिनः क्षत्रियाः पार्थ लभन्ते युद्धमीदृशम् ॥२-३२॥

yadrichchhaya chopapannam swarga dvaram apavritam
sukhinah kshatriyah Partha labhante yuddhamidrisham (2.32)

yadracchaya : on it's own/unasked for/unsought of | cha : also/and | upapapannam : offered/made available | svarga : heaven | dvaram : doors | apavratam : wide open | sukhinah : very happy/fortunate | kshatriyah : members of the warrior class | Partha : Arjuna | labhante : receive/achieve | yuddham : in battle | idrisham : like this

O Arjuna! It is only the very fortunate and happy members of the warrior class (Kshatriyas) who get such unsought opportunity of a battle which leads to the wide open doors of heaven.

(33)
अथ चेत्त्वमिमं धर्म्यं संग्रामं न करिष्यसि ।
ततः स्वधर्मं कीर्तिं च हित्वा पापमवाप्स्यसि ॥२-३३॥
*atha chetvamimam dharmyam sangramam na karishyasi
tatah svadharmam kirtim cha hitva papamavapsyasi (2.33)*

atha : so | chet : if | tvam : you | imam : this | dharmyam : in accordance with your righteous duty | sangramam : fight | na : not | karishyasi : do/perform | tatah : then | svadharmam : own righteous duty | kirtim : reputation/fame/honour | cha : also | hitva : losing | papam : sin | avapsyasi : incur

Therefore, if in accordance with your duty, you do not fight this righteous war, then, apart from failing in the performance of your own righteous duty and losing your honour, you will also be incurring sin.

(34)
अकीर्तिं चापि भूतानि कथयिष्यन्ति तेऽव्ययाम् ।
सम्भावितस्य चाकीर्तिर्मरणादतिरिच्यते ॥२-३४॥
*akirtim chapi bhutani kathayishyanti tevyayam
sambhavitasya chakirtirmaranadatirichyate (2.34)*

akirtim : disrepute/infamy/loss of honour | cha : and | api : also | bhutani : all the people | kathayishyanti : will talk about/recount/narrate | te : of you/your | avyayam : forever | sambhavitasya : for a man of honour | cha : and | akirti : infamy/ill repute | marnat : than death | atirichyate : far exceeds/is very much more

Also, all the people will forever talk about your loss of honour and for a person of honour such ill repute is much worse than even death.

(35)

भयाद्रणादुपरतं मंस्यन्ते त्वां महारथाः ।
येषां च त्वं बहुमतो भूत्वा यास्यसि लाघवम् ॥२-३५॥

bhayad ranad uparatam mansyante tvam maharathah
yesham cha tvam bahumato bhutva yasyasi laghavam (2.35)

bhayat : because of fear | ranat : from battle | uparatam : running away/retiring/leaving | mansyante : will consider | tvam : you | maharathah : great war leaders/seated on large chariots/chariot warriors | yesham : for whom | cha : and | tvam : you | bahumata : widely respected/held in high esteem | bhutva : having been | yasyasi : will be treated | laghavam : small/adversely

The great chariot warriors, who held you in high esteem, will now think of you adversely and consider you small for having run away from the battlefield out of fear.

(36)

अवाच्यवादांश्च बहून्वदिष्यन्ति तवाहिताः ।
निन्दन्तस्तव सामर्थ्यं ततो दुःखतरं नु किम् ॥२-३६॥

avachyavadanscha bahunvadishyanti tavahitah
nindantastava samarthyam tato dukhataram nu kim (2.36)

avachya : unspeakable | vadan : words | cha : and | bahun : many | vadishyanti : will speak | tava : your | ahitah : enemies | nindanta : while speaking ill | tava : your | samarthyam : potential/ability | tatah : that | dukhataram : more painful | nu : and | kim : what

Many persons will utter unspeakable bad words against you and your enemies while speaking ill will question your ability (to fight) and what could be more painful than that.

(37)

हतो वा प्राप्स्यसि स्वर्गं जित्वा वा भोक्ष्यसे महीम् ।
तस्मादुत्तिष्ठ कौन्तेय युद्धाय कृतनिश्चयः ॥२-३७॥

hato va prapsyasi swargam jitva va bhokshyase mahim
tasmaduttishtha kaunteya yuddhaya kritanishchayah (2.37)

hata : killed | va : either | prapsyasi : you will achieve | swargam : heaven | jitva : on winning/if victorious | va : or | bhokshyase : will enjoy | mahim : the earth | tasmat : therefore/for this reason | uttishtha : rise/get up | Kaunteya : son of Kunti, Arjuna | yuddhaya : for fighting | krita : having made | nishchayah: determination

O son of Kunti, Arjuna! If you are killed on the battlefield, you will attain heaven and if you emerge victorious, you will inherit and enjoy the earth. Therefore, arise firmly determined to fight.

(38)

सुखदुःखे समे कृत्वा लाभालाभौ जयाजयौ ।
ततो युद्धाय युज्यस्व नैवं पापमवाप्स्यसि ॥२-३८॥

sukhadukhe same kritva labhalabhau jayajayau
tato yuddhaya yujyasva naivam papamavapsyasi (2.38)

sukha : joy/pleasure | dukha : sorrow/pain | same : equal/same | kritva : doing | labha : profit | alabha : loss | jaya : victory | ajaya : defeat | tata : therefore | yuddhaya : for fighting | yujyasva : get ready | na : not/never | evam : thereby/in this way | papam : sin | avapsyasi : shall incur

Treating pleasure and pain (joy and sorrow), profit and loss and victory and defeat as the same (equal), you should get ready to fight (fight for the sake of fighting evil). In this way you can never incur any sin.

(39)

एषा तेऽभिहिता सांख्ये बुद्धिर्योगे त्विमां शृणु ।
बुद्ध्या युक्तो यया पार्थ कर्मबन्धं प्रहास्यसि ॥२-३९॥

esha te bhihita sankhye buddhiryoge tvimam shrinu
buddhya yukto yaya partha karmabandham prahasyasi (2.39)

aisha : this | te : you | abhihita : stated/spoken | sankhye : in sankhya (philosophy of knowledge) | buddhi : wisdom | yoge : in action | tu : but | imam : this | shrinu : listen | buddhya : by wisdom | yukta : endowed with | yaya : by which | Partha : Arjuna | karmabandham : bondage of action (and reaction) | prahasyasi : shall be relieved of

O Arjuna! So far I have spoken to you in terms of the wisdom of sankhya or the philosophy of knowledge, now listen to me about the philosophy of action endowed with wisdom by which you will be relieved of the bondage of action (and reaction).

(40)
नेहाभिक्रमनाशोऽस्ति प्रत्यवायो न विद्यते ।
स्वल्पमप्यस्य धर्मस्य त्रायते महतो भयात् ॥२-४०॥

nehabhikrama nasho sti pratyavayo na vidyate
svalpam apyasya dharmasya trayate mahato bhayat (2.40)

na : no | iha : here/in this (yoga) | abhikrama : in the attempt | nasa : loss/waste | asti : exists | pratyavaya : opposite results | na : no | vidyate : visible/seen | svalpama : a little | api : only | asya : of this | dharmasya : of righteous duty | trayate : frees/releases | mahato : great | bhayat : from fear/danger

In this yoga no attempt goes waste and no risk of opposite results is seen. Only a little of this righteous duty performed releases one from great fears.

(41)
व्यवसायात्मिका बुद्धिरेकेह कुरुनन्दन ।
बहुशाखा ह्यनन्ताश्च बुद्धयोऽव्यवसायिनाम् ॥२-४१॥

vyavasayatmika buddhir ekeha kuru nandana
bahushakha hyanantash cha buddhayo vyavasayinam (2.41)

vyavasayatmika : determined/single-minded | buddhi : intellect | eka : one | iha : here/in this approach | Kurunandana : scion of Kuru dynasty, Arjuna | bahushakha : multi-branched/moving in different directions | hi : certainly

| ananta : unending | cha : and | buddhaya : intellects/minds | vyavasayinam : those not single-minded, irresolute

O scion of the Kuru dynasty, Arjuna! Here in this approach, the intellect is determined and aimed at one goal. Irresolute minds, on the other hand, certainly move in different directions and the journey is unending.

(42)
यामिमां पुष्पितां वाचं प्रवदन्त्यविपश्चितः ।
वेदवादरताः पार्थ नान्यदस्तीति वादिनः ॥२-४२॥

yamimam pushpitam vacham pravadanty avipashchitah
vedavadaratah partha nanyadastiti vadinah (2.42)

yamimam : these persons who | pushpitam : flowery/showy | vacham : words | pravadanty : speak | avipashchitah : unwise persons/those with poor knowledge | vedvadratah : those indulging in mere letters (or rituals) of the Vedas | Partha : Arjuna | na : no | anya : other | asti : exists | iti : thus, so | vadinah : those speaking

These persons of superficial knowledge use flowery language and indulge only in letters or rituals of Vedas. O Arjuna! They talk as if nothing else exists.

(43)
कामात्मानः स्वर्गपरा जन्मकर्मफलप्रदाम् ।
क्रियाविशेषबहुलां भोगैश्वर्यगतिं प्रति ॥२-४३॥

kamatmanah swargpara janma karma phala pradam
kriya vishesha bahulam bhogaishwaryagatim prati (2.43)

kamatmanah : anxious to satisfy sensory desires | svargpara : with attainment of heavens their highest ambition | janma-karma-phala-pradam : action leading to the fruit of another birth | kriyavishesha : special ceremonies | bahulam : many/varied | bhoga : sensory pleasures | aishwarya : luxury/affluence | gatim : progress | prati : for/towards

They are anxious only to satisfy their sensory desires. Attainment of heaven is their highest ambition. Various activities lead them only to the fruit of another birth. They perform varied special ceremonies (rituals) for the sake of material progress, more luxuries and sensory enjoyments.

(44)
भोगैश्वर्यप्रसक्तानां तयापहृतचेतसाम् ।
व्यवसायात्मिका बुद्धिः समाधौ न विधीयते ॥२-४४॥

bhogaiswarya prasaktanam tayapahrita chetsam
vyavasayatmika buddhih samadhau na vidhiyate (2.44)

bhoga : sensory enjoyment | aiswarya : luxury/opulence/affluence | prasaktanam : those attached | taya : thereby/by such things | apahrita-chetsam : with lost sensitivity | vyavasayatmika-buddhih : determined mind | samadhau : in the state of concentration | na : not/never | vidhiyate : happen/achieved

For those who are attached to sensory pleasures and a life of luxury and opulence, samadhi or the state of concentration and a determined mind are never likely to be achieved.

(45)
त्रैगुण्यविषया वेदा निस्त्रैगुण्यो भवार्जुन ।
निर्द्वन्द्वो नित्यसत्त्वस्थो निर्योगक्षेम आत्मवान् ॥२-४५॥

traigunyavishaya veda nistraigunyo bhavarjuna
nirdvandvo nityasattvastho niryogakshema atmavan (2.45)

trai-gunya : the three gunas or attributes of material nature - sat, rajas and tamas.
1) sat stands for the sublime, for truth, piety and goodness leading to a stage of equanimity of mind and suspension of physical activity
2) rajas means activity, and
3) tamas means darkness, evil and the state of inactivity vishaya: subjects | Veda : the four Vedas are : Rigveda, Atharvaveda,

Yajurveda and Samaveda | nistraigunyo : beyond three attributes of the physical nature | bhava : become | Arjuna: O Arjuna | nirdvandva : beyond the duality of good and evil, pleasure and pain, light and | darkness, life and death etc. | nitya-sattvastha: in the state of pure atman (supreme soul | consciousness) | niryoga-kshema : free from feelings of profit and protection | atmavan : immersed in self (soul consciousness)

The Vedas are conditioned by considerations of the three gunas or what may be called the three attributes of physical nature. But, O Arjuna! You transcend these attributes and should get over all dualities of good and evil, pleasure and pain, light and darkness, life and death etc. and work for getting established in self and attaining the state of pure atman (supreme soul consciousness) free from all concerns of gain and loss etc.

(46)
यावानर्थ उदपाने सर्वतः संप्लुतोदके ।
तावान्सर्वेषु वेदेषु ब्राह्मणस्य विजानतः ॥२-४६॥
yavanartha udapane sarvatah samplutodake
tavansarveshu vedeshu brahmanasya vijanatah (2.46)

yavan : all that/as much | artha : purpose/meaning | uda-pane : in a well of water | sarvatah : from all sides | sampluta-udake : in a large flooding of water | tavan : in the same way | sarveshu : all | vedeshu : in Vedas | brahamanasya : of the supreme Brahamana | vijanatah : has the knowledge

When water floods all sides, a small well makes all the sense in as much as it provides drinking water. Similarly, when so much knowledge is in the Vedas, it is one person with the knowledge of the self (Brahamana, Atman) who becomes most useful.

(47)

कर्मण्येवाधिकारस्ते मा फलेषु कदाचन ।
मा कर्मफलहेतुर्भूर्मा ते सङ्गोऽस्त्वकर्मणि ॥२-४७॥

*karmanyevadhikarste ma phaleshu kadachana
ma karma phala hetur bhurma te sangostvakarmani (2.47)*

karmani : in action/in performing ones duties | eva : surely | adhikara : right/authority/jurisdiction | te : your | ma : not | phaleshu : on fruits/rewards/results | kadachana : never | ma : not | karma-phala : fruit of action | hetu : cause/purpose | bhu : become | ma : never | te : of you | sango : attachment | astu : there should be | akarmani : in not doing ones duties

For doing your duty, you certainly have every authority but you never have any control over the results of your action. Getting fruits of your action is outside your jurisdictional limits. Never think that you are the cause of the fruits of your action and never have any attachment to not doing your duty i.e. You must always continue to do your duty without any desire for results.

(48)

योगस्थः कुरु कर्माणि सङ्गं त्यक्त्वा धनंजय ।
सिद्ध्यसिद्ध्योः समो भूत्वा समत्वं योग उच्यते ॥२-४८॥

*yogasthaḥ kuru karmaṇi sangam tyaktva dhananjaya
siddhy asiddhyoh samo bhutva samatvan yoga uchyate (2.48)*

yogasthah : equipoised | kuru : do/perform | karmani : required action/duty to be performed | sangam : attachment | tyaktva : sacrificing/giving up | dhananjaya : O Arjuna | siddhi-asiddhiyoh : in success and failure | samo : same/equipoised | bhutva : becoming | samatvam : equanimity | yoga : yoga | uchyate : is called

O Arjuna! Perform your duties in a state of yoga (equipoise) giving up all attachment. Remaining equally poised in the face of success and failure, victory and defeat, is called yoga of equanimity.

(49)

दूरेण ह्यवरं कर्म बुद्धियोगाद्धनंजय ।
बुद्धौ शरणमन्विच्छ कृपणाः फलहेतवः ॥२-४९॥

durena hyavaram karma buddhiyogadh dhananjaya
buddhau sharanam anvichchha kripanah phala hetavah (2.49)

durena : from a distance | hy : surely | avaram : inferior | karma : action | buddhi -yogat : directed by wisdom and not by the desire for fruits | Dhananjaya : one who has conquered the lust for riches | buddhau : in wisdom | sharanam : take refuge | anvichchha : search/try to find | kripanah : misers/inferior | phala hetavah : for the purpose of fruits

O Arjuna, for one who has conquered the lust for riches, action done with a desire for its fruits is certainly far inferior to action directed by wisdom (budhi-yoga) without any attachment to its results.
Continue from previous line it will be the best for you to take refuge in the wisdom of buddhi-yoga (yoga of wisdom). Those who work for the purpose of fruits are misers/inferior people.

(50)

बुद्धियुक्तो जहातीह उभे सुकृतदुष्कृते ।
तस्माद्योगाय युज्यस्व योगः कर्मसु कौशलम् ॥२-५०॥

buddhiyukto jahatiha ubhe sukritadushkrite
tasmadyogaya yujyasva yogah karmasu kausalam (2.50)

buddhi-yukto : those endowed with wisdom /of doing their duty with a spirit of | detachment to rewards | jahati : gives up/becomes free of | iha : here/in this world | ubhe : both | sukrate-duskrite : good and bad of their action | tasmat : therefore | yogaya : for the sake of yoga (detached service) | ujjyasma : get ready | yogah : action dictated by wisdom and a sense of duty/without attachment to its fruits | karmasu : in work/in performance of ones duty/in action | kaushalam : skill/art

Those who act with wisdom and perform their duty with a spirit of detachment to rewards thereof become free from good and bad of their action here on earth itself. Therefore, get ready for the yoga of detached service, for doing ones duty directed by wisdom and without looking for fruits. Yoga is the skill of doing ones job well, of discharging ones responsibilities with efficiency.

(51)
कर्मजं बुद्धियुक्ता हि फलं त्यक्त्वा मनीषिणः ।
जन्मबन्धविनिर्मुक्ताः पदं गच्छन्त्यनामयम् ॥२-५१॥

karma jam buddhiyukta hi phalam tyaktva manishinah
janma bandha vinirmuktah padam gachchhanty anamayam (2.51)

karma-jam : born of action | buddhi-yukta : possessed of wisdom | hi : surely | phalam : fruits/results | tyaktva : giving up | manishinah : sages/the wise | janma-bandha : bondage of birth and death | vinirmuktah : freed | padam : position | gachchhanty : go | anamayam : beyond evil

Men of wisdom give up the fruits of their action. The sages freed from the bondage of birth and death achieve the supreme position of bliss which is free from all evil.

(52)
यदा ते मोहकलिलं बुद्धिर्व्यतितरिष्यति ।
तदा गन्तासि निर्वेदं श्रोतव्यस्य श्रुतस्य च ॥२-५२॥

yada te mohakalilam buddhirvyatitarishyati
tada gantasi nirvedam shrotavyasya shrutva say cha (2.52)

yada : when | te : your | moha : illusion | kalilam : forest/quagmire | buddhi : wisdom | vyatitarishyati : gets over | tada : then | ganta-asi : you shall go | nirvedam : indifferent | shrotavyasya : all that has to be heard | shrutasya : all that has been heard already | cha : also

Once your wisdom (discerning intellect) gets over the quagmire of illusions, you shall become indifferent to whatever has been heard as also what has yet to be heard.

(53)

श्रुतिविप्रतिपन्ना ते यदा स्थास्यति निश्चला ।
समाधावचला बुद्धिस्तदा योगमवाप्स्यसि ॥२-५३॥

shrutivipratipanna te yada sthasyati nischala
samadhavchala buddhistada yogamvapsyasi (2.53)

shrutivipratipanna : upset on hearing conflicting views | te : your | yada : when | sthasyati : stays | nischala : fixed/unmoved | samadhau : in samadhi (deep meditation)/immersed in supreme soul / consciousness completely oblivious of material surroundings | achala : unmoved | buddhi : intelligence/wisdom/mind | tada : then | yogam: yoga | avapsyasi : shall attain

Upset on hearing various conflicting views, when your mind gets fixed and stabilised in Samadhi (deep meditation) in the knowledge of the ultimate, you can be said to have attained the stage of yoga and joined in supreme soul consciousness.

(54)

अर्जुन उवाच
स्थितप्रज्ञस्य का भाषा समाधिस्थस्य केशव ।
स्थितधीः किं प्रभाषेत किमासीत व्रजेत किम् ॥२-५४॥

Arjuna uvacha
sthitapragyasya ka bhasha samadhisthasya keshava
sthitadhih kim prabhaseta kim asita vrajeta kim (2.54)

Arjuna uvacha : Arjuna said | sthitapragynasya : one whose mind is fully settled in a state of equanimity | ka : which/what bhasha : language | samadhisthasya : of one sitting in Samadhi/immersed in deep meditation and supreme soul consciousness | Keshava : Lord Krishna | sthitadhih : one whose mind is settled | kim : how | prabhaseta : talks | kim : what | asita : sits | vrajeta : walks | kim : how

Arjuna asked Lord Krishna: O Keshava! what are the symptoms of a realised soul, what kind of language is spoken by such a person whose mind is fully settled and is at peace? While in samadhi - in trance - and completely immersed in deep meditation and supreme soul consciousness, what does he talk, how does he sit and how does he walk?

(55)
श्रीभगवानुवाच
प्रजहाति यदा कामान्सर्वान्पार्थ मनोगतान् ।
आत्मन्येवात्मना तुष्टः स्थितप्रज्ञस्तदोच्यते ॥२-५५॥

Shribhagavan uvacha
prajahati yada kaman sarvan partha manogatan
atmany evatmana tushtah sthita pragyastadochyate (2.55)

Shribhagavan-uvacha : Lord Krishna replied : | prajahati : leaves/gives up | yada : when | kaman : sensory desires | sarvan : of all kinds | Partha : Arjuna | mana-gatan : settled in the mind | atmani : in atman (supreme soul consciousness) | eva : surely | tushtah : satisfied | sthita-pragyas : with steady mind/in a stage of tranquility | tado : then/at that time | cyate : is spoken

Lord Krishna replied: O Arjuna! mind can be said to have surely become tranquil and settled in supreme soul consciousness when craving for gratification of all kinds of sensory desires is completely given up and with a steady mind the Self learns to remain satisfied in Self itself. Happiness that comes from the Spirit within is different and far superior to allsensory pleasures and worldly joys.

(56)
दुःखेष्वनुद्विग्नमनाः सुखेषु विगतस्पृहः ।
वीतरागभयक्रोधः स्थितधीर्मुनिरुच्यते ॥२-५६॥

dukhesv anudvigna manah sukhesu vigatasprhah
vita raga bhaya krodhah sthita dhir muniruchyate (2.56)

dukhesu : in the midst of sorrow/suffering | anudvigna-manah : unperturbed in mind | sukhesu : in times of pleasure | vigataspṛha : free from desire/without hankering for results | vitaraga : devoid of attachment | bhaya : fear | krodhah : anger | sthitadhir : one with steady mind | munir : saint/realised soul | uchyate : is called

One who remains unperturbed in the face of suffering and free from desires of sensory gratification at times of pleasure, one who is free from fear, anger and attachment to results of action is called a saint and a realised soul.

(57)

यः सर्वत्रानभिस्नेहस्तत्तत्प्राप्य शुभाशुभम् ।
नाभिनन्दति न द्वेष्टि तस्य प्रज्ञा प्रतिष्ठिता ॥२-५७॥

yah sarvatranabhisnehas tat tat prapya subhasubham
nabhinandati na dvesti tasya pragya pratisthita (2.57)

yah : who | sarvatra : everywhere | anabhisneha : unaffected/without attachment | tat : that | prapya : getting | subha : good/pleasant | asubham : bad/unpleasant | na : not/never/neither | abhinandati : welcomes/praises | na : not/never/nor | dvesti : envies | tasya : his | pragya : wisdom/mind | pratisthita : established/fixed/stabilised

One who remains unattached everywhere and is not affected by his getting what is good or what is bad, neither praises nor envies, the mind of such a person may be said to have attained stability.

(58)

यदा संहरते चायं कूर्मोऽङ्गानीव सर्वशः ।
इन्द्रियाणीन्द्रियार्थेभ्यस्तस्य प्रज्ञा प्रतिष्ठिता ॥२-५८॥

yada sanharate chayam kurmoanganiva sarvashah
indriyanindriyarthebhyas tasya pragya pratisthita (2.58)

yada : when | sanharate : contracts/withdraws | cha : and/also | ayam : this person | kurma : tortoise | angani : limbs of its body | iva : like | sarvashah : altogether/from all sides | indriyani : sensory | indriya-arthebhya : from the interest of objects of sense gratification | tasya : his | pragya : mind | pratisthita : established

Like the tortoise withdrawing the limbs of its body from all sides into its shell, when a person brings his senses away from all objects of sensory gratification, his mind may be said to have become steady and established in supreme soul consciousness.

(59)
विषया विनिवर्तन्ते निराहारस्य देहिनः ।
रसवर्जं रसोऽप्यस्य परं दृष्ट्वा निवर्तते ॥२-५९॥

vishaya vinivartante niraharasya dehinah
rasavarjam rasoapyasya param drastva nivartate (2.59)

vishaya : objects of sensory gratification | vinivartante : fall away | niraharasya : of one without food/ a person practising abstinence | dehinah : self in body | ras-varjam : giving up the taste | rasa : taste/ sense of pleasure | api : also | asya : his | param : supreme | drastva : after seeing/experiencing | nivartate : ceases/disappears

When an embodied self leads a life of abstinence and lives without food, objects of sensory pleasures fall away. The taste for enjoyment of sense objects also disappears when the supreme is seen and the supreme soul consciousness is realised.

(60)
यततो ह्यपि कौन्तेय पुरुषस्य विपश्चितः ।
इन्द्रियाणि प्रमाथीनि हरन्ति प्रसभं मनः ॥२-६०॥

yatato hyapi Kaunteya purushasya vipashchitah
indriyani pramathini haranti prasabham manah (2.60)

yatata : while making every attempt | hi : positively | api : also | Kaunteya : Arjuna (son of Kunti) | purushasya : of man | vipashchitah : specially intelligent/wise | indriyani : senses | pramathini : agitating/creating turbulence | haranti : take away/render ineffective | prasabham : forcibly | manah : mind

O Arjuna! The senses are very powerful in creating turbulence in the minds of all those who are positively trying hard to control them. The minds of even the specially intelligent and wise men are rendered ineffective by the senses forcibly taking away their power of discrimination.

(61)
तानि सर्वाणि संयम्य युक्त आसीत मत्परः ।
वशे हि यस्येन्द्रियाणि तस्य प्रज्ञा प्रतिष्ठिता ॥२-६१॥

tani sarvani sanyamya yukta asita matparah
vashe hi yasyendriyani tasya pragya pratishthita (2.61)

tani : those | sarvani : all | sanyamya : self restraint | yukta : with | asita : sitting | mat-parah : with faith in me | vase : in control | hi : positively | yasya : whose | indriyani : senses | tasya : his | pragya : mind | pratishthita : established/steady

With self-restraint over all those senses, sitting with faith in Me (as the supreme soul consciousness), one whose senses are positively under control, his mind can be said to have become steady.

(62)
ध्यायतो विषयान्पुंसः सङ्गस्तेषूपजायते ।
सङ्गात्संजायते कामः कामात्क्रोधोऽभिजायते ॥२-६२॥

dhyayato vishayanpunshah sangas teshupaajayate
sangatsanjayate kamah kamat krodhoabhijayate (2.62)

dhyayato : when thinking of | vishayan : objects of senses | punshah : of a person | sanga : attachment | teshu : to them | upajayate : develops/grows | sangat : from attachment | sajayate : develops | kamah : desire | kamat : from desire | krodha : anger | abhijayate : grows

When a person is engaged in thinking of the objects of sensory pleasures, attachment towards them grows, from attachment grows desire and from unfulfilled desires grows anger.

(63)
क्रोधाद्भवति संमोहः संमोहात्स्मृतिविभ्रमः ।
स्मृतिभ्रंशाद्बुद्धिनाशो बुद्धिनाशात्प्रणश्यति ॥२-६३॥

krodhadbhavati sammohah sammohat smritivibhramah
smriti bhranshad buddhinasho buddhinashat pranasyati (2.63)

krodhat : from anger | bhavati : happens/is born | sammohah : delusion | sammohat : from delusion | smritivibhramah : loss of memory | smritibhranshad : from loss of memory | buddhinasho : loss of wisdom (faculty of discriminating between right and wrong) | buddhinashat : from loss of wisdom | pranasyati : is ruined

Anger breeds delusion, from delusion loss of memory follows, loss of memory leads to loss of discriminatory faculty and loss of discriminatory power means complete ruination.

(64)
रागद्वेषवियुक्तैस्तु विषयानिन्द्रियैश्चरन् ।
आत्मवश्यैर्विधेयात्मा प्रसादमधिगच्छति ॥२-६४॥

ragadvesha viyuktais tu vishayan indriyaish charan
atma vashyair vidheyatma prasadam adhigachchhati (2.64)

raga : attachment | dvesha : aversion | viyuktais : freed | tu : but | vishayan : sensory objects | indriyaish : by the senses | charan : moving about | atma-vashyair : under self control | vidheya-atma : self regulating | prasadam : divine bliss | adhigachchhati : achieves

A person who exercises full self-control and is self regulating, who is free from attachment and aversion, who keeps his senses under restraint, can be said to have achieved divine bliss.

(65)
प्रसादे सर्वदुःखानां हानिरस्योपजायते ।
प्रसन्नचेतसो ह्याशु बुद्धिः पर्यवतिष्ठते ॥२-६५॥

prasade sarva-dukhanam hanir asyopajayate
prasanna-chetaso hyashu buddhih paryavatishthate (2.65)

prasade : on receiving God's grace/bliss | sarva : all | dukhanam : sorrows/miseries | hanir : loss | asyo : his | pajayate : happens | prasanna-chetaso : with a happy heart | hi : surely | asu : soon | buddhih : mind | pary : fully | avatishthate : gets fixed

On receiving God's grace, all suffering and sorrows disappear and surely with a happy heart, soon enough mind gets firmly fixed (in supreme soul consciousness).

(66)
नास्ति बुद्धिरयुक्तस्य न चायुक्तस्य भावना ।
न चाभावयतः शान्तिरशान्तस्य कुतः सुखम् ॥२- ६६॥

*nasti buddhirayuktasya na chayuktasya bhavana
na chabhavayatah shantir ashantasya kutah sukham (2.66)*

nasti : does not exist | buddhir : mind/wisdom | ayuktasya : one not connected (with supreme soul consciousness) | na : not | cha : and | bhayuktasya : one not connected (with supreme soul consciousness) | bhavana : feeling | na : not | cha : and | abhavayatah : devoid of feelings/insensitive | shanti : peace | ashantasya : disturbed/unpeaceful | kutah : where | sukham : happiness

It is not a sign of any wisdom to be unconnected (with the supreme soul consciousness). Such a person is devoid of any feelings of peace and how is happiness possible without peace?

(67)
इन्द्रियाणां हि चरतां यन्मनोऽनु विधीयते ।
तदस्य हरति प्रज्ञां वायुर्नावमिवाम्भसि ॥२- ६७॥

*indriyanam hi charatam yanmanoanu vidhiyate
tadasya harati pragyam vayur navam ivambhasi (2.67)*

indriyanam : of senses | hi : surely | charatam : while | yan : which | mana : mind | anuvidhiyate : gets much involved | tat : that | asya : it's | harati : takes away | pragyam : wisdom/power of discrimination | vayu : wind | navam : boat | iva : like | ambhasi : on water

When the mind gets closely involved with the wandering senses, wisdom (the power of discrimination) is lost just as a boat on water is swept away by a strong wind.

(68)
तस्मादस्य महाबाहो निगृहीतानि सर्वशः ।
इन्द्रियाणीन्द्रियार्थेभ्यस्तस्य प्रज्ञा प्रतिष्ठिता ॥२-६८॥

tasmadyasya mahabaho nigrihitani sarvashah
indriyanindriyarthebhyastasya pragya pratisthita (2.68)

tasmad : therefore | yasya : whose | Mahabaho : one with strong arms, Arjuna | nigrihitani : so restrained/controlled | sarvashah : fully/completely | indriyani : senses | indriya-arthebhya : from objects of sensory pleasures | tasya : his | pragya : discrimination/wisdom | pratisthita : established/fixed

Therefore, O strong-armed warrior, Arjuna! One who has succeeded in fully restraining his senses from objects of sensory pleasures, can be said to have achieved the stage of steady wisdom (equanimity of mind, supreme soul consciousness).

(69)
या निशा सर्वभूतानां तस्यां जागर्ति संयमी ।
यस्यां जाग्रति भूतानि सा निशा पश्यतो मुनेः ॥२-६९॥

ya nisha sarvabhutanam tasyam jagarti sanyami
yasyam jagrati bhutani sa nisha pashyato muneh (2.69)

ya : what | nisha : night | sarva : all | bhutanam : living beings | tasyam : in that | jagarti : keeps awake | sanyami : one who has control over the senses | yasyam : in which | jagrati : are awake | bhutani : living beings | sa : that | nisha : night | pashyata : seeing | muneh : saint/realised soul

What is night for all living beings, in that the saint i.e. the self-realised soul (who has control over his senses) keeps awake and when all other living beings are awake, the saint sees it as night.

(70)
आपूर्यमाणमचलप्रतिष्ठं समुद्रमापः प्रविशन्ति यद्वत् ।
तद्वत्कामा यं प्रविशन्ति सर्वे स शान्तिमाप्नोति न कामकामी ॥२-७०॥

apuryamanam achala pratishtham samudramapah pravishanti yadvat
tadvatkama yam pravishanti sarve sa shantimapnoti na kamakami (2.70)

apuryamanam : filled from all sides | achala-pratistham : staying steady | samudram : ocean | apah : waters | pravishanti : enter | yadvat : as | tadvat : same way | kama : desires | yam : whom | pravishanti : enter | sarve : all | shantim : peace | apnoti : achieves | na : not | kam-kami : those who are given to pursuing sensory gratification

All the time, waters keep flowing into the ocean, yet it stays steady. In the same way, when all the desires for sensory pleasures enter, only a self-realised soul can achieve peace, not a person who keeps pining for fulfilling sensory desires.

(71)
विहाय कामान्यः सर्वान् पुमांश्चरति निःस्पृहः ।
निर्ममो निरहंकारः स शान्तिमधिगच्छति ॥२-७१॥

vihaya kamanyah savan pumanshcharti nihshprihah
nirmamo nirahankarah sa shantim adhigachchhati (2.71)

vihaya : giving up | kaman : sensory desires | yah : who | sarvan : all | puman : person | charati : moves about | nihsprihah : without longing | nirmamo : without a sense of 'my-ness' | nirahankarah : without a strong 'ego' feeling | sa : he | shantim : peace | adhigachchhati : achieves

Only a person who has abandoned all sensory desires and one who lives without any longing and without any sense of 'My'ness or a feeling of 'I'ness (strong ego) can achieve peace.

(72)
एषा ब्राह्मी स्थितिः पार्थ नैनां प्राप्य विमुह्यति ।
स्थित्वास्यामन्तकालेऽपि ब्रह्मनिर्वाणमृच्छति ॥२-७२॥

esha brhami sthitih partha nainam prapya vimuhyati
sthithvasyam antkaleapi brahama nirvanam richchhati (2.72)

esha : this | brahmi : divine | sthitih : condition | Partha : Arjuna | na : not | enam : this | prapya : having achieved | vimuhyati : is deluded | sthitva : so situated | asyam : in this | anta-kale : at the last moment of life | api : also |

brahma-nirvanam : ultimate salvation/union with the Divine | richchhati : achieves

O Arjuna! This is the divine position. Having reached this, one is no more deluded. If one is so situated at the last moment of his life, he attains the ultimate salvation and becomes one with the supreme soul consciousness (Param-atma chaitanya).

Thus ends the second Canto titled 'Yoga of Knowledge'.

Third Canto

KARAMA-YOGA
Yoga of Action

(1)

अर्जुन उवाच
ज्यायसी चेत्कर्मणस्ते मता बुद्धिर्जनार्दन ।
तत्किं कर्मणि घोरे मां नियोजयसि केशव ॥३-१॥

Arjuna uvacha
jyayasi chetkarmanaste mata buddhir janardana
tatkim karmani ghore mam niyojayasi keshava (3.1)

jyayasi : superior/better | chet : if | karmanas : as compared to action | te : you | mata : believe/consider | buddhir : knowledge | Janardana : Shri Krishna | tat : therefore | kim : why | karmani : action | ghore : terrible | mam : me | niyojayasi : involves | Keshava : Krishna

O Janardana (Shri Krishna), If you believe that knowledge is superior to action, then, O Keshava (Shri Krishna), why are you involving me in the terrible action of war?

(2)

व्यामिश्रेणेव वाक्येन बुद्धिं मोहयसीव मे ।
तदेकं वद निश्चित्य येन श्रेयोऽहमाप्नुयाम् ॥३-२॥

vyamishreneva vakyena buddhim mohayasiva me
tadekam vada nishchitya yena shreyoaham apnuyam (3.2)

vyamishrena : conflicting | iva : surely | vakyena : by words | buddhim : mind | mohayas-iva : as it were confusing | me : my | tat : therefore | ekam : one | vada : say/speak | nischitya : definite | yena : by which | shreyo : the best | aham : I | apnuyam : achieve

Seemingly conflicting words that you speak surely confuse my mind. Therefore, please tell me that one definite way by which I can achieve what is the best for me.

(3)

श्रीभगवानुवाच
लोकेऽस्मिन्द्विविधा निष्ठा पुरा प्रोक्ता मयानघ ।
ज्ञानयोगेन सांख्यानां कर्मयोगेन योगिनाम् ॥३-३॥

Shribhagavan uvacha
lokeasmindvividha nistha pura prokta mayanagha
gyanyogena sankhyanam karamyogena yoginam (3.3)

Shribhagavan : Lord Krishna | uvacha : said : | loke : in this world | asmin : this | dvi-vidha : confusion/strongly divided between two alternatives | nistha : faith | pura : old | prokta : spoken | maya : by me | anagha : sinless | gyana-yogena : by yoga of knowledge | sankhyanam : the meditative path of knowledge | karma-yogena : by the yoga of action | yoginam : of yogis

Lord Krishna said : O sinless one, Arjuna! As has been spoken by me earlier, in this world, there are two alternative paths (of reaching the supreme, getting salvation or becoming one with the soul consciousness), one is through faith in the meditative path of knowledge (gyan-yoga) and the other is that of yogis whose faith is in karma-yoga or in the life philosophy of action and performance of ones duties.

(4)

न कर्मणा मनारम्भान्नैष्कर्म्यं पुरुषोऽश्नुते ।
न च संन्यसनादेव सिद्धिं समधिगच्छति ॥३-४॥

na karmana manarambhat naiskarmyam purushosnute
na cha sanyasanadeva siddhim samadhigachchhati (3.4)

na : not | karmana : actions | manarambhat : by not initiating | naiskarmyam : not doing anything | purusha : a person | asnute : achieves | na : not | cha : and | sannyasanat : by renouncing action/worldly life | eva : only | siddhim :achievements/success| samadhigachchhati : reaches the 'samadhi ' state/ getting centred in the supreme soul consciousness

By not beginning to take action and not doing anything, a person does not become free from action, nor does one achieve the stage of samadhi and reaches the Supreme by renouncing the world. Whichever path you select, gyan or karma yoga, action is necessary. Even to reach the stage of non-action, one has to act.

(5)

न हि कश्चित्क्षणमपि जातु तिष्ठत्यकर्मकृत् ।
कार्यते ह्यवशः कर्म सर्वः प्रकृतिजैर्गुणैः ॥३-५॥

na hi kaschitkshanapi jatu tishthatyakarmakrit
karyate hyavashah karma sarva prakratijairgunai (3.5)

na : not | hi : surely | kaschit : anyone | kshanam : moment | api : even | jatu : at any time | tisthati : exists | akarmakrit : without performing any action | karyate : made to act | hi : surely | avashah : beyond control | karma : action | sarva : all | prakratijai : born of nature | gunai : quality

Surely, no one can exist at anytime, even for a moment, without performing any action. It is beyond our powers not to act because action is part of the quality born of nature.

(6)

कर्मेन्द्रियाणि संयम्य य आस्ते मनसा स्मरन् ।
इन्द्रियार्थान्विमूढात्मा मिथ्याचारः स उच्यते ॥३-६॥

karmendriyani sanyamya ya aste manasa smaran
indriyarthan vimudhatma mithyacharah sa uchyate (3.6)

karma-indriyani : the five sense organs of action | sanyamya : restraining | ya : who | aste : remains | manasa : by mind | smaran : remembrance | indriya-arthan : for sense objects | vimudha : fool | atma : soul/self | mithya-acharah : bad conduct | sa : he | uchyate : is said to be

He who restrains the five sense organs of action while his mind remains pre-occupied with remembrance of objects of sense gratification is a fool who is deluding his self. Such a person is said to be of bad character, a hypocrite.

(7)

यस्त्विन्द्रियाणि मनसा नियम्यारभतेऽर्जुन ।
कर्मेन्द्रियैः कर्मयोगमसक्तः स विशिष्यते ॥३-७॥

*yastvindriyani manasa niyamyarabhate arjuna
karmendriyaih karma yogam asakatah sa vishishyate (3.7)*

ya : who, one | tu : but | indriyani : the senses | manasa : by the mind | niyamya : disciplining | arabhate : begins | Arjuna : O Arjuna! karma-indriyaih : sense organs of action | karma-yogam : philosophy of action | asakatah : nonattached | sa : he | vishishyate : is superior

But, O Arjuna! one who disciplines the senses by his mind and begins to practice Karma-Yoga - philosophy of action without attachment - is far superior.

(8)

नियतं कुरु कर्म त्वं कर्म ज्यायो ह्यकर्मणः ।
शरीरयात्रापि च ते न प्रसिद्ध्येदकर्मणः ॥३-८॥

*niyatam kuru karma tvam karma jyayo hyakarmanah
sharira yatrapi cha te na prasiddhayed karmanah (3.8)*

niyatam : ordained/bounden | kuru : do | karma : action/duty/work | tvam : you | karma : act | jyaya : better | hi : surely | akarmanah : not doing any work | sharira : body | yatra : journey/maintenance | api : even | cha : and/also | te : your | na : not | prasiddhyet : be possible | akarmanah : without work

You should perform your bounden duties as action is definitely better than not doing any work. Also, it would not be possible to maintain even the physical body without work.

(9)

यज्ञार्थात्कर्मणोऽन्यत्र लोकोऽयं कर्मबन्धनः ।
तदर्थं कर्म कौन्तेय मुक्तसङ्गः समाचर ॥३-९॥

*yagyarthat karmanoanyatra lokoayam karmabandhanah
tadartham karma kaunteya muktasangah samachara (3.9)*

yagyarthat : for the sake of yagya/sacrificial performance | karmana : wok/action | anyatra : elsewhere | loka : world | ayam : this | karma-bandhanah : bondage of action | tat : that | artham : for the purpose of | karma : action/work | Kaunteya : son of Kunti, Arjuna | mukta-sangah : freed from the association | samachara : conduct well

O son of Kunti, Arjuna! Any work done in this world, except for sacrificial purpose only, causes bondage. Therefore, you should so conduct yourself as to be completely free from all association and attachment. Then only you can manage to be free from all bondage.

(10)
सहयज्ञाः प्रजाः सृष्ट्वा पुरोवाच प्रजापतिः ।
अनेन प्रसविष्यध्वमेष वोऽस्त्विष्टकामधुक् ॥३-१०॥

sahayagyah prajah srishtva purovacha prajapatih
anena prasavishyadhvam esha vo astvishta kama dhuk (3.10)

saha : with | yagyah : sacrifice | prajah : creation/generation | srishtva : creating | pura : at the beginning of creation | uvacha : said | prajapatih : creator of praja, Brahma | anena : by this | prasavishyadhvam : be more prosperous | esha : this | va : your | astu : so be it | ishta : desired | kama-dhuk : the milch-cow (kamadhenu) that fulfils all desires

At the beginning, the Creator, Prajapati Brahma created us, the human beings (praja) with sacrifice (yagya) and said : by this sacrifice, prosper. This will be your kamdhenu (the cow that fulfils all desires).

(11)
देवान्भावयतानेन ते देवा भावयन्तु वः ।
परस्परं भावयन्तः श्रेयः परमवाप्स्यथ ॥३-११॥

devan bhavayatanena te deva bhavayantu vah
parasparam bhavayantah shreyah param avapsyatha (3.11)

devan : gods | bhavayata : pleased | anena : by this (yagya) | te : those | deva : gods | bhavayantu : will please | vah : you | parasparam : mutually |

bhavayantah : pleasing | shreyah : good | param : the supreme | avapsyatha : achieve

By this yagya (sacrifice), the gods will be pleased and they will please you. Thus, mutually pleasing one another, you will attain the supreme good.

(12)
इष्टान्भोगान्हि वो देवा दास्यन्ते यज्ञभाविताः ।
तैर्दत्तानप्रदायैभ्यो यो भुङ्क्ते स्तेन एव सः ॥३-१२॥

ishtan bhoganhi vo deva dasyante yagya bhavitah
tair dattan apradayaibhyo yo bhunkte stena eva sah (3.12)

ishtan : desired/wished for | bhogan : objects of enjoyment | hi : definitely | va : you | deva : gods | dasyante : will give/bestow | yagya-bhavita : pleased/satisfied by yagya (sacrifice) | tai : by them | dattan : given | apradaya : without offering | ebhaya : to them (gods) | ya : who | bhunkte : enjoys | stena : thief | eva : surely/verily | sah : he

Pleased by your yagyas (sacrifices), gods will certainly bestow on you your desired objects of pleasure, but one who enjoys them without making an offering to the gods is verily a thief.

(13)
यज्ञशिष्टाशिनः सन्तो मुच्यन्ते सर्वकिल्बिषैः ।
भुञ्जते ते त्वघं पापा ये पचन्त्यात्मकारणात् ॥३-१३॥

yagyashistashinah santo muchyante sarvakilbisaih
bhunjate te tvagham papa ye pachantyatma karanat (3.13)

yagya-shista : left over/residue of yagya food | ashinah : those who eat | santa : saintly persons | muchyante : get freed | sarva : all | kilbisaih : from sins | bhunjate : enjoy/eat | te : they | tu : but | agham : grievous sins | papa : sinners | ye : who | pachanti : cook food | atma-karanat : for enjoyment of sense objects

Those saintly persons who eat the residue food at yagyas are freed from all sins but those sinners who cook food only for their sensory gratification commit grievous sins.

(14)
अन्नाद्भवन्ति भूतानि पर्जन्यादन्नसम्भवः ।
यज्ञाद्भवति पर्जन्यो यज्ञः कर्मसमुद्भवः ॥३-१४॥

annadbhavanti bhutani parjanyad annasambhavah
yagyadbhavati parjanyo yagyah karmasamudbhavah (3.14)

annant : from food-grains | bhavanti : come out/emerge | bhutani : living beings | parjanyad : from rains | anna : food-grains | sambhavah : possible | yagyat : from sacrifice (yagya) | bhavati : happens/comes out/results | parjanya : rain | yagyah : sacrifice | karma : action/performance of ones duties/obligations | samudbhavah : born of

All living beings depend on food-grains. Food-grains become possible because of rains. Rains result from yagyas (sacrifice). Sacrifice comes from action - from due performance of ones duties.

(15)
कर्म ब्रह्मोद्भवं विद्धि ब्रह्माक्षरसमुद्भवम् ।
तस्मात्सर्वगतं ब्रह्म नित्यं यज्ञे प्रतिष्ठितम् ॥३-१५॥

karma brahmodbhavam viddhi brahamakshara samudbhavam
tasmat sarvagatam brahma nityam yagye pratishthitam (3.15)

karma : action | brahma : the creator god Prajapati Brahma/Creative / Consciousness | udbhavam : produced | viddhi : know | brahma akshara : Shabdbrahma/ Word God | samudbhavam : arising from | tasmat : therefore | sarva-batam : all pervading | Brahma : the supreme/impersonal/ imperishable | nityam : eternally/always | yagye : in sacrifice | pratishthitam : situated

You should know that all action has its source in the will of the creative consciousness of Brahma, the god of creation. The god of creation himself arises from the supreme impersonal, imperishable

Brahma eternally founded in sacrifice. The ultimate goal is thus sacrifice or action without any attachment and for communion with supreme soul consciousness.

(16)

एवं प्रवर्तितं चक्रं नानुवर्तयतीह यः ।
अघायुरिन्द्रियारामो मोघं पार्थ स जीवति ॥३-१६॥

evam pravartitam chakram nanuvartayatiha yah
aghayur indriyaramo mogham partha sa jivati (3.16)

evam : thus | pravartitam : as well established | chakram : cycle | na : not | anuvartayati : adopt | iha : here/in this life | yah : who | agha-ayu : persons involved in acts of sin | indriya-arama : engaged in gratification of sensory objects | mogham : uselessly | Partha : Arjuna | sa : he | jivati : lives

O Arjuna! Thus, those persons who do not follow this well-established revolving cycle of creation, are involved in acts of sin and gratification of sensory objects and are actually living in vain.

(17)

यस्त्वात्मरतिरेव स्यादात्मतृप्तश्च मानवः ।
आत्मन्येव च सन्तुष्टस्तस्य कार्यं न विद्यते ॥३-१७॥

yas tvatma ratir eva syad atma triptash cha manavah
atmanyeva cha santustashtasya karyam na vidyate (3.17)

ya : who | tu : but | atma-rati : looking within/taking pleasure in self consciousness | eva : certainly | syat : remains | atma-triptah : self-satisfied | cha : and | manavah : man | atmani : in himself | eva : only | cha : and | santushta : contented | tasya : his | karyam : duty/obligation | na : not | vidyate : exist

But for a person who looks within, certainly takes pleasure in self-consciousness, is self-satisfied and contented in himself, there hardly seems any duty left to be performed.

(18)

नैव तस्य कृतेनार्थो नाकृतेनेह कश्चन ।
न चास्य सर्वभूतेषु कश्चिदर्थव्यपाश्रयः ॥३-१८॥

naiva tasya kritenartho nakriteneha kashchan
na chasya sarva bhuteshu kashchid artha vyapashraya (3.18)

na : not | eva : certainly | tasya : his | kritena : by doing the job/performing ones duty | artha : meaning/motive | na : nor | akritena : without doing the ordained job/discharging ones duty | iha : here/in this world | kaschana : whatever | na : not | cha : and | asya : of him | sarva-bhuteshu : for all living beings | kashchid : any | artha : purpose/motive | vyapashrayah : being dependent

Not attached to action, such a person has no motive in doing something or in not performing any duty whatsoever. He does not wish to gain anything by doing something nor does he stand to lose anything by not doing it. He need not depend on any other being.

(19)

तस्मादसक्तः सततं कार्यं कर्म समाचर ।
असक्तो ह्याचरन्कर्म परमाप्नोति पूरुषः ॥३-१९॥

tasmadasaktah satatam karyam karma samachar
asakto hyacharan karmam parmapnoti purushah (3.19)

tasmat : therefore | asakta : unattached | satatam : eternally/always | karyam : duty/something to be done as an obligation | karma : action/work | samachara : perform well | asakta : without attachment | hi : definitely | acharan : cconduct/doing | karma : action/work | param : supreme | apnoti : achieves | purushah : man

Therefore, always remaining unattached, keep doing your work as your duty, and fulfil your obligations well because a man performing his bounded duties without attachment achieves the supreme.

(20)

कर्मणैव हि संसिद्धिमास्थिता जनकादयः ।
लोकसंग्रहमेवापि संपश्यन्कर्तुमर्हसि ॥३-२०॥

karmanaiva hi sansidhim asthita janakadayah
loka sangraham evapi sampashyan kartum arhasi (3.20)

karmana : by work | eva : even | hi : definitely | sansiddhim : supreme realisation | asthita : situated | janakadayah : Janaka and others | lokasangraham : the people at large | evapi : also | sampasyan : in view of | kartum : to do | arhasi : befits you

King Janaka and his like definitely attained realisation of the supreme by their adherence to performing their duties. In the interest of the people at large also it only befits you to do your duty.

(21)

यद्यदाचरति श्रेष्ठस्तत्तदेवेतरो जनः ।
स यत्प्रमाणं कुरुते लोकस्तदनुवर्तते ॥३-२१॥

yad yad acharati shreshthastadtadevetaro janah
sa yatpramanam kurute lokas tad anuvartate (3.21)

yat yat : whatever | acharati : conduct is followed | shrestha : eminent men/icons | tattat : the same | eva : certainly | itara : other | janah : person | sa : he | yat : whichever | pramanam : example | kurute : does | loka : the world | tat : that | anuvartate : follows

What the icon does, the same is certainly done by others, whatever example of conduct he presents, the world follows.

(22)

न मे पार्थास्ति कर्तव्यं त्रिषु लोकेषु किंचन ।
नानवाप्तमवाप्तव्यं वर्त एव च कर्मणि ॥३-२२॥

na me parthasti kartavyam trishu lokeshu kinchana
nanavaptam avaptavyam varta eva cha karmani (3.22)

na : not | me : mine | Partha : Arjuna | asti : is/exists | kartavyam : duty | trishu : in the three | lokeshu : worlds | kinchana : any | na : nothing/not | anavaptam : desired | varte : engaged | eva : surely | cha : and/also | karmani : action

O Arjuna! There is nothing in the three worlds that remains to be done by me as a bounden duty nor is there any unfulfilled desire or anything that I wanted to achieve and have not achieved, yet I am all the time engaged in action.

(23)
यदि ह्यहं न वर्तेयं जातु कर्मण्यतन्द्रितः।
मम वर्त्मानुवर्तन्ते मनुष्याः पार्थ सर्वशः ॥३-२३॥

*yadi hyaham na varteyam jatu karmanyatandritah
mama vartmanuvartante manushyah partha sarvashah (3.23)*

yadi : if | hi : certainly | aham : I | na : not | varteyam : remain engaged | jatu : ever | karmani : in action/attending to my duties | atandritah : attentive | mam : my | vartma : path | anuvartante : follow | manushyah : people | Partha : Arjuna | sarvashah : in all respects

O Arjuna! If ever I do not remain fully engaged in action i.e. attentive in performing my duties, all the other people will certainly follow my example and in all respects take the same path and become careless in regard to attending to their duties.

(24)
उत्सीदेयुरिमे लोका न कुर्यां कर्म चेदहम्।
संकरस्य च कर्ता स्यामुपहन्यामिमाः प्रजाः ॥३-२४॥

*utsideyurime loka na kuryam karma chedaham
sankarasya cha karta syam upahanyam imah prajah (3.24)*

utsideyu : would be destroyed | ime : these | loka : worlds | na : not | kuryam : I do | karma : action/duty | chet : if | aham : I | sankarasya : of the population born of illegitimate unions | cha : and | karta : creator/doer | syam : would be | upahanyam : would ruin | imah : these | prajah : people

If I do not perform my bounden duties all these worlds would be destroyed. I shall be responsible for a large population born of illegitimate unions and this would ruin all the people.

(25)
सक्ताः कर्मण्यविद्वांसो यथा कुर्वन्ति भारत ।
कुर्याद्विद्वांस्तथासक्तश्चिकीर्षुर्लोकसंग्रहम् ॥३-२५॥

saktah karmanyavidwanso yatha kurvanti bharata
kuryad vidwans tathasaktash chikirshur loka sangraham (3.25)

sakta : attached | karmani : bounden duties | avidwansa : those not knowledgable/the ignorant ones | yatha : as | kurvanti : do | Bharata : descendant of Bharat, Arjuna | kuryat : do | vidvan : the learned | tatha : and/thus | asakta : non-attached | chikirshu : desiring (to present an example before the people) | lokasangraham : welfare of the people at large

O descendant of Bharata, Arjuna! As the ignorant ones do their bounden duties attached to results thereof, the learned also do so but without any attachment and only desiring to do good to the people at large or set an example before them.

(26)
न बुद्धिभेदं जनयेदज्ञानां कर्मसङ्गिनाम् ।
जोषयेत्सर्वकर्माणि विद्वान्युक्तः समाचरन् ॥३-२६॥

na buddhi bhedam janayedagyanam karmasanginam
joshayet sarvakarmani vidvanyuktah samacharan (3.26)

na : not | buddhi : intelligence/mind | bhedam : disturbance | janayet : create/generate | agyanam : of those who do not know/ignorant | karma : action | sanginam : attached to results | joshayet : engage in | sarva : all | karmani : acts/works | vidvan : learned | yuktah : engaged/steady | samacharan : acting

One should not create disturbance in the minds of the ignorant persons engaged in action with attachment to results thereof. Any confusion in that regard may lead them to stop all work. The learned and the wise should instead promote continuation of all activities.

(27)
प्रकृतेः क्रियमाणानि गुणैः कर्माणि सर्वशः ।
अहंकारविमूढात्मा कर्ताहमिति मन्यते ॥३-२७॥

prakrteh kriyamanani gunaih karmani sarvashah
ahankara vimudhatma kartaham iti manyate (3.27)

prakrte : of nature | kriyamanani : happening/getting done | gunaih : attributes/qualities | karmani : acts/activities | sarvashah : all | ahankar : false pride/ego | vimudha : deluded by | atma : self | karta : doer | aham : I | iti : thus | manyate : thinks/believes

All that is happening or is being done is a natural phenomenon. It flows from the attributes of nature. But, a person blinded by his false ego thinks that he is the doer.

(28)
तत्त्ववित्तु महाबाहो गुणकर्मविभागयोः ।
गुणा गुणेषु वर्तन्त इति मत्वा न सज्जते ॥३-२८॥

tattvavittu maha baho guna karma vibhagayoh
guna guneshu vartanta iti matva na sajjate (3.28)

tattvavit : knower of the essence of the supreme | tu : but | Mahabaho : mighty-armed Arjuna | guna-karma : attributes and actions | vibhagayoh : of different parts | guna : attributes | guneshu : senses | vartante : being involved | iti : thus | matva : believing | na : not | sajjate : get attached

O mighty-armed one, Arjuna! The learned who know the essence of the supreme truth understand the difference between the attributes of nature and the objects of sensory gratification acting on each other and, therefore, they remain unattached.

(29)
प्रकृतेर्गुणसंमूढाः सज्जन्ते गुणकर्मसु ।
तानकृत्स्नविदो मन्दान्कृत्स्नविन्न विचालयेत् ॥३-२९॥

prakriter guna sammudhah sajjante gunakarmasu
tanakritsna vido mandan kritsna vin na vichalayet (3.29)

prakrite : of nature | guna : attributes/modes | sammudhah : misled | sajjante : getting engaged/remaining attached | gunakarmasu : sensory activities | tan : those | akrtsna-vida : those not understanding fully | mandan : those with poor intelligence | krtsna-vit : those who know all | na : not | vichalayet : get upset

Those with poor intelligence, engaged in sensory activities of the material world are misled by the attributes of nature and remain attached to the results of their activities. But, the wise ones who know all should do nothing to upset them and create a situation where they abandon the path of action.

(30)
मयि सर्वाणि कर्माणि संन्यस्याध्यात्मचेतसा ।
निराशीर्निर्ममो भूत्वा युध्यस्व विगतज्वरः ॥३-३०॥
mayi sarvani karmani sannyasyadhyatmachetasa
nirashir nirmamo bhutva yudhyasva vigata jvarah (3.30)

mayi : to me | sarvani : all | karmani : actions | sannyasya : giving up/renouncing | adhyatna : knowledge of the soul/self | chetsa : consciousness | nirashi : without any hope of gain | nirmama : without a feeling of myness/devoid of egoism | bhutva : being | yudhyasva : fight/engage in battle | vigatajvarah : without feverish strain

Renounce all your actions unto me and concentrate on knowledge of self-consciousness. Devoid of egoism, without any hope for gain and free from mental fever, fight.

(31)
ये मे मतमिदं नित्यमनुतिष्ठन्ति मानवाः ।
श्रद्धावन्तोऽनसूयन्तो मुच्यन्ते तेऽपि कर्मभिः ॥३-३१॥
ye me matamidam nityamanutisthanti manavah
shraddhavanto anasuyanto muchyante api karmabhih (3.31)

Ye : those | me : my | matam : opinion/precepts | idam : these | nityam : always | anutisthanti : follow/bring into practice | manavah : human beings |

shraddhavanta : those having faith | anasuyanta : without envy | muchyante : become free | te : they | api : also | karmabhih : bondage of action

Those human beings who follow and always faithfully practice my precepts without envy are also freed from the bondage of action.

(32)

ये त्वेतदभ्यसूयन्तो नानुतिष्ठन्ति मे मतम् ।
सर्वज्ञानविमूढांस्तान्विद्धि नष्टानचेतसः ॥३-३२॥

*ye tvetadabhyasuyanto nanutishthanti me matam
sarva gyan vimuddhans tan vidhi nastanachetsah (3.32)*

ye : those | tu : however | etat : this | abhyasuyanta : decry/disregard | na : not | anutishthanti : perform | me : my | matam : precept/view/advice | sarva-gyan vimudhan : devoid of all knowledge | tan : they | vidhi : know | nashtan : finished/ruined | achetsah : fools/without consciousness

However, those who decry my advice and do not practice it are fools, devoid of all knowledge. Please know that they are bound to be ruined.

(33)

सदृशं चेष्टते स्वस्याः प्रकृतेर्ज्ञानवानपि ।
प्रकृतिं यान्ति भूतानि निग्रहः किं करिष्यति ॥३-३३॥

*sadrisham cheshtate svasyah prakriter gyanavanapi
prakritim yanti bhutani nigrahah kim karishyati (3.33)*

sadrisam : in accordance with | chestate : attempts to act | svasyah : own | prakrite : nature | gyanavana : knowledgeable/wise | api : even | prakrtim : nature | yanti : follow | bhutani : living beings | nigrahah : restraint | kim : what | karisyati : can do/will do

Even a wise man attempts to act in accordance with his nature. All living beings follow nature. What will restraints do ?

(34)

इन्द्रियस्येन्द्रियस्यार्थे रागद्वेषौ व्यवस्थितौ ।
तयोर्न वशमागच्छेत्तौ ह्यस्य परिपन्थिनौ ॥३-३४॥

indriyasyendriyasyarthe ragadveshau vyavasthitau
tayorna vashamagachchettau hyasya paripanthinau (3.34)

indriyasya : of the senses | indriyasya -arthe : for the purpose of sensory gratification | raga : attachment | dveshau : aversion | vyavasthitau : organised | tayorna : of them | na : not/never | vasham : under control | agachchhet : come | tau : those | hi : certainly | asya : his | paripanthinau : impediments/stumbling stones

It is in the nature of each one of our senses to have attachment or aversion to well organised objects of sensory gratification. One should avoid coming under their influence as they are stumbling blocks (on the spiritual path).

(35)

श्रेयान्स्वधर्मो विगुणः परधर्मात्स्वनुष्ठितात् ।
स्वधर्मे निधनं श्रेयः परधर्मो भयावहः ॥३-३५॥

shreyan sva dharmo vigunah para dharmat sv anushthitat
sva dharme nidhanam shreyah para dharmo bhayavahah (3.35)

shreyan : better | svadharma : ones own charter of duties | vigunah : with flaws | para-dharmat : as compared to duties meant for others | su-anushthitat : properly performed | sva-dharme : in the area of duties ordained for self bounden duties | nidhanam : death | shreyah : better | para-dharma : duties meant for others | bhaya-avahah : fearful

It is always better to follow ones own charter of bounden duties even with some flaws rather than properly perform duties meant for others. Even death in pursuit of ones duties is preferable. Following other's charter of duties is dangerous.

(36)
अर्जुन उवाच
अथ केन प्रयुक्तोऽयं पापं चरति पूरुषः ।
अनिच्छन्नपि वार्ष्णेय बलादिव नियोजितः ॥३-३६॥

Arjuna uvacha
atha kena prayuktoayam papam charati purushah
anicchannapi varshneya baladiva niyojitah (3.36)

Arjuna said : | atha : so/then | kena : by what | prayukta : get impelled | ayam : this one | papam : sins | charati : does | purusha : man | anicchan : unwillingly | api : also/even | varshneya : O descendant of Vrsni | balat : forcefully | iva : as if | niyojitah : pre-determined

O descendant of Vrsni, Lord Krishna! What is it that impels one, even unwillingly, to commit sins ? Is it that it is forced by pre-ordained destiny?

(37)
श्रीभगवानुवाच
काम एष क्रोध एष रजोगुणसमुद्भवः ।
महाशनो महापाप्मा विद्ध्येनमिह वैरिणम् ॥३-३७॥

Shribhagwan uvacha
kama esa krodha esa rajo guna samudbhavah
mahashano maha papma vidhyenam iha vairinam (3.37)

Shribhagvan : Lord Krishna | uvacha : said | kama : lust/desire | esa : this | krodha : anger | esa : this | raja-guna : attribute of active nature called rajoguna | samudbhavah : born of | maha-shana : all devouring | maha-papma : greatly sinful | viddhi : know | enam : this | iha : here/on earth | vairinam : enemy

Lord Krishna said : You should know that all-devouring lustful desire and anger are both born of the attributes of active nature. Here, on this earth, these constitute a very sinful enemy.

(38)

धूमेनाव्रियते वह्निर्यथादर्शो मलेन च।
यथोल्बेनावृतो गर्भस्तथा तेनेदमावृतम् ॥३-३८॥

dhumenavriyate vahmir yathadarsho malena cha
yatholbenavrito garbhas tatha tenedam avritam (3.38)

dhumena : by smoke | avriyate : is covered | vahni : fire | yatha : just as | adarsha : mirror | malena : by dust | cha : and | yatha : just as | ulbena : secundine | avrta : covered | garbha : embryo | tatha : so/similarly | tena : by that (lust) | idam : this | avrtam : covered

Just as fire is engulfed by smoke, mirror is covered by dust and embryo is enveloped by secundine, similarly, this knowledge is covered by lust.

(39)

आवृतं ज्ञानमेतेन ज्ञानिनो नित्यवैरिणा।
कामरूपेण कौन्तेय दुष्पूरेणानलेन च ॥३-३९॥

avrtam gyanmetena gyanino nitya vairina
kama rupena kaunteya dushpurenanalena cha (3.39)

avrtam : covered | gyanam : knowledge | etena : by this | gyanina : of the knower | nityavairina : by the eternal enemy | kama-rupena : in the shape of lustful desire | Kaunteya : son of Kunti, Arjuna | dushpurena : not satisfied / insatiable | analena : by the fire | cha : also

O son of Kunti, Arjuna! This knowledge is covered by the wise knower's eternal enemy in the shape of lustful desire which burns like insatiable fire.

(40)

इन्द्रियाणि मनो बुद्धिरस्याधिष्ठानमुच्यते।
एतैर्विमोहयत्येष ज्ञानमावृत्य देहिनम् ॥३-४०॥

indriyani mano buddhir asyadhishthanam uchyate
etair vimohayatyesha gyanam avrtya dehinam (3.40)

indriyani : senses | mana : mind | buddhi : intelligence | asya : of this | adhishthanam : sitting place/residence | uchyate : is said | etai : by these | vimohayati : fascinates/deludes into confusion | esha : this (lust) | gyanam : knowledge | avrityam : covering | dehinam : the embodied being/self

This lust is said to have its residence in the sense organs, the mind and the intelligence. It puts a veil on the wisdom of self and causes confusion.

(41)
तस्मात्त्वमिन्द्रियाण्यादौ नियम्य भरतर्षभ ।
पाप्मानं प्रजहि ह्येनं ज्ञानविज्ञाननाशनम् ॥३-४१॥
tasmat tvam indriyanyadau niyamya bharatarishabha
papmanam prajahi hyenam gyan vigyana nashanam (3.41)

tasmat : therefore | tvam : you | indriyani : sense organs | adau : first | niyamya : controlling by rules/discipline | Bharata-rishabha : Best (the most eminent) among descendants of Bharata, | Arjuna | papmanam : sinful | prajahi : kill | hi : certainly/definitely | enam : this | gyan : knowledge of the spirit | vigyan : knowledge of matter | nashanam : the destroyer |

Therefore, O Arjuna, the best of the descendants of Bharata ! first, you discipline your senses, (and then) definitely kill this (lust which is) sinful destroyer of the knowledge of the spiritual and the material.

(42)
इन्द्रियाणि पराण्याहुरिन्द्रियेभ्यः परं मनः ।
मनसस्तु परा बुद्धिर्यो बुद्धेः परतस्तु सः ॥३-४२॥
indriyani paranyahur indriyebhyah param manah
manasas tu para buddhir yo buddheh paratas tu sah (3.42)

indriyani : senses/sense organs | parani : superior | ahu : said to be | indriyebhyah : sense objects | param : superior | manah : mind | manasa : to mind | tu : also | para : superior | buddhi : intelligence | ya : who | buddhe : to intelligence | parata : higher | tu : but | sah : he/self

The senses are said to be superior to sense objects, mind is superior to senses, intelligence is above the mind and higher than the intelligence is the suprem econsciousness of the self (atman).

(43)
एवं बुद्धेः परं बुद्ध्वा संस्तभ्यात्मानमात्मना ।
जहि शत्रुं महाबाहो कामरूपं दुरासदम् ॥३-४३॥

evam buddheh param buddhva sanstabhyatmanam atmana
jahi shatrum maha baho kama rupam durasadam (3.43)

evam : thus | buddheh : intellect | param : supreme | buddhva : knowing | samstabhya : strengthen, stabilise | atmanam : mind/self | atmana : self | jahi : conquer/destroy | shatrum : enemy | Mahabaho : O mighty-armed one, Arjuna | kama-rupam : lust | durasadam : difficult to conquer

O mighty-armed Arjuna! Thus knowing that the supreme self (atman) that is above the intellect and controlling the mind by intelligence (self by self), destroys this difficult-to-conquer enemy called lust.

Thus ends the Third Canto titled 'Yoga of Action'.

Fourth Canto

GYANA-KARMA-SANYASA YOGA
Yoga of Knowledge, Action and Renunciation

(1)

श्रीभगवानुवाच
इमं विवस्वते योगं प्रोक्तवानहमव्ययम् ।
विवस्वान्मनवे प्राह मनुरिक्ष्वाकवेऽब्रवीत् ॥४-१॥

Shribhagavan uvacha
imam vivasvate yogam proktavanahamavyayam
vivasvanmanave praha manurikshvakave abravit (4.1)

Shribhagavan : Shri Bhagavan, Lord Krishna | uvacha : said | imam : this | vivasvate : to the sun-god | yogam : the knowledge of becoming one with the supreme self consciousness | proktavan : imparted | aham : I | avyayam : indestructible | vivasvan : Sun-god | Manave : to Manu | praha : told | Manu : the first man, father of mankind | ikshvakave : to King Ikshvaku | abravit : said

Lord Krishna said that he first imparted this indestructible knowledge of this yoga of action and realising the oneness with the supreme soul-consciousness to the Sun-god, Vivasvan who passed it on to Manu and Manu conveyed it to King Iksvaku.

(2)

एवं परम्पराप्राप्तमिमं राजर्षयो विदुः ।
स कालेनेह महता योगो नष्टः परन्तप ॥४-२॥

evam parampara praptam imam rajarshayo viduh
sa kaleneha mahata yogo nashtah parantapa (4.2)

evam : thus | parampara : by traditional succession | praptam : received | imam : this | rajarsaya : saint-like kings | viduh : knew | sa : that | kalena : with the passage of time | iha : here/on this earth | mahata : great | yoga :

the science (philosophy) of action and realising oneness with the supreme soul (self consciousness) | nastah : lost | parantapa : scorcher of foes, Arjuna

Thus, through traditional succession, from generation to generation, several saintly kings received this knowledge of yoga - philosophy of action with realisation of oneness with the supreme soul consciousness. Unfortunately, O Arjuna! With the passage of time, this knowledge was lost on this earth.

(3)

स एवायं मया तेऽद्य योगः प्रोक्तः पुरातनः ।
भक्तोऽसि मे सखा चेति रहस्यं ह्येतदुत्तमम् ॥४-३॥

sa evayam maya teadya yogah proktah puratanah
bhaktoasi me sakha cheti rahasyam hyetaduttamam (4.3)

sah : that | eva : surely | ayam : this | maya : by me | te : to you | adya : today | yogah : the science (philosophy) of non-attached action and realisation of the oneness with the supreme soul (self) consciousness | proktah : spoken | puratanah : ancient | bhakta : devotee | asi : are | me : my | sakha : dear friend | cha : and/also | iti : therefore | rahasyam : secret/mystery | hi : certainly | etat : this | uttamam : profound

You are my devotee and also a dear friend. Therefore, today, I am giving to you that very knowledge of yoga (of unattached action and realisation of oneness with the supreme soul consciousness) which is spoken of as very ancient and is certainly a profound mystery (for the other undeserving ones).

(4)

अर्जुन उवाच
अपरं भवतो जन्म परं जन्म विवस्वतः ।
कथमेतद्विजानीयां त्वमादौ प्रोक्तवानिति ॥४-४॥

Arjuna uvacha
aparam bhavato janma param janma vivasvatah
kathametadvijaniyam tvamadau proktavaniti (4.4)

Gyana-Karma-Sanyasa Yoga | 81

Arjuna : Arjuna | uvacha : said : | aparam : later/recent | bhavta : your | janma : birth | param : earlier | janma : birth | vivasvatah : Vivasvata, the Sun-god | katham : how | etat : this | vijaniyam : shall comprehend/understand | tvam : you | adau : at beginning | proktavan : spoken/imparted | iti : thus

Arjuna said: Your birth was very much subsequent to that of Vivasvata, the Sun-god. How can I then comprehend that (as claimed by you earlier) it was you who had imparted this knowledge to Vivasvata at the beginning?

(5)

श्रीभगवानुवाच
बहूनि मे व्यतीतानि जन्मानि तव चार्जुन ।
तान्यहं वेद सर्वाणि न त्वं वेत्थ परन्तप ॥४-५॥

Shribhagavan uvacha
bahuni me vyatitani janmani tava charjuna
tanyaham veda sarvani na tvam vettha parantapa (4.5)

Shribhagavan : Lord Krishna | uvacha : said : | bahuni : many | me : mine | vyatitani : have passed | janmani : births | tava : yours | cha : and | arjuna : Arjuna | tani : those | aham : I | veda : know | sarvani : all | na : not | tvam : you | vettha : know | parantapa : Arjuna

Lord Krishna said: O Arjuna! Both you and I have passed through many births. The difference between us is that I remember all my past births while you, scorcher of enemies, Arjuna, do not know about your past births.

(6)

अजोऽपि सन्नव्ययात्मा भूतानामीश्वरोऽपि सन् ।
प्रकृतिं स्वामधिष्ठाय संभवाम्यात्ममायया ॥४-६॥

ajoapi sannavyayatma bhutanamishvaroapi san
prakritim svamadhishthaya sambhavamyatmamayaya (4.6)

aja : unborn | api : although | san : so | avyaya : without any decay | atma : self | bhutanam : all living beings | ishvara : supreme lord | api : also | san : so

| prakritim : nature | svam : myself | adhishthaya : controlling | sambhavami : incarnate | atmamayaya : my intrinsic power

Although I am never born and so never decay, also, I am the supreme lord of all living beings, myself, controlling it's own nature, incarnates (from time to time) through its own intrinsic power.

(7)

यदा यदा हि धर्मस्य ग्लानिर्भवति भारत ।
अभ्युत्थानमधर्मस्य तदात्मानं सृजाम्यहम् ॥४-७॥

yada yada hi dharmasya glanir bhavati bharata
abhyutthanam adharmasya tadatmanam srijamyaham (4.7)

yada yada : whenever | hi : certainly | dharmasya : of dharma/of the code of righteous conduct | glani : fall/decline | bhavati : happens | bharata : O descendant of King Bharata, Arjuna | abhyutthanam : predominance | adharmasya : of lack of dharma/vice | tada : then/at that time | atmanam : self | srijami : manifest | aham : I

O Arjuna, descendant of Bharata! Whenever dharma (righteous conduct/virtue) declines and lack of dharma (vice) prevails widely, at that time, I manifest myself on earth.

(8)

परित्राणाय साधूनां विनाशाय च दुष्कृताम् ।
धर्मसंस्थापनार्थाय सम्भवामि युगे युगे ॥४-८॥

paritranaya sadhunam vinashaya cha dushkriatam
dharma sansthapanarthaya sambhavami yuge yuge (4.8)

paritranaya : to protect | sadhunam : the virtuous | vinashaya : to destroy | cha : and | dushkriatam : the vicious | dharma : code of righteous conduct | sansthapana : establishment | arthaya : for the purpose of | sambhavami : manifest myself/incarnate/appear | yuge yuge : age after age

To protect the virtuous and to destroy the vicious and for establishing the code of righteous conduct, I appear on earth from age to age.

(9)

जन्म कर्म च मे दिव्यमेवं यो वेत्ति तत्त्वतः ।
त्यक्त्वा देहं पुनर्जन्म नैति मामेति सोऽर्जुन ॥४-९॥

janma karma cha me divyamevam yo vetti tattvatah
tyaktava deham punarjanma naiti mameti soarjuna (4.9)

janma : birth | karma : action | cha : and | me : mine | divyam : divine | evam : and | ya : who | vetti : know | tattvatah : essentially | tyaktva : giving up/ leaving | deham : the body | puna : again | janma : birth | na : never/not | eti : achieves | mam : me | eti : achieves | sa : he | arjuna : Arjuna

O Arjuna! My birth and actions have been divine. He who gets to know essentially this and other truths like this, when he leaves the body (dies), he is freed from the bondage of rebirth and achieves me.

(10)

वीतरागभयक्रोधा मन्मया मामुपाश्रिताः ।
बहवो ज्ञानतपसा पूता मद्भावमागताः ॥४-१०॥

vitaragabhayakrodha manmaya mamupashritah
bahavo gyanatapasa puta mad bhavamagatah (4.10)

vita : freed from | raga : attachment | bhaya : fear | krodha : anger | manmaya : in me | mam : my | upashritah : dependant | bahava : many | gyana : knowledge/wisdom | tapasa : penance | puta : purified | mat-bhavam : my being | agatah : reached

Freed from attachment, fear and anger, many in the past who depended on me and were purified by wisdom and penance succeeded in reaching me.

(11)

ये यथा मां प्रपद्यन्ते तांस्तथैव भजाम्यहम् ।
मम वर्त्मानुवर्तन्ते मनुष्याः पार्थ सर्वशः ॥४-११॥

ye yatha mam prapadyante tanstathaiva bhajamy aham
mama vartmanuvartante manushyah partha sarvashah (4.11)

ye : who | yatha : as/in whatever way | mam : me | prapadyante : worship | tan : them | tatha : so/in the same way | eva : also/definitely | bhajamy : respond | aham : I | mama : my | vartma : path | anuvartante : follow | manushyah : men | partha : Arjuna | sarvashah : all/in every way

In whatever way one worships me, in the same way I respond. O Arjuna! Whichever path men may follow, it converges on my path in every way. In other words, every path is my path, is equally valid and leads unto me.

(12)

काङ्क्षन्तः कर्मणां सिद्धिं यजन्त इह देवताः ।
क्षिप्रं हि मानुषे लोके सिद्धिर्भवति कर्मजा ॥४-१२॥

kanksantah karmanam sidhim yajanta iha devatah
kshipram hi manushe loke siddhirbhavati karmaja (4.12)

kanksantah : desire | karmanam : of actions | siddhim : results | yajante : worship | iha : here/in this world | devatah : gods | kshipram : very early/much faster | hi : certainly | manushe : among men | loke : in this world | siddhi : success | bhavati : comes | karma-ja : born of action

Those in this world who are motivated by a desire for fruits of their action, worship gods. Certainly, among men here on earth, that way, success from action comes much faster.

(13)

चातुर्वर्ण्यं मया सृष्टं गुणकर्मविभागशः ।
तस्य कर्तारमपि मां विद्ध्यकर्तारमव्ययम् ॥४-१३॥

chaturvarnayam maya srishtam gunakarmavibhagashah
tasya kartaramapi mam viddhy akartaram avyayam (4.13)

chaturvarnayam : the four caste system | maya : by me | srastam : created | guna : quality/nature | karma : work | vibhagashah : division | tasya : it's/of that | kartaram : creator | api : also/although | mam : me | viddhy : know | akartaram : non-doer | avyayam : imperishable/not subject to change or decay/eternal

I have created fourfold caste divisiona based on the nature of work in each one of them. Although it's creator, I myself am a non-doer being unchanging and eternal.

(14)
न मां कर्माणि लिम्पन्ति न मे कर्मफलेस्पृहा ।
इति मां योऽभिजानाति कर्मभिर्न स बध्यते ॥४-१४॥

na mam karmani limpanti na me karmaphale spriha
iti mam yoabhijanati karmabhirna sa badhyate (4.14)

na : never | mam : me | karmani : kinds of work | limpanti : affect | na : nor | me : my | karmaphale : fruit of action | spriaha : aspiration | iti : thus | mam : me | yah : who | abhijanati : know | karmabhi : works | na : never | sa : he | badhyate : becomes involved

Different kinds of work never affect me nor do I have any aspiration to seek fruits of my action. Anyone who knows me thus will also never get involved in action with attachment to reward thereof.

(15)
एवं ज्ञात्वा कृतं कर्म पूर्वैरपि मुमुक्षुभिः ।
कुरु कर्मैव तस्मात्त्वं पूर्वैः पूर्वतरं कृतम् ॥४-१५॥

evam gyatva kritam karma purvairapi mumukshubhih
kuru karmaiva tasmatvam purvaih purvataram kritam (4.15)

evam : thus | gyatva : having known | kritam : done | karma : action | purvai : in the past | api : also | mumukshubhi : those who sought salvation/ liberation | kuru : do | karma : duty/ assigned/unattached action | eva : certainly | tasmat : from that/therefore | tvam : you | purvaih : those gone before/ancestors | purva-taram : in ancient times | kritam : done

Having thus known about the (unattached) action done in the past by those who sought liberation (from the cycle of birth and death), you should also perform your assigned duties in life (without attachment to results) as your ancestors did in ancient times.

(16)
किं कर्म किमकर्मेति कवयोऽप्यत्र मोहिताः ।
तत्ते कर्म प्रवक्ष्यामि यज्ज्ञात्वा मोक्ष्यसेऽशुभात् ॥४-१६॥

kim karma kimakarmeti kavayoapyatra mohitah
tatte karma pravakshyami yajgyatva mokshyaseashubhat (4.16)

kim : what | karma : action | kim : what | akarma : inaction | iti : thus | kavaya : the wise | api : also | atra : here | mohitah : confused | tat : that | te : you | karma : action | parvakshyami : shall clarify/explain | yat : which | gyatva : after knowing | mokshyase : will be liberated/freed | ashubhat : from all that is unpleasant/evil

Even the wise get confused on what is action here and what is inaction. I shall, therefore explain to you what constitutes that action. After knowing that you will be freed from all that is unpleasant or evil.

(17)
कर्मणो ह्यपि बोद्धव्यं बोद्धव्यं च विकर्मणः ।
अकर्मणश्च बोद्धव्यं गहना कर्मणो गतिः ॥४-१७॥

karmano hyapi boddhavyam boddhavyam cha vikarmanah
akarmanashcha boddhavyam gahana karmano gatih (4.17)

karmana : action | hi : surely | api : also | boddhavyam : should be understood | boddhavyam : should be understood | cha : also | vikarmana : foul action | akarmana : inaction | cha : also | boddhavyam : should be understood | gahana : very difficult to comprehend | karmana : of action | gati : nature

What surely constitutes action has to be understood. Also, what is foul action and what is inaction have also to be understood. Actually, the true nature of action is very difficult to comprehend.

(18)
कर्मण्यकर्म यः पश्येदकर्मणि च कर्म यः ।
स बुद्धिमान्मनुष्येषु स युक्तः कृत्स्नकर्मकृत् ॥४-१८॥

karmanyakarma yah pashyedakarmani cha karma yah
sa buddhiman manushyeshu sa yuktah kritsnakarmakrit (4.18)

karmani : in action | akarma : inaction | yah : who | pashyet : sees | akarmani : in inaction | cha : also | karma : action | yah : who | sa : he | buddhiman : intelligent/wise | manushyeshu : among men | sa : he | yuktah : yoga-yukta/yogi | kritsnakarmakrit-karma-krit : doer of all action or one who is freed from all action

He who sees action in inaction and inaction in action is really wise among men. He is a yogi and a realised soul who while being engaged as a doer of acts is freed from all action.

(19)
यस्य सर्वे समारम्भाः कामसंकल्पवर्जिताः ।
ज्ञानाग्निदग्धकर्माणं तमाहुः पण्डितं बुधाः ॥४-१९॥

yasya sarve samarambhah kamasankalpavarjitah
gyanagni dagdha karmanam tamahuh panditam budhah (4.19)

yasya : whose | sarve : all | samarambhah : well-began (actions) | kama : sensory gratification | sankalpa : longing | varjitah : devoid of | gyana : supreme knowledge | agni : fire | dagdha : burned | karmanam : whose actions | tam : him | ahuh : call | panditam : the wise | budhah : those who know/the sages

One who acts without any desire for sensory gratification and whose actions have been burnt by the fire of supreme knowledge is called by the sages a wise person.

(20)
त्यक्त्वा कर्मफलासङ्गं नित्यतृप्तो निराश्रयः ।
कर्मण्यभिप्रवृत्तोऽपि नैव किंचित्करोति सः ॥४-२०॥

tyaktva karma phalasangam nitya tripto nirashrayah
karmanyabhiprivratto api naiva kinchitkaroti sah (4.20)

tyaktva : giving up | karma : action | phala : fruit | asangam : attachment | nitya : always | tripta : satisfied | nirashrayah : not dependent on any support | karmani : activity | abhipravritta : fully engaged | api : also | na : not | eva : surely | kinchit : anything | karoti : does | sah : he

Giving up all attachment to fruits of his action, always contented (in supreme soul consciousness) and not dependent on any worldly support and although all the time fully engaged in action, he does not do anything (for getting any fruit).

(21)
निराशीर्यतचित्तात्मा त्यक्तसर्वपरिग्रहः ।
शारीरं केवलं कर्म कुर्वन्नाप्नोति किल्बिषम् ॥४-२१॥

nirashir yata chittatma tyakta sarva parigrahah
shariram kevalam karma kurvannapnoti kilbisham (4.21)

nirashi : without any hope (of result) | yata : in control | chittatma : mind and body | tyakta : giving up | sarva : all | parigrahah : sense of ownership over his worldly possessions | shariram : pertaining to body | kevalam : only | karma : action/work | kurvan : doing | na : not | apnoti : receives | kilbisham : sinful reactions

Without any hope, with mind and body in control, giving up all sense of ownership over his worldly possessions, his body only carries on some activities, one does not attract any sinful reactions.

(22)
यदृच्छालाभसंतुष्टो द्वन्द्वातीतो विमत्सरः ।
समः सिद्धावसिद्धौ च कृत्वापि न निबध्यते ॥४-२२॥

yadrachchha labha santushto dvandvatito vimatsarah
samah siddhavasiddhau cha kritvapi na nibadhyate (4.22)

yadrachchha : on it's own | labha : gain | santushta : satisfied | dvandva : duality of pleasure and pain, loss and gain etc. | atita : past | vimatsarah : free from envy | samah : steady/equipoise | siddhau : in success | asddhau : in failure | cha : and | kritva : doing | api : although | na : never | nibadhyate : becomes bonded/attached

One who remains contented with the gain that comes on its own, who has got over the feelings of envy and duality of loss and gain, pleasure and pain etc. and who retains his equipoise in success and failure, never gets bonded to fruits of action even though all the time continuing to work.

(23)

गतसङ्गस्य मुक्तस्य ज्ञानावस्थितचेतसः ।
यज्ञायाचरतः कर्म समग्रं प्रविलीयते ॥४-२३॥

gatasangasya muktasya gyanavasthita chetasah
yagyayacharatah karma samagram praviliyate (4.23)

gatasangasya : one who has got over attachment | muktasya : of the freed | gyanavasthita : situated in super consciousness | chetasah : wisdom | yagyaacharatah : performing activity with fruits thereof sacrificed | karma : action | samagram : in totality | praviliyate : merges fully

A person who has conquered his senses and got over all attachment to objects of sensory gratification and one who acts with all results of his action sacrificed, may be said to have been liberated and merged in totality into the super soul consciousness.

(24)

ब्रह्मार्पणं ब्रह्म हविर्ब्रह्माग्नौ ब्रह्मणा हुतम् ।
ब्रह्मैव तेन गन्तव्यं ब्रह्मकर्मसमाधिना ॥४-२४॥

brahmarpanam brahma havirbrahmagnau brahmana hutam
brahamaiva tena gantavyam brahma karama samadhina (4.24)

brahma : the supreme/the absolute/the self/the one/the supreme soul consciousness | arpana : ladle - the long wooden spoon with which oblation of ghee (crystalised butter) etc. is made during yagya/the ritual of sacrifice to fire-god/ | the act or the process of offering | brahma : the supreme | havi : ghee (crystalised butter) and other offering | brahma : the supreme/the one | agnau : fire | brahmana : by Brahman | hutam : offering/the act | brahma : the supreme/the one | eva : surely | tena : by him | gantavyam : destination | brahma : the supreme/the one | karma : action | samadhina : the state of being immersed in supreme soul (self) consciousness

The long spoon used for offering purified butter to fire-god during yagya ceremony is itself nothing but Brahman, the butter that is being offered is Brahman, the fire-god to which offering is made is Brahman, the person making the offering i.e. involved in action is also no other but Brahman himself and the ultimate goal of the one making the offering is also Brahman only. Thus, all that exists is Brahman. There is nothing but Brahman. The one who realises the supreme truth of unattached action and of oneness with the One has reached the ultimate destination of union with the supreme soul consciousness.

(25)
दैवमेवापरे यज्ञं योगिनः पर्युपासते ।
ब्रह्माग्नावपरे यज्ञं यज्ञेनैवोपजुह्वति ॥४-२५॥

daivamevapare yagyam yoginah parupasate
brahmagnavapare yagyam yagyenaivopajuhvati (4.25)

daivam : gods | eva : alone/only | apare : others | yagyam : sacrifice through fire god | yoginah : yogis/practitioners of yoga | paryupasate : worship | brahma : the supreme/the one/pure consciousness | agnau : in the fire | apare : others | yagyam : of the sacrifice to fire-god | yagnena : through sacrifice to fire-god | eva : only/alone | upajuhvati : gets into union with Brahma/ the supreme self/ by offering self as the sacrifice

Some yogis make sacrificial offerings to some particular gods alone. Others offer their self as sacrifice to the fire of Brahma, the supreme self.

It can be understood as the individual self merging in the collective self and in the context of one making the offering being Brahman, the offering itself being Brahman, the act or the process of offering and the fire-god through whom the sacrifice is being made also being Brahman - self sacrificing the self to the self, every self being Brahman only. The ultimate aim of yoga is union with Brahman, the Supreme Self Consciousness (vide preceding verse 24).

(26)

श्रोत्रादीनीन्द्रियाण्यन्ये संयमाग्निषु जुह्वति ।
शब्दादीन्विषयानन्य इन्द्रियाग्निषु जुह्वति ॥४-२६॥

shrotradinindriyanyanye sanyamagnishu juhvati
shabdadinvishayananya indrayagnishu juhvati (4.26)

shrotra : hearing | adini : etc/such as | indriyani : senses | sanyama : self-restraint | agnishu : in the fire | juhvati : sacrifice to fire | shabda : word/sound | adin : etc | vishayan : sensory objects | anye : others | indriya : senses | agnishu : in the fires | juhvati : offerings

Some offer their senses such as hearing as sacrifice to the fire of self restraint while others offer sensory objects of sound etc. in the fires of senses.

(27)

सर्वाणीन्द्रियकर्माणि प्राणकर्माणि चापरे ।
आत्मसंयमयोगाग्नौ जुह्वति ज्ञानदीपिते ॥४-२७॥

sarvanindriya karmani prana karmani chapre
atma sanyama yogagnau juhvati gyandipite (4.27)

sarvani : all | indriya : senses | karmani : functions/activities | prana : breathing | karmani : activity | cha : and | apare : others | atma : self | sanyama : control | yoga : realisation | agnau : in the fire | juhvati : offer as sacrifice | gyana : knowledge | dipite : lighted

Others offer all their sensory activities including breath-taking as sacrifice to the fire of realisation through self control lighted by knowledge.

(28)

द्रव्ययज्ञास्तपोयज्ञा योगयज्ञास्तथापरे ।
स्वाध्यायज्ञानयज्ञाश्च यतयः संशितव्रताः ॥४-२८॥

dravya yagyas tapo yagya yoga yagyas tathapare
svadhyaya gyana yagyash cha yatayah sanshita vratah (4.28)

dravya-yagya : sacrificing ones personal wealth and belongings | tapa-yagya : sacrificing all the penance | yoga-yagya : sacrifice for achieving the ultimate union with the supreme | tatha : and | apare : others | svadhyaya : deep self study for attaining higher knowledge | gyana-yagyash : sacrifice for gaining spiritual knowledge of the supreme soul | consciousness | cha : and | yatayah : persons who have control over their senses | sanshita vratah : committed to strong vows

There are some who offer their wealth and belongings as sacrifice, others offer penance, still others committed to strong vows and having control over their senses concentrate on deep self study and gaining spiritual knowledge of the supreme soul (self) consciousness.

(29)
अपाने जुह्वति प्राणं प्राणेऽपानं तथापरे ।
प्राणापानगती रुद्ध्वा प्राणायामपरायणाः ॥४-२९॥

apane juhvati pranam praneapanam tathapare
pranapana gati ruddhva pranayama parayanah (4.29)

apane : in the incoming breath | juhvati : offer | pranam : outgoing breath | prane : in the out going breath | apanam : incoming breath | tatha : and | apare : others | prana-apana-gati : the practice of controlling the outgoing and incoming breath | ruddhva : blocking/stopping | pranaayama-parayanah : one who is knowledgeable about the practice of breath control

Some who are good at controlling their breath offer as a sacrifice the outgoing breath in the incoming breath and the incoming breath in the outgoing breath and others do so by holding still the whole activity of incoming and outgoing breath.

(30)
अपरे नियताहाराः प्राणान्प्राणेषु जुह्वति ।
सर्वेऽप्येते यज्ञविदो यज्ञक्षपितकल्मषाः ॥४-३०॥

apare niyataharah pranan praneshu juhvati
sarvea pyete yagya vido yagya kshapita kalmashah (4.30)

apare : others | niyata : restrained | aharah : food | pranam : outgoing breath | praneshu : to outgoing breath | juhvati : offer | sarve : all | api : also/although | ete : these | yagya-vida : knowing about the yagya (the act of organising sacrificial fire) | yagya-kshapita : absolved by sacrifices made | kalmashah : sins/evil deeds

Others by regulating their food intake offer the outgoing breath unto itself and when the breath is held the vital force is under control. All these knowers of the purpose and performance of yagyas for making sacrifices through the fire-god have been absolved of their sins by their sacrifices.

(31)

यज्ञशिष्टामृतभुजो यान्ति ब्रह्म सनातनम् ।
नायं लोकोऽस्त्ययज्ञस्य कुतोऽन्यः कुरुसत्तम ॥४-३१॥

yagya shishtamrita bhujo yanti brahma sanatanam
nayam loko astyayagyasya kuto anyah kuru sattama (4.31)

yagya-shishta : remnant of sacrifice | amrita-bhuja : those who have had the nector of immortality | yanti : go/reach | brahma : the supreme/the absolute/the ultimate | sanatanam : eternal | na : not | ayam : this | loka : the world | asti : exists/is | ayagyasya : one who makes no sacrificial offerings to fire god/one who does not perform yagyas | kuta : where | anyah : other | kuru-sat-tama : the best among those of the Kuru dynasty

Those who taste the remnant of sacrifice – the nectar of immortality - go to the eternal Brahman, the ultimate. O ! Arjuna, the best of the Kuru dynasty, for those who do not sacrifice, this world has no place, what to say of others.

To be happy in this world and to reach the Supreme, one has to sacrifice. Without making sacrifices, one cannot be at peace in life or thereafter.

(32)

एवं बहुविधा यज्ञा वितता ब्रह्मणो मुखे ।
कर्मजान्विद्धि तान्सर्वानेवं ज्ञात्वा विमोक्ष्यसे ॥४-३२॥

evam bahuvidha yagya vitata brahmano mukhe
karma janvidhi tan sarvan evam gyatva vimokshyase (4.32)

evam : thus | bahu-vidha : multi-faceted/of different types | yagya : sacrifices/ offerings to fire-god | vitata : have been described | brahmana-mukhe : in the voice of Vedas | karmajan : born of action | vidhi : know | tan : them | sarvan : all | evam : thus | gyatva : knowing | vimokshyase : stands liberated

Thus various types of sacrifices have been described in the Vedas. But, we should understand that all these are born of action. One who knows them all stands liberated.

(33)

श्रेयान्द्रव्यमयाद्यज्ञाज्ज्ञानयज्ञः परन्तप ।
सर्वं कर्माखिलं पार्थ ज्ञाने परिसमाप्यते ॥४-३३॥

shreyan dravya mayad yagyata gyana yagyah parantapa
sarvam karmakhilam partha gyane parisampyate (4.33)

shreyan : superior | dravya-mayat : material objects | yagyat : as compared to sacrifice | gyana-yagyah : knowledge sacrifice | parantapa : scorcher of enemies, Arjuna | sarvam : all | karma : action | akhilam : entire | partha : Arjuna | gyane : in knowledge | parisamapyate : conclude/end

O scorcher of enemies, son of Prathu, Arjuna! Offering of knowledge as sacrifice is far superior to offering of material objects. Ultimately, all action concludes in knowledge (of the supreme).

(34)

तद्विद्धि प्रणिपातेन परिप्रश्नेन सेवया ।
उपदेक्ष्यन्ति ते ज्ञानं ज्ञानिनस्तत्त्वदर्शिनः ॥४-३४॥

tadviddhi pranipatena pariprashnena sevaya
upadekhsyanti te gyanam gyaninas tattva darshinah (4.34)

tat : that | viddhi : know | pranipatena : by properly prostrating (before the master/guru) | pariprashnena : by raising polite questions | sevaya : by rendering service | upadekshyanti : will instruct/advise/initiate | te : they | gyanam : knowledge | gyanina : the knowledgeable/realised souls | tattva-darshinah : those who have seen the essence of truth

You should try to attain the knowledge of the supreme by properly prostrating before the spiritual masters, by raising before them polite questions and by rendering to them sincere service. It is then that the realised ones who have seen the essence of truth will initiate you into the path of the spiritual truth.

(35)
यज्ज्ञात्वा न पुनर्मोहमेवं यास्यसि पाण्डव ।
येन भूतान्यशेषेण द्रक्ष्यस्यात्मन्यथो मयि ॥४-३५॥

yajgyatva na punar moham evam yasyasi pandava
yena bhutanyasheshan drakshyashyatmanyatho mayi (4.35)

yat : which | gyatva : knowing | na : not/never | puna : again | moham : illusion/delusion | evam : and | yasyasi : will get into | pandava : O son of Pandu, Arjuna | yena : by which | bhutani : living beings | asheshani : all | drakshyasi : will see | atmani : higher self/soul | atha : so | mayi : me

O son of Pandu, Arjuna! (after getting such knowledge from the realised souls and spiritual masters), you will not suffer from such delusions and will be able to understand that all living beings are part of the supreme being or reside in me.

(36)
अपि चेदसि पापेभ्यः सर्वेभ्यः पापकृत्तमः ।
सर्वं ज्ञानप्लवेनैव वृजिनं सन्तरिष्यसि ॥४-३६॥

api chedasi papebhyah sarvebhyah papakrittamah
sarvam gyana plavenaiva vrijinam santarishyasi (4.36)

api : even | chet : if | asi : you be | papebhyah : guilty of sin | sarvebhyah : of all | papakrittamah : the greatest of the sinners | sarvam : all | gyana-plavena : by the boat of higher knowledge | eva : surely | vrijinam : sin | santarishyasi : will get across safely

Even if you are the most sinful of all the sinners, you shall certainly be able to get across the sea of sins with the help of the boat of higher knowledge.

(37)

यथैधांसि समिद्धोऽग्निर्भस्मसात्कुरुतेऽर्जुन ।
ज्ञानाग्निः सर्वकर्माणि भस्मसात्कुरुते तथा ॥४-३७॥

yathaidhansi samiddho agnir bhashma-sat krute arjuna
gyanagnih sarva-karmani bhashma-sat kurute tatha (4.37)

yatha : as | edhansi : wood | samiddha : burning/blazing | agni : fire | bhashma-sat : ashes | kuru te : does/turns into | arjuna : O Arjuna | gyana-agnih : fire of knowledge | sarva-karmani : all actions | bhashma-sat : to ashes | kurute : turns into | tatha : same way

O Arjuna! Just as the blazing fire reduces wood to ashes, in the same way, the fire of (higher) knowledge turns (the results of) all our actions into ashes.

(38)

न हि ज्ञानेन सदृशं पवित्रमिह विद्यते ।
तत्स्वयं योगसंसिद्धः कालेनात्मनि विन्दति ॥४-३८॥

na hi jnanena sadrshyam, pavitramiha vidyate
tatsvayam yoga-samsiddhah kalenatmani vindati (4-38)

na: not | hi: verily | jnanena: to wisdom/higher knowledge | sadrshyam: like | pavitram: pure | iha: here (in this world) | vidyate: is | tat: that | svayam: oneself | yoga-samsiddhah : perfected in Yoga | kalen: in time | atmani : in the Self | vindati : finds

In this world, verily, there is nothing purer than higher (spiritual) knowledge. When one gets perfected in yoga (of selfless action), this realization comes on its own.

(39)

श्रद्धावाँल्लभते ज्ञानं तत्परः संयतेन्द्रियः ।
ज्ञानं लब्ध्वा परां शान्तिमचिरेणाधिगच्छति ॥४-३९॥

shraddhavanlabhate gyanam tatparah sanyatendriyah
gyanam labhdva param shantim achirenadhigachchhati (4.39)

shraddha-van : one having faith | labhate : achieves | gyanam : (higher) knowledge | tat-parah : with readiness/devoted | sanyat : controlled | indriyah : senses | gyanam : (higher) knowledge | labdhva : having attained | param : highest/supreme shantim : peace | achirena : without delay/very soon | adhigachchhati : achieves/reaches/goes to

Only a person with faith, devotion and control over his senses achieves the (higher) knowledge but having achieved it, he very soon attains supreme peace.

(40)
अज्ञश्चाश्रद्दधानश्च संशयात्मा विनश्यति ।
नायं लोकोऽस्ति न परो न सुखं संशयात्मनः ॥४-४०॥

agyash chashraddadhanash cha sanshayatma vinashyati
nayam lokoasti na paro na sukham sanshayatmanah (4.40)

agya : one who does not know | cha : and | ashraddadhanash : one who does not have faith | cha : also | sanshaya : doubt | atma : self | vinashyati : is ruined | na : never | ayam : this | loka : world | asti : is | na : not | para : next life | na : not/never | sukham : happiness | sanshaya : doubt | atmanah : of self

A person who does not know, has no faith and is full of doubts (in regard to the ultimate truth, the supreme soul consciousness), is ruined because a doubting self can never be happy either in this world or in life hereafter.

(41)
योगसंन्यस्तकर्माणं ज्ञानसंछिन्नसंशयम् ।
आत्मवन्तं न कर्माणि निबध्नन्ति धनंजय ॥४-४१॥

yoga-sannyasta-karmanam gyana- sanchhinna-sanshayam
atmavantam na karmani nibadhnanti dhananjaya (4.41)

yoga : action without attachment to its results with the full knowledge of the supreme soul consciousness | sannyasta-karmanam : one who has renounced the fruits of his action | gyana : higher knowledge | sanchhinna : dispelled | sanshayam : doubts | atma-vantam : one who has achieved self-control | na : not | karmani : acts | nibadhanti : bind | dhananjaya : conqueror of wealth, Arjuna

O conqueror of wealth, Arjuna! When with the help of higher knowledge, doubts have been dispelled, one who has achieved self-control and renounced the fruits of his action, cannot be bound by his actions.

(42)

तस्मादज्ञानसम्भूतं हृत्स्थं ज्ञानासिनात्मनः ।
छित्त्वैनं संशयं योगमातिष्ठोत्तिष्ठ भारत ॥४-४२॥

tasmada gyan sambhutam hrat-stham gyanasinatmanah
chhittvainam sanshayam yogam atishthottishtha bharata (4.42)

tasmat : therefore | agyana-sambhutam : product of ignorance | hratstham : stationed in the heart | gyana-asina : by the weapon of higher knowledge | atmanah : self | chhittva : cutting | enam : this | sanshayam : doubt | yogam : renouncing the fruits of action | atishtha : situated in | uttishtha : arise | bharat : O descendant of Bharat, Arjuna

Therefore, cutting with the help of the weapon of higher knowledge the doubt about the Self born of ignorance, stationed in the heart, O descendant of Bharat, Arjuna! Take recourse to yoga of renouncing the fruits of action, arise and fight.

Thus ends the fourth chapter titled 'Yoga of Knowledge, Action and Renunciation'.

Fifth Canto

NISHKAM KARMA - SANYASA YOGA
Yoga of Selfless Action and Renunciation

(1)

अर्जुन उवाच
संन्यासं कर्मणां कृष्ण पुनर्योगं च शंससि ।
यच्छ्रेय एतयोरेकं तन्मे ब्रूहि सुनिश्चितम् ॥५-१॥

Arjuna uvacha
sannyasam karmanam krishna punar yogam cha shansasi
yach chhreya etayor ekam tanme bruhi su-nishchitam (5-1)

arjuna : Arjuna | uvacha : said | sannyasam : renunciation | karmanam : of all action | krishna : Lord Krishna | puna : again | yogam : yoga meaning action without desiring its fruits | cha : and | shansasi : praising | yat : which | shreya : better | etayo : of the two | ekam : one | tat : that | me : unto me | bruhi : speak please | sunishchitam : definitely

Arjuna said: O Lord! once you ask me to go for renunciation of all action and then, in the same breath, you advocate yoga which also calls for action without desiring its fruits. Please tell me definitely which of the two is better.

(2)

श्रीभगवानुवाच
संन्यासः कर्मयोगश्च निःश्रेयसकरावुभौ ।
तयोस्तु कर्मसंन्यासात्कर्मयोगो विशिष्यते ॥५-२॥

Shribhagavan uvacha
sannyasah karma-yogash cha nihshreyasa-karavubhau
tayostu karma-sannyasat karama-yogo vishishyate (5.2)

Shribhagavan : Lord Krishna | uvacha : said | sannyasah : renunciation | karma yoga : yoga of action (without desiring any fruits thereof) | cha : also/and | nishreyasakarau : on way to doing good | ubhau : both | tayo

: of the two | tu : but | karmasannyasat : from renunciation of action | karmayoga : yoga of action/commitment to work | vishisyate : is better

Lord Krishna said: Renouncing all action or taking sanyas and pursuing karma yoga or action without desiring its fruits, both are good but between the two, it is better to remain dedicated to selfless action than to go for sanyasa or renunciation of all action.

(3)

ज्ञेयः स नित्यसंन्यासी यो न द्वेष्टि न काङ्क्षति ।
निर्द्वन्द्वो हि महाबाहो सुखं बन्धात्प्रमुच्यते ॥५-३॥

*geyah sa nitya-sannyasi yo na dveshti na kankhsati
nirdvandvo hi maha-baho sukham bandhat pramuchyate (5.3)*

geyah : worth knowing | sa : he | nitya : always/forever | sannyasi : one who has renounced action | ya : who | na : not | dvesti : hates | na : nor | kankshsati : desires | nirdvandva : free from the conflicts of dualities | hi : because | Mahabaho : Arjuna (one with large arms) | sukham : happily | bandhat : from bondage | pramuchyate : gets freed

O Arjuna! It should be understood that a person who does not hate anything nor does he desire anything for himself is for ever a sanyasi who has renounced action and has got liberated from all dualities and is happily free from bondage (of life and death).

(4)

सांख्ययोगौ पृथग्बालाः प्रवदन्ति न पण्डिताः ।
एकमप्यास्थितः सम्यगुभयोर्विन्दते फलम् ॥५-४॥

*sankhya-yogau priathag balah pravadanti na panditah
ekamapyasthitah samyag ubhayor vindate phalam (5.4)*

sankhya : path of knowledge | yogau : path of selfless action | prithak : separate/different | balah : children/immature or ignorant people | pravadantih : say | na : not | pandita : the learned | ekam : one | api : even | asthitah : situated | samyak : complete | ubhayo : both | vindate : enjoys | phalam : result

It is only the children or ignorant people who may say that the paths of renunciation and selfless action are different. The learned, however, know that anyone who sincerely follows either path gets to enjoy the benefits of both (i.e. achieves the realisation of supreme soul consciousness).

(5)

यत्सांड्.ख्यैः प्राप्यते स्थानं तद्योगैरपि गम्यते ।
एकं सांख्यं च योगं च यः पश्यति सः पश्यति ॥५-५॥

yat sankhyaih prapyate sthanam tadyogairapi gamyate
ekam sankhyam cha yogam cha yah pashyati sah pashyati (5.5)

yat : what | sankhyaih : by following the path of knowledge or sankhya philosophy (realising that the world of the material has to be transcended to reach the all-inclusive ultimate which is the one supreme soul or self-consciousness) | prapyate : reaches/achieves | sthanam : position/state | tat : that | yogai : by following the path of yoga (karma yoga is for remaining devoted to action selflessly and without any desire for fruits thereof. The end result there of is also the realisation of the supreme self or soul consciousness) | api : also | gamyate : can be reached | ekam : one | sankhyam : path of knowledge | cha : also | yogam : path of selfless action | cha : also | yah : who | pashyati : sees

The state of realisation that is reached by following the path of knowledge (Sankhya or Gyana Yoga) can equally well be reached through selfless action or action without any desire for its fruits (Karma Yoga). One who sees the truth of this statement really sees.

(6)

संन्यासस्तु महाबाहो दुःखमाप्तुमयोगतः ।
योगयुक्तो मुनिर्ब्रह्म नचिरेणाधिगच्छति ॥५- ६॥

sanyasas tu maha baho dukham aptum ayogatah
yoga-yukto munir brahma na chirenadhigachchhati (5.6)

sanyasa : state of renunciation | tu : but | mahabaho : O long-armed one, Arjuna | dukham : sorrow | aptum : to get | ayogatah : without performing ones duty or required action | yogayukta : one devoted to the path of selfless action | muni : saint | brahama : the Supreme/all inclusive soul consciousness | na chirena : without delay/intuitively | adhigachchhiyati : attains/goes in the direction (of the divine)

O Arjuna! Renunciation without doing ones duty, i.e. without performing the required action is bound to lead to sorrow and disappointment. But a saint devoted to the path of selfless action attains the Supreme - the all inclusive soul consciousness - intuitively, without delay. Since renunciation also requires action, the path of selfless action is quicker for reaching the goal of self-realisation.

(7)
योगयुक्तो विशुद्धात्मा विजितात्मा जितेन्द्रियः ।
सर्वभूतात्मभूतात्मा कुर्वन्नपि न लिप्यते ॥५-७॥

yoga-yukto vishudhatma vijitatma jitendriyah
sarva-bhutatma-bhutatma kurvann api na lipyate (5.7)

yogayukta : dedicated to selfless action | vishudhatma : a pure soul | vijitatma : one who has conquered the self | jitendriyah : one who has full control over his senses | sarvabhuta : to all living beings | atmabhutatma : one who sees his self in all others | kurvan : performing action | api : though | na : not | lipyate : involved

A true yogi i.e. one dedicated to selfless action, with a pure soul, who has conquered his self, who has full control over his senses and who sees his self in all living beings performs action without being involved therein.

(8-9)
नैव किंचित्करोमीति युक्तो मन्येत तत्त्ववित् ।
पश्यञ्शृण्वन्स्पृशञ्जिघ्रन्नश्नन्गच्छन्स्वपञ्श्वसन् ॥५-८॥
प्रलपन्विसृजन्गृह्णन्नुन्मिषन्निमिषन्नपि ।
इन्द्रियाणीन्द्रियार्थेषु वर्तन्त इति धारयन् ॥५-९॥

naiva kincht karomiti yukto manyeta tattva-vit
pashyanshrivan sprishanjighrann ashnangachchhan svapanshvasan (5.8)

pralapan visriajan grihnann unmishan nimishann api
indriyanindriyartheshu vartanta iti dharayan (5.9)

na : not | eva : definitely/positively | kinchit : anything | karomi : I do | iti : this | yukta : centred (the yogi who knows) | manyeta : believes | tattva-vit : one who knows the essential truth | pashyan : seeing | shrivan : hearing | sprishan : touching | jighran : smelling | ashnan : eating | gachchhan : walking | svapan : dreaming | shvasan : breathing | pralapan : speaking | visrijan : excreting | grihanan : accepting | unmishan : opening (the eyes) | nimishan : closing (the eyes) | api : also/though | indriyani : senses | indriya-artheshu : for the gratification of senses | vartante : engaged | iti : thus | dharayan : holding

The yogi (devoted to selfless action) positively knows the quintessential truth that it is not he who is doing anything while seeing, hearing, touching, smelling, eating, walking, dreaming, breathing, speaking, excreting, accepting something, opening or closing eyes, it is actually the senses that are doing all this for sensory gratification.

(10)
ब्रह्मण्याधाय कर्माणि सङ्गं त्यक्त्वा करोति यः ।
लिप्यते न स पापेन पद्मपत्रमिवाम्भसा ॥५-१०॥

brahmanyadhaya karmani sangam tyaktva karoti yah
lipyate na sa papena padma-patram ivambhasa (5.10)

brahmani : unto the Supreme | adhaya : surrendering | karmani : all action | sangam : attachment | tyaktva : giving up | karoti : does | yah : who | lipyate : gets involved | na : never | sa : he | papena : by the sins | padma-patram : lotus leaf | iva : like | ambhasa : by the water

A person who surrenders all his deeds to the Supreme and performs all the action (discharges all his duties) selflessly, without attachment, is never affected by the sins (or virtues) involved therein just as the lotus leaf remains unaffected by the water.

(11)

कायेन मनसा बुद्ध्या केवलैरिन्द्रियैरपि ।
योगिनः कर्म कुर्वन्ति सङ्गं त्यक्त्वात्मशुद्धये ॥५-११॥

kayena manasa buddhya kevalair indriyair api
yoginah karma kurvanti sangam tyaktvatma-shuddhaye (5.11)

kayena : with the body | manasa : with the mind | buddhya : with the intelligence | kevalai : only | indriyai : with the senses | api : even | yoginah : those committed to selfless action | karma : actions | kurvanti : perform action | sangam : attachment | tyaktva : giving up | atma : self | shuddhaye : for the sake of purification of the self

Yogis - those committed to selfless action and non-attachment - may also use action by the body, mind, intellect and even the senses for the sake of purification of the self.

(12)

युक्तः कर्मफलं त्यक्त्वा शान्तिमाप्नोति नैष्ठिकीम् ।
अयुक्तः कामकारेण फले सक्तो निबध्यते ॥५-१२॥

yuktah karma-phalam tyaktva shantim apnoti naishthikim
ayuktah kama-karena phale sakto nibadhyate (5-12)

yuktah : yogi committed to selfless action | karma-phalam : fruits of action | tyaktva : giving up | shantim : peace | apnoti : attains | naishthikim : steadfast | ayuktah : those not committed to selfless action | kama-karena : for enjoying the fruits of action | phale : fruit | sakta : attached | nibadhyate : remain bound

The yogi committed to selfless action achieves peace by his steadfastness in giving up all desire for fruits of action. Those not committed to selfless action and anxious to enjoy the fruits of action remain bound to them.

(13)
सर्वकर्माणि मनसा संन्यस्यास्ते सुखं वशी ।
नवद्वारे पुरे देही नैव कुर्वन्न कारयन् ॥५-१३॥

sarva-karmani manasa sannyasyaste sukham vashi
nava-dvare pure dehi naiva kurvan na karayan (5.13)

sarva : all | karmani : actions | manasa : by the mind | sanyasya : by renouncing | aste : lives | sukham : happily | vashi : controller of the senses | nava-dvare : at nine gates | pure : in the city | dehi : soul in the body | na : never | eva : certainly | kurvan : acting | na : not | karayan : causing to act

The embodied soul as the controller of the senses, having mentally renounced all actions, lives happily in the body with nine gates (two eyes, two nostrils, two ears, two organs of excretion and procreation and a mouth) neither acting nor causing the senses to act. (He does not identify his self with the body and knows that he is not the doer; the on-going activities of the senses do not concern or bother him. Mentally renouncing all action makes the mind indifferent and detached).

(14)
न कर्तृत्वं न कर्माणि लोकस्य सृजति प्रभुः ।
न कर्मफलसंयोगं स्वभावस्तु प्रवर्तते ॥५-१४॥

na kartritvam na karmani lokasya srijati prabhuh
na karma-phala-sanyogam svabhavastu pravartate (5.14)

na : never | kartritvam : the feeling of being the doer | na : nor | karmani : of actions | lokasya : of the people | srijati : creates | prabhuh : master (of the body) | na : nor | karma-phala : with the fruits of activities | sanyogam : relationship | svabhava : nature | tu : but | pravartate : does

The embodied soul, the master of the body, does not perform actions nor does he induce people to act or create relationships, feeling of being the doer or seeker of fruits of action. But, the nature does all this.

(15)

नादत्ते कस्यचित्पापं न चैव सुकृतं विभुः ।
अज्ञानेनावृतं ज्ञानं तेन मुह्यन्ति जन्तवः ॥५-१५॥

nadatte kasyachit papam na chaiva sukritam vibhuh
agyanenavritam gyanam tena muhyanti jantavah (5.15)

na : never | adatte : accepts | kasyachit : of anyone | papam : sin | na : nor | cha : and | eva : definitely | sukritam : good deeds | vibhuh : God | agyanena : by ignorance | avritam : covered | gyanam : knowledge | tena : that | muhyanti : deluded | jantavah : living beings/people

God does not accept anybody's sins or noble deeds. Knowledge is covered by ignorance and, therefore, people get deluded.

(16)

ज्ञानेन तु तदज्ञानं येषां नाशितमात्मनः ।
तेषामादित्यवज्ज्ञानं प्रकाशयति तत्परम् ॥५-१६॥

gyanena tu tad agyanam yesham nashitam atmanah
tesham aditya-vaj gyanam prakashayati tat param (5.16)

gyanena : through knowledge | tu : but | tat : that | agyanam : ignorance | yesham : whose | nashitam : destroyed | atmanah : the self | tesham : their | aditya-vat : like the rising sun | gyanam : knowledge | prakashayati : brings to light | tat : that | param : the supreme soul consciousness

But, when through knowledge, that ignorance is destroyed, the self brings to light the knowledge of the ultimate, the supreme soul consciousness just as the rising sun destroys all darkness.

(17)

तद्बुद्धयस्तदात्मानस्तन्निष्ठास्तत्परायणाः ।
गच्छन्त्यपुनरावृत्तिं ज्ञाननिर्धूतकल्मषाः ॥५-१७॥

tad-buddhayas tad-atmanas tan-nishthas tat-parayanah
gachchhantyapunar-avrittim gyana-nirdhuta-kalmashah (5.17)

tat-buddhaya : whose intelligence is engrossed in that Supreme | tat-atmana

: whose mind is always thinking of that Supreme | tat-nishtha : whose full faith is in that Supreme | tat-parayanah : who have completely surrendered to that Supreme | gachchhanti : get | apuna : avrittim : liberation from the cycle of birth and death | gyana : knowledge of the Self (Supreme) | nirdhuta : cleansed | kalmashah : sins

Those whose intelligence is engrossed in that (Supreme), whose mind is always thinking of that, who have full faith in that and who have completely surrendered to that, get liberated from the cycle of birth and death and by their knowledge of the Self, they are cleansed of all their sins. [This is the stage of the realisation of the Supreme Soul (Self) Consciousness.]

(18)
विद्याविनयसंपन्ने ब्राह्मणे गवि हस्तिनि ।
शुनि चैव श्वपाके च पण्डिताः समदर्शिनः ॥५-१८॥

vidya-vinaya-sampanne brahmane gavi hastini
shuni chaiva shva-pake cha panditah sama-darshinah (5-18).

vidya : education/learning | vinaya : humility | sampanne : equip | brahmane : in the Brahmin | gavi : cow | hastini : elephant | suni : dog | cha : and | eva : definitely | shva-pake : dog eater (outcaste) | cha : and | panditah : the wise | sama-darshinah : those who look upon all with an equal eye/treat all equally

The brahmin equipped with learning and humility, the cow, the elephant, the dog, and the dog-eater (the outcast), are all treated equally by the wise (who have attained self-realisation). Once one has realised the self in him knows that the same self exists within all others.

(19)
इहैव तैर्जितः सर्गो येषां साम्ये स्थितं मनः ।
निर्दोषं हि समं ब्रह्म तस्माद्ब्रह्मणि ते स्थिताः ॥५-१९॥

ihaiva tairjitah sargo yesham samye sthitam manah
nirdosham hi samam brahma tasmad brahmani te sthitah (5-19).

iha : here (in this life) | eva : even | tai : by them | jitah : conquered | sarga : birth and death | yesham : whose | samye : equanimity | sthitam : situated |

manah : mind | nirdosham : without any flaw or shortcoming | hi : because | samam : equally | brahma : the Supreme | tasmat : at that/therefore | brahmani : in the Supreme | te : they | sthitah : are established

Those whose mind is stationed in equanimity, they have conquered in this life itself the cycle of birth and death and the whole world because they are firmly established in that Supreme that is flawless, perfect and the same for all. In other words, those who have realised self consciousness stand emancipated in this life itself and feel one with the same self in all others. This is the stage of the ultimate realisation of the supreme soul consciousness.

(20)

न प्रहृष्येत्प्रियं प्राप्य नोद्विजेत्प्राप्य चाप्रियम् ।
स्थिरबुद्धिरसंमूढो ब्रह्मविद्ब्रह्मणि स्थितः ॥५-२०॥

na prahrishyetpriyam prapya nodvijetprapya chapriyam
sthira buddhir asammudho brahma-vid brahmani sthitah (5-20)

na : neither | prahrishyet : rejoices | priyam : pleasing | prapya : receiving | na : nor | udvijet : get agitated | prapya : on getting | cha : and | apriyam : unpleasant | sthira-buddhi : one with stable mind | asammudha : undisturbed/without any doubts or delusion | brahma-vid : one who has known the Supreme | brahmani : in Brahma/in the Supreme | sthitah : situated/staying

One who does not get overjoyed when he receives something pleasant nor does he get agitated in the face of an unpleasant experience, who has known the Supreme and rests in the Supreme and whose mind is steady remains undisturbed (with pleasure or pain, gain or loss, success or failure etc.

(21)

बाह्यस्पर्शेष्वसक्तात्मा विन्दत्यात्मनि यत्सुखम् ।
स ब्रह्मयोगयुक्तात्मा सुखमक्षयमश्नुते ॥५-२१॥

bahya-sparsheshv asaktatma vindatyatmani yat sukham
sa brahma-yoga-yuktatma sukham akshayam ashnute (5-21)

bahya-sparsheshu : external objects of sense gratification | asakta-atma : one who is not attached | vindati : rejoices | atmani : in the self | yat : that | sukham : happiness | sa : he | brahma-yoga : by meditating on the Supreme | yukta-atma : equipped with the knowledge of the Self | sukham : happiness | akshayam : eternal/not subject to decay or diminution | asnute : enjoys

A person who is not attached to external objects of sensory gratification enjoys bliss within the Self. Equipped with the knowledge of the Self, the happiness that he gets by meditating on the Supreme is eternal and not subject to diminution or decay. For, he has become one with Supreme Soul Consciousness.

(22)
ये हि संस्पर्शजा भोगा दुःखयोनय एव ते ।
आद्यन्तवन्तः कौन्तेय न तेषु रमते बुधः ॥५-२२॥

ye hi sansparsha-ja bhoga dukha-yonaya eva te
adyantavantah kaunteya na teshu ramate budhah (5-22)

ye : these | hi : definitely | sansparsha-ja : by contact of the senses | bhoga : joys | dukha : sorrows | yonaya : sensory sources | eva : certainly | te : they | adi : beginning | anta : end | vanta : upto/subject to | kaunteya : O Arjuna, son of Kunti | na : not | teshu : those | ramate : enjoy | budhah : the wise

O son of Kunti, Arjuna! These joys that certainly come from contact with the senses lead to sorrows. The pleasures derived from sensory sources do not last, they certainly have a beginning and an end. The wise, therefore, do not enjoy them.

(23)
शक्नोतीहैव यः सोढुं प्राक्शरीरविमोक्षणात् ।
कामक्रोधोद्भवं वेगं स युक्तः स सुखी नरः ॥५-२३॥

shaknotihaiva yah sodhum prak sharira-vimokshanat
kama-krodhodbhavam vegam sa yuktah sa sukhi narah (5-23).

shaknoti : can do/is able to | iha eva : here itself/in this world | yah : who | sodhum : withstand | prak : before | sharira : body | vimokshanat : liberation from this body | kama : lust | krodha : anger | udbhavam : beginning from/born of | vegam : tide of the cravings of the senses | sa : he | yuktah : yogi | sa : he | sukhi : happy | narah : person

A person who is able to withstand the high tide of the cravings of the senses born of anger and lust in this world itself, before leaving this body, is a yogi and poised to be a happy person.

(24)

योऽन्तःसुखोऽन्तरारामस्तथान्तर्ज्योतिरेव यः ।
स योगी ब्रह्मनिर्वाणं ब्रह्मभूतोऽधिगच्छति ॥५-२४॥

yo antah-sukho antararamas tathantar jyotireva yah
sa yogi brahma-nirvanam brahma bhuto adhigachchhati (5-24)

ya : who | antah-sukha : inner happiness/bliss | antarama : enjoying within | tatha : and | anta-jyoti : inner light | eva : certainly | yah : who | sa : he | yogi : a person who has mastered his senses and is committed to selfless action and to reaching the Supreme Self Consciousness | brahma-nirvanam : reaching the Supreme | brahma-bhuta : becoming one with the Supreme Self | adhigachchhati : attains

One who is endowed with inner bliss and enjoys happiness within as well as inner light is certainly a yogi who can reach the Supreme and attain the ultimate stage of becoming one with the Supreme Self Consciousness.

(25)

लभन्ते ब्रह्मनिर्वाणमृषयः क्षीणकल्मषाः ।
छिन्नद्वैधा यतात्मानः सर्वभूतहिते रताः ॥५-२५॥

labhante brahma-nirvanam rishayah kshina kalmashah
chhinna-dvaidha yatatmanah sarva-bhuta-hite ratah (5-25)

labhante : benefit/achieve | brahma-nirvanam : salvation by reaching the Supreme | rishayah : rishis/seers | kshina-kalmashah : freed of sins | chhinna : torn | dvaidha : duality/doubts | yata-atmanah : those who have control over their minds | sarva-bhuta : all living beings | hite : in the interests of/in serving | ratah : engaged

Those seers who have been freed of all sins and of all the dualities and doubts, who are engaged in serving all living beings and have achieved control over their minds, achieve salvation in the realisation of the Supreme.

(26)
कामक्रोधवियुक्तानां यतीनां यतचेतसाम् ।
अभितो ब्रह्मनिर्वाणं वर्तते विदितात्मनाम् ॥५-२६॥
kama-krodha-viyuktanam yatinam yata-chetasam
abhito brahma nirvanam vartate viditatmanam (5-26).

kama : lust | krodha : wrath | viyuktanam : liberated ones | yatinam : saints/seers | yata-chetasam : who have full control over their mind | abhita : early | brahma-nirvanam : salvation by reaching the Supreme (Soul Consciousness) | vartate : appears/is there | vidita-atmanam : those who are known to have realised the Self

Those who have been liberated from the evils of lust and wrath, the saints who are in full control of their mind and senses and who have achieved Self-realisation are assured of early salvation in the Supreme.

(27-28)
स्पर्शान्कृत्वा बहिर्बाह्यांश्चक्षुश्चैवान्तरे भ्रुवोः ।
प्राणापानौ समौ कृत्वा नासाभ्यन्तरचारिणौ ॥५- २७॥
यतेन्द्रियमनोबुद्धिर्मुनिर्मोक्षपरायणः ।
विगतेच्छाभयक्रोधो यः सदा मुक्त एव सः ॥५- २८॥
sparshan kritva bahir bahyamsh chakshush chaivantare bhruvoh
pranapanau samau kritva nasabhyantara-charinau (5-27)
Yatendriya-mano-budhhir munir moksha-parayanah
vigatechchha-bhaya-krodho yah sada mukta eva sah (5-28)

sparshan : sensory contacts (objects) | kritva : keeping | bahi : out | bahyan

: external | chakshu : eyes | cha : and | eva : certainly | antare : between | bhruvoh : the eye-brows | prana-apanau : breathing in and out | samau : even | kritva : keeping | nasa-abhyantara : through the nostrils | charinau : blowing | yata : controlled | indriya : senses | mana : mind | buddhi : intellect | muni : saint/sage | moksha : salvation/liberation | parayanah : destined | vigata : got over/won | ichchha : wishes/desires | bhaya : fear | krodha : anger | yah : who | sada : always | mukta : freed | eva : certainly | sah : he

Keeping out all external sense objects, fixing the eyes between the two eyebrows, taking breaths in and out through the nostrils with evenness, controlling the senses, mind and intellect, a sage who has won desires, anger and fear shall achieve liberation, realise the Supreme and reach salvation.

(29)

भोक्तारं यज्ञतपसां सर्वलोकमहेश्वरम् ।
सुहृदं सर्वभूतानां ज्ञात्वा मां शान्तिमृच्छति ॥५-२९॥

bhoktaram yagyatapasam sarvaloka maheshvaram
suhradam sarvabhutanam gyatva mam shantim richchhati (5-29)

bhoktaram : receiver | yagya : sacrifice | tapasam : penances | sarva-loka : all the planets of the universe | maha-ishvaram : the Supreme Reality/Lord | suhradam : friend/benefactor | sarva-bhutanam : all the living beings | gyatva : knowing | mam : Me (Lord Krishna) | shantim : peace (bliss and relief from worldly woes) | rachchhati : achieves

One who knows Me as the receiver of all the sacrifices and penances, as the Supreme Lord of all the planets of the universe and as the friend and benefactor of all living beings, achieves peace (bliss and relief from worldly woes).

Thus ends the fifth Canto titled 'Yoga of Selfless Action and Renunciation'.

Sixth Canto

DHYANA-YOGA
Yoga of Meditation

(1)

श्रीभगवानुवाच
अनाश्रितः कर्मफलं कार्यं कर्म करोति यः ।
स संन्यासी च योगी च न निरग्निर्न चाक्रियः ॥६-१॥

Shribhagavan uvacha
anashritah karmaphalam karyam karma karoti yah
sa sanyasi cha yogi cha na niragnirna chakriyah (6.1)

Shribhagvan : Lord Krishna | uvacha : said | anashritah : not dependent | karma-phalam : fruits of action | karyam : bounden/obligatory | karma : action/work/duties | karoti : does/performs (action) | yah : who | sa : he | sanyasi : saint who leads a life of renunciation | cha : and | yogi : one devoted to selfless action/seeking no fruits of action | cha : also | na : not | ni : without | agni : fire | na : nor | cha : also | akriyah : non-doer

Lord Krishna said: One who is devoted to work and performs his bounden duties as an obligation without depending on any rewards or fruits of action, is a true sanyasi (saint committed to a life of renunciation) and also a yogi (devoted to selfless action). A non-doer and one who does not keep the sacrificial fire burning is neither a sanyasi nor a yogi.

(2)

यं संन्यासमिति प्राहुर्योगं तं विद्धि पाण्डव ।
न ह्यसंन्यस्तसंकल्पो योगी भवति कश्चन ॥६-२॥

yam sanyasamiti prahuryogam tam viddhi pandava
na hyasannyasta-sankalpo yogi bhavati kashachna (6.2)

yam : what | sanyasam : renunciation | iti : thus | prahu : say | yogam : the way to the Supreme/selfless action | tam : that | viddhi : know | pandava :

son of Pandu, O Arjuna | na : never | hi : definitely | asannyasta : without renouncing | sankalpa : determination | yogi : a person committed to selfless action and seeking union with the Supreme Soul (Self) Consciousness | bhavati : becomes | kashchana : anybody

O Arjuna! What is called sanyas (renunciation of worldly desires for objects of sense gratification) and what is spoken of as yoga (commitment to selfless action and seeking union with the Supreme Soul (Self) Consciousness) are actually one and the same. It can be said definitely that no one can become a yogi without a determination to renounce the objects of sensory gratification.

(3)
आरुरुक्षोर्मुनियोंगं कर्म कारणमुच्यते ।
योगारूढस्य तस्यैव शमः कारणमुच्यते ॥६-३॥

arurukshor muner yogam karma karnamuchyate
yogarudhasya tasyaiva shamah karanamuchyate (6.3)

aruruksho : wishing to climb (the ladder of yoga) | mune : sage | yogam : of yoga | karma : action/performance of ones bounden duty | karanam : means | uchyate : is spoken of as | yogarudhasya : one who has reached a high position on the yoga ladder | tasya : his | eva : certainly | shamah : inaction | karanam : ground/justification (for cessation of action) | uchyate : is said to be

For a sage wishing to scale the heights of yoga, the ladder is said to be action or performance of ones bounden duty but as one reaches a high position on the way to self-realisation, certainly one can speak of the ground or justification for cessation of activity.

(4)
यदा हि नेन्द्रियार्थेषु न कर्मस्वनुषज्जते ।
सर्वसंकल्पसंन्यासी योगारूढस्तदोच्यते ॥६-४॥

yada hi nendriyartheshu na karamasv-anushajjate
sarva sankalpa sannyasi yogarudhas tadochyate (6.4)

yada : when | hi : verily | na : neither | indriya-artheshu : for the purpose of sensory gratification | na : nor | karmasu : in actions | anushajjate : is attached | sarva-sankalpa : all thoughts or plans for fruitive action | sannyasi : sage who has renounced sensory desires | yoga-arudha : one who has achieved a high position on the ladder of yoga | tada : then | uchyate : is said to be

Verily, one may be said to have attained a high position on the ladder of yoga or sanyasa when he or she is no more attached to or interested in either objects of sensory gratification or thoughts of fruit-oriented actions.

(5)
उद्धरेदात्मनात्मानं नात्मानमवसादयेत् ।
आत्मैव ह्यात्मनो बन्धुरात्मैव रिपुरात्मनः ॥६- ५॥

uddhared atmanatmanam natmanam avasadayet
atmaiva hyatmano bandhur atmaiva ripur atmanah (6.5)

uddharet : raise | atmana : self | atmanam : oneself | na : never | atmanam : oneself | avasadayet : weaken/degrade | atma : self | eva : certainly | hi : verily | atmana : of oneself | bandhu : friend | atma : self | eva : certainly | ripu : enemy | atmanah : of oneself

One should raise one's self by oneself alone. One should never degrade or weaken one's self. For, self only is the friend of oneself and also the enemy. (Since the ultimate aim of yoga and sannyasa is to realise union with the Supreme Self, it is only through the individual self that it can be achieved.)

(6)
बन्धुरात्मात्मनस्तस्य येनात्मैवात्मना जितः ।
अनात्मनस्तु शत्रुत्वे वर्ते तात्मैव शत्रुवत् ॥६- ६॥

bandhur atmatmanas tasya yenatmaivatmana jitah
anatmanastu shatrutve vartetatmaiva shatru vat (6.6)

bandhu : brother/friend | atma : self | atmana : of oneself | tasya : his | yena : by whom | atma : self | eva : certainly | atmana : by oneself | jitah : conquered

| anatmana : one not having control over self | tu : but | shatrutve : because of the enmity | varteta : remains | atma eva : only the self | shatruvat : like an enemy

For one who has conquered his self, the self is certainly the best friend, but one who has failed to control the self will find that it is only the self who behaves like an enemy.

(7)

जितात्मनः प्रशान्तस्य परमात्मा समाहितः ।
शीतोष्णसुखदुःखेषु तथा मानापमानयोः ॥६- ७॥

jitatmanah prashantasya paramatma samahitah
shitoshna-sukha-dukheshu tatha manapamanayoh (6.7)

jitatmanah : one who has conquered his self | prashantasya : who has achieved peace/tranquility | paramatma : the Supreme Soul | samahitah : fully attained | shita : cold | ushna : heat | sukha : happiness | dukheshu : in times of sorrow | tatha : and | mana : honour | apmanayoh : dishonor

One who has conquered his self and achieved peace in the Supreme Self remains tranquil and maintains equanimity in the face of cold or heat, happiness or sorrow as also honour and dishonour. (All these dualities do not disturb the yogi whose self has achieved oneness with Supreme Self Consciousness.)

(8)

ज्ञानविज्ञानतृप्तात्मा कूटस्थो विजितेन्द्रियः ।
युक्त इत्युच्यते योगी समलोष्टाश्मकाञ्चनः ॥६- ८॥

gyana-vigyana-triptatma kutastho vijitendriyah
yukta ityuchyate yogi sama-loshtrashma-kanchanah (6.8)

gyana : knowledge | vigyana : specialised knowledge | traptatma : satisfied self (soul) | atma : self | kutastha : unshaken | vijita-indriyah : who has won over the senses | yukta : accomplished/steadfast | iti : thus | uchyate : it is said | yogi : sage committed to selfless action | sama : same | loshta : pebbles | ashma : stones | kanchanah : gold

One who is fully satisfied with the knowledge and specialised knowledge of the self, remains unshaken and in full control of the senses is said to be a steadfast yogi for whom pebbles, stones and gold are the same.

(9)
सुहृन्मित्रार्युदासीनमध्यस्थद्वेष्यबन्धुषु ।
साधुष्वपि च पापेषु समबुद्धिर्विशिष्यते ॥ ६- ९॥

*suhrin mitraryudasina madhyastha dveshya bandhushu
sadhushvapi cha papeshu sama buddhir vishishyate (6.9).*

suhrin : well-wishers | mitra : friends | ary : enemies | udasina : neutrals | madhyastha : mediators | dveshya : the envious | bandhushu : relatives | sadhushv : the spiritual beings/the saintly ones | api : as well | cha : and | papeshu : the sinners | samabuddhi : with the same mind | vishishyate : stands out as more distinguished

One further stands out as a more distinguished yogi when he considers with the same mind i.e. equally all persons - whether well-wishers, friends, enemies, neutrals, mediators, envious ones, relatives, the saintly ones as also the sinners.

(10)
योगी युञ्जीत सततमात्मानं रहसि स्थितः ।
एकाकी यतचित्तात्मा निराशीरपरिग्रहः ॥ ६- १०॥

*yogi yunjita satatam atmanam rahasi sthithah
ekaki yata-chittatma nirashir aparigrahah (6.10).*

yogi : a person who is in control of his sensory desires/is committed to selfless action and is on the way to attain union of his self with the Supreme Self Consciousness | yunjita : engaged in concentration | satatam : constantly | atmanam : oneself | rahasi : in solitude | sthitah : seated | ekaki : alone | yat-chitta-atma : self in control of mind and sensory desires | nirashi : without hoping for any benefits | aparigrahah : rising above all feelings of possessiveness of material things

A yogi has to constantly practice keeping oneself engaged in concentration, seated alone and in solitude, with mind and sensory desires under control, without hoping for any benefits and rising above all feelings of possessiveness in regard to material things.

(11 - 12)
शुचौ देशे प्रतिष्ठाप्य स्थिरमासनमात्मनः ।
नात्युच्छ्रितं नातिनीचं चैलाजिनकुशोत्तरम् ॥६-११॥
तत्रैकाग्रं मनः कृत्वा यतचित्तेन्द्रियक्रियः ।
उपविश्यासने युञ्ज्याद्योगमात्मविशुद्धये ॥६-१२॥

shuchau dese pratishthapya sthiram asanam atmanah
natyuchchhritam natinicham chailajina kushottaram (6.11)
tatraikagram manah kritva yata chittendriya kriyah
upavishyasane yunjyad yogam atma vishuddhaye (6.12)

shuchau : clean | dese : ground/place | pratishthapya : set up | sthiram : stable/firm | asanam : seat | atmanah : self | na : not | ati : too | ucchritam : high | na : nor | ati : too | nicham : low | chaila-ajina : deer-skin | kusha : kusha grass | uttaram : cloth | tatra : there | ekagram : with single-minded attention | manah : mind | kritva : having done | yat-chitta : controlling the mind | indriya : senses | kriyah : activities | upavishya : sitting | asane : on the seat | yunjyat : should practice | yogam : the discipline of selfless action and commitment to joining the Supreme Self Consciousness | atma : self | vishuddhaye : purification

A person interested in yoga practice should select a clean place, over it spread kusha grass, deer-skin and soft cloth in that order and establish a stable seat for himself. The seat should not be too high nor should it be too low. Sitting on this seat, after having achieved control over his mind and sensory activities, the yoga aspirant should practice with single minded attention the discipline of self-purification and selfless action and commitment to joining the Supreme Self Consciousness.

(13)

समं कायशिरोग्रीवं धारयन्नचलं स्थिरः ।
सम्प्रेक्ष्य नासिकाग्रं स्वं दिशश्चानवलोकयन् ॥६- १३॥

samam kaya-shiro-grivam dharayann achalam sthirah
samprekshya nasikagram svam dishash chanavlokayan (6.13)

samam : straight | kaya : body | shira : head | grivam : neck | dharayan : holding | achalam : motionless | sthirah : steady | samprekshya : looking | nasika : nose | agram : front tip of the nose | svam : own | disha : direction | cha : and | anavalokayan : not looking

Let him hold his body, head and neck straight, steady and motionless, with his eyes fixed on the front tip of his own nose and without his looking in any other direction.

(14)

प्रशान्तात्मा विगतभीर्ब्रह्मचारिव्रते स्थितः ।
मनः संयम्य मच्चित्तो युक्त आसीत मत्परः ॥६- १४॥

prashantatma vigata-bhir brahmachari vrate sthitah
manah sanyamya machchitto yukta asita mat parah (6.14)

prashanta : tranquil | atma : mind | vigatbhi : free from fear | brahmachari-vrate : under a vow of celibacy | sthitah : situated | mana : mind | sanyamya : under control | mat : me | chitta : thinking | yukta : yogi | asita : remain | matparah : committed to me

With the tranquil mind under control, free from fear, under a vow of celibacy, always thinking of me, a yogi should remain committed to union with me (the Supreme) as the final goal.

(15)

युञ्जन्नेवं सदात्मानं योगी नियतमानसः ।
शान्तिं निर्वाणपरमां मत्संस्थामधिगच्छति ॥६- १५॥

yunjann evam sadatamanam yogi niyata manasah
shantim nirvana paramam mat-sanstham adhigachchhati (6.15)

yunjan : practicing (yoga) | evam : this way | sada : always | atmanam : self | yogi : one committed to selfless action/abstaining from sensory temptations and striving for union of Self with the Supreme Self consciousness | niyata-manasah : one who has achieved control over the mind | shantim : peace | nirvana-paramam : ultimate salvation | mat-sanstham : residing within me | adhigachchhati : attains

Always practising yoga in this manner and having achieved full control over mind, the yogi attains the peace that resides in me and reaches the ultimate stage of salvation (union of the self with the Supreme Self Consciousness).

(16)
नात्यश्नतस्तु योगोऽस्ति न चैकान्तमनश्नतः ।
न चाति स्वप्नशीलस्य जाग्रतो नैव चार्जुन ॥६-१६॥

*natyashnatastu yogoasti na chaikantam anashnatah
na chati svapana shilasya jagrato naiva charjuna (6.16)*

na : never | ati : too much | ashnata : who eats | tu : but | yoga : selfless action as the way to reach the Supreme | asti : exists | na : not | cha : also/and | ekantam : at all | anashnatah : who does not eat | na : nor | cha : also | ati : too much | svapana-shilasya : of one who is habituated to sleep | jagrata : one keeps nightvigil/sleeps very little | na : not | eva : ever | cha : also/and | arjuna : O Arjuna

O Arjuna! Yoga is not for one who eats too much, nor for the one who does not eat at all. It is not for one who is habituated to too much sleep nor for one who sleeps very little.

(17)
युक्ताहारविहारस्य युक्तचेष्टस्य कर्मसु ।
युक्तस्वप्नावबोधस्य योगो भवति दुःखहा ॥६-१७॥

*yuktahara viharasya yukta cheshtasya karmasu
yukta svapnavabodhasya yogo bhavati dukhaha (6.17)*

yukta : regulated | ahara : eating | viharasya : recreation | yukta : regulated |

cheshtasya : making efforts | karmasu : to work | yukta : regulated | svapna-avabodhasya : of the sleeping and the awake | yoga : the way to selfless action and reaching the Supreme | bhavati : becomes | dukha-ha : mitigating sorrow

For one who is well regulated in matters of eating, recreation, efforts at work, sleeping and keeping awake, yoga becomes the way to mitigate sorrow and pain.

(18)
यदा विनियतं चित्तमात्मन्येवावतिष्ठते ।
निःस्पृहः सर्वकामेभ्यो युक्त इत्युच्यते तदा ॥६-१८॥

yada viniyatam chittam atmanyevavatishthate
nihsprahah sarva kamebhyo yukta ityuchyate tada (6.18)

yada : when | viniyatam : disciplined/regulated | chittam : mind | atmani : in the self | eva : definitely | avatishthate : is situated | nihsprahah : free from desires | sarva : for all | kamebhya : objects of sensory gratification | yukta : well established | iti : thus | uchyate : is said to be | tada : then

When the mind is fully disciplined, is free from desires of all objects of sensory gratification and is definitely situated in the self, then only can one be said to be established in yoga.

(19)
यथा दीपो निवातस्थो नेङ्गते सोपमा स्मृता ।
योगिनो यतचित्तस्य युञ्जतो योगमात्मनः ॥६-१९॥

yatha dipo nivatastho nengate sopama smrita
yogino yatachittasya yunjato yogam atmanah (6.19)

yatha : as | dipa : lamp | nivata-stha : placed at a spot free from winds | na : not | ingate : waver/flicker | sa : that | upama : example | smrita : remembered | yogina : of the yogi | yata-chittasya : with a controlled mind | yunjata : practicing | yogam : concentration | atmanah : in the self

The flame of a lamp placed in a spot free from winds does not flicker.

That example applies to the yogi with a controlled mind practising yoga of the self.

(20)
यत्रोपरमते चित्तं निरुद्धं योगसेवया ।
यत्र चैवात्मनात्मानं पश्यन्नात्मनि तुष्यति ॥ ६- २०॥

yatroparamate chittam niruddham yoga sevaya
yatra chaivatmanatmanam pashyann atmani tushyati (6.20).

yatra : where/when | uparamate : attains tranquility | chittam : mind | niruddham : controlled | yoga-sevaya : by practising yoga | yatra : where/in which state | cha : and | eva : only | atmana : by the self | atmanam : the self | pashyan : seeing | atmani : in the self | tushyati : is satisfied

When by practising yoga, the mind is fully controlled and a state of tranquility is reached and the self is satisfied when it sees only the Self in the self. (The seer is the self. What is seen is the Self. And, where it is seen is also the self. There is nothing but the Self. This is the state of Supreme Self (Soul) Consciousness.)

(21)
सुखमात्यन्तिकं यत्तद् बुद्धिग्राह्यमतीन्द्रियम् ।
वेत्ति यत्र न चैवायं स्थितश्चलति तत्त्वतः ॥ ६- २१॥

sukham atyantikam yat tad buddhi grahyam atindriyam
vetti yatra na chaivayam sthitash chalati tattvatah (6.21)

sukham : bliss | atyantikam : the Supreme/the unlimited | yat : which | tat : that | buddhi : pure intelligence | grahyam : understandable | atindriyam : transcendental | vetti : knows | yatra : where | na : never | cha : and | eva : only | ayam : this (yogi) | sthitash : situated | chalati : moves away | tattvatah : from the essential/truth (of Supreme Self (Soul) Consciousness)

When the yogi experiences the supreme bliss which transcends the senses and can be understood only by pure intelligence, he gets fixed in that state and never wants to move away from the quintessence of the ultimate truth of Supreme Self (Soul) Consciousness.

(22)
यं लब्ध्वा चापरं लाभं मन्यते नाधिकं ततः ।
यस्मिन्स्थितो न दुःखेन गुरुणापि विचाल्यते ॥६- २२॥

yam labdhva chaparam labham manyate nadhikam tatah
yasminsthito na dukhena guru api vichalyate (6.22)

yam : that | labdhva : having received/having obtained/having reached | cha : and | aparam : the other | labham : gain | manyate : accepts/respects | na : never | adhikam : more | tatah : than that | yasmin : in which | sthita : situated | na : never | dukhena : by sorrows | gurunahatva-api : even by the heaviest of sorrows | vichalyate : gets shaken

After having reached that supreme state of bliss, the yogi never accepts (desires) any other gain, nothing more than that. He does not get shaken in this resolve even by the heaviest of sorrows.

(23)
तं विद्याद्दुःखसंयोगवियोगं योगसंज्ञितम् ।
स निश्चयेन योक्तव्यो योगोऽनिर्विण्णचेतसा ॥६- २३॥

tam vidyad dukha-sanyoga-viyogam yogasangitam
sa nishchayena yuktavyo yogo anirvinna chetasa (6.23)

tam : that | vidyat : known | dukha-sanyoga : sorrows of coming in contact (with the material world of sensory objects) | viyogam : absence of contact with the material world | yoga-sangitam : called by the name 'yoga' | sa : that | nishchayena : with determination | yoktavya : to be practiced | yoga : the way to reach the Supreme Self through selfless action and control over the senses | anirvinna-chetasa : without getting disheartened

We should know that what is called yoga frees one from the sorrows that result from contact with the material world of sensory objects. That yoga needs to be practised as a bounden duty, with determination, without getting disheartened.

(24)

संकल्पप्रभवान्कामांस्त्यक्त्वा सर्वानशेषतः ।
मनसैवेन्द्रियग्रामं विनियम्य समन्ततः ॥६- २४॥

sankalpa prabhavan kamams tyaktva sarvan asheshatah
manasaivendriya gramam viniyamya samantatah (6.24)

sankalpa : plannings | prabhavan : born of | kaman : sensory desires | tyaktva :abandoning | sarvan : all | sheshatah : fully | manasa : by the mind | eva : definitely | indriya-gramam : all the senses | viniyamya : regulating | samantatah : from all sides

Abandoning fully all plans born of sensory desires and the mind definitely regulating all the senses from all sides (are part of the yoga practice).

(25)

शनैः शनैरुपरमेद्बुद्ध्या धृतिगृहीतया ।
आत्मसंस्थं मनः कृत्वा न किंचिदपि चिन्तयेत् ॥६- २५॥

shanai shanair uparamed buddhya dhriti grihitaya
atma sanstham manah kritva na kinchid api chintayet (6.25)

shanai-shanai : slowly-slowly/gradually/step by step | uparamet : tranquility | buddhya : by intelligence | dhriti grihitaya : holding firmly and with patience | atma-sanstham : situated in the self | mana : mind | kritva : making | na : not | kinchit : anything else | api : even | chintayet : should consider

Gradually, step by step, one should attain by the use of ones intelligence, the state of tranquility. Once attained, it should be held firmly and with patience and the mind should not even think of anything else.

(26)

यतो यतो निश्चरति मनश्चञ्चलमस्थिरम् ।
ततस्ततो नियम्यैतदात्मन्येव वशं नयेत् ॥६- २६॥

yato yato nishcharati manash chanchalam asthiram
tatas tato niyamyaitad atmanyeva vasham nayet (6.26)

yata yata : wherever | nishcharati : gets agitated | mana : mind | chanchalam : fickle | asthiram : unstable | tata tata : there | niyamya : regulating | etat : this | atmanmni : in the self | eva : certainly | vasham : control | na yet : bring under

Wherever the mind gets agitated due to its fickle and unstable nature, every time it is necessary to regulate and discipline it and bring it back under the control of the self.

(27)
प्रशान्तमनसं ह्येनं योगिनं सुखमुत्तमम् ।
उपैति शान्तरजसं ब्रह्मभूतमकल्मषम् ॥६-२७॥

prashanta manasam hyenam yoginam sukham uttamam
upaitti shantarajasam brahma bhutam akalmasham (6.27)

prashanta : peaceful | manasam : mind | hi : definitely | enam : this | yoginam : yogi | sukham : happiness | uttamam : the highest | upaitti : achieves | shanta-rajasam : passions stilled | brahma-bhutam : attached to the Supreme | akalmasham : absolved of all past sins

This yogi achieves the highest happiness when his mind definitely becomes peaceful and passions are stilled. Once his mind is tranquil and attached to the Supreme, he stands absolved of all past sins.

(28)
युञ्जन्नेवं सदात्मानं योगी विगतकल्मषः ।
सुखेन ब्रह्मासंस्पर्शमत्यन्तं सुखमश्नुते ॥६-२८॥

yunjanevam sadatmanam yogi vigatakalmashah
sukhena brahma sansparsham atyantam sukham asnute (6.28)

yunjan : engaged in yoga | evam : thus | sada : always | atmanam : self | yogi : one committed to selfless action/control over senses and union with the Supreme | vigata : relieved of | kalmashah : all the sins/taints of good and evil | sukhena : in happiness | brahma-sansparsham : in contact with the Supreme | atyantam : the highest | sukham : happiness | asnute : attains

Thus, the yogi who is always engaged in yogic practices is absolved of all sins and taints of good and evil and other dualities. The self in contact with the Supreme, in full control of the mind, attains bliss - the highest happiness (of union with the Supreme).

(29)

सर्वभूतस्थमात्मानं सर्वभूतानि चात्मनि ।
ईक्षते योगयुक्तात्मा सर्वत्र समदर्शनः ॥६-२९॥

sarva bhuta stham atmanam sarva bhutani chatmani
ikshate yoga yuktatma sarvatra samadarshanah (6.29)

sarva : all | bhuta : living beings | sthma : situated in | atmanam : the Self (Soul) | sarva : all | bhutani : living beings | cha : and | atmani : in the self | ikshate : sees | yogayuktatma : the self merged in the Supreme Self (Soul) Consciousness | sarvatra : everywhere | sama-darshanah : looking at and treating all equally

(For a true yogi), all the living beings are situated in the Self and the Self lives in all beings. The Self merged in the Supreme, everywhere sees all living beings in the Self and treats them equally.

(30)

यो मां पश्यति सर्वत्र सर्वं च मयि पश्यति ।
तस्याहं न प्रणश्यामि स च मे न प्रणश्यति ॥६-३०॥

yo mam pashyati sarvatra sarvam cha mayi pashyati
tasyaham na pranashyami sa cha me na pranashyati (6.30)

ya : who | mam : me | pashyati : sees | sarvatra : everywhere | sarvam : all | cha : and | mayi : in Me | pashyati : sees | tasya : his | aham : I | na : not | pranashyami : lost | sa : he | cha : also | me : to Me | na : nor | Pranashyati : is lost

For one who sees me everywhere, in everything and also sees all in me, I am never lost nor is He ever lost to me. (The two are always close to each other and, in fact, one.)

(31)

सर्वभूतस्थितं यो मां भजत्येकत्वमास्थितः ।
सर्वथा वर्तमानोऽपि स योगी मयि वर्तते ॥६-३१॥

sarva bhuta sthitam yo mam bhajatyekatvam asthitah
sarvatha vartamanoapi sa yogi mayi vartate (6.31)

sarva : all | bhuta : living beings | asthitah : situated | ya : who | mam : me | bhajati : worships | ekatva oneness | asthitah : situated | sarvatha : in every way/always | vartamana : being present | api : also/even | sa : he | yogi : sage devoted to selfless action with his senses under control | mayi : in me | vartate : abides

The yogi who, having realised the oneness in all living beings, worships Me (the Supreme Soul) always abides in Me. He has risen above all dualities and knows that the same supreme self consciousness pervades all beings, nay, all are one and the same.

(32)

आत्मौपम्येन सर्वत्र समं पश्यति योऽर्जुन ।
सुखं वा यदि वा दुःखं स योगी परमो मतः ॥६-३२॥

atmaupamyena sarvatra samam pashyati yoarjuna
sukham va yadi va dukham sa yogi paramo matah (6.32)

atma : self | aupamyena : by comparison with himself | sarvatra : everywhere | samam : in the same way | pashyati : sees | ya : who | arjuna : O Arjuna | sukham : happiness | va : or | yadi : if | va : or | dukham : sorrow | sa : he/that | yogi : the person who has mastered his senses/is committed to selfless action and has realised his oneness with the Supreme | parama : the best | matah : considered

O! Arjuna, the yogi who, in comparison with himself, sees happiness and sorrow in the same way everywhere, is considered to be the best. Such a true yogi has realised the oneness of his self with the supreme self consciousness.

(33)

अर्जुन उवाच
योऽयं योगस्त्वया प्रोक्तः साम्येन मधुसूदन ।
एतस्याहं न पश्यामि चञ्चलत्वात्स्थितिं स्थिराम् ॥६- ३३॥

Arjuna uvacha
yoayam yogastvaya proktah samyena madhusudana
etasyaham na pashyami chanchalatvat sthitim sthiram (6.33)

arjuna : Arjuna | uvacha : said | ya : which | ayam : this | yoga : system of selfless action/maintaining equanimity and the individual self joining the Supreme Self-Consciousness | tvaya : you | proktah : spoken of | samyena : equanimity | madhusudana : Lord Krishna | etasya : of this | aham : I | na : not | pashyami : see | chanchalatvat : restlessness | sthitim : situation | sthiram : stable/lasting

Arjuna said: O ! Lord Krishna, the yoga of equanimity that you have spoken of does not seem to me to be of a lasting nature because of the existing situation of restlessness (in my mind).

(34)

चञ्चलं हि मनः कृष्ण प्रमाथि बलवद्दृढम् ।
तस्याहं निग्रहं मन्ये वायोरिव सुदुष्करम् ॥६- ३४॥

chanchalam hi manah krishna pramathi balavad dridham
tasyaham nigraham manye vayoriva sudushkaram (6.34)

chanchalam : restless | hi : verily | manah : mind | krishna : Lord Krishna | pramathi : turbulent | balavat : strong | dridham : firm/unbending | tasya : of that | aham : I | nigraham : subduing | manye : think | vayo : of the wind | iva : like | sudushkaram : difficult

O! Lord Krishna, verily, it is more difficult to subdue the mind than controlling the wind because the mind is certainly strong, turbulent and unbending.

(35)

श्रीभगवानुवाच
असंशयं महाबाहो मनो दुर्निग्रहं चलम् ।
अभ्यासेन तु कौन्तेय वैराग्येण च गृह्यते ॥६- ३५॥

Shribhagavan uvacha
asanshayam mahabaho mano durnigraham chalam
abhyasena tu kaunteya vairagyena cha grihyate (6.35)

Shribhagavan : Lord Krishna | uvacha : said | asanshayam : without any doubt | mahabaho : O large-armed one, Arjuna | mana : mind | durnigraham : not easy to control | chalam : restless | abhyasena : through practice | tu : but | kaunteya : son of Kunti, Arjuna | vairagyena : through detachment | cha : and | grihyate : gets controlled

Lord Krishna said: O! mighty-armed, son of Kunti, Arjuna Mind is undoubtedly restless and so very difficult to control but through practice (of Yoga) and an approach of detachment (from fruits of action), it may be possible to control it.

(36)

असंयतात्मना योगो दुष्प्राप इति मे मतिः ।
वश्यात्मना तु यतता शक्योऽवाप्तुमुपायतः ॥६- ३६॥

asanyatatmana yogo dushprapa iti me matih
vashyatmana tu yatata sakyo avaptum upayatah (6.36)

asanyata : unrestrained/uncontrolled | atmana : mind | yoga : control over the senses/selfless action and realisation of oneness with the Supreme Self | dusprapa : difficult to achieve | iti : thus | me : my | matih : view/opinion | vashya : under control | atmana : mind | tu : but | yatata : while attempting | sakya : doable/practical | avaputam : to attain | upayatah : right means

In my (Lord Krishna's) view, it is difficult to achieve yoga with a mind that is not under control but with a controlled mind, through right means, it is possible to do so.

(37)

अर्जुन उवाच
अयतिः श्रद्धयोपेतो योगाच्चलितमानसः ।
अप्राप्य योगसंसिद्धिं कां गतिं कृष्ण गच्छति ॥ ६-३७॥

Arjuna uvacha
ayatih shraddhayopeto yogach chalita manasah
aprapya yoga sansiddhim kam gatim krishna gachchhati (6.37)

arjuna uvacha : Arjuna said | ayatih : one who is unable to control his mind and senses | shraddhaya : with faith | upeta : avowed/possessed | yogat : from yoga | chalita : moved away | manasah : mind | aprapya : not gaining | yoga-sansiddhim : perfection in yoga/achieving the ultimate goal of yoga and reaching the state of the self realising its oneness with the Supreme Self (Soul) Consciousness | kam : what | gatim : end/fate | krishna : Lord Krishna | gachchhati : goes/meets

Arjuna said: O! Lord Krishna, one who begins with faith in yoga but is not able to control his mind and sensory desires, moves away from his faith in yoga and fails to achieve the ultimate goal of yoga, what fate does he meet?

(38)

कच्चिन्नोभयविभ्रष्टश्छिन्नाभ्रमिव नश्यति ।
अप्रतिष्ठो महाबाहो विमूढो ब्रह्मणः पथि ॥ ६-३८॥

kacchin nobhaya vibhrashtash chhinnabhramiva nashyati
apratishtho mahabaho vimudho brahmanah pathi (6.38)

kacchit : whether | na : not | ubhaya : both | vibhrashtash : fallen from | chinna : shattered | abhram : cloud | iva : like | nashyati : perishes | apratishtho: without a position of honour | mahabaho : mighty-armed one (Lord Krishna) | vimudha : deluded | brahmanah : of Brahamana (the Supreme) | pathi : one on the path

O! Mighty-armed Lord Krishna, whether a person deluded on the path of the Supreme Brahaman falls from both (yoga and pursuit of sensory objects) and perishes without honours like a shattered cloud.

(39)

एतन्मे संशयं कृष्ण छेत्तुमर्हस्यशेषतः ।
त्वदन्यः संशयस्यास्य छेत्ता न ह्युपपद्यते ॥६-३९॥

*etanme sanshayam krishna chhettum arhashyashesatah
tvadanyah sanshayasyasya chetta na hyupapadyate(6.39)*

etat : this | me : my | sanshayam : doubt | krishna : Lord Krishna | chhettum : dispel | arhasi : request | sheshatah : completely | tvat : you | anyah : other | sanshayasya : of the doubt | asya : of this | chetta : remover | na : no | hi : certainly | upapadyate : is able to

O! Lord Krishna, you are requested to dispel completely this doubt of mine. Certainly, no one other than you is able to remove my doubt.

(40)

श्रीभगवानुवाच
पार्थ नैवेह नामुत्र विनाशस्तस्य विद्यते ।
न हि कल्याणकृत्कश्चिद्दुर्गतिं तात गच्छति ॥६-४०॥

*Shribhagavan uvacha
partha naiveha namutra vinashastasya vidyate
na hi kalyana krit kashchid durgatim tata gachchhati (6.40)*

Shribhagavan uvacha : God Himself, Lord Krishna said | partha : son of Prathu, Arjuna | na : never | eva : verily | iha : here/in this world | na : never | amutra : in the next life/in the other world | vinasha : destruction | tasya : his | vidyate : exists/appears | na : never | hi : surely | kalyanakriat : engaged in welfare of others | kashchit : anyone | durgatim : bad state/degradation/state of grief | gachchhati : goes/reaches

Lord Krishna said: O! Son of Prathu, Arjuna, verily, he never appears to face destruction either here in this life or hereafter in the other world, for one engaged in doing good to others never reaches a state of grief.

(41)

प्राप्य पुण्यकृतां लोकानुषित्वा शाश्वतीः समाः ।
शुचीनां श्रीमतां गेहे योगभ्रष्टोऽभिजायते ॥६-४१॥

prapya punyakritam lokanushitva shashvatih samah
shuchinam shrimatam gehe yoga bhrashto abhijayate (6.41)

prapya : after having achieved | punyakritam : of those who have done pious deeds | lokan : worlds | ushitva : having lived | shashvatih : for long | samah : periods of time/years | shuchinam : of the virtuous | shrimatam : the prosperous/the affluent | gehe : in the house | yoga-bhrashtha : one who has fallen from the path of yoga | abhijayate : is born

After reaching the worlds of those who had done pious deeds and having lived there for long years, one who has fallen from the path of yoga is born again in the house of the virtuous or the prosperous.

(42)

अथवा योगिनामेव कुले भवति धीमताम् ।
एतद्धि दुर्लभतरं लोके जन्म यदीदृशम् ॥६-४२॥

athava yoginameva kule bhavati dhimatam
etaddhi durlabhataram loke janma yadidrisham (6.42)

athava : or | yoginam : of yogis | eva : certainly | kule : in the family | bhavati : is born | dhimatam : the wise | etat : this | hi : surely | durlabha-taram : extremely rare | loke : in this world | janma : birth | yat : that | idrisham : like this

While it is possible that the fallen yogi may be reborn in a family of yogis who are surely wise, such a birth is extremely rare in this world.

(43)

तत्र तं बुद्धिसंयोगं लभते पौर्वदेहिकम् ।
यतते च ततो भूयः संसिद्धौ कुरुनन्दन ॥६-४३॥

tatra tam buddhisanyogam labhate paurva dehikam
yatate cha tato bhuyah sansiddhau kuru nandana (6.43)

tatra : there | tam : that | buddhi-sanyogam : union with intelligence/wisdom | labhate : gains | paurva-dehikam : from the former body | yatate : strives/endeavours | cha : and | tata: that | bhuyah : again | sansiddhau : ultimate realisation of union with the Supreme Self Consciousness | kuru-nandana : O! son of Kuru, Arjuna

Thereupon, a person so born gains wisdom from what was already acquired in the previous body and O! son of Kuru, Arjuna, he strives harder to achieve the ultimate aim of realising oneness with the Supreme Self Consciousness.

(44)
पूर्वाभ्यासेन तेनैव ह्रियते ह्यवशोऽपि सः।
जिज्ञासुरपि योगस्य शब्दब्रह्मातिवर्तते ॥६-४४॥

*purvabhyasena tenaiva hriyate hyavashoapi sah
jigyasur api yogasya shabda brahmativartate (6.44)*

purva : former/previous | abhyasena : by practice | tena : by that | eva : verily | hriyate : is attracted | hi : surely | avasha : helpless | api : also | sah : he | jigyasu : inquisitive/anxious to know | api : even | shabda-brahma : Word-God (the concept of), the Vedas | ativartate : goes beyond

Verily, by virtue of his previous practice alone, he surely gets attracted to the truths of yoga even without trying. Such a person who is anxious to know goes beyond even the followers of the Word-God of the Vedas.

(45)
प्रयत्नाद्यतमानस्तु योगी संशुद्धकिल्बिषः।
अनेकजन्मसंसिद्धस्ततो याति परां गतिम् ॥६-४५॥

*prayatnad yatamanas tu yogi sanshuddha kilbishah
aneka janma sansiddhas tato yati param gatim (6.45)*

prayatnat : by assiduously | yatamana : striving | tu : but | yogi : devoted to the pursuit of self-realisation | sanshuddhakilbishah : one who has washed all his sins | aneka : many | janma : births | sansiddha : having achieved union with the Supreme Self | tata : thereupon | yati : achieves | param : the highest | gatim : state

But, the yogi striving assiduously, having washed all his sins, after many many births, achieves union with the Supreme Self which is the highest state and the ultimate goal.

(46)

तपस्विभ्योऽधिको योगी ज्ञानिभ्योऽपि मतोऽधिकः ।
कर्मिभ्यश्चाधिको योगी तस्माद्योगी भवार्जुन ॥ ६- ४६॥

tapasvibhyoadhiko yogi gyanibhyoapi matoadhikah
karmibhyashchadhiko yogi tasmat yogi bhavarjuna (6.46)

tapasvibhya : than ascetics | adhika : greater/superior | yogi : engaged in the pursuit of achieving union with the Supreme Self | gyanibhya : than the learned | api : also | mata : deemed/considered | adhikah : greater | karmibhya : the worker for fruits of action | cha : also | adhiko : greater | yogi : yogi | tasmat : thus | yogi : yogi | bhava : become | arjuna : Arjuna

O! Arjuna, the yogi is greater than the ascetic, he is superior to the learned (gyani), he is also deemed to be greater than the worker who is attached to the fruits of his action. Thus, O! Arjuna, you should become only a yogi (one committed to selfless action).

(47)

योगिनामपि सर्वेषां मद्गतेनान्तरात्मना ।
श्रद्धावान् भजते यो मां स मे युक्ततमो मतः ॥ ६- ४७॥

yoginamapi sarvesham mad gatenantar atmana
shraddhavan bhajate yo mam sa me yukttamo matah(6.47)

yoginam : of yogis | api : also | sarvesham : all | mad-gatena : merged in me | antaratmana : with his inner self | shraddha-van : having full faith (in me) | bhajate : worships (me) | ya : who | mam : to me | sa : he | me : by me | yukta-tama : the greatest | matah : is considered

Also, among all the yogis, the one fully devoted to me (the Supreme Self), one who with his inner self is fully merged in me, one who has full faith in me, one who worships me, is considered by me to be the greatest.

Thus ends the Sixth Canto titled 'Yoga of Meditation'.

Seventh Canto

GYANA-VIGYANA YOGA
Yoga of Higher Knowledge and Science

(1)

श्रीभगवानुवाच
मय्यासक्तमनाः पार्थ योगं युञ्जन्मदाश्रयः ।
असंशयं समग्रं मां यथा ज्ञास्यसि तच्छृणु ॥७-१॥

*Shribhagavan uvacha
mayyasakta manah partha yogam yunjan madashrayah
asanshayam samagram mam yatha gyasyasi tach chhrinu (7.1)*

Shribhagavan uvacha: Lord Krishna said | mayi : in me | asaktamanah : attached mind | Partha : son of Prathu, Arjuna | yogam : yoga | yunjan : practicing | madashrayah : depending on me | asanshayam : undoubtedly | samagram : wholly | mam : me | yatha : as/in the manner that | gyasyasi: you know | tat : that | chhrinu : listen

Lord Krishna said: O! Arjuna, listen, when mind is attached to me ('Me' throughout meaning' the Supreme i.e. the Supreme Soul consciousness') and yoga is practiced wholly with dependence on Me, in the manner that you can undoubtedly know Me fully.

(2)

ज्ञानं तेऽहं सविज्ञानमिदं वक्ष्याम्यशेषतः ।
यज्ज्ञात्वा नेह भूयोऽन्यज्ज्ञातव्यमवशिष्यते ॥७-२॥

*gyanam te aham sa vigyanam idam vakshyamyasheshatah
yajgyatva neha bhuyo anyaj gyatavayam avashishyate (7.2)*

gyanam : knowledge | te : to you | aham : I | sa : with | vigyanam : specialised knowledge (of self-realisation) | idam : this | vakshyami : shall explain | asheshatah : without leaving out anything/ in full | yat : which | gyatva : after knowing | na : not | iha : here/in this world | bhuya : further/more | anyat : anything else | gyatavyam : worthy of knowing | avashishyate : remains

I shall explain to you fully this knowledge (about how to get to Me through yoga) along with the highly specialised knowledge (of self-realisation). After knowing all this (all inclusive knowledge), there will be nothing more left in this world that is worth knowing.

(3)

मनुष्याणां सहस्रेषु कश्चिद्यतति सिद्धये ।
यततामपि सिद्धानां कश्चिन्मां वेत्ति तत्त्वतः ॥७-३॥

*manushyanam sahasreshu kashchidyatati siddhaye
yatatam api siddhanam kashchin mam vetti tattvatah (7.3)*

manushyanam : men | sahasreshu : among thousands | kashchit : someone | yatati : attempts | siddhaye : for achieving | yatatam : of those attempting | api : certainly | siddhanam : of those who have achieved (self-realisation) | kashchit : someone | mam : me | vetti : knows | tattvatah : in essence/really fully

Of thousands of men, someone attempts self-realisation (unity of the self with the supreme soul consciousness) and of those who have achieved it, hardly some one really knows me fully.

(4)

भूमिरापोऽनलो वायुः खंमनो बुद्धिरेव च ।
अहंकार इतीयं मे भिन्ना प्रकृतिरष्टधा ॥७-४॥

*bhumirapoanalo vayuh khammano buddhireva cha
ahankara itiyam me bhinna prakritirashtadha (7.4)*

bhumi : earth | apa : water | anala : fire | vayuh : air | kham : ether | mana : mind | buddhi : intelligence | eva : definitely | cha : and | ahankara : ego | iti : thus | iyam : these | me : my | bhinna : different | prakriti : nature | ashtadha : eightfold

My nature is definitely divided eightfold into earth, water, fire, air, ether, mind, intelligence and ego.

(5)

अपरेयमितस्त्वन्यां प्रकृतिं विद्धि मे पराम् ।
जीवभूतां महाबाहो ययेदं धार्यते जगत् ॥७-५॥

apareyam itas tvanyam prakritim viddhi me param
jivabhutam mahabaho yayedam dharyate jagat (7.5)

apara : lower (aparaprakrati : lower nature) | iyam : this | ita : apart from | tu : but | anyam : another | prakritim : nature | viddhi : know | me : my | para : higher (paraprakrati : higher nature) | jiva-bhutam : living beings | maha-baho : mighty-armed, Arjuna | yaya : which | idam : this | diary ate : holds | jagat : world

This is my lower nature but apart from this, O! Mighty-armed Arjuna, know that there is my other higher nature which holds this world of living beings.

(6)

एतद्योनीनि भूतानि सर्वाणीत्युपधारय ।
अहं कृत्स्नस्य जगतः प्रभवः प्रलयस्तथा ॥७-६॥

etadyonini bhutani sarvanityupadharaya
aham kritsnasya jagatah prabhavah pralayas tatha (7.6)

etat : these | yonini : natures/sources | bhutani : beings | sarvani : all | iti : thus | upadharaya : know/understand | aham : I | kritsnasya : of the whole | jagatah : universe | prabhavah : the beginning | pralaya : the end (of the universe) | tatha : and

All living beings have their source in these two. Thus, you should understand that I am both the beginning and the end of the whole of the universe. (Whatever exists, comes out of the sea of the supreme soul or self consciousness and merges in the same).

(7)

मत्तः परतरं नान्यत्किंचिदस्ति धनंजय ।
मयि सर्वमिदं प्रोतं सूत्रे मणिगणा इव ॥७-७॥

*mattah parataram nanyat kinchid asti dhananjaya
mayi sarvam idam protam sutre mani-gana iva (7.7)*

mattah : than me | para-taram : higher | na : not | anyat : other | kinchit : anything | asti : is/exists | dhananjaya : one who has conquered the greed for wealth, Arjuna | mayi : in me | sarvam : all | idam : this | protam : strung | sutre : on a thread | mani-gana : pearls | iva : like

O! Arjuna, there is nothing higher than Me that exists. All this universe is strung in me like the pearls in a thread. (It is the invisible thread of the supreme consciousness that holds all beings together).

(8)

रसोऽहमप्सु कौन्तेय प्रभास्मि शशिसूर्ययोः ।
प्रणवः सर्ववेदेषु शब्दः खे पौरुषं नृषु ॥७-८॥

*rasoahamapsu kaunteya prabhasmi shashisuryayoh
pranavah sarvavedeshu shabdah khe paurusham nrishu (7.8)*

rasa : taste | aham : I | apsu : in water | kaunteya : son of Kunti, Arjuna | prabha : light/radiance | asmi : am | shashi : moon | suryayoh : sun | pranavah : the syllable Om, Onkar | sarva : all | vedeshu : Vedas | shabdah : word (with sound vibration) | khe : in ether/space (akash) | paurusham : strength and valour | nrishu : among human beings

O! Son of Kunti, Arjuna, I am the feeling of taste in water, radiance in the moon and the sun, the syllable Om in all the Vedas, the sound in ether and strength and valour among human beings.

(9)

पुण्यो गन्धः पृथिव्यां च तेजश्चास्मि विभावसौ ।
जीवनं सर्वभूतेषु तपश्चास्मि तपस्विषु ॥७-९॥

punyo gandhah prithivyam cha tejashchasmi vibhavasau
jivanam sarvabhuteshu tapashchasmi tapasvishu (7.9)

punya : pure | gandhah : smell/odour/fragrance | prathivyam : in the earth | cha : and | tejah : brightness | cha : also | asmi : am | vibhavasau : in the fire | jivanam : life force | sarva : in all | bhuteshu : living beings | tapa : penance/austerity | cha : and | asmi : am | tapasvishu : ascetics

I am pure fragrance in earth and brightness in fire. Also, I am life force in all living beings and austerity in ascetics.

(10)

बीजं मां सर्वभूतानां विद्धि पार्थ सनातनम् ।
बुद्धिर्बुद्धिमतामस्मि तेजस्तेजस्विनामहम् ॥७-१०॥

bijam mam sarva bhutanam viddhi partha sanatanam
buddhir buddhimatam asmi tejas tejasvinam aham (7.10)

bijam : seed | mam : me | sarva-bhutanam : all living beings | viddhi : understand | partha : son of Prathu, Arjuna | sanatanam : eternal | buddhi : intelligence | buddhi-matam : of the intelligent | asmi : am | teja : radiance | tejasvinam : of the powerful | aham : I

O! Son of Prathu, Arjuna, please understand, I am the eternal seed in all living beings. I am the intellect in all the intelligent ones and the radiance of the powerful.

(11)

बलं बलवतां चाहं कामरागविवर्जितम् ।
धर्माविरुद्धो भूतेषु कामोऽस्मि भरतर्षभ ॥७-११॥

balam balavatam chaham kamaragavivarjitam
dharmaviruddho bhuteshu kamoasmi bharatarshabha (7.11)

balam : strength | bala-vatam : of the strong | cha : and | aham : I | kama

: sensory desire | raga : attachment | vivarjitam : devoid of | dharma : righteous duty | aviruddha : not against/not opposed to | bhuteshu : in all living beings | kama : desire/passion | asmi : am | bharatarshabha : O! bull (eminent) among the Bharatas, Arjuna

O! Eminent one of the Bharata dynasty, Arjuna, I am the strength of the strong devoid of sensory desire and attachment. I am also the passion in all living beings so long as it is not opposed to righteous duty.

(12)
ये चैव सात्त्विका भावा राजसास्तामसाश्च ये ।
मत्त एवेति तान्विद्धि न त्वहं तेषु ते मयि ॥७-१२॥

ye chaiva sattvika bhava rajasas tamasash cha ye
matt aeveti tanviddhi na tvaham teshu te mayi (7.12)

Ye : which | cha : and | eva : certainly | sattvika : in the realm of the good | bhava : state/nature | rajas : in the realm of passion | tamasash : in the realm of darkness (ignorance/evil) | cha : also | ye : which | matta : from me | eva : certainly | iti : thus | tan : those | viddhi : know/understand | na : not | tu : but | aham : I | teshu : in them | te : they | mayi : in me

All the states of sattva, rajas and tamas (the good, the passion and the evil) all certainly emanate from me but please understand that they are within me but I am not in them.

(13)
त्रिभिर्गुणमयैर्भावैरेभिः सर्वमिदं जगत् ।
मोहितं नाभिजानाति मामेभ्यः परमव्ययम् ॥७-१३॥

tribhir gunamayair bhavair ebhih sarvam idam jagat
mohitam nabhijanati mamebhayh param avyayam (7-13)

tribhi : three | guna-mayai : constituted of the qualities/modes (gunas) | bhavai : nature/state | ebhih : these | sarvam : whole | idam : this | jagat : world | mohitam : deluded | na : not | abhijanati : knows | mam : me | ebhyah : above/beyond these | param : supreme | avyayam : inexhaustible/immutable

Deluded by these three states constituted of the three gunas (qualities) - sattoguna (quality of the good), rajoguna (quality of the passion) and tamoguna (quality of the evil), this whole world does not know me. As the Supreme, I am beyond these three states and qualities and am immutable.

(14)

दैवी ह्येषा गुणमयी मम माया दुरत्यया ।
मामेव ये प्रपद्यन्ते मायामेतां तरन्ति ते ॥७- १४॥

*daivi hyesha guna mayi mama maya duratyaya
mam eva ye prapadyante mayam etam taranti te (7.14)*

daivi : divine | hi : verily | esha : this | guna-mayi : constituted of the three gunas (qualities) | mama : my | maya : illusion | duratyaya : difficult to overcome | mam : to me | eva : only | ye : who | prapadyante : take refuge(in me)/surrender (to me) | mayametam : this illusion | taranti : get over | te : they

Verily, this divine illusion of mine constituted of the three gunas (modes or qualities of the world of matter) is difficult to overcome. But, those who take refuge in me alone are able to get over this illusion.

(15)

न मां दुष्कृतिनो मूढाः प्रपद्यन्ते नराधमाः ।
माययापहृतज्ञाना आसुरं भावमाश्रिताः ॥७- १५॥

*na mam dushkritino mudhah prapadyante naradhamah
mayayapahritagyana asuram bhavamashritah (7.15)*

na : not | mam : to me | duskritina : bad characters/wrong-doers/evil-doers | mudhah : fools/ignorant | prapadyante : take refuge/shelter | naradhamah : undesirable human beings/men of poor morals/lowest among men | mayaya : by illusion | apahrita : deprived of | gyana : knowledge/discrimination | asuram : demonic/wicked | bhavam : nature | ashritah : dependent

The evil-doers, the ignorant, the lowest of human beings who have been deprived of higher knowledge by illusion and those dependent on demonic nature do not take shelter in me.

(16)
चतुर्विधा भजन्ते मां जनाः सुकृतिनोऽर्जुन ।
आर्तो जिज्ञासुरर्थार्थी ज्ञानी च भरतर्षभ ॥७-१६॥

*chaturvidha bhajante mam janah sukritino arjuna
arto jigyasurartharthi gyani cha bharatarshabha (7.16)*

chatur-vidha : four kinds of | bhajante : worship | mam : me | janah : persons/people | sukritina : those doing good deeds/the good | Arjuna : O! Arjuna | arta : the distressed | jigyasu : the inquisitive/the seeker of knowledge | artha-arthi : those seeking material benefit | gyani : the knower/the wise | cha : also | bharatarshabha : the eminent one of the Bharata dynasty

O! The eminent one among the scions of Bharata, Arjuna, four kinds of good people worship me : the distressed, the seekers of knowledge, those in the pursuit of material gains and the wise.

(17)
तेषां ज्ञानी नित्ययुक्त एकभक्तिर्विशिष्यते ।
प्रियो हि ज्ञानिनोऽत्यर्थमहं स च मम प्रियः ॥७-१७॥

*tesham gyani nitya yukta eka bhaktir vishishyate
priyo hi gyaninoa tyartham aham sa cha mama priyah (7.17)*

tesham : of them | gyani : wise | nitya-yukta : daily engaged/always busy in | eka : only/single | bhakti : devotion | vishishyate : is special | priya : dear | hi : certainly | gyanina : to the wise | atyartham : highly | aham : I | sa : he | cha : also | mama : to me | priyah : dear

Of them, the wise who is always engaged in devotional worship of the only One is special. I am certainly very dear to him and he is dear to me.

(18)

उदाराः सर्व एवैते ज्ञानीत्वात्मैव मे मतम् ।
आस्थितः स हि युक्तात्मा मामेवानुत्तमां गतिम् ॥७-१८॥

udarah sarv aevaite gyanityatmaiva me matam
asthitah sa hi yuktatma mam evanuttamam gatim (7.18)

udarah : noble | sarve : all | eva : surely | ete : these | gyani : the wise | tu : but | atma-eva : like myself | me : my | matam : opinion | asthitah : situated/established | sa : he | hi : certainly | yukta-atma : steadfastly engaged | mam : in me | eva : certainly | anuttamam : the supreme | gatim : destination/goal

Surely, all of them are noble but I regard the wise gyani like myself. For, in my opinion, they are certainly steadfastly engaged and established in me alone as the supreme goal.

(19)

बहूनां जन्मनामन्ते ज्ञानवान्मां प्रपद्यते ।
वासुदेवः सर्वमिति स महात्मा सुदुर्लभः ॥७-१९॥

bahunam janmanamante gyanvanmam prapadyate
vasudevah sarvamiti sa mahatma sudurlabhah (7.19)

bahunam : many | janmanamante : recurring births | ante : after | gyanvan : the wise | mam : to me | prapadyate : takes shelter | vasudevah : Lord Krishna (representing the Supreme) | sarvam : all/everything | iti : thus | sa : that | mahatma : great soul | su-durlabhah : extremely rare

After many recurring births, the wise man takes shelter in Me, thus realising that everything is ultimately only the same Supreme (Self Consciousness). But, such great souls are extremely rare.

(20)

कामैस्तैस्तैर्हृतज्ञानाः प्रपद्यन्तेऽन्यदेवताः ।
तं तं नियममास्थाय प्रकृत्या नियताः स्वया ॥७-२०॥

kamais tais tair hritagyanah prapadyanteanya devatah
tam tam niyamam asthaya prakritya niyatah svaya (7.20)

Gyana-Vigyana Yoga | 145

kamai : by desires | tai tai : various | hrita : deprived of/robbed of | gyanah : knowledge/discretion/wisdom | prapadyante : take shelter | anya : other | devatah : gods | tam tam : corresponding/respective | niyamamasthaya : rules/regulations | asthaya : following | prakritya : by nature | niyatah : established/fixed | svaya : by self

Those who have been robbed of wisdom by various sensory desires, surrender to other gods and follow their respective rules and regulations as established by themselves according to their nature.

(21)
यो यो यां यां तनुं भक्तः श्रद्धयार्चितुमिच्छति ।
तस्य तस्याचलां श्रद्धां तामेव विदधाम्यहम् ॥७-२१॥

yo yo yam yam tanum bhaktah shraddhayarchitum ichchhati
tasya tasyachalam shraddham tam eav vidadhamyaham (7.21)

yaya : whoever | yam yam : whatever | tanum : form | bhaktah : devotee | shraddhya : with faith | architum : to worship | ichchhati : wishes | tasyatasya : of him | achalam : steady/firm/unwavering | shraddham : by faith | tam : that | eva : definitely | vidadhami : make | aham : I

In whatever form, any devotee wishes to worship (the Supreme) with faith, I definitely make his faith firm in that very form (of the Supreme).

(22)
स तया श्रद्धया युक्तस्तस्याराधनमीहते ।
लभते च ततः कामान्मयैव विहितान्हि तान् ॥७-२२॥

sa taya shraddhaya yuktastasyaradhanam ihate
labhate cha tatah kamanmayaiva vihitanhi tan (7.22)

sa : he | taya : with that | shraddhaya : by faith | yukta : endowed | tasya : his | aradhanam : worship | ihate : engages | labhate : gains | cha : and | tatah : that | kaman : desires | maya : by me | eva : alone | vihitan : arranged | hi : certainly | tan : those

Endowed with that faith, he engages in the worship of that form (of the Godhead, the Supreme) and gets his desires fulfilled. (But) all that is certainly arranged by me alone (by the same Supreme).

(23)

अन्तवत्तु फलं तेषां तद्भवत्यल्पमेधसाम् ।
देवान्देवयजो यान्ति मद्भक्ता यान्ति मामपि ॥७- २३॥

antavattu phalam tesham tad bhavatyalpa medhasam
devan deva-yajo yanti mad-bhakta yanti mam api (7.23)

ant-vat : limited/short-lived | tu : but | phalam : fruit | tesham : their | tat : that | bhavati : happens/becomes | alpa-medhasam : those of little intelligence | devan : gods | deva-yaja : those worshipping the gods | yanti : go | mat : my | bhakta : devotees | yanti : go | mam : to me | api : also

Those of little intelligence who worship various gods go to those gods only and the fruits they get are limited and short-lived. On the other hand, my devotees come to me (the Supreme).

(24)

अव्यक्तं व्यक्तिमापन्नं मन्यन्ते मामबुद्धयः ।
परं भावमजानन्तो ममाव्ययमनुत्तमम् ॥७- २४॥

avyaktam vyaktim apannam manyante mam abuddhayah
param bhavam ajananto mamavyayam anuttamam (7.24)

avyaktam : unmanifest | vyaktim : individuality (the person of Lord Krishna) | appannam : achieved | manyante : accept | mam : me | abuddhayah : persons with little intelligence/the ignorant | param : higher | bhavam : state/nature | ajananta : without knowing | mama : my | avyayam : immutable | anuttamam : supreme

Persons with little intelligence think of me as being the manifestation (in individual form) of the unmanifest. They do not know my higher nature which is that of the immutable Supreme.

(25)
नाहं प्रकाशः सर्वस्य योगमायासमावृतः ।
मूढोऽयं नाभिजानाति लोको मामजमव्ययम् ॥७- २५॥

naham prakashah sarvasya yog maya samavritah
mudhoayam nabhijanati loko mam ajam avyayam (7.25)

na : not | aham : I | prakashah : manifest/visible | sarvasya : all pervading | yog-maya : divine illusion | samavritah : covered/veiled | mudha : foolish | ayam : these | na : not | abhijanati : know/understand | loka : world/people | mam : me | ajam : unborn | avyayam : not subject to death/immutable

I am not visible to the foolish because of the all pervading divine illusion. These people do not understand me as one not subject to birth and death.

(26)
वेदाहं समतीतानि वर्तमानानि चार्जुन ।
भविष्याणि च भूतानि मां तु वेद न कश्चन ॥७- २६॥

vedaham samatitani vartamanani charjuna
bhavishyani cha bhutani mam tu veda na kashchana (7.26)

veda : know | aham : I | samatitani : all the happenings in the past | vartamanani : in the present | cha : and | arjuna : O! Arjuna | bhavishyani : in the future | cha : also | bhutani : living beings | mam : me | tu : but | veda : knows | na : not | kashchana : no one

O! Arjuna, I know all that has happened in the past, is happening now and will happen in the future. Also, I know all the living beings. But, no one knows me.

(27)
इच्छाद्वेषसमुत्थेन द्वन्द्वमोहेन भारत ।
सर्वभूतानि संमोहं सर्गे यान्ति परन्तप ॥७- २७॥

ichchha dvesha samutthena dvandva mohena bharata
sarva bhutani sammoham sarge yanti parantapa (7.27)

iccha : desire/longing | dvesha : enmity/aversion | samutthena : arising from | dvandva : duality | mohena : deluded | bharata : descendent of Bharata, the great king | sarva : all | bhutani : living beings | sammohan : delusion | sarge : while being born in this world | yanti : go | parantapa : conqueror of enemies/scorcher of foes

O! Descendent of the great king Bharata, all living beings are deluded by the duality arising from desire and enmity. O! Scorcher of foes, all stand overtaken by delusion at birth.

(28)
येषां त्वन्तगतं पापं जनानां पुण्यकर्मणाम् ।
ते द्वन्द्वमोहनिर्मुक्ता भजन्ते मां दृढव्रताः ॥७- २८॥

*yesham tvanta gatam papam jananam punya karmanam
te dvandva moha nirmukta bhajante mam dridha vratah (7.28)*

yesham : whose | tu : but | anta-gatam : fully gone/eradicated | papam : sin | jananam : of the people | punya : pious | karmanam : activities/deeds | te : they | dvandva : duality | moha : delusion | nirmukta : free from | bhajante : worship | mam : to me | dridha-vratah : of firm determination

Those persons whose sins stand fully eradicated by pious deeds and who are freed from the delusion of dualities, worship me with firm determination.

(29)
जरामरणमोक्षाय मामाश्रित्य यतन्ति ये ।
ते ब्रह्म तद्विदुः कृत्स्नमध्यात्मं कर्म चाखिलम् ॥७- २९॥

*jara marana mokshaya mam ashritya yatanti ye
te brahma tadviduh kritsnam adhyatmam karma chakhilam (7.29)*

jara : old age | marana : death | mokshaya : salvation | mam : me | ashritya : shelter of | yatanti : strive | ye : who | te : those | brahma : Brahman (the Supreme) | tat : that | viduh : know | kritsnam : everything/in full | adhyatmam : transcendental | karma : action | cha : also | akhilam : completely

Those who take shelter in me while striving for salvation from old age and death, get to know Brahman (the Supreme) and everything about transcendental reality (of supreme soul consciousness) and selfless action.

(30)
साधिभूताधिदैवं मां साधियज्ञं च ये विदुः ।
प्रयाणकालेऽपि च मां ते विदुर्युक्तचेतसः ॥७- ३०॥

sadhibhutadhidaivam mam sadhiyajnam cha ye viduh
prayana kalea pi cha mam te vidur yukta chetasah (7.30)

sa-adhibhuta : what concerns all living beings in this material world | adhidaivam : about the various gods | mam : me | sadhiyajnam : about sacrifices | cha : also | ye : those | viduh : know | prayana-kale : at the time of departure from the world/at the time of death | api : even | cha : and | mam : me | te : they | vidu : know | yukta-chetasah : minds engaged

Those who know me, also know about all the living beings in this material world, various gods as also sacrifices. Even at the time of final departure from this world (death), they know me and their minds are steadfast and engaged in me.

Thus ends the Seventh Canto titled 'Yoga of Higher Knowledge and Science'.

Eighth Canto

AKSHAR-BRAHMA YOGA
Yoga of Imperishable Supreme

(1)

अर्जुन उवाच
किं तद्ब्रह्म किमध्यात्मं किं कर्म पुरुषोत्तम ।
अधिभूतं च किं प्रोक्तमधिदैवं किमुच्यते ॥८-१॥

arjuna uvacha
kim tad brahma kim adhyatmam kim karma purushottama
adhibhutam cha kim proktam adhidaivam kim uchyate (8.1)

arjunauvacha : Arjuna asked | kim : what | tat : that | brahma : Brahman (the Supreme Soul/Self) | kim : what | adhyatmam : the Self (the knowledge of the same self-consciousness permeating all beings) | kim : what | karma : action | purushottama : O! Supreme (the best among men)/Lord Krishna | adhibhutam : consciousness manifesting in physical form | cha : and | kim : what | proktam : is spoken of as | adhidaivam : consciousness in the form of celestial bodies or gods | kim : what | uchyate : is called

Arjuna asked : O! Lord Krishna, the Supreme One! What is that Brahman (the Supreme Soul Consciousness), what is Self (the same consciousness permeating all beings), what is action, what is spoken of as the same consciousness manifesting in physical form and what is called consciousness in the form of celestial bodies or gods?

(2)

अधियज्ञः कथं कोऽत्र देहेऽस्मिन्मधुसूदन ।
प्रयाणकाले च कथं ज्ञेयोऽसि नियतात्मभिः ॥८-२॥

adhiyagyah katham ko tra dehe asmin madhusudana
prayana kale cha katham geyoa si niyatatmabhih (8.2)

adhiyagyah : the lord of the sacrificial fire | katham : how | ka : who | atra : here | deheasmin : in this body | madhusudana : killer of demon Madhu, Lord Krishna | prayan-kale : at the time of departure (death) | cha : and

| katham : how | geya-asi : is to be known | niyata-atmabhih : those with self-control

Who is the Lord of the sacrificial fire (yagya) and how does it work in this body and O! Lord Krishna, how can those with self-control know it at the time of departure from this world.

(3)

श्रीभगवानुवाच
अक्षरं ब्रह्म परमं स्वभावोऽध्यात्ममुच्यते ।
भूतभावोद्भवकरो विसर्गः कर्मसंज्ञितः ॥ ८- ३॥

Shribhagavan uvacha
aksharam brahma paramamsvabhavoadhyatmamuchyate
bhutabhavodbhavakarovisargakarmasangita (8.3)

Shribhagavana-uvacha : Lord Krishna said | aksharam : indestructible/ imperishable/what never decays | brahma : Brahaman (the Supreme) | paramam : the highest | svabhava : it's own nature | adhyatmam : the self | uchyate : is called | bhuta-bhava-udbhava-kara : the process of creation/ existence and growth of living beings | visarga : offering in sacrifice | karma : action | sangita : is called

The Supreme (Brahman) is indestructible. By its own nature, it dwells in every individual and is called the Self. The offering in sacrifice leading to the process of creation, existence and growth of living beings is spoken of as action.

(4)

अधिभूतं क्षरो भावः पुरुषश्चाधिदैवतम् ।
अधियज्ञोऽहमेवात्र देहे देहभृतां वर ॥ ८- ४॥

adhibhutam ksharo bhavah purushash chadhidaivatam
adhiyagyo ahamevatra dehe deha bhritama vara (8.4)

adhibhutam : the physical manifestation of the Supreme (soul consciousness) in all beings | kshara : subject to change/decay | bhavah : nature | purusha : the indweller | cha : and | adhidaivatam : the universal Self | adhiyagya :

the Supreme Self Consciousness/the Lord of the sacrificial fire | aham : I | eva : certainly | atra : here/in this (body) | dehe : body | deha-bhritam : of the embodied | vara : best

Adhibhutam is my manifestation in physical form which is subject to change and is perishable. Adhidaivam is the universal Self (soul) in each individual. O! best of the embodied ones, Arjuna, I am certainly the Lord of the sacrificial fire, the Supreme Self Consciousness. (Yoga seeks to realise the union between the Self in our individual beings and the Supreme Self).

(5)

अन्तकाले च मामेव स्मरन्मुक्त्वा कलेवरम् ।
यः प्रयाति स मद्भावं याति नास्त्यत्र संशयः ॥८-५॥

antakale cha mameva smaranmuktva kalevaram
ya prayati sa madbhavam yati nastyatra sanshayah (8.5)

Anta-kale : at the time of death | cha : also | mam : me | eva : definitely | smaran : remembers | muktva : leaving | kalevaram : the body | ya : who | prayati : goes | sa : he | mat-bhavam : my nature | yati : achieves | na : not | asti : is | atra : here | sanshayah : doubt

One who at the time of death also definitely remembers me while leaving the body, undoubtedly achieves my nature (his Self becomes one with the Supreme Self).

(6)

यं यं वापि स्मरन्भावं त्यजत्यन्ते कलेवरम् ।
तं तमेवैति कौन्तेय सदा तद्भावभावितः ॥८-६॥

yam yam vapi smaran bhavam tyajatyante kalevaram
tam tamevaite kaunteya sada tad bhava bhavitah (8.6)

yam yam : whichever | va-api : that also | smaran : remembering | bhavam : nature/object | tyajati : gives up | ante : at the end/at the time of death | kalevaram : body | tam tam : those ones | eva : certainly | eti : gets/achieves | kaunteya : son of Kunti, Arjuna | sada : always | tat : that | bhava : object |

bhavitah : remembering/thinking/being

O! Arjuna, whatever object one is thinking of at the time of leaving the body, he/she certainly achieves that because of its being always with him.

(7)
तस्मात्सर्वेषु कालेषु मामनुस्मर युध्य च ।
मय्यर्पितमनोबुद्धिर्मामेवैष्यस्यसंशयम् ॥ ८- ७॥

tasmat sarveshu kaleshu mam anusmara yudhya cha
mayyarpita mano budhir mam evaishyasyasanshayam (8.7)

tasmat : from that | sarveshu kaleshu : at all times | mam : me | anusmara : remember | yudhya : fight | cha : also | mayi : to me | arpita : dedicated | mana : mind | buddhi : intelligence | mam : to me | eva : certainly | asanshaya : undoubtedly

It follows, O! Arjuna, that you should at all times remember me. The fight also should be dedicated to me. With your mind and intelligence fixed on me, you shall certainly achieve me.

(8)
अभ्यासयोगयुक्तेन चेतसा नान्यगामिना ।
परमं पुरुषं दिव्यं याति पार्थानुचिन्तयन् ॥ ८- ८॥

abhyasa yoga yuktena chetasa nanya gamina
paramam purusham divyam yati parthanuchintayan (8.8)

abhyasa-yoga : in the practice of yoga | yuktena : engaged | chetasa : actively with mind and intelligence | nanyagamina : without going wayward | paramam : the highest | purusham : personality of the Supreme | divyam : divine | yati : achieves | partha : son of Pratha, Arjuna | anuchintayan : always thinking of

O! Arjuna, one who is actively engaged in the practice of yoga with all his mind and intelligence and without going wayward is always thinking of me as the highest personality of the Supreme definitely succeeds in reaching me.

(9-10)

कविं पुराणमनुशासितार-मणोरणीयांसमनुस्मरेद्यः ।
सर्वस्य धातारमचिन्त्यरूप-मादित्यवर्ण तमसः परस्तात् ॥८- ९॥
प्रयाणकाले मनसाचलेन भक्त्या युक्तो योगबलेन चैव ।
भ्रुवोर्मध्ये प्राणमावेश्य सम्यक् स तं परं पुरुषमुपैति दिव्यम् ॥८- १०॥

kavim puranam anushasitaram anor aniyamsam anusmared yah
sarvasya dhataram achintya rupam
aditya varnam tamasah parastat (9.9)
prayana kale manasa chalena bhaktya yukto yoga balena chaiva
bhruvor madhye pranam avesyas amyak sa tam param purusham upaiti
divyam (9.10)

kavim : all knowing/omniscient | puranam : the ancient | anushasitaram : ruler of all | ano-aniyamsam : smaller than the smallest (nuclear) | anusmaret : remembers/meditates | yah : who | sarvasya : of all | dhataram : the holder/sustainer | achintya : inconceivable | rupam : form | aditya-varnam : effulgent like the sun | tamasah : darkness | parastat : above the physical world | prayan-kale : at the time of death | manasa : with the mind | achalena : fixed | bhaktya : with devotion | yukta : engaged in | yoga-balena : by the power of yoga | cha : also | eva : certainly | bhruvo : eyebrows | madhye : midway between | pranam : life breath | avesya : establishing | samyak : properly | sa : he | tam : that | param : the highest | purusham : personality of the Supreme | upaiti : achieves | divyam : divine/resplendent

One who meditates on the omniscient, the ancient, the ruler of all and smaller than the smallest (nuclear), who sustains all, is inconceivable, self-effulgent like the sun and beyond the darkness of the physical world, if at the time of death, he remembers with full devotion and an unwavering mind as also with the power of yoga , properly fixing the life breath midway between the eyebrows, for sure, achieves oneness with the highest resplendent personality (the Divine Purusha), the Supreme universal soul (Supreme Self Consciousness).

(11)

यदक्षरं वेदविदो वदन्ति विशन्ति यद्यतयो वीतरागाः ।
यदिच्छन्तो ब्रह्मचर्यं चरन्ति तत्ते पदं संग्रहेण प्रवक्ष्ये ॥८- ११॥

yad aksharam veda vido vadanti vishanti yad yatayo vita ragah
yadicchanto brahmacharyam charanti
tatte padam sangrahena pravakshye (8.11)

yat : that | aksharam : syllable (Om)/the imperishable | ved-vida : scholars in Vedas/those who know the Vedas | vadanti : speak | vishanti : enter | yat : which | yataya : the self-controlled ones | vita-ragah : those who have risen above sensory objects/who have gone beyond / feelings of pleasure and pain, love and hatred, gain and loss etc., who are completely unattached | yat : which | icchanta : desiring | brahmacharyam : celibacy/abstinence from sex | charanti : practice | tat : that | te : to you | padam : steps/state | sangrahena : in brief | pravakshy : shall explain

I shall explain to you in brief the steps for achieving that which the knowers of the Vedas call the imperishable, which the self-controlled and unattached ones desire to enter into and for desiring which they practice abstinence.

(12)

सर्वद्वाराणि संयम्य मनो हृदि निरुध्य च ।
मूर्ध्याधायात्मनः प्राणमास्थितो योगधारणाम् ॥८- १२॥

sarva dvarani sanyamya mano hrdi nirudhya cha
murdhnyadhyatamanah pranam asthito yoga dharanam (8.12)

sarva : all | dvarani : doors (sensory doorways in the body, meaning the sensory inlets) | sanyamya : controlling | mana : mind | hrdi : heart | nirudhya : confining/concentrating | cha : and | murdhni : on the head | adhaya : fixing | atmanah : of the Self (Soul) | pranam : the life breath | asthita : established in | yoga-dharanam : practice of meditation in yoga state

Controlling all the senses, mind concentrating on the heart, drawing the life-breath into the head, the Self gets established in yogic meditation.

(13)
ओमित्येकाक्षरं ब्रह्म व्याहरन्मामनुस्मरन् ।
यः प्रयाति त्यजन्देहं सयाति परमां गतिम् ॥८-१३॥

om ityekaksharam brahma vyaharan mamanusmaran
yah prayati tyajandeham sa yati paramam gatim (8.13)

om : syllable 'om' | iti : thus | ekaksharam : the one syllable (akshar) 'om' literally meaning the imperishable | brahma : the Absolute/the Supreme | vyaharan : uttering | mam : me | anusmaran : remembering | yah : who | prayati : goes/departs | tyajan : leaving | deham : this body | sa : he | yati : reaches/attains | paramam : the supreme | gatim : state

Thus, while leaving this body and departing, one who remembers me (the Supreme) and keeps uttering the divine syllable Om (akshar literally meaning the imperishable, Brahma) attains the highest state (of union with the supreme soul consciousness).

(14)
अनन्यचेताः सततं यो मां स्मरति नित्यशः ।
तस्याहं सुलभः पार्थ नित्ययुक्तस्य योगिनः ॥८-१४॥

ananya chetah satatam yo mam smarati nityashah
tasyaham sulabhah partha nitya yuktasya yoginah (8.14)

ananya-chetah : without the mind deviating attention elsewhere | satatam : always | ya : who | mam : me | smarati : remembers | nityashah : daily/always | tasya : his/to him | aham : I | sulabhah : easily achievable/easy to reach | partha : son of Pratha, Arjuna | nitya : daily/regularly | yuktasya : engaged | yoginah : for the yogi

O Arjuna! I am easily achievable by one who remembers me always, regularly and with single-minded devotion and who is everyday engaged in yoga (selfless action to reach Krishna consciousness or the Supreme Self Consciousness).

(15)

मामुपेत्य पुनर्जन्म दुःखालयमशाश्वतम् ।
नाप्नुवन्ति महात्मानः संसिद्धिं परमां गताः ॥८- १५॥

*mam upetya punar janma dukhalayam ashashvatam
napnuvanti mahatmanah sansiddhim paramam gatah (8.15)*

mam : me | upetya : having reached | punarjanma : rebirth | dukha-alayam : abode of sorrows | ashashvatam : ephemeral/temporary/transitory | na : never/no | apnuvanti : achieve | maha-atmanah : great souls | sansiddhim : perfection | paramam : supreme | gatah : having reached

Great souls who have reached me and achieved supreme perfection are no more subject to the process of rebirth in this ephemeral world which is an abode of sorrows.

(16)

आब्रह्मभुवनाल्लोकाः पुनरावर्तिनोऽर्जुन ।
मामुपेत्य तु कौन्तेय पुनर्जन्म न विद्यते ॥८- १६॥

*a brahma bhuvanat lokah punar avartino arjuna
mam upetya tu kaunteya punar janma na vidyate ((8.16)*

a-brahma-bhuvanatlokah : upto Brahmaloka planet (the abode of the Supreme) | puna : again | avertina : returning | arjuna : O Arjuna! | mam : to me | upetya : arriving | tu : but | kaunteya : son of Kunti, O Arjuna | punarjanma : rebirth | na : not | vidyate : known

O Arjuna! In all the planets including the Brahmaloka which is the highest, none can escape the cycle of rebirth but those who have realised me (the Supreme) do not have to be reborn.

(17)

सहस्रयुगपर्यन्तमहर्यद्ब्रह्मणो विदुः ।
रात्रिं युगसहस्रान्तां तेऽहोरात्रविदो जनाः ॥८- १७॥

*sahasra yuga paryantam ahar yad brahmano viduh
ratrim yugasahasrantam te horatra vido janah (8.17)*

sahasra : a thousand | yugasahasrantam : ages/millenniums | paryantam : till the end of | aha : day | yat : that | brahmana : of Brahma (the Supreme) | viduh : know | ratrim : night | yuga : ages/millenniums | sahasra-antam : ending at one thousand | te : they | aharatra : day and night | vida : know | janah : people

The duration of a thousand ages (yugas) constitutes a day for Brahma and another thousand ages (yugas) constitute Brahma's night. Those who know this truth really understand the meaning of day and night.

(18)
अव्यक्ताद्व्यक्तयः सर्वाः प्रभवन्त्यहरागमे ।
रात्र्यागमे प्रलीयन्ते तत्रैवाव्यक्तसंज्ञके ॥८- १८॥

avyaktad vyaktavyah sarvah prabhavantyahar agame
ratryagame praliyante tatraivavyakta sangyake (8.18)

avyaktat : from what is not manifest | vyaktayah : to what is manifest (the living beings) | sarvah : all | prabhavanti : become effective | aha-agame : as the day dawns | rati-agame : to the fall of the night | praliyante : become extinct | tatra : there | eva : certainly | avyakta : unmanifest | sangyake : is named

As the Brahma's day dawns, all the unmanifest turn into manifest living beings. As Brahma's night falls these again become what is definitely called unmanifest. (Like the cycle of life and death for individual lives, the entire creation also comes into being and disappears at the will of Brahma).

(19)
भूतग्रामः स एवायं भूत्वा भूत्वा प्रलीयते ।
रात्र्यागमेऽवशः पार्थ प्रभवत्यहरागमे ॥८- १९॥

bhutagramah sa evayam bhutva bhutva praliyate
ratryagamea vashah partha prabhavatyahar agame (8.19)

bhuta-gramah : all living beings | sa : these | eva : definitely | ayam : this | bhutvabhutva : being born again and again | praliyate : get destroyed |

ratri : night | agame : on the coming of | avashah : helplessly | partha : O son of Pratha, Arjuna! | prabhavati : is manifest | aha : day | agame : on the beginning of

O Arjuna! At the beginning of Brahma's day, all living beings are born again and again and get helplessly destroyed on the arrival of Brahma's night.

(20)
परस्तस्मात्तु भावोऽन्योऽव्यक्तोऽव्यक्तात्सनातनः ।
यः स सर्वेषु भूतेषु नश्यत्सु न विनश्यति ॥८- २०॥
*paras tasmat tu bhavo anyoavyakto avyaktat sanatanah
ya sa sarveshu bhuteshu nashyatsu na vinashyati (8.20)*

para : transcending/beyond | tasmat : from that | tu : but | bhava : nature | anya : another | avyakta : unmanifest | avyaktat : from the unmanifest | sanatanah : everlasting/eternal | yasa : that which | sarveshu : all | bhuteshu : living beings | nashyatsu : being destroyed | na : never | vinashyati : is destroyed

Going beyond that unmanifest, there is another unmanifest nature that is everlasting and transcends both manifest and unmanifest. While all other living beings perish, this unmanifest never perishes.

(21)
अव्यक्तोऽक्षरइत्युक्तस्तमाहुः परमां गतिम् ।
यं प्राप्य न निवर्तन्ते तद्धाम परमं मम ॥८- २१॥
*avyakto akshara ityuktastamahuh paramam gatim
yam prapya na nivartante tad dhama paramam mama (21)*

avyakta : unmanifest | akshara : indestructible/imperishabie | iti : thus | ukta : spoken | tam : that | ahuh : said to be | paramam : the highest | gatim : stage/destination | yam : which | prapya : on getting | na : never | nivartante : return | tat : that | dhama : residence/abode | paramam : supreme | mama : my

Described as the unmanifest and imperishable, the same is said to be the highest destination (that can be sought by anyone) and after reaching that stage one never returns from what happens to be my supreme abode.

(22)

पुरुषः स परः पार्थ भक्त्या लभ्यस्त्वनन्यया ।
यस्यान्तः स्थानि भूतानि येन सर्वमिदं ततम् ॥८- २२॥

purushah sa parah partha bhaktya labhyas tvananyaya
yasyantah sthani bhutani yena sarva midam tatam (8.22).

purushah : the Supreme Person/the Godhead | sa : he/that | parah : transcendental/above the phenomenal world/Supreme | partha : Arjuna | bhaktya : through devotion | labhya : is achievable | tu : also | ananyaya : whole-hearted | yasya : of whom | antah sthani : dwelling within | bhutani : living beings | yena : by whom | sarvam : all | idam : this | tatam : pervades

O Arjuna! That Supreme Person, the Godhead can be reached (is achievable) only by whole-hearted devotion to Him alone. All living beings dwell within Him and He pervades all this (existence).

(23)

यत्र काले त्वनावृत्तिमावृत्तिं चैव योगिनः ।
प्रयाता यान्ति तं कालं वक्ष्यामि भरतर्षभ ॥८- २३॥

yatra kale tvanavrattim avrattim chaiv yoginah
prayata yanti tam kalam vakshyami bharatarshabha (8.23)

yatra : where/which | kale : time | tu : and | anavarttim : one who does not return | avarttim : who returns | cha : and | eva : definitely | yoginah : practitioner of yoga | prayata : after departing | yanti : achieve | tam : that | kalam : time | vaksyami : shall describe | bharartarshabha : great (most powerful) of the Bharat dynasty

O great of the Bharatas, Arjuna! I shall now explain to you the time by departing at which yogis do not have to return and also the time by departing at which they have got to return.

(24)

अग्निर्ज्योतिरहः शुक्लः षण्मासा उत्तरायणम् ।
तत्र प्रयाता गच्छन्ति ब्रह्म ब्रह्मविदो जनाः ॥ ८-२४॥

agnir jyotir ahah shuklah shan masa uttarayanam
tatra prayata gachchhanti brahma brahma vido janah (8.24)

agni : fire | jyoti : radiance/light | ahah : day | shuklah : shuklapaksha - the fortnight of moonlight | Shan-masa : the six months | uttara-ayanam : the period of the year when the sun passes to the North | tatra : there | prayata : the departed | gacchanti : go | brahma : the Supreme/the Absolute | brahma-vida : those who know the Brahma | janah : persons

Those persons who are knowledgeable about Brahma succeed in reaching him by departing from this world at a time (by the path) during the day, when the fire-god (sun) is in full radiance, when we are in shukla-paksha i.e. in the fortnight of moonlight and during the part of the year when the sun passes to the North.

(25)

धूमो रात्रिस्तथा कृष्णः षण्मासा दक्षिणायनम् ।
तत्र चान्द्रमसं ज्योतिर्योगी प्राप्य निवर्तते ॥ ८-२५॥

dhumo ratris tatha krishnah shan masa dakshinayanam
tatr achandramasam jyotir yogi prapya nivartate (8.25)

dhuma : smoke | ratri : night | tatha : also/and | krishnah : krishna-paksha - the fortnight of the dark moon | shanmasa : the six months | dakshinayanam : when the sun moves towards the south | tatra : there | chandramasam : the moon planet | jyoti : light | yogi : the practitioner of yoga | prapya : having achieved | nivartate : returns

A yogi who departs from this world by the path of smoke, at night, in the fortnight of the dark moon and during the period when the sun moves towards the south, he also reaches the planet moon but comes back i.e. remains subject to the cycle of birth and death.

(26)

शुक्लकृष्णे गती ह्येते जगतः शाश्वते मते ।
एकया यात्यनावृत्तिमन्ययावर्तते पुनः ॥८-२६॥

shukla krishne gati hyete jagatah shashvate mate
ekaya yatyanavrattim anyayavartate punah (8.26)

shukla : light | krishne : in darkness | gati : state/way of departing | hi : definitely | ete : these | jagatah : the world | shashvate : of the eternal | mate : in the opinion | ekaya : by one | yati : goes | anavrattim : not coming back | a yaya : by the other | a vartate : comes back | punah : again

According to the eternal (ancient or Vedic) opinion, there are two ways of departing from this world - in one the person goes by the path of light and in the other he goes in darkness, in one he goes never to come back while in the other he returns i.e. remains involved in the cycle of birth and death.

(27)

नैते सृती पार्थ जानन्योगी मुह्यति कश्चन ।
तस्मात्सर्वेषु कालेषु योगयुक्तो भवार्जुन ॥८-२७॥

nate sriti partha janan yogi muhyati kashchana
tasmat sarveshu kaleshu yoga yukto bhavarjuna (8.27)

na : never | ete : these | sriti : paths | partha : Arjuna | janan : know | yogi : practitioner of yoga | muhyati : intrigued/astonished/deluded | kashchana : any | tasmat : from that/therefore | sarveshu kaleshu : at all times | yoga-yukta : engaged in the practice of yoga | bhava : be/remain | arjuna : Arjuna

O son of Pratha, Arjuna! Any yogi knowing these two paths is never deluded. Therefore, Arjuna! Always remain engaged in the practice of yoga.

(28)
वेदेषु यज्ञेषु तपःसु चैव: दानेषु यत्पुण्यफलं प्रदिष्टम् ।
अत्येति तत्सर्वमिदं विदित्वा: योगी परं स्थानमुपैति चाद्यम् ॥८-२८॥

vedeshu yagyeshu tapahsu chaivah
daneshu yat punya phalam pradishtam
atyeti tat sarvam idam viditvah
yogi param sthanam upaiti chadyam (8.28)

vedeshu : from the Vedas | yagyeshu : by offering sacrifices to fire-god | tapahsu : by penance | chaivahS : and also | daneshu : by giving charities | yat : that/which | punya-phalam : fruits of good deeds | pradishtam : indicated | atyeti : rises above | tat sarvam : all those | idam : this | viditvah : knowing | yogi : practitioner of yoga | param : supreme | sthanam : place | upaiti : reaches | cha : also/and | adyam : primeval

Knowing the essence of the fruits of all the good deeds accruing from the study of Vedas, sacrifices, penances and acts of charity, the yogi rises above all those and reaches the primeval supreme abode.

Thus ends the Eighth Canto titled 'Yoga of Imperishable Supreme'.

Ninth Canto
RAJVIDYA-RAJGUHYA YOGA
Yoga of Royal Knowledge and Royal Secret

(1)

श्रीभगवानुवाच
इदं तु ते गुह्यतमं प्रवक्ष्याम्यनसूयवे ।
ज्ञानं विज्ञानसहितं यज्ज्ञात्वा मोक्ष्यसेऽशुभात् ॥९-१॥

Shribhagavan uvacha
idam tu te guhyatamam pravakshyamy anasuyave
gyanam vigyansahitam yaj gyatva mokshyaseashubhat (9.1)

Shribhagavan uvacha : Lord Krishna said | idam : this | tu : really | te : to you | guhyatamam-tamam : the most secret | pravakshyami : I am saying | anusuyave : to one free from envy | gyanam : knowledge | vigyan : realisation | sahitam : with | yat : which | gyatva : knowing | mokshyase : shall be relieved | ashubhat : from this unfortunate existence

Lord Krishna said: Since you are free from envy, I shall really convey to you this most secret knowledge with ways of its realisation. Knowing this, you shall be relieved of the unfortunate existence on earth (shall attain Moksha or ultimate salvation).

(2)

राजविद्या राजगुह्यं पवित्रमिदमुत्तमम् ।
प्रत्यक्षावगमं धर्म्यं सुसुखं कर्तुमव्ययम् ॥९-२॥

raja vidya raja guhyam pavitramid muttamam
pratyakshavagamam dharmyam susukham kartumavyayam (9.2)

raj-vidya : King of knowledge/the highest of sciences | raj-guhyam : kingly (the deepest) secrets | pavitram : very pure | idam : this | uttamam : best | pratyakshavagamam : realisable (understandable) by direct experience | dharmyam : righteous | su-sukham : happily | kartum : to achieve | avyayam : imperishable

This (knowledge Lord Krishna is speaking about) is the best, the highest of the sciences, reveals the deepest secrets, is very pure, understandable by direct experience, righteous, happily achievable and imperishable.

(3)

अश्रद्दधानाः पुरुषा धर्मस्यास्य परन्तप ।
अप्राप्य मां निवर्तन्ते मृत्युसंसारवर्त्मनि ॥९- ३॥

ashraddadhanah purusha dharmasyasya parantapa
aprapya mam nivartante mrityu sansara vartmani (9.3)

ashraddadhanah : those having no faith | purusha : persons | dharmasya : of rightful conduct | asya : this | parantapa : destroyer of enemies (Arjuna) | aprapya : without achieving | mam : me | nivartante : return | mrityu : death | sansara : the material world | vartmani : to the path of

O destroyer of enemies, Arjuna! Those persons who have no faith in this rightful conduct (principles of dharma) fail to reach me and return to the path of (birth and) death in the material world.

(4)

मया ततमिदं सर्वं जगदव्यक्तमूर्तिना ।
मत्स्थानि सर्वभूतानि न चाहं तेष्ववस्थितः ॥९- ४॥

maya tatamidam sarvam jagad avyakta murtina
matsthani sarvabhutani na chaham teshvavasthitah (9.4)

maya : by me | tatam : full of/pervaded by | idam : this | sarvam : all | jagat : the material world | avyakta : unmanifest | murtina : form | mat-sthani : situated in me | sarva-bhutani : all living beings | na : not | cha : also/and | aham : I | tesu : in them | avasthitah : situated

All this material world is pervaded by me in my unmanifest form. All living beings are situated in me but I am not in them.

(5)

न च मत्स्थानि भूतानि पश्य मे योगमैश्वरम् ।
भूतभृन्न च भूतस्थो ममात्मा भूतभावनः ॥९- ५॥

na cha matsthani bhutani pashya me yogamaishvaram
bhutabhrinna cha bhutastho mamatma bhutabhavanah (9.5)

na : not | cha : also | mat-sthani : situated in me | bhutani : living beings | pashya : behold | me : my | yogam : of yoga | aishvaram : divine | bhuta-bhrat : sustainer of living beings | na : never | cha : also/and | bhuta-stha : stationed in the living beings | mama : my | atma : self | bhuta-bhavanah : source of creation/bringing the beings into existence

The living beings are also (really) not situated in me. Behold my divine power of yoga, although I sustain all living beings, I am never stationed in them. My Self is the source of all beings.

(6)

यथाकाशस्थितो नित्यं वायुः सर्वत्रगो महान् ।
तथा सर्वाणि भूतानि मत्स्थानीत्युपधारय ॥९- ६॥

yathakasha sthito nityam vayuh sarvatrago mahan
tatha sarvani bhutani matsthanity upadharaya (9.6)

yatha : as | akasha-sthita : situated in the sky/in the ether | nityam : always | vayuh : wind/air | sarvatra-ga : blowing everywhere | mahan : great | tatha : accordingly | sarvani-bhutani : all living beings | mat-sthani : situated in me | iti : thus | upadharaya : understand

(The apparent contradiction in the statements in verse (9.4) and (9.5) above, Lord Krishna saying that all living beings are situated in Him and that all living beings really are not situated in Him, is sought to be explained by giving the analogy of wind. The wind which fills space is not in it.)

As the great wind which is blowing everywhere is always situated in ether but is not in it, understand thus that all living beings are situated in me and are yet not in me.

(7)
सर्वभूतानि कौन्तेय प्रकृतिं यान्ति मामिकाम् ।
कल्पक्षये पुनस्तानि कल्पादौ विसृजाम्यहम् ॥९-७॥

sarva-bhutani kaunteya prakritim yanti mamikam
kalpakshye punastani kalpadau visrijamyaham (9.7)

sarva : all | bhutani : living beings | kaunteya : son of Kunti, Arjuna | prakritim : nature | yanti : enter | mamikam : my | kalpakshye : at the end of the millennium (kalpa) | puna : again | tani : those | kalpadau : at the beginning of the kalpa (the millennium) | visrijami : create | aham : I

O son of Kunti, Arjuna! At the end of each millennium, all living beings merge in my nature. At the beginning of the (next) millennium, I again create them.

(8)
प्रकृतिं स्वामवष्टभ्य विसृजामि पुनः पुनः ।
भूतग्राममिमं कृत्स्नमवशं प्रकृतेर्वशात् ॥९-८॥

prakritim svam avashtabhya visrijami punah punah
bhuta gramam imam kritsnam avasham prakriter vashat (9.8)

prakritim : nature | svam : my own | avastabhya : accepting/according to | visrajami : create | punah punah : again and again | bhuta-gramam : all these creatures | imam : these | kratsnam : in totality/all | avasham : helpless/powerless/dependent | prakriti : nature | vasat : by the force of

In accordance with my own nature, I again and again create all these creatures rendered dependent by the force of their nature.

(9)
न च मां तानि कर्माणि निबध्नन्ति धनंजय ।
उदासीनवदासीनमसक्तं तेषु कर्मसु ॥९-९॥

na cha mam tani karmani nibadhnanti dhananjaya
udasina vad asinam asaktam teshu karmasu (9.9)

na : never | cha : also/and | mam : me | tani : these | karmani : acts | nibadhnanti : do not bind | dhananjaya : conqueror of wealth, Arjuna | udasina-vad : as neutral | asinam : sitting | asaktam : without attachment | teshu : these | karmasu : acts

Also, O conquerer of wealth, Arjuna! All these acts never bind me. Sitting as a neutral person, I am without attachment to these acts.

(10)
मयाध्यक्षेण प्रकृतिः सूयते सचराचरम् ।
हेतुनानेन कौन्तेय जगद्विपरिवर्तते ॥९-१०॥

mayadhyakshena prakritih suyate sacharacharam
hetunanena kaunteya jagad viparivartate (9.10)

maya : by me | adhyakshena : presided | prakritih : nature | suyate : creates | sa-characharam : all the animate and inanimate objects | hetuna : for the purpose of | anena : this | kaunteya : son of Kunti, Arjuna | jagat : the (material) world | viparivartate : revolves the cycle of creation and annihilation

O son of Kunti, Arjuna! The nature, with me presiding, creates all the animate and inanimate beings. For this purpose, the world of matter keeps revolving the cycle of creation and annihilation.

(11)
अवजानन्ति मां मूढा मानुषीं तनुमाश्रितम् ।
परं भावमजानन्तो मम भूतमहेश्वरम् ॥९-११॥

avajananti mam mudha manushim tanum ashritam
param bhavam ajananto mama bhuta maheshvaram (9.11)

avajananti : do not know | mam : me | mudha : fools | manushim : in human form | tanum : body | ashritam : dwelling | param : supreme | bhavam : nature | ajananta : not knowing | mama : my | bhuta : every living being | maha-ishvaram : the Great Lord

Those fools who do not know me disregard my supreme nature

dwelling in human form not realising that I am the Great Lord of all living beings.

(12)
मोघाशा मोघकर्माणो मोघज्ञाना विचेतसः ।
राक्षसीमासुरीं चैव प्रकृतिं मोहिनीं श्रिताः ॥९- १२॥
*moghasha moghakarmano moghagyana vichetasah
rakshasimasurim chaiv prakritim mohinim shritah (9.12)*

mogha-asha : vain hopes | mogha-karmana : vain actions | mogha-gyana : vain knowledge | vichetasah : unhealthy mind | rakshasim : demons | asurim : devils | cha : and | eva : certainly | prakritim : nature | mohinim : delusive | shritah : sheltered in

Those of unhealthy minds with vain hopes, vain actions and vain knowledge certainly take shelter in the delusive nature of demons and devils.

(13)
महात्मानस्तु मां पार्थ दैवीं प्रकृतिमाश्रिताः ।
भजन्त्यनन्यमनसो ज्ञात्वा भूतादिमव्ययम् ॥९- १३॥
*mahatmanastu mam parth daivim prakritimashritah
bhajantyananyamanaso gyatva bhutadimavyayam (9.13)*

maha-atmana : the great souls | tu : but | mam : my | partha : son of Pratha, Arjuna | daivim : divine | prakritim : nature | ashritah : taking shelter in/dependent | bhajanti : worship | anananyamanasa : with a mind devoted only to me (the Supreme) | gyatva : knowing | bhuta-adim : origin of living beings | avyayam : immutable

O son of Partha, Arjuna! Those with great souls and divine nature take shelter in me and worship me with a mind devoted only to me knowing that I am the origin of all living beings and immutable.

(14)
सततं कीर्तयन्तो मां यतन्तश्च दृढव्रताः ।
नमस्यन्तश्च मां भक्त्या नित्ययुक्ता उपासते ॥९-१४॥

*satatam kirtayanto mam yatantashcha dradhavratah
namasyantashcha mam bhaktya nityayukta upasate (9.14).*

satatam : always | kirtayanta : glorifying/chanting praises | mam : me | yatantash : trying | cha : also | dradha-vratah : with strong determination | namasyantash : offering respects | cha : and | mam : me | bhaktya : with devotion | nitya-yukta : ever steadfast | upasate : worship

Always chanting my praises, also striving with strong determination to offer respects and ever being steadfast, they worship me with devotion.

(15)
ज्ञानयज्ञेन चाप्यन्ये यजन्तो मामुपासते ।
एकत्वेन पृथक्त्वेन बहुधा विश्वतोमुखम् ॥९-१५॥

*gyanayagyena chapyanye yajanto mam upasate
ekatvena prithaktvena bahudha vishvatomukham (9.15)*

gyana-yagyena : sacrifice by imparting knowledge | cha : and | api : also | anye : others | yajanta : sacrificing | mam : me | upasate : worship | ekatvena : in oneness | prithaktvena : in duality | bahudha : in diversity | vishvata-mukham : universal form

Others who offer sacrifice by imparting knowledge also certainly worship me (in my various forms) as the only One, in duality, in diversity and as universal.

(16)
अहं क्रतुरहं यज्ञः स्वधाहमहमौषधम् ।
मन्त्रोऽहमहमेवाज्यमहमग्निरहं हुतम् ॥९-१६॥

*aham kraturaham yagyah svadhaham aham aushadham
mantro aham aham evajyam aham agniraham hutam (9.16)*

aham : I | kratu : a Vedic ritual | aham : I | yagyah : worship through sacrificial fire | svadha : oblation | aham : I | aham : I | aushadham : medicine | mantra : sacred chant | aham : I | aham : I | eva : certainly | ajyam : ghee (melted butter) | aham : I | agni : fire | aham : I | hutam : offering

I am the Vedic ritual (kratu), I am the worship through sacrificial fire (yagya), I am the oblation to the ancestors, I am the medicine, I am the sacred chant (mantra), I am the ghee, I am the fire and I am also the offering.

(17)
पिताहमस्य जगतो माता धाता पितामहः ।
वेद्यं पवित्रमोंकार ऋक्साम यजुरेव च ॥९-१७॥

pitahamasya jagato mata dhata pitamahah
vedyam pavitram onkara rik sama yajur eva cha (9.17)

pita : father | aham : I | asya : of this | jagata : world/universe | mata : mother | dhata : sustainer | pitamahah : grandfather | vedyam : to be known | pavitram : purifier | onkara : om | rik : the Rigveda | sama : the Samaveda | yaju : the Yajurveda | eva : certainly | cha : and

I am the father of this universe, the mother, the sustainer and the grandfather. I am all that is there to be known, the purifier and the syllable Om (transcendental sound vibration). I am also the three Vedas - the Rigveda, the Samaveda and the Yajurveda.

(18)
गतिर्भर्ता प्रभुः साक्षी निवासः शरणं सुहृत् ।
प्रभवः प्रलयः स्थानं निधानं बीजमव्ययम् ॥९-१८॥

gatirbharta prabhuh sakshi nivasah sharnam suhrit
prabhavah pralayah sthanam nidhanam bijam avyayam (9.18)

gati : goal | bharta : sustainer | prabhuh : lord | sakshi : witness | nivasah : dwelling | sharanam : shelter/refuge | suhrit : dear friend | prabhavah : the source/the origin | pralayah : destroyer (of the universe) | sthanam : the (ultimate) resting place | nidhanam : storehouse | bijam : seed | avyayam : imperishable

I am the goal to be reached, the sustainer, the Lord, the witness, the dwelling place, the refuge, the dear friend, the source of all creation, the destroyer of the universe, the ultimate resting place, the storehouse, also I am the imperishable seed (of all that exists).

(19)
तपाम्यहमहं वर्षं निगृह्ञाम्युत्सृजामि च ।
अमृतं चैव मृत्युश्च सदसच्चाहमर्जुन ॥९- १९॥

tapamyaham aham varsham nigrihnamyutsrijami cha
amritam chaiva mrityushcha sad asachchahamarjuna (9.19)

tapami : give heat | aham : I | aham : I | varsam : rain | nigrihnami : withhold | utsrijami : send forth | cha : and | amritam : immortal/imperishable | cha : and | eva : certainly | mriyush : death | cha : and | sat : spirit | asat : material world/matter | cha : and | aham : I | arjuna : Arjuna

O Arjuna! I give heat, I withhold and give rain, I am the imperishable and certainly I am also death, spirit and matter.

(20)
त्रैविद्या मां सोमपाः पूतपापा यज्ञैरिष्ट्वा स्वर्गतिं प्रार्थयन्ते ।
ते पुण्यमासाद्य सुरेन्द्रलोकमश्नन्ति दिव्यान्दिवि देवभोगान् ॥९- २०॥

traividya mam somapah putapa
yagyairishtva svargatim prarthayante
te punyamasadya surendralokah
mashnanti divyandivi devabhogan (9.20)

trai-vidya : the learned in three Vedas | mam : me | somapah : soma juice (somaras) | puta : purified/redeemed | papa : sins | yagyai : with sacrificial offerings | ishtva : worshipping | sva-gatim : passage to heaven | prarthayante : pray for | te : they | punyam : pious | asadya : achieving | sura-indra : of Indra | lokam : world/planet | ashnanti : enjoy | divyam : divine | divi : in heaven | deva-bhogan : the godly pleasures

The learned in the Vedas and those who have been redeemed of all sins by drinking somaras (the soma juice) and who seek heavenly abodes worship me by making sacrificial offerings. They are reborn on the pious and heavenly planet of Indra and enjoy godly pleasures there.

(21)
ते तं भुक्त्वा स्वर्गलोकं विशालं
क्षीणे पुण्ये मर्त्यलोकं विशन्ति ।
एवं त्रयीधर्ममनुप्रपन्ना
गतागतं कामकामा लभन्ते ॥९-२१॥

te tam bhuktva svargalokam vishalam
kshine punye martyalokam vishanti
evam trayi dharmam anuprapanna
gatagatam kamakama labhante (9.21)

te : they | tam : that | bhuktva : after enjoying | svarga-lokam : heaven | vishalam : vast | kshine : exhausted | punye : pious deeds | martya-lokam : this mortal world | vishanti : return | evam : thus | trayi : three Vedas | dharmam : righteous obligations (as ordained by the Vedas) | anuprapanna : abiding by | gata-agatam : going and coming (dying and being born again) | kama-kama : desiring sensory gratification | labhante : achieve

After enjoying the vast pleasures of the heavens, on the exhaustion of the credits earned by them for their pious deeds, they return to this mortal world. Thus, those desiring sensory gratification by discharging the righteous obligations ordained by the three Vedas achieve only the continuation of the cycle of life and death.

(22)
अनन्याश्चिन्तयन्तो मां ये जनाः पर्युपासते ।
तेषां नित्याभियुक्तानां योगक्षेमं वहाम्यहम् ॥९-२२॥

ananyashchintayanto mam ye janah paryupasate
tesham nityabhiyuktanam yoga-kshemam vahamy aham (9.22)

ananya : as the only one object | chintayanta : of thought | mam : me | ye : those | janah : persons | paryupasate : worship | tesham : of them | nitya : always | abhiyuktanam : those engaged in yoga | yoga-kshema : selfless action/welfare | vahamy : carry | aham : I

Of persons who always worship me as the only object of thought, I carry with me those engaged in selfless yogic action.

(23)

येऽप्यन्यदेवताभक्ता यजन्ते श्रद्धयान्विताः ।
तेऽपि मामेव कौन्तेय यजन्त्यविधिपूर्वकम् ॥९-२३॥

yeapyanyadevatabhakta yajante shraddhayanvitah
tepi mameva kaunteya yajantyavidhipurvakam (9.23)

ye : those | api : also | anya : other | devata : gods | bhaktas : devotees | yajante : worship | shraddhaya-anvitah : with full faith | te : they | api : also | mam : me | eva : only | kaunteya : son of Kunti, Arjuna | yajanti : worship | avidhi-purva kam : not in accordance with proper process

O Arjuna! Those devotees who worship other gods with full faith also worship me only but they do not follow the correct procedure.

(24)

अहं हि सर्वयज्ञानां भोक्ता च प्रभुरेव च ।
न तु मामभिजानन्ति तत्त्वेनातश्च्यवन्ति ते ॥९-२४॥

aham hi sarva yagyanam bhokta cha prabhureva cha
na tu mam abhijananti tattvenatash chyavanti te (9.24)

aham : I | hi : surely | sarva : all | yagyaam : sacrifices | bhokta : enjoyer | cha : and | prabhu : the God/the Supreme Lord | eva : also | cha : and | na : not | tu : but | mam : me | abhijananti : know/are aware of/realise | tattvena : the essential truth | ata : therefore | chyavanti : fall down | te : they

Surely, I alone am the enjoyer and the Lord of all the sacrifices (yagyam). Therefore, those who do not realise this essential truth fail (to reach me and remain subject to birth and death).

(25)

यान्ति देवव्रता देवान्पितृन्यान्ति पितृव्रताः ।
भूतानि यान्ति भूतेज्या यान्ति मद्याजिनोऽपि माम् ॥९-२५॥

yanti devavrata devanpitrin yanti pitri vratah
bhutani yanti bhutejya yanti madyajinoapi mam (9.25)

yanti : go | deva-vrata : those devoted to different gods | devan : gods | pitran : the ancestors | yanti : go | pitrivratah : those devoted to ancestors | bhutani : ghosts and spirits | yanti : go | bhutejya : believers in ghosts and spirits | yanti : go | mat : my | yajina : devotees | api : but | mam : me

The devotees of different gods go to them, those devoted to worshipping the ancestors go to them, the believers in ghosts and spirits go to them but my devotees come to me.

(26)

पत्रं पुष्पं फलं तोयं यो मे भक्त्या प्रयच्छति ।
तदहं भक्त्युपहृतमश्नामि प्रयतात्मनः ॥९-२६॥

patram pushpam phalam toyam yo me bhaktya prayachchhati
tadaham bhaktyupahritam ashnami prayatnatmanah (9.26)

patram : leaf | pushpam : flower | phalam : fruits | toyam : water | ya : who | me : me | bhaktya : with devotion | prayacchati : offers | tat : that | aham : I | bhakti-upahritam : offered in worship | ashnami : accept | prayata-atmanah : from ones mind

A simple leaf, a flower, a fruit or water or whatever is offered to me with love and devotion, I accept.

(27)

यत्करोषि यदश्नासि यज्जुहोषि ददासि यत् ।
यत्तपस्यसि कौन्तेय तत्कुरुष्व मदर्पणम् ॥९-२७॥

yatkaroshi yadashnasi yajjuhoshi dadasi yat
yattapasyasi kaunteya tatkurushva mad-arpanam (27).

yat : whatever | karoshi : you do | yat : whatever | ashnasi : you eat | yat : whatever | juhoshi : is offered by you | dadasi : gives away | yat : whatever | tapasyasi : penance you practice | kaunteya : son of Kunti, Arjuna | tat : that | kurushva : do | mat : unto me | arpanam : as an offering

Whatever you do, whatever you eat, whatever you offer in sacrifice, whatever you give away, whatever penance you practise, O son of Kunti, Arjuna all that you present to me, I accept as an offering to me.

(28)
शुभाशुभफलैरेवं मोक्ष्यसे कर्मबन्धनैः ।
संन्यासयोगयुक्तात्मा विमुक्तो मामुपैष्यसि ॥९- २८॥

shubhashubha phalairevam mokshyase karmabandhanaih
sanyasa yoga yuktatma vimukto mamupaishyasi (9.28)

shubha : auspicious | ashubhat : inauspicious | phalai : fruits | evam : thus | mokshyase : get salvation/get freed | karma : action | bandhanaih : bondage | sanyasa : renunciation | yoga : selfless action | yukta-atma : mind engaged | vimukta : freed | mam : me | upaishyasi : reach

Thus, you will be emancipated from the bondage of action and its auspicious and inauspicious fruits. With your mind fully engaged in yoga and renunciation, you will be freed and shall reach me.

(29)
समोऽहं सर्वभूतेषु न मे द्वेष्योऽस्ति न प्रियः ।
ये भजन्ति तु मां भक्त्या मयि ते तेषु चाप्यहम् ॥९- २९॥

samoaham sarvabhuteshu na me dveshyoasti na priyah
ye bhajanti tu mam bhaktya mayi te teshu chapyaham (9.29)

sama : equal | aham : I | sarva- bhuteshu : to all living beings | na : not/neither | me : me | dveshya : full of hatred | asti : is | na : nor | priyah : dear | ye : those who | bhajanti : worship | tu : but | mam : me | bhaktya : by devotion | mayi : in me | te : they | teshu : in them | cha : also | api : certainly | aham : I

All living beings are equal to me. Neither I hate anyone nor is anyone dear to me. But those who are devoted to me and worship me are in me and I am also certainly in them.

(30)
अपि चेत्सुदुराचारो भजते मामनन्यभाक् ।
साधुरेव स मन्तव्यः सम्यग्व्यवसितो हि सः ॥९- ३०॥

api chetsuduracharo bhajate mamananyabhak
sadhureva sa mantavyah samyagvyavasito hi sah (9.30)

api : even | chet : if | su-durachara : one of very bad character/a very wicked person | bhajate : worships | mam : me | ananya-bhak : with single-minded devotion | sadhu : good | eva : verily | sa : he | mantavyah : should be regarded | samyak : rightly | vyavasita : resolved | hi : indeed | sah : he

Even if a very wicked person worships me with single-minded devotion, he should be verily regarded as good, for he has indeed made a right mental resolution.

(31)
क्षिप्रं भवति धर्मात्मा शश्वच्छान्तिं निगच्छति ।
कौन्तेय प्रति जानीहि न मे भक्तः प्रणश्यति ॥९- ३१॥

kshipram bhavati dharamatma shashvach chhantim nigachchhati
kaunteya prati janihi na me bhaktah pranashyati (9.31)

kshipram : very soon | bhavati : becomes | dharma-atma : a righteous person | shashvat-shantim : eternal peace | nigachchhati : achieves | kaunteya : son of Kunti, Arjuna | pratijanihi : proclaim | na : never | me : my | bhaktah : devotee | pranashyati : perishes

He very soon becomes a righteous person and achieves eternal peace. O Arjuna! Proclaim that my devotee never perishes.

(32)

मां हि पार्थ व्यपाश्रित्य येऽपि स्युः पापयोनयः ।
स्त्रियो वैश्यास्तथा शूद्रास्तेऽपि यान्ति परां गतिम् ॥९-३२॥

mam hi partha vyapashritya yeapi syuh papayonayah
striyo vaishyastatha shudrasteapi yanti param gatim (9.32)

mam : me | hi : surely | partha : son of Pratha, Arjuna | vyapashritya : taking refuge | ye : who | api : also | syuh : might be | papa-yonayah : born in sin | striya : women | vaishyas : the merchant caste | tatha : and | shudra : the lowest service caste people | te api : they also | yanti : reach | param : the supreme | gatim : goal

O Arjuna! Those who take refuge in me even if they happen to be women, merchants or the lowest service caste people born in the womb of sin also reach the supreme goal.

(33)

किं पुनर्ब्राह्मणाः पुण्या भक्ता राजर्षयस्तथा ।
अनित्यमसुखं लोकमिमं प्राप्य भजस्व माम् ॥९-३३॥

kim punarbrahmanah punya bhakta rajarshayastatha
anityamasukham lokamimam prapya bhajasva mam (9.33)

kim : what | puna : again | brahamanah : the caste supposed to consist of holy and learned persons | punya : pious deeds | bhakta : devotees | rajarshaya : righteous kings | tatha : and | anityam : transient | asukham : sorrowful | lokam : world | imam : this | prapya : arrived | bhajasva : worship | mam : me

(When even the wicked can be saved by taking refuge in me), what is there for the holy Brahmanas with their pious deeds and the devoted righteous kings. Having arrived in this transient world full of sorrows, (it is best to worship the Lord).

(34)

मन्मना भव मद्भक्तो मद्याजी मां नमस्कुरु ।
मामेवैष्यसि युक्त्वैवमात्मानं मत्परायणः ॥९- ३४॥

manmana bhava madbhakto madyaji mam namaskuru
mamevaishyasi yuktvaivam atmanam matparayanah (9.34)

mat-mana : mind engaged in thinking of me | bhava : become | mat : my | bhakta : devotee | mat : my | yaji : worshiper | mam : to me | namaskuru : offer homage/respect/obeisance | mam : to me | eva : surely | eshyasi : will come | yuktva : being engaged in | evam : thus | atmanam : soul | mat-parayanah : devoted to me

(It is, therefore, most advisable to) keep your mind engaged in thinking of me, become my devotee and worshiper and offer obeisance to me. Thus, engaged in me, your soul will surely reach me (and your individual soul will become one with the supreme soul consciousness).

Thus ends the Ninth Canto titled 'Yoga of Royal Knowledge and Royal Secret'.

Tenth Canto

VIBHUTI YOGA
Yoga of Divine Glory

(1)

श्रीभगवानुवाच
भूय एव महाबाहो शृणु मे परमं वचः ।
यत्तेऽहं प्रियमाणाय वक्ष्यामि हितकाम्यया ॥१०-१॥

*Shribhagavan uvacha
bhuya eva mahabaho shrinu me paramam vachah
tatte aham priyamanaya vakshyami hitakamyaya (10.1).*

Shribhagavan uvacha : Lord Krishna said | bhuya : again | eva : verily | mahabaho : long-armed, Arjuna | shrinu : listen | me : my | paramam : supreme/important | vachah : words/statement | yat : which | te : to you | aham : I | priyamanaya : dear to me | vakshyami : say | hita-kamyaya : wish your well being

Lord Krishna said: O Arjuna! verily listen to my important words again. I say these to you because you are dear to me and I wish your well being.

(2)

न मे विदुः सुरगणाः प्रभवं न महर्षयः ।
अहमादिर्हि देवानां महर्षीणां च सर्वशः ॥१०-२॥

*na me viduh suraganah prabhavam na maharashayah
ahamadirhi devanam maharashinam cha sarvashah (10.2)*

na : never/neither | me : my | viduh : know | suraganah : the gods | prabhavam : origin | na : never/nor | maharshayah : great saints | aham : I | adi : beginning/origin | hi : certainly | devanam : of the gods | maharshaya : of the great saints | cha : and | sarvashah : in all respects

Neither the many gods nor the great saints know my origin for certain. I am certainly the origin of the many gods and the great sages in all respects.

(3)

यो मामजमनादिं च वेत्ति लोकमहेश्वरम् ।
असंमूढः स मर्त्येषु सर्वपापैः प्रमुच्यते ॥१०-३॥

yo mamajamanadim cha vetti lokamaheshvaram
asammuddhah sa martyeshu sarva-papaih pramuchyate (10.3)

ya : who | mam : me | ajam : unborn | anadim : without beginning | cha : also/and | vetti : knows | loka : worlds/planets | maha-ishvaram - the supreme Lord | asammudhah : undeluded | sa : he | martyeshu : among mortals | sarva-papaih : from all sins | pramuchyate : is freed

He who knows me as one who is unborn and had no beginning and is the supreme lord of all the worlds, he among mortals is undeluded and freed from all sins.

(4-5)

बुद्धिर्ज्ञानमसंमोहः क्षमा सत्यं दमः शमः ।
सुखं दुःखं भवोऽभावो भयं चाभयमेव च ॥१०-४॥
अहिंसा समता तुष्टिस्तपो दानं यशोऽयशः ।
भवन्ति भावा भूतानां मत्त एव पृथग्विधाः ॥१०-५॥

budhirgyanamasammohah kshama satyam damah shamah
sukham dukham bhavoabhavo bhayam chabhayameva cha (10.4)
ahinsa samata tushtistapo danam yashoayashah
bhavanti bhava bhutanam matta eva prithagvidhah (10.5)

buddhi : intelligence | gyanam : knowledge | asammohah : freedom from doubt/non-delusion | kshama : forgiveness | satyam : truthfulness | damah : sensory control | shamah : calmness of mind | sukham : happiness | dukham : sorrow/misery | bhava : birth/existence | abhava : death/non-existence | bhayam : fear | cha : also | abhayam : fearlessness | eva : also | cha : and | ahinsa :non-violence | samata : equality | tushti : contentment | tapa : penance | danam : benevolence | yasha : fame | ayashah : ill-fame | bhavanti : are born | bhava : qualities | bhutanam : of living beings | matta : from me

| eva : certainly | prithak-vidhah : of different kinds

Intellect, knowledge, non-delusion, forgiveness, truthfulness, sensory control, calmness of mind, happiness, sorrow, birth, death, fear and also fearlessness, non-violence, equality, contentment, penance, benevolence, fame and ill-fame, all these different kinds of qualities are certainly born of me alone.

(6)
महर्षयः सप्त पूर्वे चत्वारो मनवस्तथा ।
मद्भावा मानसा जाता येषां लोक इमाः प्रजाः ॥१०- ६॥

maharshayah sapta purve chatvaro manavastatha
madbhava manasa jata yesham loka imah prajah (10.6)

maha-rshayah : great sages | sapta : seven | purve : before | chatvara : four | manava : Manus (beginners of the human race) | tatha : also | mat-bhava : created by me | manasa : from the mind | jata : born | yesham : of them | loke : in the worlds around | imah : all this | prajah : people

The seven great sages and before them the four Manus (the beginners of the human race) were also created by me from my mind and all the people inhabiting the worlds around come from them.

(7)
एतां विभूतिं योगं च मम यो वेत्ति तत्त्वतः ।
सोऽविकम्पेन योगेन युज्यते नात्र संशयः ॥१०- ७॥

etam vibhutim yogam cha mama yo vetti tattvatah
soavikampena yogena yujyate natra sanshayah (10.7)

tam : these | vibhutim : manifestations | yogam : power of yoga | cha : and | mama : mine | ya : who | vetti : knows | tattvatah : in essence | sa : he | avikampena : unshakable | yujyate : is established | na : never | atra : here | sanshayah : doubt

Those who understand these manifestations of mine and my essential yogic powers, get unshakeably established in yoga. There is no doubt about it.

(8)

अहं सर्वस्य प्रभवो मत्तः सर्वं प्रवर्तते ।
इति मत्वा भजन्ते मां बुधा भावसमन्विताः ॥१०-८॥

aham sarvasya prabhavo mattah sarvam pravartate
iti matva bhajante mam budha bhavasamanvitah (9.8)

aham : I | sarvasya : of all | prabhava : the origin | matah : from me | sarvam : all | pravartate : evolves | iti : thus | matva : accepting this | bhajante : worship | mam : me | budha : the wise | bhavasamanvita : with warm devotion

I am the origin of all. Everything evolves from me. Accepting this, the wise worship me with warm devotion.

(9)

मच्चित्ता मद्गतप्राणा बोधयन्तः परस्परम् ।
कथयन्तश्च मां नित्यं तुष्यन्ति च रमन्ति च ॥१०-९॥

machchitta madgataprana bodhayantah parasparam
kathayantascha mam nityam tushyanti cha ramanti cha (10.9)

mat-chitta : minds fixed in me | mat-gata-prana : life devoted to me | bodhayanta : talking | parasparam : among themselves | kathayanta : speaking about me | cha : and | mam : me | nityam : always | tusyanti : get satisfied | cha : and | ramanti : enjoy bliss | cha : and

With their minds fixed in me and their lives devoted to me, they keep talking about me and having discourses among themselves and thus remain always satisfied, happy and enjoy the bliss.

(10)

तेषां सततयुक्तानां भजतां प्रीतिपूर्वकम् ।
ददामि बुद्धियोगं तं येन मामुपयान्ति ते ॥१०-१०॥

tesham satatayuktanam bhajatam pritipurvakam
dadami buddhi yogam tam yena mamupayanti te (10.10)

yesham : to those | satata-yuktanam : always engaged in | bhajatam :

worshipping | priti-purvakam : ecstatic in love | dadami : give | buddhi-yogam : yogic intelligence | tam : that | yena : by which | mam : to me | upayanti : come | te : they

To those who are always engaged in worshipping me and getting ecstatic in my love, I gift yogic intelligence by which they can reach me.

(11)
तेषामेवानुकम्पार्थमहमज्ञानजं तमः ।
नाशयाम्यात्मभावस्थो ज्ञानदीपेन भास्वता ॥१०- ११॥

tesham evanukampartham aham ajnana jam tamah
nashayamymatmabhavostho gyandipenan bhasvata (11.11)

tesam : for them | eva : only | anukampartham : to show special consideration | aham : I | ajnana-jam : born of ignorance | tama : darkness | nashayami : destroy | atma-bhavastha : situated in their hearts | gyana-dipena : with the lamp of knowledge | bhasvata : glowing/radiant/luminous

Only to show special consideration for them, I destroy with the luminous lamp of knowledge the darkness born of ignorance in their hearts.

(12-13)
अर्जुन उवाच
परं ब्रह्म परं धाम पवित्रं परमं भवान् ।
पुरुषं शाश्वतं दिव्यमादिदेवमजं विभुम् ॥१०- १२॥
आहुस्त्वामृषयः सर्वे देवर्षिर्नारदस्तथा ।
असितो देवलो व्यासः स्वयं चैव ब्रवीषि मे ॥१०- १३॥

arjuna uvacha
param brahma param dhama pavitram paramam bhavan
purusham shashvatam divyamadidevamajam vibhum (10.12)
ahustvamrishayah sarve devarshir naradas tatha
asito devalo vyasah svayam chaiva bravishi me (10.13)

arjuna uvacha : Arjuna said | param brahma : the supreme being | param dhama : the ultimate abode | pavitram : the pure | paramam : the highest/ the Absolute | bhavan : you | purusham : persons | shashvatam : everlasting | divyam : divine | adi-devam : the original Godhead | ajam : unborn | vibhum : great | ahu : say | tvam : you | rishiyah : the sages | sarve : all | devarishi : the sage among the gods/the godly Rishi | narada : Narada | tatha : and | asita : Asita | devala : Devala | vyasah : Vyasa | svayam : personally | cha : also | eva : surely | bravishi : say | me : to me

Arjuna said: You are the Supreme Brahman, the ultimate abode, the pure, the highest, the eternal divine person (Purusha), the unborn, great, original Godhead. All the sages, the godly Rishi Narada, as also Asita, Devala and Vyasa say so about you and you also personally confirm this to me.

(14)

सर्वमेतदृतं मन्ये यन्मां वदसि केशव ।
न हि ते भगवन्व्यक्तिं विदुर्देवा न दानवाः ॥१०- १४॥

sarvametadritam manye yanmam vadasi keshava
na hi te bhagavanvyaktim vidurdeva na danavah (10.14)

sarvam : all | etat : this | ritam : truth | manye : agreed | yat : which | mam : to me | vadasi : you say | keshava : Lord Krishna | na : neither | hi : verily | te : your | bhagavan : God | vyaktim : manifestations | vidu : know | deva : gods | na : nor | danavah : the demons

O! Krishna! All this that you say to me is agreed to be true. Verily, my God! Neither the gods nor the demons know your (various) manifestations (expressions in different forms).

(15)

स्वयमेवात्मनात्मानं वेत्थ त्वं पुरुषोत्तम ।
भूतभावन भूतेश देवदेव जगत्पते ॥१०- १५॥

svayam evatmanatmanam vettha tvam purushottama
bhuta bhavana bhutesha devadeva jagatpate (10.15)

svayam : self | eva : verily | atmana : by yourself | atmanam : yourself | vettha

: know | tvam : you | purusha-uttama : best of persons | bhuta-bhavana : source of beings | bhutesha : Lord of all beings | deva-deva : God of gods | jagat-pate : Master of the universe

O the best of persons, the source of all beings, Lord of all beings, God of gods, Master of the universe! verily, (only) you yourself know yourself by yourself.

(16)
वक्तुमर्हस्यशेषेण दिव्या ह्यात्मविभूतयः ।
याभिर्विभूतिभिर्लोकानिमांस्त्वं व्याप्य तिष्ठसि ॥१०- १६॥

vaktum arhasyaseshena divya hyatmavibhutayah
yabhir vibhutibhir lokan imamstvam vyapya tishthasi (10.16)

vaktum : to speak | arhasi : able to | aseshena : without leaving anything/ in detail/fully | divya : divine | hi : surely/verily | atma : own | vibhutayah : attributes | yabhi : by which | vibhutibhi : attributes | lokan : all the planets (worlds) | imam : these | tvam : you | vyapya : pervading/permeating | tishthasi : exist

Verily, you alone are able to speak fully about your own divine attributes by which attributes you exist by permeating all the worlds.

(17)
कथं विद्यामहं योगिंस्त्वां सदा परिचिन्तयन् ।
केषु केषु च भावेषु चिन्त्योऽसि भगवन्मया ॥१०- १७॥

katham vidyamaham yogintvam sada parichintayan
keshu keshu cha bhaveshu chintyoasi bhagavan maya (10.17)

katham : how | vidyam : know | aham : I | yogin : practitioner of yoga | tvam : you | sada : always | parichintayan : thinking/meditating | keshu : in which | keshu : in which | cha : and | bhaveshu : forms | chintya asi : to be thought | bhagavan : God | maya : by me

O Great Yogi, Lord Krishna! How should I keep ameditating on you all the time and how can I know you. In what different forms, O

God, you are to be thought of by me.

(18)

विस्तरेणात्मनो योगं विभूतिं च जनार्दन ।
भूयः कथय तृप्तिर्हि शृण्वतो नास्ति मेऽमृतम् ॥१०-१८॥

vistarenatmano yogam vibhutim cha janardana
bhuyah kathaya triptirhi shrinvato nasti meamritam (10.18)

vistarena : in extensor/in detail | atmana : your | yogam : power of yoga | vibhutim : attributes | cha : and | janardana : Lord Krishna | bhuyah : again/once more | kathaya : describe | tripti : satisfaction | hi : verily | shrinvata : hearing | na asti : does not exist/is not | me : my | amritam : nectar (like speech)

O Janardana! Describe to me again in extensor your yogic powers and their attributes. Verily, I am never satisfied hearing your nectar like speech.

(19)

श्रीभगवानुवाच
हन्त ते कथयिष्यामि दिव्या ह्यात्मविभूतयः ।
प्राधान्यतः कुरुश्रेष्ठ नास्त्यन्तो विस्तरस्य मे ॥१०-१९॥

Shribhagavan uvacha
hanta te kathayishyami divya hyatmavibhutayah
pradhanyatah kurushreshtha nastyanto vistarasya me (10.19)

Shribhagavan uvacha : Lord Krishna said | hanta : so now | te : to you | kathayishyami : I shall describe | divya : divine | hi : surely | atma-vibhutayah : personal qualities | pradhanyatah : principal ones | kuru-shreshtha : best of the descendants of Kuru | na asti : does not exist/is not there | anta : end | vistarasya : to the extent | me : my

Lord Krisna said: So now, O best of the descendants of Kuru, I shall describe to you the principal ones of my divine personal attributes. There does not exist any end to my extent.

(20)

अहमात्मा गुडाकेश सर्वभूताशयस्थितः ।
अहमादिश्च मध्यं च भूतानामन्त एव च ॥१०- २०॥

ahamatma gudakesha sarva bhutashaya sthitah
ahamadishcha madhyam cha bhutanamanta eva cha (10.20)

aham : I | atma : self/soul | gudakesha : Arjuna | sarva-bhuta : all living beings | ashaya-sthitah : situated in the heart | aham : I | adi : the beginning/ origin | cha : and | madhyam : middle | cha : also | bhutanam : of all living beings | anta : the end | eva : certainly | cha : and

O Arjuna! I am the Supreme Soul (Self) situated in the hearts of all living beings. Also, I am certainly the beginning, the middle and the end of all living beings.

(21)

आदित्यानामहं विष्णुर्ज्योतिषां रविरंशुमान् ।
मरीचिर्मरुतामस्मि नक्षत्राणामहं शशी ॥१०- २१॥

adityanamaham vishnurjyotisham raviranshuman
marichir marutamasmi nakshatranamaham shashi (10.21)

adityanam : of the 12 sons of Aditi (Adityas) | aham : I | vishnu : Godhead Vishnu, the preserver | jyotisham : of the radiances | ravi : sun (Sun-God) | anshuman : radiant | marichi : Marichi | marutam : of the winds | asmi : I am | nakshatranam : of the planets | aham : I | shashi : moon

Of the Adityas (the 12 sons of Aditi), I am god Vishnu, of the Radiances, I am the sun, of the winds, I am Marichi, of the planets, I am the moon.

(22)

वेदानां सामवेदोऽस्मि देवानामस्मि वासवः ।
इन्द्रियाणां मनश्चास्मि भूतानामस्मि चेतना ॥१०- २२॥

vedanam samavedoasmi devanamasmi vasavah
indriyanam manashchasmi bhutanamasmi chetana (10.22)

vedanam : among the Vedas | sama-veda : the Sama Veda | asmi : I am | devanam : among the gods | asmi : I am | vasava : Indra | indriyanam : among the senses | mana : the mind | cha : and | asmi : I am | bhutanam : among living beings | asmi : I am | chetana : consciousness

Among the Vedas I am the Samaveda, among the gods I am Indra, among the senses I am the mind and among living beings I am consciousness.

(23)

रुद्राणां शंकरश्चास्मि वित्तेशो यक्षरक्षसाम् ।
वसूनां पावकश्चास्मि मेरुः शिखरिणामहम् ॥१०-२३॥

rudranam shankarashchasmi vittesho yaksharakshasam
vasunam pavakashchasmi meruh shikharinamaham (10.23)

rudranam : among the (eleven) rudras (gods of destruction) | shankara : Shiva | cha : also/and | asmi : I am | vitta-isa : Lord of wealth | yaksha-rakshasam : demons | vasunam : gods of eight seasons | pavaka : fire-god | cha : and/also | asmi : I am | meru : (mountain) Meruh | shikharinam : among all the mountain peaks | aham : I am

Among the Rudras I am Shiva and among the Yakshas and Rakshasas I am the Lord of Wealth (Kubera), among the Vasus I am fire-god and among the mountain peaks I am Meru.

(24)

पुरोधसां च मुख्यं मां विद्धि पार्थ बृहस्पतिम् ।
सेनानीनामहं स्कन्दः सरसामस्मि सागरः ॥१०-२४॥

purodhasam cha mukhyam mam viddhi partha brihaspatim
senaninamaham skandah sarasamasmi sagarah (10.24)

purodhasam : of the priests | cha : and/also | mukhyam : the chief | mam : me | viddhi : know | partha : Arjuna (son of Pratha) | brahaspatim : Brahaspati | senaninam : of all the army commanders | aham : I | skandah : Kartikeya | sarasam : of all the water bodies | asmi : I am | sagarah : sea

O Arjuna! Know me, of all the priests I am Brahaspati, the Chief of all the army commanders I am Kartikeya and of all the water bodies I am the sea.

(25)
महर्षीणां भृगुरहं गिरामस्म्येकमक्षरम् ।
यज्ञानां जपयज्ञोऽस्मि स्थावराणां हिमालयः ॥१०- २५॥

maharishinam bhriguraham giramasmyekamaksharam
yagyanam japayagyoasmi sthavaranam himalayah (10.25)

maharishinam : of the Maharishis (the great saints) | bhrigu : the sage Bhrigu | aham : I am | giram : words | asmi : I am | ekam : one | aksharam : letter, the syllable (OM) | yagyanam : of the sacrificial fires/modes of worship | japa-yagya : chanting the name of God | asmi : I am | sthavaranam : of the immovable | himalayah : the Himalaya

Of the great sages I am Bhrigu, of all the words I am the one syllable OM, of the modes of worship I am chanting, of the immovables I am the Himalaya.

(26)
अश्वत्थः सर्ववृक्षाणां देवर्षीणां च नारदः ।
गन्धर्वाणां चित्ररथः सिद्धानां कपिलो मुनिः ॥१०- २६॥

asvatthah sarvavrikshanam devarshinam cha naradah:
gandharvanam chitrarathah siddhanam kapilo munih (10.26)

asvatthah : peepul tree | sarvavriakshanam : of all the trees | devarshinam : of all the godly sages | cha : and | naradah : Narada Muni | gandharvanam : of the Gandharvas | chitrarathah : Chitraratha | siddhanam : of all the saints who have achieved self-realisation | kapila munih : Kapila Muni

Of all the trees I am the Peepul and of all the godly sages I am Narada Muni, of the Gandharvas I am Chitraratha, of all the realised souls I am Kapila Muni.

(27)

उच्चैः श्रवसमश्वानां विद्धि माममृतोद्भवम् ।
ऐरावतं गजेन्द्राणां नराणां च नराधिपम् ॥१०- २७॥

*uchchaih shravasam ashvanam viddhi mamamritodbhavam
airavatam gajendranam naranam cha naradhipam (10.27)*

uchchaihshravasam : the horse named Uchchaishravasam | ashvanam : among the horses | viddhi : know | mam : me | amritodbhavam : born of nectar that came from the churning of the ocean | airavatam : elephant named Airavata, also born of nectar that came from the churning of the ocean (samudra-manthan) | gaja-indranam : among the celestial elephants | naranam : among human beings | cha : and | nara-adhipam : ruler of men/ king

(O Arjuna!) Know me, among the horses I am the horse named Uchchaishravasam (born of nectar that emerged at the samudra-manthan - the great churning of the ocean), among the heavenly elephants I am the elephant named Airavata (who also was born of the same nectar) and among human beings I am their ruler.

(28)

आयुधानामहं वज्रं धेनूनामस्मि कामधुक् ।
प्रजनश्चास्मि कन्दर्पः सर्पाणामस्मि वासुकिः ॥१०- २८॥

*ayudhanamaham vajram dhenunamasmi kamadhuk
prajanashchasmi kandarpah sarpanamasmi vasukih (10.28)*

ayudhanam : of the weapons | vajram : thunderbolt | dhenunam : of the cows | asmi : I am | kama-dhuk : Kama-dhenu (the cow fulfilling all wishes) | prajana : the cause of procreation | cha : and | asmi : I am | kandarpah : Cupid, Kamadeva | sarpanam : of the serpents | asmi : I am | vasukih : Vasuki

Of the weapons I am the thunderbolt, of the cows I am Kamadhenu, as the cause of procreation I am Kamadeva (Cupid) and of the serpents I am Vasuki.

(29)

अनन्तश्चास्मि नागानां वरुणो यादसामहम् ।
पितृणामर्यमा चास्मि यमः संयमतामहम् ॥१०-२९॥

anantaschasmi naganam varuno yadsamaham
pitrinamaryama chasmi yamah sanyamatamaham (10.29)

ananta : Ananta | cha : also | asmi : I am | naganam : of the serpents (Nagas) | varuna : Varuna (the god of water) | yadasam : of aquatic beings | aham : I am | pitrinam : of the departed ancestors | aryama : Aryama | cha : also | asmi : I am | yamah : god of death | sanyamatam : among the regulators | aham : I am

Of the Nagas I am Ananta, of aquatic beings I am Varuna and of the departed ancestors I am Aryama and among the regulators I am Yama - the god of death.

(30)

प्रह्लादश्चास्मि दैत्यानां कालः कलयतामहम् ।
मृगाणां च मृगेन्द्रोऽहं वैनतेयश्च पक्षिणाम् ॥१०-३०॥

prahladas chasmi daityanam kalah kalayatamaham
mriganam cha mrigendroaham vainateyash cha pakshinam (10.30)

prahlada : Prahlada | cha : also | asmi : I am | daityanam : of the demons | kalah : time | kalayatam : of the reckoners | aham : I am | mriganam : among the animals | cha : and | mriga-indra : the lion | aham : I am | vainateya : Garuda | cha : also | pakshinam : among the birds

Among the demons I am Prahlada, of the reckoned I am time, among the animals I am the lion and among the birds I am Garuda.

(31)

पवनः पवतामस्मि रामः शस्त्रभृतामहम् ।
झषाणां मकरश्चास्मि स्रोतसामस्मि जाह्नवी ॥१०-३१॥

pavanah pavatamasmi ramah shastrabhritamaham
jhashanam makarashchasmi srotasamasmi jahnavi (10.31)

pavanah : air | pavatam : of purifiers | asmi : I am | ramah : Rama | shastrabhritam : of the holders of weapons/warriors | aham : I am | jhashanam : of the fish | makarash : shark | cha : also | asmi : I am | srotasam : of all the streames | asmi : I am | jahnavi : the Ganges

Of all the purifiers I am air, of the holders of weapons I am Rama, of the fishes I am shark and of the streams I am the Ganges.

(32)
सर्गणामादिरन्तश्च मध्यं चैवाहमर्जुन ।
अध्यात्मविद्या विद्यानां वादः प्रवदतामहम् ॥१०- ३२॥

sarganam adir antash cha madhyam chaivaham arjuna
adhyatmavidya vidyanam vadah pravadatamaham (10.32)

sarganam : of all creations | adi : beginning | anta : end | cha : and | madhyam : middle | cha : also | eva : certainly | aham : I am | arjuna : Arjuna | adhyatma-vidya : spiritual knowledge/knowledge of the Self | vidyanam : of all education | vadah : the concluding statement | pravadatam : of all the argumentation | aham : I am

Of all creations I am the beginning, the end and also the middle. O Arjuna! Of all knowledge I am spiritual knowledge or the knowledge of the Self and of all the argumentation I am the concluding statement.

(33)
अक्षराणामकारोऽस्मि द्वन्द्वः सामासिकस्य च ।
अहमेवाक्षयः कालो धाताहं विश्वतोमुखः ॥१०- ३३॥

aksharnamakaroasmi dvandvah samasikasya cha
ahamevakshayah kalo dhataham visvato-mukhah (10.33)

aksharnam : among letters | akara : the first letter A | asmi : I am | dvandvah : duality | samasikasya : among the compounds | cha : and | aham : I am | eva : certainly | akshayah : indestructible | kala : time (eternal) | dhata : the creator | aham : I am | visvata-mukhah : the all-formed (Brahma)

Among the letters I am the first letter A, among the duality of all compounds I am certainly the indestructible time (eternal) and of all the creator beings I am the all-formed (four-headed) Brahma.

(34)

मृत्युः सर्वहरश्चाहमुद्भवश्च भविष्यताम् ।
कीर्तिः श्रीर्वाक्च नारीणां स्मृतिर्मेधा धृतिः क्षमा ॥१०-३४॥

mrityuh sarva harash chaham udbhavash cha bhavishyatam
kirtih shrirvakcha narinam smritirmedha dhritih kshama (10.34)

mrityuh : death | sarva-hara : all ending | cha : also/and | aham : I am | udbhava : origin/source | cha : also/and | bhavishyatam : of future happenings | kirtih : fame | shrivak : excellence in speech | cha : and | narinam : among the women | smriti : memory | medha : intelligence | dhritih : firmness | kshama : forgiveness

I am myself the death that ends everything and am the source and the future of all that may happen. I am fame, excellence in speech and among women I am memory, intelligence, firmness and forgiveness.

(35)

बृहत्साम तथा साम्नां गायत्री छन्दसामहम् ।
मासानां मार्गशीर्षोऽहमृतूनां कुसुमाकरः ॥१०-३५॥

brihatsama tatha samnam gayatri chhandasamaham
masanam marga shirsho hamritunam kusumakarah (10.35)

brahatsama : Brahatsama (hymns of the Samaveda) | tatha : and | samnam : of the Samaveda | gayatri : the Gayatri hymns | chhandasam : of all poetry metres | aham : I am | masanam : of months | marga-shirsha : spring season/month of flower bloom | aham : I am | ritunam : of the seasons | kusumakarah : spring season

Of the hymns, I am the Brahat-sama in Samaveda, of all poetry metres I am the Gayatri hymn, of months I am Margasirsa and of seasons I am the spring (when flowers are in full bloom).

(36)

द्यूतं छलयतामस्मि तेजस्तेजस्विनामहम् ।
जयोऽस्मि व्यवसायोऽस्मि सत्त्वं सत्त्ववतामहम् ॥१०-३६॥

dyutam chalayatamasmi tejastejasvinamaham
jayoasmi vyavashayoasmi sattvam sattvavatamaham (10.36).

dyutam : game of gambling | chalayatam : of the fraudulent | asmi : I am | teja : power | tejasvinam : of the powerful | aham : I am | jaya : victory | asmi : I am | vyavasaya : enterprise | asmi : I am | sattvam : strength | sattva-vatam : of the strong | aham : I am

Of the fraudulent, I am the game of gambling, I am the power of the powerful, I am victory for the enterprising, I am the strength of the strong.

(37)

वृष्णीनां वासुदेवोऽस्मि पाण्डवानां धनंजयः ।
मुनीनामप्यहं व्यासः कवीनामुशना कविः ॥१०-३७॥

vrishninam vasudevoasmi pandavanam dhananjayah
muninamapyaham vyasah kavinamushana kavih (10.37)

vrashninam : of the Vrashni dynasty | vasudeva : Vasudeva Krishna | asmi : I am | pandavanam : of the Pandavas | dhananjaya : Arjuna | muninam : of the saints | api : also | aham : I am | vyasah : the great compiler of the Vedas, Rishi Vedavyasa | kavinam : of the great sages/thinkers | usana : Usana (Sukracharya) | kavih : sage/thinker

Among the descendants of Vrashni I am Vasudeva, among the Pandavas I am Arjuna, among the saints I am Rishi Vedvyasa, among the sages I am Usana (Sukracharya).

(38)

दण्डो दमयतामस्मि नीतिरस्मि जिगीषताम् ।
मौनं चैवास्मि गुह्यानां ज्ञानं ज्ञानवतामहम् ॥१०-३८॥

dando damayatamasmi nitirasmi jigishatam
maunam chaivasmi guhyanam gyanam gyanavatamaham (10.38)

danda : punishment | damayatam : of the means of controlling lawlessness | asmi : I am | niti : morality | asmi : I am | jigisatam : of those aspiring to win | maunam : silence | cha : and | eva : also | asmi : I am | guhyanam : of secrets | gyanam : knowledge (of the spirit) | gyanavatam : of the knowers | aham : I am

As the means of controlling lawlessness I am punishment, for those aspiring to win I am morality, for keeping secrets I am silence and among the knowers I am the one with spiritual knowledge.

(39)
यच्चापि सर्वभूतानां बीजं तदहमर्जुन ।
न तदस्ति विना यत्स्यान्मया भूतं चराचरम् ॥१०-३९॥

yachchapi sarvabhutanam bijam tadahamarjuna
na tadasti vina yatsyanmaya bhutam characharam (10.39)

yat : what | cha : and | api : also | sarva-bhutanam : of all living beings | bijam : seed | tat : that | aham : I am | arjuna : O Arjuna ! | na : not | tat : that | asti : it exists | vina : without | yat : which | syat : is there | maya : me | bhutam : living beings | chara : moving/sentient/conscient | achara : non-moving/non-sentient/non-conscient

O Arjuna! Of whatever exists and also of all the living beings I am the seed, nothing that is there, whether sentient or non-sentient - conscient or non-conscient - can exist without me.

(40)
नान्तोऽस्ति मम दिव्यानां विभूतीनां परन्तप ।
एष तूद्देशतः प्रोक्तो विभूतेर्विस्तरो मया ॥१०-४०॥

nantoasti mama divyanam vibhutinam parantapa
esha tuddesatah prokta vibhutervistaro maya (10.40)

na : no | anta : end | asti : is | mama : my | divyanam : divine | vibhutinam : attributes | parantapa : conqueror of foes, Arjuna | esha : all this | tu : but | uddesatah : for example | prokta : spoken | vibhute : of attributes | vistara : the expanse | maya : by me

O conqueror of foes, Arjuna! There is no end of my attributes. All this that I have spoken to you is only by way of an example to indicate the vast expanse of my attributes.

(41)
यद्यद्विभूतिमत्सत्त्वं श्रीमदूर्जितमेव वा ।
तत्तदेवावगच्छ त्वं मम तेजोंऽशसंभवम् ॥१०-४१॥

yad yad vibhutimat sattvam shrimad urjitam eva va
tat tad evavagachchha tvam mama tejoanshashambhavam (10-41)

yat yat : whatever | vibhuti : greatness | mat : having | sattvam : being | shrimat : prosperous | urjitam : powerful | eva : also | va : or | tat tat : all those | eva : also | avagaccha : know | tvam : you | mama : my | teja : splendor | ansha : a part | sambhavam : born of

You should know that whatever distinction any being achieves in terms of prosperity or power is only a part of my splendour.

(42)
अथवा बहुनैतेन किं ज्ञातेन तवार्जुन ।
विष्टभ्याहमिदं कृत्स्नमेकांशेन स्थितो जगत् ॥१०-४२॥

athava bahunaitena kim jnaten tavarjuna
vishtabhyaham idam kritsnamekanshena sthita jagat (10.42)

athava : or | bahuna : many | etena : by this | kim : what | jnatena : by knowing | tava : your | arjuna : Arjuna! | vishtabhya : supporting | aham : I | idam : this | kritsnam : the whole | eka-anshena : by one part | sthita : situated/existing | jagat : world

O Arjuna! Of what avail is knowing all this for you? You should know that I am there and can support the whole world by a part of myself.

Thus, ends the 10th Canto titled 'Yoga of Divine Glory'.

Eleventh Canto
VISHWAROOP DARSHAN
Vision of the Universal Form

(1)

अर्जुन उवाच
मदनुग्रहाय परमं गुह्यमध्यात्मसंज्ञितम् ।
यत्त्वयोक्तं वचस्तेन मोहोऽयं विगतो मम ॥११-१॥

Arjuna uvacha
mad anugrahaya paramam guhyam adhyatma sanjnitam
yat tvayoktam vachas tena moho 'yam vigato mama (11.1).

arjuna: Arjuna | uvacha : said | mat-anugrahaya : out of regard for me | paramam : supreme | guhyam : secret | adhyatma : spiritual science | sanjnitam : on the subject/in the matter of/in regard to | yat : which | tvaya : by you | uktam : said | vacha : discourse | tena : by that | moha : delusion | ayam : this | vigata : gone away/removed/dispelled | mama : my

Arjuna said : Out of regard for me, you have spoken about the supremely secret spiritual science of the Self (of my Self and your Self being the same and one with the Supreme Self). After hearing your discourse, my delusion (of distinction between you and me) stands fully dispelled.

(2)

भवाप्ययौ हि भूतानां श्रुतौ विस्तरशो मया ।
त्वत्तः कमलपत्राक्ष माहात्म्यमपि चाव्ययम् ॥११-२॥

bhavapyayau hi bhutanam shrutau vistarasho maya
tvattah kamala-patr-aksa mahatmyam api chavyayam (11.2)

bhava : birth/origin/creation | apyayau : death/end/destruction | hi : verily | bhutanam : beings | shrutau : heard | vistarasha : in extensor/in detail | maya : by me | tvatta : from you | kamala-patra-aksa : Lotus-eye —one | mahatmyam : greatness | api : also | cha : and | avyayam : inexhaustible

O Lotus-eyed I have heard from you in detail about the birth and death of beings as also about your inexhaustible greatness.

(3)
एवमेतद्यथात्थ त्वमात्मानं परमेश्वर ।
द्रष्टुमिच्छामि ते रूपमैश्वरं पुरुषोत्तम ॥११-३॥

evam etad yathattha tvam atmanam parameshvara
drashtum icchami te rupam aishvaraim purushottama (11.3)

evam : thus | etat : this | yatha : as | attha : say | tvam : you | atmanam : yourself | parama-ishvara : Supreme Lord | drashtum : to see | icchami : I wish | te : your | rupam : form | aishvaram : divine | purusha-uttama : superb human being/best of men/ideal person

O the best of men! You are thus as you say you are (but) O my Supreme Lord, I wish to see you in your divine form.

(4)
मन्यसे यदि तच्छक्यं मया द्रष्टुमिति प्रभो ।
योगेश्वर ततो मे त्वं दर्शयात्मानमव्ययम् ॥११-४॥

manyase yadi tachchhakyam maya drashtumiti prabho
yogeshvara tatah me tvam darshayatmanam avyayam (11.4)

manyase : you believe/it seems to you/you think | yadi : if | tat : that | shakyam : can be | maya : by me | drashtum : be seen | iti : thus/that | prabho : O Lord | yoga-ishvara : Lord of yogic powers | tatah : then | me : to me | tvam : you | darshaya : show | atmanam : Self | avyayam : eternal/imperishable/immutable

O Lord! If you think that it is possible for the immutable form of your Self to be seen by me , then O God of yogis, show that to me.

(5)
श्रीभगवानुवाच
पश्य मे पार्थ रूपाणि शतशोऽथ सहस्रशः ।
नानाविधानि दिव्यानि नानावर्णाकृतीनि च ॥११-५॥

Shribhagavan uvaacha
pashya me partha rupani shatashotha sahasrashah
nanavidhani divyani nana-varnakrtini cha (11.5)

Shribhagavan uvacha : Lord Krishna said | pashya : see | me : my | partha : son of Pratha, Arjuna | rupani : forms | shatasha : hundreds | atha : also | sahasrasha : thousands | nanavidhani : in various ways | divyani : divine | nana : various | varna : colour | akritini : shapes | cha : and

Lord Krishna said: O Arjuna! see the hundreds and thousands of divine forms in which I appear in various ways, colours and shapes.

(6)

पश्यादित्यान्वसून्रुद्रानश्विनौ मरुतस्तथा ।
बहून्यदृष्टपूर्वाणि पश्याश्चर्याणि भारत ॥११-६॥

pashyadityan vasun rudran ashvinau marutas tatha
bahuny adrshta-purvani pashyashcharyani bharata (11.6)

pashya : see | adityan : (the twelve) sons of Aditi | vasun : (the eight) Vasus | rudran : (the eleven) Rudras | ashvinau : (the two) Asvini Kumars | maruta : Maruts (the 49 wind gods) | tatha : and | bahuni : many | adrashta : not seen | purvani : before | pashya : see | ashcharyani : wonders | bharata : O descendant of Bharata

O descendant of the great king Bharata! see (in me) the twelve Adityas (sons of Aditi), the eight Vasus, eleven Rudras, two Asvins and forty-nine Maruts (wind gods) and many other wonders never seen before.

(7)

इहैकस्थं जगत्कृत्स्नं पश्याद्य सचराचरम् ।
मम देहे गुडाकेश यच्चान्यद् द्रष्टुमिच्छसि ॥११-७॥

ihaikastham jagat kritsnam pashyadya sa-characharam
mama dehe gudakesha yachchanyad drashtumichchhasi (11.7)

iha : in this | ekastham : in one place | jagat : the world | kritsnam : fully | pashya : see | adya : at once | sa : with | chara : moving | acharam : non-moving | mama : my | dehe : in the body | gudakesha : Arjuna | yat : that | cha : also | anyat : other | drashtum : to see | ichchhasi : you wish

O Arjuna ! In this one place, in my body, at once, you can see fully the whole world with all the moving and non-moving objects. Also, you can see anything else that you may wish to see.

(8)
न तु मां शक्यसे द्रष्टुमनेनैव स्वचक्षुषा ।
दिव्यं ददामि ते चक्षुः पश्य मे योगमैश्वरम् ॥११-८॥
na tu mam shakyase drashtum anenaiva sva-chakshusha
divyam dadami te chakshuh pashya me yogam aishvaram (11.8).

na : never | tu : but | mam : me | shakyase : am | drashtum : to see | anena : with these | eva : certainly | sva-chakshusha : with own eyes | divyam : divine | dadami : I will give you | te : to you | chaksuh : eyes/vision | pashya : see | me : my | yogam aishvaram : the supreme richness of yoga.

But, you certainly can never see me with your own existing eyes. I will give you divine vision to enable you to experience my supreme richness of yoga.

(9)
संजय उवाच
एवमुक्त्वा ततो राजन्महायोगेश्वरो हरिः ।
दर्शयामास पार्थाय परमं रूपमैश्वरम् ॥११-९॥
sanjaya uvacha
evamuktva tato rajanmaha yogeshvaro harih
darshahyamasa parthaya paramam rupamaishvaram (11.9)

sanjaya uvacha : Sanjaya said | evam : thus | uktva : speaking | tata : then | rajan : King | maha-yoga-ishvara : the supreme Lord of yoga | harih : Lord Krishna | darshayam asa : showed | parthaya : to Arjuna | paramam : the ultimate | rupam aishvaram : cosmic form

Sanjaya said: O King! After speaking thus, the supreme yogi, Lord

Krishna showed Arjuna the ultimate cosmic form.

(10)
अनेकवक्त्रनयनम्, अनेकाद्भुतदर्शनम्,
अनेकदिव्याभरणम्, दिव्यानेकोद्यतायुधम्॥११-१०॥

aneka-vaktra-nayanam anekadbhuta-darshanam
aneka-divyambara-bharam divya-nekodyat yudham (11.10)

aneka : many | vaktra : mouths | nayanam : eyes | aneka : many | adbhuta : wonderful/miraculous | darshanam : seeing/view/vision | aneka : many | divya : celestial | abharanam : ornaments | divya : divine | aneka : many | udyata : uplifted/raised | ayudham : weapons

It was a miraculous vision of many mouths, many eyes, body decorated with many celestial ornaments and many raised weapons.

(11)
दिव्यमाल्याम्बरधरं दिव्यगन्धानुलेपनम् ।
सर्वाश्चर्यमयं देवमनन्तं विश्वतोमुखम् ॥११- ११॥

divya malyambara dharam divya gandhanulepanam
sarvashcharya mayam devam anantam vishvatomukham (11.11)

divya : celestial | malya : garlands | ambara : dresses | dharam : wearing | divya : divine | gandha : perfumes | anulepanam : smeared with | sarva : all | ashcharya-mayam : wonderful | devam : shining | anantam : unlimited/eternal | vishvatah-mukham : with mouths opening on all sides

The Lord was wearing celestial garlands and dresses and many divine perfumes were smeared all over the body. With mouths opening on all sides, it was the most miraculous sight of the Eternal.

(12)
दिवि सूर्यसहस्रस्य भवेद्युगपदुत्थिता ।
यदि भाः सदृशी सा स्याद्भासस्तस्य महात्मनः ॥११- १२॥

divi suryasahasrasya bhaved yugapad utthita
yadi bhaah sadrishii sa syad bhasastasya mahatmanah (11.12)

divi : in the sky | surya : sun | sahasrasya : of thousands of | bhavet : there were | yugapat : at the same time/at once | utthita : present/rise up/born of the rise of | yadi : if | bhah : light/splendor/luminosity | sadrishi : like | sa : that | syat : would be | bhasah : effulgence/radiance | tasya : of that | maha-atmanah : of the Supreme Self

Even the luminosity that might result from a thousand suns arising in the sky all at once would be no match to the effulgence of the cosmic (universal) form of the Lord (Supreme Self).

(13)
तत्रैकस्थं जगत्कृत्स्नं प्रविभक्तमनेकधा ।
अपश्यद्देवदेवस्य शरीरे पाण्डवस्तदा ॥११-१३॥

tatraikastham jagatkritsnam pravibhaktam anekadhaa
apashyaddevadevasya sharire pandavastadaa (11.13)

tatra : there | eka-stham : at one place | jagat : universe | kritsnam : full/complete/entire | pravibhaktam : divided | anekadha : into many | apashyat : could see | deva-devasya: of the God of gods (the cosmic self) | sharire : in the body | pandava : Arjuna | tada : then

Arjuna could then see at one place in the body of the One, the God of gods (the cosmic Self) the entire universe even though it was divided into many.

(14)
ततः सविस्मयाविष्टो हृष्टरोमा धनंजयः ।
प्रणम्य शिरसा देवं कृताञ्जलिरभाषत ॥११-१४॥

tatah sa vismayavishto hrishtaroma dhananjayah
pranamya shirasa devam kritanjalirabhashata (11.14)

tata : then | sa : he | vismaya-avishta : greatly astonished/filled with wonder | hrista-roma : with hair standing on end | dhananjayah : Arjuna | pranamya : bending forward to offer respects | shirasa : with the head | devam : Godhead | krita-anjali : with hands folded | abhashata : spoke thus

Then, filled with wonder, with his hair standing on end, hands folded and head bending (to offer obeisance) to the Godhead, Arjuna spoke thus.

(15)

अर्जुन उवाच
पश्यामि देवां स्तवदेव देहे: सर्वांस्तथा भूतविशेषसंघान् ।
ब्रह्माणमीशं कमलासनस्थमृषींश्च सर्वानुरगांश्च दिव्यान् ॥११-१५॥

arjuna uvacha
pashyami devan stavadeva deheh
sarvans tatha bhuta vishesha sanghan
brahmanam isham kamalasana stham
rishinsh cha sarvan uragamsh cha divyan (11.15)

arjuna uvacha : Arjuna said | pashyami : I see | devan : gods | tava : your | deva : O God, My Lord Krishna | dehe : in the body | sarvan : all | tatha : and | bhuta : living beings | vishesha-sanghan : all the special kinds of | brahmanam-isam : Lord Brahma | kamala-asana-stham : seated on the lotus | rishin : sages | cha : also | sarvan : all | uragan : serpents | cha : also | divyan : divine

Arjuna said: O My Lord Krishna! I see in your (cosmic) body all the gods and all the other kinds of living beings with Lord Brahma seated on the lotus as also the great sages and divine serpents.

(16)

अनेकबाहूदरवक्त्रनेत्रं पश्यामि त्वां सर्वतोऽनन्तरूपम् ।
नान्तं न मध्यं न पुनस्तवादिं पश्यामि विश्वेश्वर विश्वरूप ॥११-१६॥

aneka bahudara vaktra netram
pashyami tvam sarvato nanta rupam
nantam na madhyam na punas tavadim
pashyami vishveshvara vishvarupa (11.16)

aneka : many/multiple | bahu : arms | udara : bellies | vaktra : mouths | netram : eyes | pashyami : I see | tvam : you | sarvata : everywhere | ananta-rupam : infinite forms | na antam : unending | na madhyam : with no middle

| no punah : no repetition | tava : your | adim : beginning | pashyami : I see | vishva-ishvara : Lord of the universe | vishva-rupa : universal (cosmic) form

O Supreme Lord of the universe! I am seeing you in infinite forms, boundless from all sides, with multiple arms, bellies, mouths and eyes. O Cosmic Form! I do not see your beginning, middle or end.

(17)
किरीटिनं गदिनं चक्रिणं चतेजोराशिं सर्वतो दीप्तिमन्तम् ।
पश्यामि त्वां दुर्निरीक्ष्यं समन्ता-द्दीप्तानलार्कद्युतिमप्रमेयम् ॥११-१७॥

kiritinam gadinam chakrinam cha
tejo rashim sarvato diptimantam
pashyami tvam durnirikshyam samantad
diptanalarka dyutim aprameyam (11.17)

kiritinam : crown | gadinam : mace/club | chakrinam : disc/discus | cha : and | teja-rashim : lot of radiance/effulgence | sarvata : from all sides/everywhere | dipti-mantam : shining/glowing | pashyami : I see | tvam : you | durnirikshyam : difficult to look at | samantat : all around/on all sides | dipta-anala : burning fire | arka : sun | dyutim : sunshine | aprameyam : immeasurable/incomprehensible

I see you with a crown, a mace and a disc, glowing from all sides with lot of radiance. Very much like burning fire and immeasurably bright sunshine all around, it is difficult for anyone to look towards you (in that cosmic form).

(18)
त्वमक्षरं परमं वेदितव्यं त्वमस्य विश्वस्य परं निधानम् ।
त्वमव्ययः शाश्वतधर्मगोप्ता सनातनस्त्वं पुरुषो मतो मे ॥११-१८॥

tvam aksharam paramam veditavyam
tvam asya vishwasya param nidhanam
tvam avyayah shashvata dharma gopta
sanatanas tvam purusho mato me (18.18)

tvam : you | aksharam : the indestructible | paramam : Supreme Being |

veditavyam : to be known | tvam : you | asya : this | vishvasya : of the universe | param : ultimate/supreme | nidhanam : shelter/refuge/resting place | tvam : you | avyayah : imperishable/immortal | shashvata-dharma gopta : guardian of the eternal Dharma | sanatana : ancient/eternal | tvam : you | purusah : the Supreme Lord | matah me : it is my view

O Lord! In my view, you are the supreme indestructible being to be known. You are the ultimate refuge of this universe. You are the immortal guardian of eternal Dharma. You are the Supreme Lord.

(19)

अनादिमध्यान्तमनन्तवीर्य-मनन्तबाहुं शशिसूर्यनेत्रम् ।
पश्यामि त्वां दीप्तहुताशवक्त्रं स्वतेजसा विश्वमिदं तपन्तम् ॥११- १९॥

anadi madhyaantam ananta viryam
ananta baahum shashi surya netram
pashyami tvam dipta hutasha vaktram
svatejasa vishvam idam tapantam (11.19)

anadi : without a beginning | madhya : middle | antam : end | ananta : infinite/unlimited | viryam : vigour/power/glory | ananta : unlimited | bahum : arms | shashi : moon | surya : sun | netram : eyes | pashyami : I see | tvam : you | dipta : blazing | hutasa-vaktram : fire coming out of your mouth | sva-tejasa : self-radiance | vishvam : universe | idam : this | tapantam : heating

I see that you are without any beginning, middle or end, with infinite powers, unlimited number of arms, the sun and the moon as your eyes, your mouth emitting blazing fire and the entire universe getting heated by your radiance.

(20)

द्यावापृथिव्योरिदमन्तरं हि व्याप्तं त्वयैकेन दिशश्च सर्वाः ।
दृष्ट्वाद्भुतं रूपमुग्रं तवेदं लोकत्रयं प्रव्यथितं महात्मन् ॥११-२०॥

dyava a prithivyor idam antaram hi
vyaptam tvayaikena dishash cha sarvah
drishtvadbhutam rupam ugram tavedam
loka trayam pravyathitam mahatman (11.20)

dyau-a-prithivyoh : of heaven and earth | idam : this | antaram : space in between | hi : certainly | vyaptam : pervaded/filled with | tvaya : by you | ekena : alone | dishah : direction | cha : and | sarvah : all | drishtva : seeing | adbhutam : wonderful | rupam : form | ugram : terrible/awful | tava : your | idam : this | loka : planets/worlds | trayam : three | pravyathitam : upset/struck with fear | maha-atman : Supreme Soul (Self)

O Supreme Soul! This whole space between heaven and earth and in all directions is filled only by you alone and seeing this wonderful and awful form of yours, the three worlds stand stricken with fear.

(21)
अमी हि त्वां सुरसंघा विशन्ति केचिद्भीताः प्राञ्जलयो गृणन्ति ।
स्वस्तीत्युक्त्वा महर्षिसिद्धसंघाः स्तुवन्ति त्वां स्तुतिभिः पुष्कलाभिः ॥११-२१॥

ami hi tvam surasangha vishanti
kechid bhitah pranjalayo grinanti
svastityuktva maharishi siddha sanghah
stuvanti tvam stutibhih pushkalabhih (11.21)

ami : those | hi : verily | tvam : you | sura-sangha : groups of gods | vishanti : are entering | kechit : some | bhitah : afraid/frightened | pranjalaya : folded hands | grinanti : extolling | svashti : may all be well | iti : thus | uktva : saying/reciting | maharishi : great sages | siddha-sanghah : hosts of realised souls | stuvanti : are praising/praying/worshipping | tvam : you | stutibhi : with hymns | pushkalabhih : excellent

Verily, (I am seeing) groups of gods are entering into your cosmic body. Some of them appear frightened and have folded hands. Hosts of great sages and realised souls reciting 'may all be well' wishes are worshipping you with excellent hymns.

(22)
रुद्रादित्या वसवो ये च साध्या विश्वेऽश्विनौ मरुतश्चोष्मपाश्च ।
गन्धर्वयक्षासुरसिद्धसंघा वीक्षन्ते त्वां विस्मिताश्चैव सर्वे ॥११-२२॥

rudraditya vasavo ye cha sadhya
vishve 'shvinau marutash choshmapash cha

gandharva yakshasura siddha sangha
vikshante tvam vismitash chaiva sarve (11.22)

rudra : reincarnations of Lord Shiva | aditya : the Adityas | vasava : the Vasus | ye : all these | cha : and | sadhya : the Sadhyas | vishve : the Vishvedevas | ashvinau : the Asvini Kumars | maruta : the Maruts | cha : and | ushma-pah : the forefathers | cha : and | gandharva : the Gandharvas | yaksha : the Yaksas | asura : demons | siddha : the Siddhas | sangha : groups/bands | vikshante : are looking | tvam : you | vismita : in wonder | cha : and | eva : certainly | sarve : all

All the divinities - the (11) Rudras, (12) Adityas, (8) Vasus - and the Sadhyas, the Vishvedevas, the (2) Asvini Kumaras, the (49) Maruts and the forefathers and the hosts of Gandharvas, the Yaksas, the demons and the Siddhas, all of them are certainly looking at you in wonder.

(23)

रूपं महत्ते बहुवक्त्रनेत्रं महाबाहो बहुबाहूरुपादम् ।
बहूदरं बहुदंष्ट्राकरालं दृष्ट्वा लोकाः प्रव्यथितास्तथाहम् ॥११-२३॥

rupam mahatte bahuvaktra netram
maha abaho bahuru padam
bahudaram bahu damshtra karalam
drishtva lokah pravyathitas tathaham (11.23)

rupam : form | mahat : great | te : you | bahu : many | vaktra : faces | netram : eyes | maha-baho : O Big-armed one, Lord Krishna | bahu : arms | uru : thighs | padam : legs | bahu-udaram : many stomachs | bahu-danshtra : many teeth | kara lam : terrible/awe-inspiring | drishtva : seeing | lokah : the planets | pravyathita : upset | tatha : and | aham : I

O Big-armed one, Lord Krishna! Seeing your great cosmic form with multiple faces, eyes, arms, thighs, legs, stomachs and the many awe-inspiring teeth, all the planets are upset and so am I.

(24)

नभःस्पृशं दीप्तमनेकवर्णं व्यात्ताननं दीप्तविशालनेत्रम् ।
दृष्ट्वा हि त्वां प्रव्यथितान्तरात्मा धृतिं न विन्दामि शमं च विष्णो ॥११-२४॥

nabhah sprisham deptam aneka varnam
vyattananam depta vishala netram
drishtva hi tvam pravyathitantar atma
dhritim na vindami shamam cha vishno (11.24)

nabhah-sprisham : touching the sky | diptam : radiant | aneka : many | varnam : colours | vyatta : open | ananam : mouths | dipta : shining/glowing | vishala : big | netram : eyes | drishtva : seeing | hi : verily | tvam : you | pravyathita : disturbed/upset | antah : within | atma : self | dhritim : firmness/steadiness | na : not | vindami : I have | shamam : tranquility | cha : and | vishno : Lord Vishnu

O Lord Vishnu! Verily seeing you in your cosmic form with the many radiant colours touching the sky, open mouths and glowing big eyes, I am disturbed within myself and am not able to maintain the firmness and tranquillity of mind.

(25)

दंष्ट्राकरालानि च ते मुखानि दृष्ट्वैव कालानलसन्निभानि ।
दिशो न जाने न लभे च शर्म प्रसीद देवेश जगन्निवास ॥११-२५॥

danshtra karaalani cha te mukhani
drishtvaiva kalanala sannibhani
disho na jane na labhe cha sharma
prasida devesha jagan nivasa (11.25)

danshtra : teeth | karalam : terrible/awe-inspiring/awesome | cha : and | te : your | mukhani : faces | drshtva : seeing | eva : thus | kala-anala : the fire of death | sannibhani : as if | disha : direction | na : not | jane : I know | na : not | labhe : I get/find | cha : and | sharma : peace | prasida : be pleased | deva-isa : Lord of Lords | jagat-nivasa : in whom the universe dwells

O Lord of Lords, in whom the universe dwells, seeing your awesome teeth and your many faces with blazing fire of death, I have lost the sense of direction and find no peace. Be pleased/ have mercy.

(26-27)

अमी च त्वां धृतराष्ट्रस्य पुत्राः सर्वे सहैवावनिपालसंघैः ।
भीष्मो द्रोणः सूतपुत्रस्तथासौ सहास्मदीयैरपि योधमुख्यैः ॥११-२६॥
वक्त्राणि ते त्वरमाणा विशन्ति दंष्ट्रा करालानि भयानकानि ।
केचिद्विलग्ना दशनान्तरेषु संदृश्यन्ते चूर्णितैरुत्तमाङ्गैः ॥११-२७॥

ami cha tvam dhritarashtrasya putrah
sarve sahaivavani pala sanghaih
bhishmo dronah suta putras tatha'sau
sahasmadeyair api yodha mukhyaih (11.26)
vaktrani te tvaramana vishanti
danshtra karalani bhayanakani
kechid vilagna dashanantharesu
sandhrishyante churnitair uttamangaih (11.27)

ami : those | cha : and | tvam : you | dhrtarastrasya : of Dhratarastra | putrah : sons | sarve : all | saha : with | eva : also | avani-pala : kings | sanghaih : groups/bands/hosts | bhisma : Pitamaha Bhishma | dronah : Dronacharya | suta-putrah : Karna | tatha : and | asau : that | saha : with | asmadiyai : our | api : also | yodha-mukhyai : chiefs of warriors | vaktrani : mouths | te : your | tvaramana : rushing | vishanti : entering | danstra : teeth | karalani : terrible | bhayanakani : fearful | kechit : some | vilagna : clinging | dashana-antaresu : between the teeth | sandrishyante : are seen | churnitai : smashed | uttama-angai : heads

(I am seeing that) all of them, the sons of Dhritarashtra along with the bands of kings (on their side) are entering into you and Bhishma Pitamaha, Dronacharya and that Karna as also those on our side with the warrior-chief sare all rushing into your mouths made fearful by the terrible teeth. Heads of some of them are seen clinging between the teeth and getting smashed.

(28)

यथा नदीनां बहवोऽम्बुवेगाः समुद्रमेवाभिमुखा द्रवन्ति ।
तथा तवामी नरलोकवीरा-विशन्ति वक्त्राण्यभिविज्वलन्ति ॥११-२८॥

yatha nadinam bahavo mbu vegah
samudram evabhimukhah dravanti
tatha tavami naraloka vira
vishanti vaktrany abhivijvalanti (11.28)

yatha : as | nadinam : of the rivers | bahava : the many/various | ambuvegah : waves of water | samudram : ocean | eva : verily | abhimukha : towards | dravanti : rush towards | tatha : and | tava : your | ami : all these | nara-loka-vira : kings of the people's world | vishanti : are entering | vaktrani : the mouths | abhivijvalanti : blazing

As the waves of the waters of various rivers verily rush towards the ocean, all these kings of the world of the people are entering your blazing mouth.

(29)

यथा प्रदीप्तं ज्वलनं पतङ्गाविशन्ति नाशाय समृद्धवेगाः ।
तथैव नाशाय विशन्ति लोका-स्तवापि वक्त्राणि समृद्धवेगाः ॥११-२९॥

yatha pradeptam jvalanam patanga
vishanti nashaya samriddha vegah
tathai va naashaya vishanti lokas
tavapi vaktrani samriddha vegah (11.29)

yatha : as | pradiptam : blazing | jvalanam : fire | patanga : moths | vishanti : enter | nashya : for destruction | samriddha : with full | vegah : speed | tatha-eva : in the same way | nasaya : for getting destroyed/dying | vishanti : are entering | loka : people | tava : your | api : also | vaktrani : mouths | samriddha-vegah : with full force/speed

(I am seeing) all the people rushing at full speed towards your mouth for getting destroyed just as the moths enter the blazing fire with full force only to die.

(30)

लेलिह्यसे ग्रसमानः समन्ता-ल्लोकान्समग्रान्वदनैर्ज्वलद्भिः ।
तेजोभिरापूर्य जगत्समग्रंभासस्तवोग्राः प्रतपन्ति विष्णो ॥११-३०॥

lelihyase grasamanah samantal lokan samagran vadanair jvaladbhih
tejobhir apurya jagat samagram bhasas tavograh pratapanti vishno (11.30)

lelihyase : licking repeatedly | grasamanah : devouring | samantat : from all sides | lokan : people/planets | samagran : all | vadanair : by the mouths | jvaladbhih : blazing | tejobhi : effulgence | apurya : covering | jagat : world | samagram : all | bhasa : rays | tava : your | ugrah : terrible | pratapanti : are scorching | vishno : O Lord Vishnu

O Lord Vishnu! (I see) you are devouring all the people in your blazing mouths, repeatedly licking them from all sides, covering the whole world with your effulgence and terrible scorching rays.

(31)

आख्याहि मे को भवानुग्ररूपोनमोऽस्तु ते देववर प्रसीद ।
विज्ञातुमिच्छामि भवन्तमाद्यं न हि प्रजानामि तव प्रवृत्तिम् ॥११-३१॥

akhyahi me ko bhavan ugra rupo
namo'stu te deva vara prasida
viyanatum ichchhami bhavantam adyam
na hi prajanami tava pravrittim (11.31)

akhyahi : speak/explain | me : to me | ka : who | bhavan : you | ugra-rupa : fierce form | nama astu : greetings | te : to you | deva-vara : great among gods | prasida : be pleased | viynatum : to know | ichchhami : I wish | bhavantam : you | adyam : original | na : not | hi : verily | prajanami : comprehend | tava : your | pravrttim : purpose

O the great among gods, of fierce form, please tell me who you are? Greetings to you. Please be pleased. You are the primal Lord. I wish to know you. Verily, I am not able to comprehend your purpose.

(32)

श्रीभगवानुवाच
कालोऽस्मि लोकक्षयकृत्प्रवृद्धो लोकान्समाहर्तुमिह प्रवृत्तः ।
ऋतेऽपि त्वां न भविष्यन्ति सर्वेयेऽवस्थिताः प्रत्यनीकेषु योधाः ॥११-३२॥

Shribhagavan uvacha
kalo'smi lokakshayakrit pravriddho
lokan samahartumiha pravrittah
ritepi tvam na bhavishyanti sarve
ye'vasthitah pratyanekeshu yodhah (11.32)

Shribhagavan uvacha : Lord Krishna said | kala : time | asmi : I am | loka : worlds | kshaya-krit : the destroyer | pravriddha : mighty | lokan : all people | samahartum : in destroying | iha : here/in this world | pravrittah : engaged | rite : without | api : even | tvam : you | na : never | bhavishyanti : will be | sarve : all | ye : who | avasthita : situated | prati-anikeshu : on the opposite side | yoddhah : warriors

Lord Krishna said : I am the mighty time, the great destroyer of the worlds. At this time, I am engaged in destroying these worlds. These warriors on the opposite side will not last even without you.

(33)

तस्मात्त्वमुत्तिष्ठ यशो लभस्व जित्वा शत्रून् भुङ्क्ष्व राज्यं समृद्धम् ।
मयैवैते निहताः पूर्वमेव निमित्तमात्रं भव सव्यसाचिन् ॥११-३३॥

tasmat tvam uttishtha yasho labhasva
jitva shatrun bhungkshva rajyam samriddham
mayaivaite nihatah purvam eva
nimitta matram bhava savya sachin (11.33)

tasmat : therefore | tvam : you | uttishtha : rise/get up | yasho : fame/glory | labhasva : gain | jitva : winning/conquering | shatrun : enemies | bhungkshva : enjoy | rajyam : kingdom | samriddham : flourishing/prosperous | maya : by me | eva : verily | ete : these | nihatahh : killed/slain | purvam eva : pre-ordained | nimitta-matram : only the excuse/means/instrument | bhava : become | savya-sachin : O Savyasachi (good left-handed archer, Arjuna)

Therefore, O good archer, Arjuna! Arise achieve glory by conquering your enemies and enjoy a prosperous kingdom. Verily, all these warriors already stand slain by me, you are becoming only an instrument.

(34)

द्रोणं च भीष्मं च जयद्रथं चकर्णं तथान्यानपि योधवीरान् ।
मया हतांस्त्वं जहि मा व्यथिष्ठा युध्यस्व जेतासि रणे सपत्नान् ॥११-३४॥

dronam cha bhishmam cha jayadratham cha
karnam tatha'nyanapi yodha viran
maya hatamstvam jahi ma vyathishtha
yudhyasva jetasi rane sapatnan (11.34)

dronam : Dronacharya | cha : also | bhishma : Bhishma Pitamaha | cha : also | jayadratham : Jayadratha | karnam : Karna | tatha : and | anyan : others | api : also | yoddha-viran : great fighters | maya : by me | hatan : killed | tvam : you | jahi : destroy | ma : do not | vyathishtha : be disturbed | yudhyasva : just fight | jeta asi : you will conquer | rane : in the fight | sapatnan : enemies

O Arjuna! Destroy Dronacharya, Bhishma Pitamaha, Jayadratha, Karna and other great warriors. They have all been already killed by me. Do not be disturbed, just fight. You will conquer the enemies in the fight.

(35)

संजय उवाच
एतच्छ्रुत्वा वचनं केशवस्य कृताञ्जलिर्वेपमानः किरीटी ।
नमस्कृत्वा भूय एवाह कृष्णं सगद्गदं भीतभीतः प्रणम्य ॥११-३५॥

sanjaya uvacha
etachchhrutva vachanam keshavasya
kritanjalir vepamanah kirete
namaskritva bhuya evaha krishnam
sa gadgadam bhita-bhitah pranamya (11.35)

sanjaya : Sanjaya | uvacha : said | etat : thus | shrutva : hearing | vachanam : speech | keshavasya : of Keshava (Lord Krishna) | krita-anjali : with folded hands | vepamanah : trembling | kiriti : Crown-wearing Arjuna | namaskritva : after offering greetings | bhuya : again | eva : also | aha : said | krishnam :

unto Krishna | sa-gadgadam : with a faltering (choked with emotion) voice | bhita-bhitah : fearful | pranamya : offering respectful greetings

Sanjaya said: Hearing these words of Lord Krishna, trembling Arjuna greeted Him with folded hands and in a faltering (choked with emotion) voice, fearfully bowing down, again said to him.

(36)
अर्जुन उवाच
स्थाने हृषीकेश तव प्रकीर्त्या जगत्प्रहृष्यत्यनुरज्यते च ।
रक्षांसि भीतानि दिशो द्रवन्तिसर्वे नमस्यन्ति च सिद्धसंघाः ॥११-३६॥

arjuna uvacha
sthane hrishikesha tava prakertiya
jagat prahrishyaty anurajyate cha
rakshansi bhitani disho dravanti
sarve namasyanti cha siddha sanghah (11.36)

arjuna uvacha : Arjuna said | sthane : rightly/it is only proper | hrishikesha : master of senses, Lord Krishna | tava : your | prakirtya : praises | jagat : world | prahrshyati : is rejoicing/is delighted | anurajyate : is getting attached | cha : and | rakshansi : the demons | bhitani : out of fear | dishah : directions | dravanti : are fleeing | sarve : all | namasyanti : are offering respects | cha : also | siddha-sanghah : hosts of Siddhas (noble/realised souls)

Arjuna said: O master of the senses, Lord Krishna! It is only proper that the world takes delight in singing your praises, the demons flee in fear in different directions and hosts of Siddhas (noble souls) are bowing down to offer respects.

(37)
कस्माच्च ते न नमेरन्महात्मन् गरीयसे ब्रह्मणोऽप्यादिकर्त्रे ।
अनन्त देवेश जगन्निवास त्वमक्षरं सदसत्तत्परं यत् ॥११-३७॥

kasmachcha te na nameran mahatman
gareyase brahmano'py adi kartre
ananta devesha jagan nivasa
tvam aksharam sad asat tat param yat (11.37)

kasmat : why/how | cha : also | te : for you | na : not | nameran : show respect/pay obeisance | maha-atman : great soul | gariyase : better/greater | brahmana : than Brahma | api : also | adi-kartre : to the creator | ananta : unlimited/infinite | deva-isha : God of gods | jagat-nivasa : abode of the universe | tvam : you | aksharam : imperishable | sat-asat : truth and falsehood/good and evil | tat param : transcendental/beyond that | yat : that

How is it possible not to pay obeisance to you, O great soul, you are greater than Brahma and also his creator. O the infinite, God of gods, the abode of the universe, you only are that imperishable one who is beyond good and evil (being and non-being).

(38)

त्वमादिदेवः पुरुषः पुराण-स्त्वमस्य विश्वस्य परं निधानम् ।
वेत्तासि वेद्यं च परं च धाम त्वया ततं विश्वमनन्तरूप ॥११-३८॥

tvam adi devah purushah puranas
tvamasya vishvasya param nidhanam
vettasi vedyam cha param cha dhama
tvaya tatam vishvam ananta rupa (11.38)

tvam : you | adi-devah : the primeval God | purushah : Purusha | puranah : old/ancient | tvam : you | asya : of this | vishvasya : universe | param : ultimate | nidhanam : refuge/sanctuary | vetta : knower | asi : you are | vedyam : the knowable | cha : and | param : final/supreme | cha : and | dhama : shelter/abode/destination/goal | tvaya : by you | tatam : permeated | vishvam : universe | ananta-rupa : infinite form

You are the primeval God and ancient Purusha. You are the ultimate sanctuary of this universe. You are the knower and all that is knowable. You are the supreme destination. O infinite (cosmic) form! This universe is permeated by you.

(39)
वायुर्यमोऽग्निर्वरुणः शशाङ्कः प्रजापतिस्त्वं प्रपितामहश्च ।
नमो नमस्तेऽस्तु सहस्रकृत्वः पुनश्च भूयोऽपि नमो नमस्ते ॥११-३९॥

vayu ryamo 'gnir varunah shashankah
prajapatis tvam prapitamahash cha
namo namas te' stu sahasra kritvah
punash cha bhuyo'pi namo namaste (11.39)

vayu : air | Yama : the destroyer/god of death | agni : fire | varuna : water | shasha-anka : the moon | prajapati : Brahma | tvam : you | prapitamaha : the great-grandfather | cha : and | nama : respects | namah : again my respects | te : to you | astu : so it be | sahasra-kritva : a thousand times | puna : again | cha : and | bhuya : again | api : also | nama : offering respects | namaste : obeisance to you

You are the air, the destroyer, the fire, the water, the moon, lord of the people - Brahma and the great-grandfather, I bow to you and pay my respects again and again, my obeisance to you again and again.

(40)
नमः पुरस्तादथ पृष्ठतस्तेनमोऽस्तु ते सर्वत एव सर्व ।
अनन्तवीर्यामितविक्रमस्त्वं सर्वं समाप्नोषि ततोऽसि सर्वः ॥११-४०॥

namah purastad atha prishthatas te
namostu te sarvata eva sarva
ananta veryamita vikramas tvam
sarvam samapnoshi tato'si sarvah (11.40)

namah : offering respects | purastat : from the front | atha : also | prishthata : from behind | te : to you | nama astu : offer my respects | te : to you | sarvatah eva : from all sides | sarva : all/everything | ananta-virya : unlimited potency/capacity/prowess | amita-vikrama : unlimited valour | tvam : you | sarvam : everything | samapnosi : pervades | tatah : wherefore | asi : you are | sarvah : everything

O Lord with unlimited prowess! Respects to you from the front and from behind; O universal Self, for you obeisance from all sides. You are possessed of unlimited valour, you permeate the entire universe. Wherefore, you are everything.

(41- 42)
सखेति मत्वा प्रसभं यदुक्तं हे कृष्ण हे यादव हे सखेति ।
अजानता महिमानं तवेदमया प्रमादात्प्रणयेन वापि ॥११-४१॥
यच्चावहासार्थमसत्कृतोऽसि विहारशय्यासनभोजनेषु ।
एकोऽथवाप्यच्युत तत्समक्षं तत्क्षामये त्वामहमप्रमेयम् ॥११-४२॥

sakheti matva prasabham yad uktam
he krishna he yadava he sakheti
ajanata mahimanam tavedam
maya pramadat pranayena vapi (11.41)
yach chavahasartham asat krit' si
vihara shayyasana bhojaneshu
eko'tha vapy achyuta tat samaksham
tat kshamaye tvam aham aprameyam (11.42)

sakha : friend | iti : thus | matva : assuming/considering/taking | prasabham : presumptuously | yat : whatever | uktam : said | he krishna : O Lord Krishna | he yadava : O Yadava | he sakhe : O my friend | iti : thus | ajanata : not knowing/oblivious of | mahimanam : glories/greatness | tava : your | idam : this | maya : by me | pramadat : in mindlessness | pranayena : out of affection | va api : or merely | yat : whatever | cha : also | avahasa-artham : for fun/only in humour/just in jest | asat-kritah : insulted/dishonoured/slighted | asi : have been | vihara : relaxing | shayya : in bed | asana : sitting | bhojaneshu : while eating | ekah : alone | athava : or | api : also/even | achyuta : infallible one | tat-samaksham : in their presence | tat : that | kshamaye : beg to be excused | tvam : from you | aham : I | aprameyam : incomprehensible

O Infallible One, Lord Krishna! Oblivious of your greatness and this (cosmic form of yours) and taking you to be my friend, out of affection or in sheer mindlessness, I kept addressing you presumptuously as 'O Krishna!', 'O Yadava!', 'O friend' and so on whatever. Also, while you were walking, in bed, sitting or eating, alone or even in the presence of your friends, merely for fun, I have been disrespectful to you. For all that, O incomprehensible one, I seek your pardon.

(43)
पितासि लोकस्य चराचरस्य त्वमस्य पूज्यश्च गुरुर्गरीयान् ।
न त्वत्समोऽस्त्यभ्यधिकः कुतोऽन्योलोकत्रयेऽप्यप्रतिमप्रभाव ॥११-४३॥

pitasi lokasya characharasya
tvam asya pujyash cha gurur gariyan
na tvat samo sty abhyadhikah kuto' nyo
loka traye'py apratima prabhava (11.43)

pita : father | asi : you are | lokasya : of the world | chara : moving | acharasya : non-moving | tvam : you | asya : of this | pujyah : venerable/worship worthy | cha : and | guru : spiritual master | gariyan : glorious/great | na : never | tvat-samana : equal to you/like you | asti : is | abhyadhikah : greater | kutah : where/how | anyah : other | loka-traye : in the three planets | api : also | apratima-prabhava : unique power

You are father of the world, of all the moving and the non-moving. You are the great and venerable spiritual master. O one with unique powers! in all the three planets there is none equal to you, where then is the question of anyone being greater?

(44)
तस्मात्प्रणम्य प्रणिधाय कायं प्रसादये त्वामहमीशमीड्यम् ।
पितेव पुत्रस्य सखेव सख्युः प्रियः प्रियायार्हसि देव सोढुम् ॥११-४४॥

tasmat pranamya pranidhaya kayam
prasadaye tvam aham isham idyam
piteva putrasya sakheva sakhyuh
priyah priyayarhasi deva sodhum (11.44)

tasmat : therefore | pranamya : saluting | pranidhaya : prostrating | kayam : the body | prasadaye : to beg mercy | tvam : you | aham : I | isam : the God head | idyam : adorable | pita iva : like father | putrasya : the son | sakha-iva : like friend | sakhyuh : the friend | priyah : lover | priyayah : the beloved | arhasi : you should | deva : my Lord | sodhum : tolerate me

So, after prostrating the body at your feet and saluting you, I pray to you, my adorable Lord, to be pleased. As the father tolerates the son, friend tolerates the friend and the lover tolerates the beloved, I beg of you to forgive me and tolerate me.

(45)

अदृष्टपूर्वं हृषितोऽस्मि दृष्ट्वाभयेन च प्रव्यथितं मनो मे ।
तदेव मे दर्शय देव रूपंप्रसीद देवेश जगन्निवास ॥११-४५॥

adrishta purvam hrishito 'smi drishtva
bhayena cha pravyathitam mano me
tad eva me darshaya deva rupam
prasida devesha jagan nivasa (11.45)

adriasta-purvam : not seen before | hristah : gladdened/thrilled | asmi : I am | drishtva : by seeing | bhayena : out of fear | cha : and | pravyathitam : disturbed | manah : mind | me : my | tat : that | eva : certainly | me : to me | darshaya : show | deva : divine | rupam : form | prasida : be pleased/be gracious | deva-isa : O Lord of Lords/God of gods | jagat-nivasa : O abode of the universe

After seeing your universal (cosmic) form like of which I had never seen before, I am thrilled. Also, my mind is certainly very much disturbed with fear. (Therefore) O God of gods, abode of the universe, be pleased and once again show me (Your normal divine form).

(46)

किरीटिनं गदिनं चक्रहस्त-मिच्छामि त्वां द्रष्टुमहं तथैव ।
तेनैव रूपेण चतुर्भुजेनसहस्रबाहो भव विश्वमूर्ते ॥११-४६॥

kiritinam gadinam chakrahastam
ichchhaami tvam drashtumaham tathaiva
tenaiva rupena chatur bhujena
sahasra baaho bhava vishva murte (11.46)

kiritinam : helmet/crown | gadinam : with mace | chakra-hastam : disc in hand | icchami : I wish | tvam : you | drastum : to see | aham : I | tatha eva : in that position | tena eva : in that | rupena : form | chatuhbhujena :

four-handed | sahasra-baho : one with a thousand arms | bhava : become | visva-murte : the universal form

I wish to see you as before with the crown on your head and mace and disc in your hands. O Lord! Do appear in that universal form with a thousand arms and four-hands.

(47)

श्रीभगवानुवाच
मया प्रसन्नेन तवार्जुनेदं रूपं परं दर्शितमात्मयोगात् ।
तेजोमयं विश्वमनन्तमाद्यं यन्मे त्वदन्येन न दृष्टपूर्वम् ॥११-४७॥

Shribhagavan uvacha
maya prasannena tavarjunedam
rupam param darshitam atma yogat
tejo mayam vishvam anantam adhyam
yan me tvad anyena na drishta purvam (11.47)

Shribhagavan : God | uvacha : said | maya : me | prasannena : happily/gladly | tava : to you | arjuna : O Arjuna | idam : this | rupam : form | param : supreme | darshitam : shown | atma-yogat : my yogic powers | teja-mayam : full of radiance | vishvam : universe | anantam : infinite | adyam : original | yat : which | me : my | tvat anyena : other than you | na drishtva-purvam : never previously seen by anyone before

Lord Krishna said: O Arjuna! Using my yogic powers I have shown to you gladly this, my supreme universal form full of radiance, beginning of all, infinite, grand cosmic form which no one else (other than Arjuna) had ever seen.

(48)

न वेदयज्ञाध्ययनैर्न दानै-र्न च क्रियाभिर्न तपोभिरुग्रैः ।
एवंरूपः शक्य अहं नृलोकेद्रष्टुं त्वदन्येन कुरुप्रवीर ॥११-४८॥

na veda yajnaadhyayanairna daanair
na cha kriyaabhir na tapobhir ugraih
evam roopah shakya aham nri
loke drashtum twad anyena kuru pravira (11.48)

na : never | veda-yajna : by sacrifice | adhyayanai : study of vedas | na : never | danai : through charity | na : never | cha : and | kriyabhi : by pious acts | na : never | tapobhi : by penance | ugrai : severe | evam-rupa : in this form | shakya : can | aham : I | nri-loke : in this world | drastum : be seen | tvat : you | anyena : by another | kuru-pravira : best among Kuru warriors

O the best among the Kuru warriors, Arjuna! In this world none other than you can see me in this universal form of mine because it can never be done by offering sacrifices to fire, by studying Vedas, by charity, by doing pious acts or by severe penances.

(49)

मा ते व्यथा मा च विमूढभावो दृष्ट्वा रूपं घोरमीदृङ्ममेदम् ।
व्यपेतभीः प्रीतमनाः पुनस्त्वं तदेव मे रूपमिदं प्रपश्य ॥ ११- ४९॥

maa te vyatha maa cha vimudha bhavo
drishtva rupam ghoram idrin mamedam
vyapeta bhih prita manah punas tvam
tad eva me rupam idam prapashya (11.49)

ma : never let it be | te : to you | vyatha : pain/suffering | ma : never let it come about | cha : also | vimudha-bhava : delusion | drishtva : by seeing | rupam : form | ghoram : terrible | idrk : as it is | mama : my | idam : this | vyapeta-bhi : free from fear | prita-manah : glad at heart | puna : again | tvam : you | tat : that | eva : thus | me : my | rupam : form | idam : this | prapashya : see

By seeing this terrible form of mine you should never let yourself be subjected to suffering nor should you let delusion overtake you, again feel free from fear and glad at heart and see me in this usual form of mine.

(50)

संजय उवाच
इत्यर्जुनं वासुदेवस्तथोक्त्वा स्वकं रूपं दर्शयामास भूयः।
आश्वासयामास च भीतमेनं भूत्वा पुनः सौम्यवपुर्महात्मा ॥११-५०॥

sanjaya uvacha
ity arjunam vasudevas tathoktva
svakam rupam darshayamasa bhuyah
ashvasayam asa cha bhitam enam
bhutva punah saumya vapur mahatma (11.50)

sanjaya uvacha : Sanjaya said | iti :thus | arjunam : to Arjuna | vasudeva : Lord Krishna | tatha : that way | uktva : speaking | svakam : his own | rupam : form | darshayam asa : showed | bhuyah : again | ashvasayam asa : assured/encouraged | cha : and | bhitam : afraid/fearful | enam : him | bhutva : becoming | punah : again | saumya vapur : lovely form | maha-atma : the great soul

Sanjaya said: Speaking thus to Arjuna, Lord Krishna again showed his (usual human) figure and again the great soul assumed his lovely form and reassured the fearful Arjuna.

(51)

अर्जुन उवाच
दृष्ट्वेदं मानुषं रूपं तव सौम्यं जनार्दन।
इदानीमस्मि संवृत्तः सचेताः प्रकृतिं गतः ॥११-५१॥

arjuna uvacha
drishtvedam manusham rupam tava saumyam janardana
idanimasmi samvrittah sachetah prakritim gatah (11.51)

arjuna uvacha : Arjuna said | drishtva : seeing | idam : this | manusham : human | rupam : form | tava : your | saumyam : very lovely | janardana : Janardana, Lord Krishna | idanim : now | asmi : I am | samvrittah : settled/stable | sa-chetah : in my consciousness | prakritim : to my nature | gatah : gone/returned

Seeing Lord Krishna in his usual human form, Arjuna said: O Janardana, Lord Krishna! Seeing you in this serene human form, now I find my mind is settled and I am back to my original nature.

(52)
श्रीभगवानुवाच
सुदुर्दर्शमिदं रूपं दृष्टवानसि यन्मम ।
देवा अप्यस्य रूपस्य नित्यं दर्शनकाङ्क्षिणः ॥११-५२॥

Sribhagavan uvacha
su durdarsham idam rupam drishtvanasi yanmama
devapyasya rupasya nityam darshana kangkshinah (11.52)

Shribhagavan uvacha : Lord Krishna said | sudurdarsham : one difficult to be seen | idam : this | rupam : form | drishtavan asi : as seen by you | yat : which | mama : of mine | devah : gods | api : also | asya : this | rupasya : form | nityam : eternally | darshana-kankshinah : anxious to see

Lord Krishna said: It is extremely rare to see the form of mine that you have seen. Even gods are eternally anxious to see it.

(53)
नाहं वेदैर्न तपसा न दानेन न चेज्यया ।
शक्य एवंविधो द्रष्टुं दृष्टवानसि मां यथा ॥११-५३॥

naa ham vedairna tapasaa na danena na chejyaya
shakya evamvidho drashtum drishtavanasi mam yatha (11.53)

na : never/not | aham : I | vedai : by the study of Vedas | na : not | tapasa : by penances | na : not | danena : by charity | na : not | cha : also | ijyaya : by worship/sacrifices in fire | shakya : can | evam-vidha : in this way | drashtum : to see | drishtavan : seeing | asi : you are | mam : me | yatha : as

In this way as you have seen me, I can never be seen by the study of Vedas, not by penances, not by charity, also not by worship.

(54)

भक्त्या त्वनन्यया शक्य अहमेवंविधोऽर्जुन ।
ज्ञातुं द्रष्टुं च तत्त्वेन प्रवेष्टुं च परंतप ॥११-५४॥

bhaktya tu ananyaya shakya aham evam vidho arjuna
gyatum drashtum cha tattvena praveshtum cha parantapa (11.54)

bhaktya : by devotion | tu : but | ananyaya : single-minded | shakya : possible | aham : I | evam-vidha : this way/ in this manner | arjuna : O Arjuna | gyatum : to know | drashtum : to see | cha : and | tattvena : in essence | praveshtum : to enter into/to realise | cha : also | parantapa : scorcher of enemies

But, O scorcher of enemies, Arjuna! This way, by single-minded devotion, it is possible to know, to see and, in essence, also to enter into me (in this cosmic form).

(55)

मत्कर्मकृन्मत्परमो मद्भक्तः सङ्गवर्जितः ।
निर्वैरः सर्वभूतेषु यः स मामेति पाण्डव ॥११-५५॥

mat karma-krin mat-paramo madbhaktah sangavarjitah
nirvairah sarva-bhuteshu yah sa mam eti pandava (11.55)

mat : my | karma : action/work | krit : doing | mat : me | param : supreme | mat : me | bhaktah : devotion | sanga-varjitah : without attachment to fruits of action | nirvairah : without opposition/with no enemies | sarva-bhutesu : all living beings | yah : who | sa : he | mam : me | eti : comes/reaches | pandava : O son of Pandu, Arjuna

O son of Pandu, Arjuna! One who performs all his acts only for me, regards me as supreme, is devoted to me, is not attached to fruits of action and who is devoid of any ill-will (or feelings of enmity) towards any living beings, only such a person reaches me.

Thus ends the Eleventh Canto titled 'Vision of the Universal Form'.

Twelfth Canto

BHAKTI YOGA
Yoga of Devotion

(1)

अर्जुनउवाच
एवं सततयुक्ता ये भक्तास्त्वां पर्युपासते।
ये चाप्यक्षरमव्यक्तं तेषां के योगवित्तमाः॥१२-१॥

Arjunauvacha
evam satata-yukta ye bhaktas tvam paryupasate
ye chapy aksharam avyaktam teshamke yoga-vittamah (12.1)

arjuna : Arjuna | uvacha : said | evam : thus | satata : always/constantly | yukta : engaged | ye : those | bhakta : devotees | tvam : you | paryupasate : worship | ye : those | cha : and | api : only/also/again | aksharam : indestructible/immortal/imperishable | avyaktam : unmanifest | tesham : among them | ke : who | yoga-vit-tamah : well-versed in the knowledge of yoga

Arjuna said : Among those devotees who are thus (as stated earlier) all the time engaged in worshipping you and those who believe only in the imperishable and unmanifest (impersonal), who is better-versed in the knowledge of yoga.

(2)

श्रीभगवानुवाच
मय्यावेश्य मनो ये मां नित्ययुक्ता उपासते।
श्रद्धया परयोपेतास्ते मे युक्ततमा मताः॥१२-२॥

Shribhagavan uvacha
mayyaveshyamano ye mam nitya-yuktaupasate
shraddhayaparayopetaste me yuktatamamatah (12.2)

Shribhagavan : Lord Krishna | uvacha : said | mayi : on me | aveshya : fixing/concentrating | mana : mind | ye : those | mam : me | nitya : all the time/constantly | yuktah : engaged | upasate : worship | shraddhaya : with faith/

devotion | paraya : supreme/highest | upetah : equipped with/endowed with | te : they | me : by me | yukta-tama : best of yogis | matah : regarded/accepted

Lord Krishna said: Those who fix their mind on me all the time remain engaged in worshiping me with the highest devotion are regarded by me as the best of yogis.

(3-4)

ये त्वक्षरमनिर्देश्यमव्यक्तं पर्युपासते।
सर्वत्रगमचिन्त्यं च कूटस्थमचलं ध्रुवम्॥ १२- ३॥
संनियम्येन्द्रियग्रामं सर्वत्र समबुद्धयः।
ते प्राप्नुवन्ति मामेव सर्वभूतहिते रताः॥ १२- ४॥

*ye tv aksharam anirdeshyam avyaktam paryupasate
sarvatra-gam achintyam cha kuta-stham achalamdhruvam (12.3)
sanniyamyendriya-gramam sarvatra sama-buddhayah
te prapnuvanti mam eva sarva-bhuta-hite ratah (13.4)*

ye : those | tu : but | aksharam : imperishable | anirdeshyam : indefinite/directionless/indescribable/undefinable | avyaktam : unmanifest | paryupasate : worship | sarvatra-gam : all pervading/omnipresent | achintyam : unthinkable/inconceivable | cha : and | kuta-stham : unchanging | achalam : immovable | dhruvam : constant/eternal | sanniyamya : bringing under proper control/having appropriately subdued | indriya-gramam : group of senses | sarvatra : everywhere | sama-buddhayah : of similar thinking/even-minded | te : they | prapnuvanti : attain/reach | mam : me | eva : certainly | sarva-bhuta-hite : for the welfare of all living beings | ratah : engaged

But, those who, after appropriately controlling their senses, remaining even-minded and engaged in the welfare of all living beings everywhere, worship the imperishable, indescribable, unmanifest, omnipresent, inconceivable, unchanging, immovable and eternal, they certainly reach only me.

(5)

क्लेशोऽधिकतरस्तेषामव्यक्तासक्तचेतसाम्।
अव्यक्ता हि गतिर्दुःखं देहवद्भिरवाप्यते॥१२-५॥

klesho 'dhikataras tesham avyaktasakta-chetasam
avyakta hi gatir duhkham dehavadbhir avapyate (12.5)

klesha : trouble | adhika-tara : greater | tesham : those | avyakta : unmanifest | asakta : attached | chetasam : mind | avyakta : unmanifest | hi : certainly | gati : movement/speed/goal/progress | duhkham : sorrow/pain | deha-vadbhi : with a body | avapyate : is achieved

Those whose minds are attached to the unmanifest certainly face greater trouble because it is difficult for the embodied to achieve the goal of the unmanifest.

(6-7)

ये तु सर्वाणि कर्माणि मयि संन्यस्य मत्पराः।
अनन्येनैव योगेन मां ध्यायन्त उपासते॥१२-६॥
तेषामहं समुद्धर्ता मृत्युसंसारसागरात्।
भवामि न चिरात्पार्थ मय्यावेशितचेतसाम्॥१२-७॥

ye tu sarvani karmani mayi sannyasya mat-parah
ananyenaiva yogena mam dhyayanta upasate (12.6)
tesham aham samuddharta mrityu-samsara-sagarat
bhavami na chirat partha mayy aveshita-chetasam (12.7)

ye : who | tu : but | sarvani : all | karmani : acts | mayi : in me | sannyasya : giving up/renouncing | mat-para : devoted to me | ananyena : single-minded | eva : certainly/verily | yogena : by yoga | mam : me | dhyayanta : meditating | upasate : worship | tesham : them | aham : I | samuddharta : saviour/deliverer | mrityu : death/mortal | samsara : world | sagarat : from the ocean | bhavami : become | na : not | chirat : for a long time | partha : O son of Pratha, Arjuna ! | mayi : on me | aveshita : fixed | chetasam : of those minds

But, those who worship me, renounce all their acts to me, are single-minded in their devotion to me, meditate on me by yoga and whose minds are fixed on me, O son of Pratha, Arjuna! Verily, I do not take long to become their saviour from the ocean of this mortal world.

(8)

मय्येव मन आधत्स्व मयि बुद्धिं निवेशय।
निवसिष्यसि मय्येव अत ऊर्ध्वं न संशयः॥१२- ८॥

mayy eva mana adhatsva mayi buddhim niveshaya
nivasishyasi mayy eva ata urdhvam na sanshayah (12.8)

mayi : on me | eva : only | mana : mind | adhatsva : fix | mayi : in me | buddhim : intellect | niveshaya : place/invest | nivasishyasi : you will reside | mayi : in me | eva : only | atahurdhvam : hereafter | na : no | sanshayah : doubt

Fix your mind on only me and invest your intelligence in me, no doubt, hereafter (always) you will reside in me only.

(9)

अथ चित्तं समाधातुं न शक्नोषि मयि स्थिरम्।
अभ्यासयोगेन ततो मामिच्छाप्तुं धनंजय॥१२- ९॥

atha chittam samadhatum na shaknoshi mayi sthiram
abhyasa-yogena tato mam ichchhaptum dhananjaya (12.9)

atha : if | chittam : mind | samadhatum : to fix | na : not | shaknoshi : able to/can | mayi : on me | sthiram : steadily | abhyasa-yogena : by the practice of yoga | tata : then | mam : me | ichchha : wish/desire/hope | aptum : to get/reach | dhanan-jaya : winner of wealth, Arjuna

O winner of wealth, Arjuna! If you cannot fix your mind steadily on me, then you may hope to reach me by the practice of yoga.

(10)

अभ्यासेऽप्यसमर्थोऽसि मत्कर्मपरमो भव।
मदर्थमपि कर्माणि कुर्वन्सिद्धिमवाप्स्यसि॥१२- १०॥

abhyase 'py asamartho 'si mat-karma-paramo bhava
mad-artham api karmani kurvan siddhim avapsyasi (12.10)

abhyase : by practice | api : also/even | asamartha : unable | asi : are | mat-karma-parama : doing all action for my sake | bhava : become | mat-artham : for me | api : even | karmani : acts | kurvan : doing/performing | siddhim : perfection | avapsyasi : will reach

If you are unable to practice also, you can do all your acts for my sake. Even by acting for my sake, you can achieve perfection (and reach me).

(11)
अथैतदप्यशक्तोऽसि कर्तुं मद्योगमाश्रितः।
सर्वकर्मफलत्यागं ततः कुरु यतात्मवान्॥१२-११॥

athaitad apy ashakto 'si kartum mad-yogam ashritah
sarva-karma-phala-tyagam tatah kuru yatatmavan (12.11)

atha : if | etat : this | api : also/even | ashakta : unable to do | asi : you are | kartum : to do | madyogam : refuge in me | ashrita : dependent | sarva-karma : of all acts | phala : result/fruits | tyagam : sacrifice/renunciation | tata : then | kuru : do | yata-atma-van : self-controlled

If you are unable to do even this, depend on refuge in me, renounce fruits of all action and do self-control.

(12)
श्रेयो हि ज्ञानमभ्यासाज्ज्ञानाद्ध्यानं विशिष्यते।
ध्यानात्कर्मफलत्यागस्त्यागाच्छान्तिरनन्तरम्॥१२-१२॥

shreyo hi gynanam abhyasaj gyananad dhyanam vishishyate
dhyanat karma-phala-tyagas tyagach chhantir anantaram (10.12)

shreya : better | hi : certainly | gyananam : knowledge | abhyasat : than practice | gynanat : than knowledge | dhyanam : meditation | vishishyate : is specially valued | dhyanat : than meditation | karma-phala-tyagah : renunciation of fruits of all action | tyagat : from renunciation | shanti : peace | anantaram : thereafter/immediately

Knowledge is certainly better than practice, meditation is more specially valued than knowledge, renunciation of fruits of all action is superior to meditation. From renunciation follows peace.

(13-14)

अद्वेष्टा सर्वभूतानां मैत्रः करुण एव च।
निर्ममो निरहंकारः समदुःखसुखः क्षमी॥१२-१३॥
संतुष्टः सततं योगी यतात्मा दृढनिश्चयः।
मय्यर्पितमनोबुद्धिर्यो मद्भक्तः स मे प्रियः॥१२-१४॥

adveshta sarva-bhutanam maitrah karuna eva cha
nirmamo nirahankarah sama-duhkha-sukhah kshami (12.13)
santushtah satatam yogi yatatma dridha-nishchayah
mayy arpita-mano-buddhir yo mad-bhaktah sa me priyah (12.14)

adveshta : free from envy/hatred/ill feelings | sarva-bhutanam : for all living beings | maitrah : friendliness | karuna : compassion | eva : certainly | cha : and/also | nirmama : free from feelings of I and mine | nirahankarah : without false ego | sama : equal/same | duhkha : in sorrow/pain/distress | sukhah : in pleasure/happiness | kshami : forgiving/forbearing/tolerant | santushtah : satisfied/contented | satatam : always | yogi : practitioner of yoga | yata-atma : self-controlled | dridhanishchayah : strong-willed/with determination | mayi : in me | arpita : set on/devoted to/fixed/settled | mana : mind | buddhi : intelligence | ya : who | mat bhaktah : my devotee | sa : he | me : to me | priyah : dear

He who has no ill feelings towards any living being, is friendly and compassionate to all and also free from feelings of I and mine and false ego, is same in pleasure and pain, is always forgiving and contented, practitioner of yoga, self-controlled, strong-willed, of settled mind and intelligence and who is my devotee, such a person is dear to me.

(15)

यस्मान्नोद्विजते लोको लोकान्नोद्विजते च यः।
हर्षामर्षभयोद्वेगैर्मुक्तो यः स च मे प्रियः॥१२-१५॥

yasman nodvijate loko lokan nodvijate cha yah
harshamarsha-bhayodvegair mukto yah sa cha me priyah (12.15)

yasmat : by whom | na : not | udvijate : are agitated/afflicted | loka : people | lokat : by people | na : not | udvijate : is disturbed/agitated | cha : and | yah : who | harsha : happiness/joy | amarsha : envy | bhaya : fear | udvegai : anxiety | mukta : freed from | yah : who | sa : he | cha : also | me : to me | priyah : dear

One by whom the people are not agitated and who does not agitate the people, also who is freed from joy, envy, fear and anxiety, he is dear to me.

(16)
अनपेक्षः शुचिर्दक्ष उदासीनो गतव्यथः।
सर्वारम्भपरित्यागी यो मद्भक्तः स मे प्रियः॥१२-१६॥

anapekshah shuchir daksha udasino gata-vyathah
sarvarambha-parityagi yo mad-bhaktah sa me priyah (11.16)

anapeksha : neutral/independent | shuchi : pure | daksha : expert/competent | udasina : indifferent/unconcerned | gata-vyathah : freed from sorrow | sarva-arambha : of all beginnings/commencements/undertakings | parityagi : renouncer | ya : who | madbhaktah : my devotee | sa : he | me : to me | pariyah : dear

One who is independent, pure, competent, unconcerned, freed from sorrow, renouncer of all undertakings and who is my devotee is dear to me.

(17)
यो न हृष्यति न द्वेष्टि न शोचति न काङ्क्षति।
शुभाशुभपरित्यागी भक्तिमान्यः स मे प्रियः॥१२-१६॥

yo na hrshyati na dveshti na shochati na kankshati
shubhashubha-parityagi bhaktiman yah sa me priyah (11.17)

ya : who | na : never | hrshyati : enjoys/rejoices | na : never | dvesti : hates/detests/grieves | na : never | shochati : laments | na : never | kankshati : wishes/desires | shubha : auspicious | ashubha : inauspicious | parityagi : renouncer | bhakti-man : devotee | yah : who | sa : he | me : to me | priyah : dear

One who never rejoices, never hates (anyone), never laments, never desires (anything), renounces both the auspicious and the inauspicious and who is my devotee is dear to me.

(18 - 19)
समः शत्रौ च मित्रे च तथा मानापमानयोः।
शीतोष्णसुखदुःखेषु समः सङ्गविवर्जितः॥१२- १८॥
तुल्यनिन्दास्तुतिर्मौनी सन्तुष्टो येन केनचित्।
अनिकेतः स्थिरमतिर्भक्तिमान्मे प्रियो नरः॥१२- १९॥

*samh ahshatrau cha mitre cha tatha manapamanayoh
shitoshna-sukha-duhkheshu samah sanga-vivarjitah (12.18)
tulya-ninda-stutir mauni santushto yena kenachit
aniketah sthira-matir bhaktiman me priyo narah (12.19)*

samah : equal/same | shatrau : to enemy | cha : and | mitre : to a friend | cha : also | tatha : and | mana : honour | apamana : dishonor | shita : in cold | ushna : heat | sukha : happiness/joy | duhkheshu : in sorrow | samah : equipoised | sanga-vivarjitah : free from all attachment | tulya : equal | ninda : defamation | stuti : praise | mauni : silent | santushta : satisfied/contented | yenakenachit : with anything | aniketah : without a residence | sthira : fixed/steadfast | mati : determination | bhakti-man : devotee | me : to me | priya : dear | narah : man

One who is the same to an enemy and to a friend, equipoised in honour and dishonour, in cold and in heat, in joy and sorrow, free from all attachment, equal in defamation and praise, silent, satisfied with anything, having no residence, steadfast and determined, such a devotee is dear to me.

(20)
ये तु धर्म्यामृतमिदं यथोक्तं पर्युपासते।
श्रद्दधाना मत्परमा भक्तास्तेऽतीव मे प्रियाः॥१२- २०॥

*ye tu dharma mrtam idam yathoktam paryupasate
shraddadhana mat-parama bhaktas te 'tiva me priyah (12.20)*

ye : who | tu : really | dharma : righteousness | amrtam : nectar | idam : this | yatha : as | uktam : said/stated | paryupasate : follow | shraddadhana : with faith | mat-parama : taking me as the Supreme | bhakta : devotees | te : they | ativa : very much | me : to me | priyah : dear

Those who really follow this path of nectar of dharma as stated, with faith and take me as the Supreme, such devotees are very much dear to me.

Thus ends the Twelfth Canto titled 'Yoga of Devotion'.

Thirteenth Canto

BRAHMA-VIDYA
Knowledge of the Brahaman

(1)

अर्जुन उवाच।
प्रकृतिं पुरुषं चैव क्षेत्रं क्षेत्रज्ञमेव च।
एतद्वेदितुमिच्छामि ज्ञानं ज्ञेयं च केशव ॥१३-१॥

Arjunauvacha
prakritim purusham chaiva kshetram kshetra-jnam eva cha
etad veditum ichchhami jnanam jneyam cha keshava (13.1)

Arjuna uvacha : Arjun said | prakritim : material nature | purusham : the enjoyer | cha : and | eva : indeed | kshetram : the field of activities | kshetra-jñam : the knower of the field | eva : even | cha : also | etat : this | veditum : to know | ichchhami : I wish | jñanam : knowledge | jñeyam : the goal of knowledge | cha : and | keshava : Krishna, the killer of the demon named Keshi

(2)

श्रीभगवानुवाच
इदं शरीरं कौन्तेय क्षेत्रमित्यभिधीयते।
एतद्यो वेत्ति तं प्राहुः क्षेत्रज्ञ इति तद्विदः॥१३-२॥

Shribhagavan uvacha
idam shariram kaunteya kshetram ity abhidhiyate
etad yo vetti tam prahuh kshetra-jna iti tad-vidah (13.2)

Shribhagavan : God (Lord Krishna) | uvacha : said | idam : this | shariram : body | kaunteya : son of Kunti, Arjuna | kshetram : the field | iti : thus | abhidhiyate : is called | etat : this | yah : who | vetti : knows | tam : he | prahuh : is called | Kshetra-jna : the knower of the field | iti : thus | tat-vidha : those who know this

O son of Kunti, Arjuna! According to those who know, this body is called the field and one who knows this is called the knower of the field.

(3)

क्षेत्रज्ञं चापि मां विद्धि सर्वक्षेत्रेषु भारत।
क्षेत्रक्षेत्रज्ञयोर्ज्ञानं यत्तज्ज्ञानं मतं मम॥१३- ३॥

kshetra-jnam chapi mam viddhi sarva-kshetreshu bharata
kshetra-kshetrajnayor jnanam yat taj jnanam matam mama (13.3)

Kshetra-jnam : knower of the field | cha : and | api : also | mam : me | viddhi : know | sarva : all | kshetresu : in the fields (bodies) | bharata : O scion of the great king Bharata | kshetra : the field | kshetra-jnayo : the knower of the field | jnanam : knowledge | yat : which | tat : that | jnanam : knowledge | matam : opinion | mama : my

O scion of the great King Bharata, Arjuna! I am also the knower in the fields of all bodies and what is known i.e. knowledge. This is my opinion.

(4)

तत्क्षेत्रं यच्च याहक्च यद्विकारि यतश्च यत्।
स च यो यत्प्रभावश्च तत्समासेन मे शृणु॥१३- ४॥

tat kshetram yach cha yadirk cha yad-vikari yatash cha yat
sa cha yo yat-prabhavash cha tat samasena me shrinu (13.4)

tat : that | kshetram : field | yat : what | cha : and | yadrik : as it is/with what properties it is constituted | cha : and | yat : what | vikari : deficiencies/changes/modifications | yatash : which | cha : and | yat : what | sa : he | cha : and | ya : who | yat : what | prabhavash : impact/effect/influence | cha : and | tat : that | samasena : in brief | me : me | shrinu : listen

What is the field, how it is constituted and with what properties, what are its deficiencies and what would be the effect of modifications, listen to me in brief.

(5)

ऋषिभिर्बहुधा गीतं छन्दोभिर्विविधैः पृथक्।
ब्रह्मसूत्रपदैश्चैव हेतुमद्भिर्विनिश्चितैः॥१३- ५॥

rishibhir bahudha gitam chandobhir vividhaih prithak
brahma-sutra-padaish chaiva hetumadbhir vinishchitaih (13.5)

rishibhi : by the sages | bahudha : in many ways | gitam : sung | chhandobhi : by chants | vividhaih : various | prithak : separate/distinct | brahma-sutra-padai : by Vedantic aphorisms from the Brahmasutra | cha : and | eva : also | hetu-madbhi : with cause and effect/reasoned | vinishchitaih : certain/conclusive/convincing

In this regard, sages have sung Vedic hymns in various ways and distinct chants from the Brahmasutra which are well-reasoned and convincing.

(6-7)
महाभूतान्यहंकारो बुद्धिरव्यक्तमेव च।
इन्द्रियाणि दशैकं च पञ्च चेन्द्रियगोचराः॥१३- ६॥
इच्छाद्वेषः सुखं दुःखं संघातश्चेतना धृतिः।
एतत्क्षेत्रं समासेन सविकारमुदाहृतम्॥१३- ७॥

maha-bhutany ahankaro buddhir avyaktam eva cha
indriyani dashaikam cha pancha chendriya-gocharah (13.6)
ichchha dveshah sukham duhkham sanghatash chetana dhritih
etat kshetram samasena sa-vikaram udahritam (13.7)

maha-bhutani : (five) great elements viz. air, fire, water, earth and ether | ahankara : false ego | buddhi : intelligence | avyaktam : unmanifest (primordial nature) | eva : also | cha : and | indriyani : the (ten) senses | dasha-ekam : the ten senses and the mind | cha : and | pancha: five | indriya-go-charah : objects of the senses | ichchha : desire | dveshah : hatred/enmity/envy | sukham : happiness | duhkham : sorrow/distress | sanghatash : body as the aggregate of elements | chetana : consciousness/symptom of life | dhriti : conviction/fortitude | etat : this | kshetram : the field (of activities) | samasena : in short | sa-vikaram : with interactions/modifications/attributes | udahritam : for example

The five great elements (air, water, fire, earth and ether), false ego, intelligence and also the unmanifest (primordial) nature plus the ten senses and the mind, the five sense objects (smell, taste, form, touch and sound), desire, hatred, happiness, sorrow, body as the aggregate of elements, consciousness as the symptom of life and fortitude may be briefly described as the field of activities with all the attributes, interactions and modifications.

(8 - 12)

अमानित्वमदम्भित्वमहिंसा क्षान्तिरार्जवम्।
आचार्योपासनं शौचं स्थैर्यमात्मविनिग्रहः॥१३-८॥
इन्द्रियार्थेषु वैराग्यमनहंकार एव च।
जन्ममृत्युजराव्याधि दुःख दोषानुदर्शनम्॥१३-९॥
असक्तिरनभिष्वङ्गःपुत्रदारगृहादिषु।
नित्यंचसमचित्तत्वमिष्टानिष्टोपपत्तिषु॥१३-१०॥
मयिचानन्ययोगेनभक्तिरव्यभिचारिणी।
विविक्तदेशसेवित्वमरतिर्जनसंसदि॥१३-११॥
अध्यात्मज्ञाननित्यत्वंतत्त्वज्ञानार्थदर्शनम्।
एतज्ज्ञानमितिप्रोक्तमज्ञानंयदतोऽन्यथा॥१३-१२॥

amanitvam adambhitvam ahinsa kshantir arjavam
acharyopasanam shaucham sthairyam atma-vinigrahah (13.8)
indriyartheshu vairagyam anahankara eva cha
janma-mrityu-jara-vyadhi- duhkha-doshanudarshanam (13.9)
asaktir anabhishvangah putra-dara-grihadishu
nityam cha sama-chittatvam ishtanishtopapattisu (13.10)
mayi chananya-yogena bhaktir avyabhicharini
vivikta-desha-sevitvam aratir jana-sansadi (13.11)
adhyatma-jnana-nityatvam tattva-jnanartha-darshanam
etajjnanam iti proktam ajnanam yad ato 'nyatha (13.12)

amanitvam : humility | adambhitvam : unpretentiousness | ahinsa : non-violence | kshanti : forgiveness/tolerance | arjavam : simplicity in thought and speech/uprightness | acharya-upasanam : service to the Guru with a sense of devotion | shaucham : cleanliness/purity | sthairyam : steadiness/stability/poise | atma-vinigrahah : self-control | ▪ indriya-arthesu : objects of sensory gratification | vairagyam : renunciation/non-attachment | anahankara : free from false egoism | eva : also | cha : and | janma : birth | mrityu : death | jara : old age | vyadhi : disease | duhkha : sorrow/distress | dosha : faults/evil | anudarshanam : seeing/realisation of/observing | ▪ ashakti : without attachment | anabhishvangah : non-identification of oneself | putra : son | dara : wife | griha-adishu : home, etc. | nityam : always | cha : and | samachittatvam : mental equipoise/equilibrium in thinking/equanimity | ishta : desirable/pleasant | anishta : undesirable/ unpleasant | upapattishu : having received | ▪ mayi : in me | cha : and | ananya yogena : by the yoga of oneness (there is no other) or non-dualism | bhakti : devotion | avyabhicharini : without any break | vivikta : solitary | desha : place | sevitvam : aspiring/desire to live | aratih : lack of love/ attachment, aversion | jana-sansadi : among the people at large | ▪ adhyatma : spiritual/concerning the self | jnana : knowledge | nityatvam : always | tattva-jnana : quintessential knowledge/knowledge of basic truth | artha : object | darshanam : philosophy | etat : this | jnanam : knowledge | iti : end/ thus | proktam : spoken | ajnanam : ignorance | yat : which | atah : therefore | anyatha : otherwise

Humility, unpretentiousness, non-violence, forgiveness, simplicity, devoted service to the Guru, cleanliness, steadiness, self-control, non-attachment to objects of sensory gratification and free from false egoism, seeing evil and sorrow in birth, death, old age and disease, non-identification of oneself with son, wife, home etc., always maintaining equanimity in the face of pleasant and unpleasant and unbroken devotion in me through the yoga of oneness or non-dualism, aspiration to living in solitude, aversion to living in crowds, always devoted to search for knowledge of the self (spiritual knowledge) and the quintessential or the basic truth, this knowledge alone is the object of philosophy, everything otherwise is spoken of as only ignorance.

(13)
ज्ञेयं यत्तत्प्रवक्ष्यामि यज्ज्ञात्वामृतमश्नुते।
अनादिमत्परं ब्रह्म न सत्तन्नासदुच्यते॥१३- १३॥

jneyam yat tat pravakshyami yaj jnatvamritam ashnute
anadi mat-param brahma na sat tan nasad uchyate (13.13)

jneyam : the knowable/what is worth knowing | yat : which | tat : that | pravakshyami : shall speak/shall describe | yat : which | jnatva : on knowing | amritam : nectar/the state of bliss | ashnute : attains/reaches | anadimat : one without beginning | param-brahma : the Supreme Soul | na : not/neithe | sat : being/existence/truth | tat : that | na : nor | asat : non-being/non-existence/untruth | uchyate : is said to be

I shall describe that which is worth knowing and on knowing that one reaches the state of bliss in Brahman - the Supreme Soul - which is without any beginning and is said to be neither being nor non-being.

(14)
सर्वतः पाणिपादं तत्सर्वतोऽक्षिशिरोमुखम्।
सर्वतः श्रुतिमल्लोके सर्वमावृत्य तिष्ठति॥१३-१४॥

sarvatah pani-padam tat sarvato 'kshi-shiro-mukham
sarvatah shrutimal loke sarvam avritya tishthati (13.14)

sarvatah : everywhere | pani : hands | padam : feet | tat : that | sarvata : everywhere | akshi : eyes | shira : heads | mukham : mouths | sarvatah : everywhere | shruti-mat : with ears | loke : in the world | sarvam : all/everything | avritya : covering | tishthati : exists

Hands and feet everywhere, eyes, heads and mouths everywhere, ears in the world everywhere, that (the Supreme Soul) exists covering all.

(15)
सर्वेन्द्रियगुणाभासं सर्वेन्द्रियविवर्जितम्।
असक्तं सर्वभृच्चैव निर्गुणं गुणभोक्तृ च॥१३- १५॥

sarvendriya-gunabhasam sarvendriya-vivarjitam
asaktam sarva-bhrich caiva nirgunam guna-bhoktri cha (13.15)

sarva-indriya : all the senses | guna : qualities | abhasam : source | sarva-indriya : all the senses | vivarjitam : being without | asaktam : without attachment | sarva-bhrit : the sustainer of all | cha : and | eva : also | nirgunam : without material qualities | guna-bhokta : experiencer of gunas (qualities) | cha : also/and

Source of the qualities of all the senses, yet without any senses, the

Supreme Soul is devoid of all attachment and is without material qualities yet it sustains and experiences all.

(16)
बहिरन्तश्च भूतानामचरं चरमेव च।
सूक्ष्मत्वात्तदविज्ञेयं दूरस्थं चान्तिके च तत्।।१३- १६।।

bahir antash cha bhutanam acharam charam eva cha
sukshmatvat tad avijneyam dura-stham chantike cha tat (13.16)

bahi : outside | anta : within | cha : and | bhutanam : all beings | acharam : unmoving beings | charam : moving beings | eva : also | cha : and | sukshmatvat : very subtle | tat : that | avijneyam : incomprehensible | durastham : far | cha : and | antike : near | cha : and | tat : that

It (the Supreme Soul) is within and outside all beings - moving and unmoving. On account of being very subtle, it is incomprehensible, far and also near.

(17)
अविभक्तं च भूतेषु विभक्तमिव च स्थितम्।
भूतभर्तृ च तज्ज्ञेयं ग्रसिष्णु प्रभविष्णु च।।१३- १७।।

avibhaktam cha bhuteshu vibhaktam iva cha sthitam
bhuta-bhartri cha tajjneyam grasishnu prabhavishnu cha (13.17)

avibhaktam : indivisible | cha : and | bhuteshu : in all living beings | vibhaktam : divided | iva : as if | cha : also | sthitam : situated/stands | bhuta-bhartri : the sustainer of all living beings | cha : also | tat : that | jneyam : to be known | grasishnu : destroy | prabhavishnu : creator | cha : and

Though indivisible, (the Supreme Soul) seems to stand as if divided in all living beings. Though sustainer of all living beings, it also needs to be known that it is the destroyer and creator of all.

(18)
ज्योतिषामपि तज्ज्योतिस्तमसः परमुच्यते।
ज्ञानं ज्ञेयं ज्ञानगम्यं हृदि सर्वस्य विष्ठितम्।।१३- १८।।

jyotisham api taj jyotis tamasah param uchyate
jnanam jneyam jnana-gamyam hridi sarvasya vishthitam (13.18)

jyotisham : of lights | api : also | tat : that/it | jyoti : light | tamasah : darkness | param : beyond/para | uchyate : is spoken of as | jnanam : knowledge | jneyam : what is to be known/the object of knowledge | jnana-gamyam : the goal of knowledge | hridi : in the heart | sarvasya : of all | vishthitam : dwelling/residing

It (the Supreme Soul) is the light also of lights, is spoken of as being beyond darkness, as knowledge, object of knowledge and the goal of knowledge residing in the hearts of all.

(19)
इति क्षेत्रं तथा ज्ञानं ज्ञेयं चोक्तं समासतः।
मद्भक्त एतद्विज्ञाय मद्भावायोपपद्यते॥१३-१९॥
iti kshetram tatha jnanam jneyam coktam samasatah
mad-bhakta etad vijnaya mad-bhavayopapdyate (13.19)

iti : thus | kshetram : field | tatha : and | jnanam : knowledge | jneyam : knowable | cha : and | uktam : stated/described/explained | samasatah : in brief | mat-bhakta : my devotee | etat : this | vijnaya : after knowing | mat-bhavaya : my being | upapadyate : reaches/attains

Thus, (the body as) the field (of our actions), the knowledge and the knowable have been explained by me in brief. After knowing this, my devotee can reach me (my being).

(20)
प्रकृतिं पुरुषं चैव विद्ध्यनादी उभावपि।
विकारांश्च गुणांश्चैव विद्धि प्रकृतिसंभवान्॥१३-२०॥
prakritim purusham chaiva viddhy anadi ubhav api
vikaransh cha gunansh chaiva viddhi prakriti-sambhavan (13.20)

prakrtim : primordial nature of matter | purusham : primordial intelligence (mind)/the active agent | cha : and | eva : certainly/definitely | viddhi : know

| anadi : without a beginning | ubhau : both | api : also | vikaran : changes | cha : and | gunan : qualities | cha : also | eva : certainly | viddhi : know | prakriti : nature | sambhavan : born of

Matter and mind both are without a beginning. Also, know that the changes and the qualities are definitely born of nature.

(21)
कार्यकरणकर्तृत्वे हेतुः प्रकृतिरुच्यते।
पुरुषः सुखदुःखानां भोक्तृत्वे हेतुरुच्यते॥१३- २१॥

karya-karana-kartritve hetuh prakritir uchyate
purusah sukha-duhkhanam bhoktritve heturuchyate (13.21)

karya : action | karana : the cause | kartritve : creation | hetuh : the instrument of | prakriti : the world of material nature | uchyate : it is stated | purushah : the primordial mind/the active agent | sukha : happiness/joys | duhkhanam : sorrows | bhoktritve : experience | hetu : the means | uchyate : is said to be

In the creation of cause and action, nature (Prakrti) is stated to be the instrument. The joys and sorrows are said to be experienced by Purusha. (Action is caused by nature and mind experiences joy and sorrow).

(22)
पुरुषः प्रकृतिस्थो हि भुङ्क्ते प्रकृतिजान्गुणान्।
कारणं गुणसङ्गोऽस्य सदसद्योनिजन्मसु॥१३- २२॥

purushah prakriti-stho hi bhunkte prakriti-jan gunan
karanam guna-sango 'sya sad-asad-yoni-janmasu (13.22)

purushah : the primordial intelligence (mind)/the active agent | prakriti-stha : situated (residing) in primordial energy of matter (Prakrti) | hi : verily | bhunkte : experiences | prakriti-jan : born of material energy (Prakrti) | gunan : qualities | karanam : the cause | guna-sanga : in association with the qualities | asya : of this | sat-asat : good and evil | yoni : wombs (born in different species) | janmasu : in births

Purusha residing in Prakrti (Mind in Body) experiences the qualities (of senses) born of Prakrti. Because of the good and evil deeds committed by this Purusha in association with the qualities (of senses), births of beings take place in wombs of different species.

(23)

उपद्रष्टानुमन्ता च भर्ता भोक्ता महेश्वरः।
परमात्मेति चाप्युक्तो देहेऽस्मिन्पुरुषः परः॥१३- २३॥

upadrashtanumanta cha bharta bhokta maheshvarah
paramatmeti chapy ukto dehe 'smin purushah parah (13.23)

upadrashta : overseer | anumanta : permitter | cha : and | bharta : supporter | bhokta : enjoyer | maha-ishvarah : the Great Lord | parama-atma : the Supreme Self (Soul) | iti : thus | cha : and | api : also | ukta : is said | dehe : in the body | asmin : this | purushah : primordial intelligence | parah : beyond/supreme

In this body, the supreme Purusha is said to be also the overseer, the permitter, the supporter, the experiencer and the Great Lord and thus the Supreme Self (Soul).

(24)

य एवं वेत्ति पुरुषं प्रकृतिं च गुणैः सह।
सर्वथा वर्तमानोऽपि न स भूयोऽभिजायते॥१३- २४॥

ya evam vetti purusham prakritim cha gunaih saha
sarvatha vartamano 'pi na sa bhuyo 'bhijayate (13.24)

ya : who | evam : thus | vetti : knows | purusham : primordial intelligence/Purusha | prakritim : nature/primordial material energy/Prakrti | cha : and | gunaih : qualities | saha : with | sarvatha : fully/in every way | vartamana : existing/present/living | api : even/also | na : never/not | sa : he | bhuya : again | abhijayate : is born

One who thus knows Purusha and Prakrti along with their qualities, even while living fully in every way, is never born again.

(25)

ध्यानेनात्मनि पश्यन्ति केचिदात्मानमात्मना।
अन्ये सांख्येन योगेन कर्मयोगेन चापरे॥१३-२५॥

dhyanenatmani pashyanti kechid atmanam atmana
anye sankhyena yogena karma-yogena chapare (13.25)

dhyanena : by meditation | atmani : within the Self | pashyanti : see | kechit : some | atmanam : Supreme Self (Soul) | atmana : by the Self | anye : others | sankhyena : through Sankhya philosophy | yogena : by yoga | karma-yogena : by karma-yoga i.e. by performing action without attachment to fruits thereof | cha : and | apre : others

Some see the Supreme Self (Soul) within their individual selves through meditation. Others do it by yoga through knowledge of Sankhya philosophy, and still others reach the Supreme Self by following the path of Karma-yoga and performing action without attachment to its fruits.

(26)

अन्ये त्वेवमजानन्तः श्रुत्वान्येभ्य उपासते।
तेऽपि चातितरन्त्येव मृत्युं श्रुतिपरायणाः॥१३-२६॥

anye tv evam ajanantah shrutvanyebhya upasate
te 'pi chatitaranty eva mrityum shruti-parayanah (13.26)

anye : others | tu : but | evam : thus | ajanantah : those who do not know | shrutva : by hearing | anyebhya : from others | upasate : worship | te : they | api : also | cha : and | atitaranti : swim across/transcend/go beyond | eva : verily | mrityum : death | shruti-paranayah : faithfully devoted to ear-to-ear knowledge

But, others who do not know this take to worship on hearing from others and for being faithfully devoted to ear-to-ear knowledge, they also verily swim across and get over the cycle of birth and death.

(27)

यावत्संजायते किंचित्सत्त्वं स्थावरजङ्गमम्।
क्षेत्रक्षेत्रज्ञसंयोगात्तद्विद्धि भरतर्षभ॥ १३- २७॥

yavat sanjayate kinchit sattvam sthavara-jangamam
kshetra-kshetrajna-sanyogat tad viddhi bharatarshabha (13.27)

yavat : whatever | sanjayate : is born | kinchit : any | sattvam : existence/being | sthavara : unmoving | jangamam : moving | kshetra : field (body, Prakrti) | kshetra-jna : knower of the field (mind, Purusha) | sanyogat : coming together | tat : that | viddhi : know | bharat-rishabha : O Arjuna! (the bull/chief of Bharata dynasty)

O Arjuna! Know that whatever is born - moving or unmoving - is the result of the field and the knower of the field (the material body and the active agent - mind, Purusha and Prakriti) coming together.

(28)

समं सर्वेषु भूतेषु तिष्ठन्तं परमेश्वरम्।
विनश्यत्स्वविनश्यन्तं यः पश्यति स पश्यति॥ १३- २८॥

samam sarveshu bhuteshu tishthantam parameshvaram
vinashyatsv avinashyantam yah pashyati sa pashyati (13.28)

samam : equally | sarveshu : in all | bhuteshu : living beings | tishthantam : residing | parama-ishvarah : the Supreme Self (Soul) | vinashyatsu : destructible/mortal | avinashyantam : indestructible/immortal | yah : who/any one | pashyati : sees | sa : he | pashyati : sees

Only he really sees who sees the indestructible Supreme Soul equally present in all the destructible living beings.

(29)

समं पश्यन्हि सर्वत्र समवस्थितमीश्वरम्।
न हिनस्त्यात्मनात्मानं ततो याति परां गतिम्॥ १३- २९॥

samam pashyan hi sarvatra samavasthitam ishvaram
na hinasty atmanatmanam tato yati param gatim (13.29)

samam : equally | pashyan : seeing | hi : because/since/verily | sarvatra : everywhere | samavasthitam : existing | ishvaram : God/the Lord | na : never/not | hinasti : inures/hurts | atmana : the self | atmanam : by the self | tata : then | yati : reaches | param : supreme | gatim : goal/ultimate destination

Seeing the Lord existing everywhere equally, self not hurting the self, he reaches the supreme goal.

(30)
प्रकृत्यैव च कर्माणि क्रियमाणानि सर्वशः।
यः पश्यति तथात्मानमकर्तारं स पश्यति॥१३-३०॥
prakrtyaiva cha karmani kriyamanani sarvasah
yah pashyati tathatmanam akartaram sa pashyati (13.30)

prakrtya : nature (material body) | eva : verily | cha : and | karmai : acts | kriyamanani : being done | sarvasa : fully/in all respects | ya : who | pashyati : sees | tatha : and | atmanam : self | akartaram : the non-doer | sa : he | pashyati : sees

Verily, only he sees who sees all the acts in all respects being done only by the material body (Prakrti) and the self being the non-doer.

(31)
यदा भूतपृथग्भावमेकस्थमनुपश्यति।
तत एव च विस्तारं ब्रह्म संपद्यते तदा॥१३-३१॥
yada bhuta-prithag-bhavam eka-stham anupashyati
tata eva cha vistaram brahma sampadyate tada (13.31)

yada : when | bhuta : living beings | prithak-bhavam : separate existence | ekastham : situated in the One | anupashyati : sees | tata : from that | eva : One | cha : and | vista ram : the expanse | brahma : the Supreme Soul (Self) Consciousness/the Absolute/Brahaman | sampadyate : achieves | tada : then

When one sees the separate existence of all living beings in the One and from that One the expanse, he achieves the stage of the Supreme Soul Consciousness (the Brahaman or the Absolute).

(32)

अनादित्वान्निर्गुणत्वात्परमात्मायमव्ययः।
शरीरस्थोऽपि कौन्तेय न करोति न लिप्यते॥१३- ३२॥

anaditvan nirgunatvat paramatmayam avyayah
sharira-stho 'pi kaunteya na karoti na lipyate (13.32)

anadivat : being without beginning | nirgunatvat : without any gunas (qualities) | parama : supreme | atma : soul/self | ayam : this | avyayah : inexhaustible/immutable | sharira-stha : situated in the body | api : though | kaunteya : O son of Kunti, Arjuna | na karoti : does not do anything | na : nor | lipyate : gets affected

O Arjuna! Being without a beginning and without any gunas (qualities), this Supreme Soul is immutable. It does not do anything nor does it get affected (not being involved with fruits of action).

(33)

यथा सर्वगतं सौक्ष्म्यादाकाशं नोपलिप्यते।
सर्वत्रावस्थितो देहे तथात्मा नोपलिप्यते॥१३- ३३॥

yatha sarva-gatam saukshmyad akasham nopalipyate
sarvatravasthito dehe tathatma nopalipyate (13.33)

yatha : as | sarva-gatam : all pervasive | saukshmyat : because of being subtle | akasham : sky/ether | na : never | upalipyate : is polluted | sarvatra : everywhere | avasthita : situated | dehe : in the body | tatha : so/and | atma : the self | na : never | upalipyate : polluted

Just as the all pervasive ether because of being so subtle, does not get polluted so the Self dwelling everywhere in the body, never gets polluted.

(34)

यथा प्रकाशयत्येकः कृत्स्नं लोकमिमं रविः।
क्षेत्रं क्षेत्री तथा कृत्स्नं प्रकाशयति भारत॥१३- ३४॥

yatha prakashayaty ekah kritsnam lokam imam ravih
kshetram kshetri tatha kritsnam prakashayati bharata (13.34)

yatha : as | prakashayati : illumines | ekah : one | kritsnam : the whole | lokam : universe/world | imam : this | ravih : sun | kshetram : field (the body) | kshetri : (one residing in the kshetra - field) the soul | tatha : and | kritsnam : all | prakashayati : illumines | bharata : O son of Bharata, Arjuna

O Arjuna! As this one sun illumines the whole world, so does the soul in every body illumine the bodies.

(35)
क्षेत्रक्षेत्रज्ञयोरेवमन्तरंज्ञानचक्षुषा।
भूतप्रकृतिमोक्षंचयेविदुर्यान्तितेपरम्॥१३- ३५॥

kshetra-kshetrajnayor evam antaram jnana-chakshusha
bhuta-prakriti-moksham cha ye vidur yanti te param (35).

kshetra : field (body) | kshetra-jnayo : the owner of the field / body | evam : thus | antaram : difference | jnana-chakshusha : through the eyes of knowledge | bhuta : living being | prakirti : nature | moksham : salvation/emancipation | cha : and | ye : who | vidu : know/perceive | yanti : go to | te : they | param : supreme

Thus, those seeing through the eyes of knowledge perceive a difference between the field and its owner (the body and the soul) and on emancipation from the nature of living beings, reach the Supreme.

Thus ends the Thirteenth Canto titled 'Knowledge of the Brahaman'.

Fourteenth Canto

GUNATRIYA-VIBHAG YOGA
Yoga of Discrimination of Three Qualities

(1)

श्रीभगवानुवाच
परंभूयः प्रवक्ष्यामि ज्ञानानां ज्ञानमुत्तमम्।
यज्ज्ञात्वा मुनयः सर्वे परांसिद्धिमितो गताः॥१४-१॥

Shribhagavan uvacha
param bhuyah pravakshyami jnananam jnanam uttamam
yaj jnatva munayah sarve param siddhimito gatah (14.1).

Shribhagavan uvacha : Lord Krishna said | param : supreme | bhuyah : again | pravakshyami : shall speak | jnananam : of all kinds of knowledge | jnanam : knowledge | uttamam : highest | yat : still/which | jnatva : knowing | munayah : the saints | sarve : all | param : supreme | siddhim : perfection | itah : from here (this world) | gata : reached/achieved

Lord Krishna said: I shall again speak to you of the highest of all knowledge knowing which all the saints from here achieved supreme perfection.

(2)

इदं ज्ञानमुपाश्रित्य मम साधर्म्यमागताः।
सर्गेऽपि नोपजायन्ते प्रलये न व्यथन्ति च॥१४-२॥

idam jnanam upashritya mama sadharmyam agatah
sarge 'pi nopajayante pralaye na vyathanti cha (14.2)

idam : this | jnanam : knowledge | upasritya : having acquired | mama : my | sadharmyam : form/nature/level | agatah : having achieved | sargeapi : even at the time of new creation of the world | na : never | upajayante : are born | pralaye : at dissolution | na : not | vyathanti : distressed/disturbed | cha : also

Having acquired this knowledge and having achieved my level, they are never born even at the time of creation of the world, also they are not distressed at the time of its dissolution (Pralaya).

(3)
मम योनिर्महद्ब्रह्म तस्मिन्गर्भं दधाम्यहम्।
संभवः सर्वभूतानां ततो भवति भारत॥१४-३॥

mama yonir mahad brahma tasmin garbham dadhamyaham
sambhavah sarva-bhutanam tato bhavati bharata (14.3)

mama : my | yoni : womb | mahat : great | brahma : the Supreme | tasmin : in that | garbham : the germ/pregnancy | dadhami : place/implant | aham : I | sambhavah : possible | sarva-bhutanam : of all living beings | tata : thereafter | bhavati : becomes | bharata : Scion of Bharata, O Arjuna!

O scion of Bharata, Arjuna! My womb is the great Brahma. In that I implant the germ and that is how the birth of all living beings becomes possible.

(4)
सर्वयोनिषु कौन्तेय मूर्तयः संभवन्ति याः।
तासां ब्रह्म महद्योनिरहं बीजप्रदः पिता॥१४-४॥

sarva-yonishu kaunteya murtayah sambhavanti yah
tasam brahma mahad yonir aham bija-pradah pita (14.4)

sarva-yonishu : from all wombs | kaunteya : O son of Kunti, Arjuna | murtayah : forms/bodies/manifestations/beings | sambhavanti : appear/are produced/are born | yah : which/whatever | tasam : of them/their | brahma : prakrti/nature | mahat yoni : great womb | aham : I | bija-pradah : seed-giving | pita : father

O Arjuna! For all the animate and inanimate creations born from any wombs, prakrti (nature) is the great womb and I am the seed-giving father.

(5)

सत्त्वं रजस्तम इति गुणाः प्रकृतिसंभवाः।
निबध्नन्ति महाबाहो देहे देहिनमव्ययम्॥१४-५॥

sattvam rajas tama iti gunah prakriti-sambhavah
nibadhnanti maha-baho dehe dehinam avyayam (14.5)

sattvam : goodness/truthfulness/righteousness/purity | raja : passion | tama : darkness/ignorance/evil | iti : thus/these/end | gunah : qualities | prakriti : nature | sambhavah : born of | nibadhnanti : binds/conditions/confines | mahabaho : one with large arms | dehe : in the body | dehinam : the Soul (Self) embodied | avyayam : eternal/indestructible

O large-armed one, Arjuna! These nature-born qualities of sattva, rajas and tamas (righteousness, passion and evil) confine the indestructible atman (Soul/Self) inside the body.

(6)

तत्र सत्त्वं निर्मलत्वात्प्रकाशकमनामयम्।
सुखसङ्गेन बध्नाति ज्ञानसङ्गेन चानघ॥१४-६॥

tatra sattvam nirmalatvat prakashakam anamayam
sukha-sangena badhnati jnana-sangena chanagha (14.6)

tatra : there (of the three natural qualities) | sattvam : goodness | nirmalatvat : like the pure | prakashakam : luminous | anamayam : free from evil | sukha : happiness | sangena : being in association | badhnati : conditions/binds | jnana : knowledge | sangena : by association/attachment to | cha : and | anagha : free from all sin

Free from all sin, O Arjuna! Of the three natural qualities, goodness because of its purity, luminousness and freedom from evil, binds by being attached to happiness and knowledge.

(7)

रजो रागात्मकं विद्धि तृष्णासङ्गसमुद्भवम्।
तन्निबध्नाति कौन्तेय कर्मसङ्गेन देहिनम्॥ १४- ७॥

rajo ragatmakam viddhi trishna-sanga-samudbhavam
tan nibadhnati kaunteya karma-sangena dehinam (14.7)

raja : quality of rajas/rajo-guna | raga-atmakam : nature of passion | viddhi : know | trishna : thirst/desire | sanga : association/attachment | samudbhavam : born of | tat : that | nibadhnati : binds | kunteya : Son of Kunti, Arjuna | karma-sangena : association with action | dehinam : the soul in the body

O Son of Kunti, Arjuna! Know that rajoguna (quality of rajas) is of the nature of passion born of desire (for acquiring objects of sensory gratification) and attachment (to objects acquired) that puts the Self (the soul in the body) to bondage through association with action (giving to Self the feeling of being the doer).

(8)

तमस्त्वज्ञानजं विद्धि मोहनं सर्वदेहिनाम्।
प्रमादालस्यनिद्राभिस्तन्निबध्नाति भारत॥ १४- ८॥

tamas tv ajnana-jam viddhi mohanam sarva-dehinam
pramadalasya-nidrabhis tan nibadhnati bharata (14.8)

tama : quality of tamas/rajo-guna | tu : and | ajnana-jam : resulting from ignorance | viddhi : know | mohanam : delusion/attraction | sarvadehinam : all the embodied souls | pramada : madness | alasya : idleness | nidrabhi : and sleep | tat : that | nibadhnati : binds | bharata : descendant of king Bharata, Arjuna

O descendant of King Bharata, Arjuna! Know that tamo-guna (quality of tamas) born of ignorance is a matter of delusion for all the embodied souls. It is sheer madness, idleness and sleep that binds. (Like sattva and rajas, tamas also leads to bondage of the embodied soul.)

(9)
सत्त्वं सुखे संजयति रजः कर्मणि भारत।
ज्ञानमावृत्य तु तमः प्रमादे संजयत्युत॥१४- ९॥
sattvam sukhe sanjayati rajah karmani bharata
jnanam avritya tu tamah pramade sanjayatyuta (14.9)

sattvam : quality of sattva (truth, goodness, virtue) | sukhe : in happiness | sanjayati : binds | rajah : quality of rajas/mode of passion | karmani : in action | bharata : O son of King Bharata, Arjuna | jnanam : knowledge | avritya : covering | tu : but/and | tamah : quality of tama/mode of ignorance | pramade : in madness | sanjayati : binds | uta : etc/and the like

O descendant of King Bharata, Arjuna! The quality of sattva (goodness) binds one to happiness, the quality of rajas (passion) to action (with desire for its fruits) and tamas (ignorance) by covering knowledge binds one to madness and the like.

(10)
रजस्तमश्चाभिभूय सत्त्वं भवति भारत।
रजः सत्त्वं तमश्चैव तमः सत्त्वं रजस्तथा॥१४- १०॥
rajas tamash chabhibhuya sattvam bhavati bharata
rajah sattvam tamash chaiva tamah sattvam rajas tatha (14.10)

rajah : mode of passion | tamah : mode of ignorance | cha : and | abhibhuya : overtaking/dominating/overpower | sattvam : goodness/righteousness | bhavati : happens | bharata : O descendant of King Bharata, Arjuna! | rajah : mode of passion | sattvam : goodness/righteousness | tamah : darkness/ignorance | cha : and | eva : also/likewise | sattvam : goodness/righteousness | raja : mode of passion | tatha : thus

O descendant of King Bharata, Arjuna! Goodness (satoguna) may happen to overpower passion (rajoguna) and ignorance (tamoguna). Similarly, at another time, passion may dominate over goodness and ignorance. Also, thus ignorance may likewise come to overtake both goodness and passion.

(11)
सर्वद्वारेषु देहेऽस्मिन्प्रकाश उपजायते।
ज्ञानं यदा तदा विद्याद्विवृद्धं सत्त्वमित्युत॥१४- ११॥

*sarva-dvareshu dehe 'smin prakasa upajayate
jnanam yada tada vidyadvivriddham sattvam ity uta (14.11)*

sarva-dvareshu : from all doors (sense openings) | dehe : in the body | asmin : this | prakasha : light/illumination | upajayate : shines/manifests/radiates | jnanam : knowledge | yada : when | tada : then | vidyat : know | vivrddham : prevails/is dominant | sattvam : goodness | itiuta : that it

When from all the doors (sense openings) in this body light of knowledge manifests, then it is known that it is goodness that is dominant.

(12)
लोभः प्रवृत्तिरारम्भः कर्मणामशमः स्पृहा।
रजस्येतानि जायन्ते विवृद्धे भरतर्षभ॥१४- १२॥

*lobhah pravrittir arambhah karmanam ashamah spriha
rajasyetani jayante vivriddhe bharatarshabha (14.12)*

lobhah : greed | pravritti : tendency | arambhah : beginning/undertaking | karmanam : actions/works | ashamah : unrest | spriha : desire/longing | rajasi : of passion (rajo-guna) | etani : all these | jayante : grow | vivriddhe : on increasing/when it becomes predominant | bharata-rishabha : bull (chief) among those of the Bharata dynasty, Arjuna

O chief of the Bharata dynasty, Arjuna! When rajo-guna (mode of passion) becomes predominant, greed, activity, undertaking of works, unrest (and) longing - all these grow.

(13)
अप्रकाशोऽप्रवृत्तिश्च प्रमादो मोह एव च।
तमस्येतानि जायन्ते विवृद्धे कुरुनन्दन॥१४- १३॥

*aprakasho 'pravrittish cha pramado moha eva cha
tamasye tani jayante vivrddhe kuru-nandana (13.14)*

aprakasha : darkness | apravritti : inactivity/idleness/tendency to avoid performance of ones duty | cha : and | pramda : madness/inability to understand | moha : delusion | eva : also | cha : and | tamasi : ignorance (tamas) | etani : all these | jayante : are born/arise | vivrddhe : on getting a position of predominance | kuru-nandana : O son of the Kuru dynasty, Arjuna!

Son of the Kuru dynasty, O Arjuna !when the mode of ignorance (tamo-guna) becomes predominant, darkness, idleness (tendency to avoid performing ones duty), lack of understanding and also delusion - all these - arise.

(14)
यदा सत्त्वे प्रवृद्धे तु प्रलयं याति देहभृत्।
तदोत्तमविदां लोकानमलान्प्रतिपद्यते॥१४-१४॥

yada sattve pravriddhe tu pralayam yati deha-bhrit
tadottama-vidam lokan amalan pratipadyate (14.14)

yada : when | sattve : quality of goodness (sat) | pravriddhe : becomes predominant | tu : but | pralayam : death/dissolution | yati : comes | deha-bhrit : embodied (soul) | tada : then | uttama-vidam : knowers of the Supreme | lokan : planets/worlds | amalan : pure | pratipadyate : achieves/reaches

But, if death comes at a time when the mode of goodness (sato-guna) has become predominant, then the embodied soul achieves the pure planets of the knowers of the Supreme.

(15)
रजसि प्रलयं गत्वा कर्मसङ्गिषु जायते।
तथा प्रलीनस्तमसि मूढयोनिषु जायते॥१४-१५॥

rajasi pralayam gatva karma-sangishu jayate
tatha pralinas tamasi mudha-yonishu jayate (14.15)

rajasi : in the mode of passion (rajo-guna) | pralayam : dissolution/death | gatva : having attained/getting/meeting | karma-sangishu : in the society of those attached to action | jayate : is born | tatha : and so/likewise | pralina : dying | tamasi : in the mode of ignorance (tamo-guna) | mudha-yonishu : in irrational species like animals, insects etc. | jayate : is born

If one meets death when the mode of passion (rajo-guna) is predominant, he or she is born in the society of those attached to action, likewise if one is dying in the mode of ignorance (when tamo-guna is predominant), he or she takes birth amongst irrational species like animals, insects etc.

(16)
कर्मणः सुकृतस्याहुः सात्त्विकं निर्मलं फलम्।
रजसस्तु फलं दुःखमज्ञानं तमसः फलम्॥१४-१६॥

karmanah sukritasyahuh sattvikam nirmalam phalam
rajasastu phalam duhkham ajnanam tamasah phalam (14.16)

karmanah : of action | su-kritasya : good/virtuous | ahu : is said | sattvikam : in the mode of goodness (sato-guna) | nirmalam : pure | phalam : fruit/result | rajasa : mode of passion (rajo-guna) | tu : but | phalam : fruit/result | duhkham : sorrow/misery/suffering | ajnanam : ignorance/complete lack of knowledge | tamasah : in the mode of ignorance (tamo-guna) | phalam : fruit/result

In the mode of goodness (sato-guna), the result of virtuous action is said to be pure but the result of action taken in the mode of passion (rajo-guna) is sorrow and action taken in the mode of ignorance (tamo-guna) results in compete lack of knowledge.

(17)
सत्त्वात्संजायते ज्ञानं रजसो लोभ एव च।
प्रमादमोहौ तमसो भवतोऽज्ञानमेव च॥१४-१७॥

sattvat sanjayate jnanam rajaso lobha eva cha
pramada-mohau tamaso bhavato 'jnanam eva cha (14.17)

sattvat : mode of goodness | sanjayate : results/arises | jnanam : knowledge/wisdom | rajasa : mode of passion | lobha : greed | eva : indeed | cha : and

| pramada : loss of comprehension or understanding/madness | mohau : delusion | tamasa : mode of ignorance | bhavata : arise | ajnanam : lack of knowledge/ignorance | eva : also | cha : and

From the mode of goodness (sato-guna) arises wisdom and from the mode of passion (rajo-guna) indeed comes greed and from the mode of ignorance (tamo-guna) results loss of comprehension, delusion and also lack of knowledge.

(18)

ऊर्ध्वं गच्छन्ति सत्त्वस्था मध्ये तिष्ठन्ति राजसाः।
जघन्यगुणवृत्तिस्था अधो गच्छन्ति तामसाः॥१४-१८॥

urdhvam gachchhanti sattva-stha madhye tishthanti rajasah
jaghanya-guna-vritti stha adho gachchhanti tamasah (14.18)

urdhvam : upwards (to higher spheres) | gachchhanti : go | sattva-stha : those adhering to the mode of goodness (sattva) | madhye : in the middle | tishthanti : stay | rajasah : those who follow the mode of passion (rajas) | jaghanya-guna-vritti-stha : engaged in the lowest (abominable) quality of roles | adha : downwards | gachchhanti : go | tamasah : those in the mode of ignorance (tamas)

Those adhering to the mode of goodness (sattva) go upwards i.e. to higher spheres, those who follow the mode of passion (rajas) stay in the middle and those in the mode of ignorance (tamas) engaged in the lowest (abominable) quality functions go down (to hellish spheres).

(19)

नान्यं गुणेभ्यः कर्तारं यदा द्रष्टानुपश्यति।
गुणेभ्यश्च परं वेत्ति मद्भावं सोऽधिगच्छति॥१४-१९॥

nanyam gunebhyah kartaram yada drashtanupashyati
gunebhyash cha param vetti mad-bhavam so 'dhigachchhati (14.19)

na : no | anyam : other | gunebhyah : than the gunas (qualities) | kartaram : the doer/the agent for action/performer | yada : when | drashta : seer | anupashyati: sees well | gunebhya : as per the gunas (nature) | cha : and |

param : higher/above the three gunas | vetti : knows | mat-bhavam : my nature | sa : he | adhigachchhatti : goes up/reaches

When the seer realises adequately that none can be seen performing any act beyond the three modes (qualities or gunas of sattva, rajas and tamas) and rises above them, he gets to know the essence of my nature and reaches me.

(20)
गुणानेतानतीत्य त्रीन्देही देहसमुद्भवान्।
जन्ममृत्युजरादुःखैर्विमुक्तोऽमृतमश्नुते॥१४- २०॥
gunanetanatityatrindehideha-samudbhavan
janma-mrityujara-duhkhairvimukto 'mrtamashnute (14.20)

gunan : qualities | etan : these | atitya : going beyond | trin : three | dehi : embodied (soul) | deha : body | samudbhavan : emerging out of/evolving from | janma : birth | mrityu : death | jara : old age | duhkhai : sorrows | vimukta : freed | amritam : nectar/immortality | ashnute : attains/acquires

Going beyond the three gunas from which the body has evolved, the embodied Soul (Self) freed from birth, death, old age and sorrows, attains immortality.

(21)
अर्जुन उवाच
कैर्लिङ्गैस्त्रीनगुणानेतानतीतो भवति प्रभो।
किमाचारः कथं चैतां स्त्रीन्गुणानतिवर्तते॥१४- २१॥
arjuna uvacha
kair lingais trin gunan etan atito bhavati prabho
kim acharah katham chaitam strin gunan ativartate (14.21)

Arjuna uvacha : Arjuna said | kath : which/what | lingai : marks/indicators/characteristics | trin : three | gunan : qualities | etan : these | atitah : having gone beyond | bhavati : happens | prabho : O Lord | kim : what | acarah : conduct | katham : how | cha : and | etan : these | trin : three | gunan : qualities | ativartate : transcends

Arjuna said: O Lord! What are the indicators of one who has gone beyond these three gunas, what kind of conduct distinguishes him and how does he transcend the three gunas.

(22)

श्रीभगवानुवाच
प्रकाशं च प्रवृत्तिं च मोहमेव च पाण्डव।
न द्वेष्टि संप्रवृत्तानि न निवृत्तानि काङ्क्षति॥१४-२२॥

Shribhagavan uvacha
prakasham cha pravrittim cha mohameva cha pandava
na dveshti sampravrittani na nivrittani kankshati (14.22)

Shribhagavan uvacha : Lord said | prakasha : light | cha : and | pravrittim : activity | cha : and | moham : delusion | eva cha : and also | pandava : O son of Pandu, Arjuna! | na dveshti : does not hate | sampravrittani : (when) these appear | na nivrittani : (when) these are absent | kankshati : desires/pines/longs

Lord Krishna said: O son of Pandu, Arjuna! One who does not hate light (of knowledge resulting from the quality of sattva), activity (resulting from the quality of rajas) and delusion (resulting from the quality of tamas) when these appear nor does he pine for them when these are absent.

(23)

उदासीनवदासीनो गुणैर्यो न विचाल्यते।
गुणा वर्तन्त इत्येवं योऽवतिष्ठति नेङ्गते॥१४-२३॥

udasina-vad asino gunair yo na vichalyate
guna vartanta ity evam yo vatishthati nengate (14.23)

udasinavat : as if indifferent/unconcerned | asina : sitting | gunai : by gunas (qualities) | ya : who | na : not | vichalyate : is moved | guna : qualities | vartante : operate/function | itieva : knowing this | ya : who | avatishthati : stays firm | na : never | ingate : wavers

One who keeps sitting as if unconcerned, who is not moved by the three qualities (gunas) and who knowing that qualities alone operate still stays firm and never wavers.

(24)
समदुःखसुखः स्वस्थः समलोष्टाश्मकाञ्चनः।
तुल्यप्रियाप्रियो धीरस्तुल्यनिन्दात्मसंस्तुतिः॥ १४- २४॥

sama-duhkha-sukhah sva-sthah sama-loshtashma-kanchanah
tulya-priyapriyo dhiras tulya-nindatma-sanstutih (14.24)

sama : equal/same | dukha : sorrow | sukhah : pleasure | sva-sthah : situated in self | sama : equally | losta : clod of earth | asma : stone | kanchana : gold | tulya : equal/alike | priya : endearing | apriya : disagreeable | dhira : steady | tulya : equal/alike | ninda : defamation/condemnation | atma-sanstuti : praise of self

Same in sorrow and pleasure, situated in self, treating equally a clod of earth, stone and gold, alike in the face of the endearing and the disagreeable and staying steady in the face of condemnation and praise of self.

(25)
मानापमानयोस्तुल्यस्तुल्यो मित्रारिपक्षयोः।
सर्वारम्भपरित्यागी गुणातीतः स उच्यते॥ १४- २५॥

manapamanayos tulyastulyo mitrari-pakshayoh
sarvarambha-parityagi gunatitah sa uchyate (14.25)

mana : honour | apamanayo : dishonor | tulya : equal/same | mitra : friends | ari : enemies | paksayoh : sides | sarva : all | arambha : endeavours | parityagi : renouncer | guna-atita : going beyond the gunas | sah : he | uchyate : is said

One who remains the same in honour and dishonour, alike towards the sides of friends and enemies and who renounces all (worldly) endeavours, is said to have gone beyond the three gunas.

(26)

मां च योऽव्यभिचारेण भक्तियोगेन सेवते।
स गुणान्समतीत्यैतान्ब्रह्मभूयाय कल्पते॥१४- २६॥

mam cha yo 'vyabhicarena bhakti-yogena sevate
sa gunan samatityaitan brahma-bhuyaya kalpate (14.26)

mam : me | cha : and | ya : who | avyabhicarena : without fail/unflinching | bhakti-yogena : with devotion | sevate : serves | sa : he | gunan : qualities | samatitya : going beyond | etan : these | brahma-bhuyaya : becoming Brahman | kalpate : suited

And one who serves me with unflinching devotion (through Bhakti-yoga), he goes beyond these three gunas and suited to become Brahman.

(27)

ब्रह्मणो हि प्रतिष्ठाहममृतस्याव्ययस्य च।
शाश्वतस्य च धर्मस्य सुखस्यैकान्तिकस्य च॥१४- २७॥

brahmano hi pratisthaham amritasyavyayasya cha
shashvatasya cha dharmasya sukhasyaikantikasya cha (14.27)

brahmana : Brahman/the Absolute/the Supreme | hi : because | pratishtha : the dwelling | aham : I am | amrtasya : of the immortal | avyayasya : of the immutable | cha : and | shashvatasya : eternal | cha : and | dharmasya : of Dharma | sukhasya : of happiness/Bliss | aikantikasya : ultimate/absolute | cha : also

Because I am the dwelling place of the Supreme (Brahman), the immortal and immutable and of the eternal Dharma and the ultimate Bliss.

Thus ends the Fourteenth Canto titled 'Yoga of Discrimination of Three Qualities'.

Fifteenth Canto

PUROSHOTTAM YOGA
Yoga of the Supreme

(1)

श्रीभगवानुवाच
ऊर्ध्वमूलमधः शाखमश्वत्थं प्राहुरव्ययम्।
छन्दांसि यस्य पर्णानि यस्तं वेद स वेदवित्॥१५-१॥

Shribhagavan uvacha
urdhva-mulam adhah-shakham ashvattham prahur avyayam
chhandansi yasya parnani yastam veda sa veda-vit (15.1)

Shribhagavan uvacha : Lord Krishna said | urdhva-mulam : with roots going upwards | adhah : downwards | shakham : branches | ashvattham : Peepal tree | prahu : is said to be | avyayam : eternal/everlasting | chhandansi : hymns of the Vedas | yasya : of which | parnani : leaves | ya : who | tam : that | veda : knows | sa : he | veda-vit : one well-versed in Vedic knowledge

Lord Krishna said: (The universe is) spoken of as an eternal peepal tree with its roots going upwards and it's branches downwards. Its leaves are the hymns of the Vedas. One who knows this is a knower of the Vedas.

(2)

अधश्चोर्ध्वं प्रसृतास्तस्य शाखा गुणप्रवृद्धा विषयप्रवालाः।
अधश्च मूलान्यनुसंततानि कर्मानुबन्धीनि मनुष्यलोके॥१५-२॥

adhash chordhvam prasritas tasya shakha
guna-pravriddha vishaya-pravalah
adhash cha mulany anusantatani
karmanubandhini manushya-loke (15.2)

adha : downward | cha : and | urdhvam : upward | prasrita : extending | tasya : of that | shakha : branches | guna : quality/mode of nature | pravriddha : nourished by | vishaya : sense objects | pravalah : shoots | adha : downward |

cha : and | mulani : roots/sources | anusantatani : spread out | karma : action | anubandhini : bound/tied | manushya-loke : the planet (world) inhabited by human beings

Branches of that tree extending upward and downward are nourished by the modes of nature (the three gunas of sattva, rajas and tamas), it's shoots are sensory objects and in the human world tied to action. it's sources are spread out above and below.

(3-4)
न रूपमस्येह तथोपलभ्यते नान्तो न चादिर्न च संप्रतिष्ठा।
अश्वत्थमेनं सुविरूढमूल-मसङ्गशस्त्रेण दृढेन छित्त्वा॥१५-३॥
ततः पदं तत्परिमार्गितव्यं यस्मिन्गता न निवर्तन्ति भूयः।
तमेव चाद्यं पुरुषं प्रपद्ये यतः प्रवृत्तिः प्रसृता पुराणी॥१५-४॥

na rupam asyeha tathopalabhyate
nanto na chadir na cha sampratishtha
ashvattham enam su-virudha-mulam
asanga-shastrena dridhena chhittva (15.3)
tatah padam tat parimargitavyam
yasmin gata na nivartanti bhuyah
tam eva chadyam purusham prapadye
yatah pravrttih prasrita purani (15.4)

na : not | rupam : form | asya : its/of this | iha : here (in this world) | tatha : and | upalabhyate : is understood/perceived | na : neither | anta : end | na : nor | cha : also | adi : beginning | na : nor | cha : also | sampratishtha : continued existence | ashvattham : peepal tree | enam : this | suvirudha : firmly | mulam : rooted | asanga-shastrena : with the weapon of non-attachment | dridhena : strong | chhittva : cutting down | tata : then | padam : goal | tat : that | parimargitavyam : has to be sought | yasmin : where | gata : having gone | na : never | nivartanti : return | bhuyah : again | tam : in that | eva : so | cha : also | adyam : primeval (Adi) | purusham : Purusha | prapadye : surrender | yatah : from whom | pravrittih : beginning | prasrita : spread out | purani : old/eternal

Here (in this material world), the form of this tree (universe) is not understood, neither its end, nor its beginning, nor also its continued existence. This firmly rooted peepal tree having been cut down with the strong weapon of non-attachment, then that goal ought to be sought from where there is no coming back and where one surrenders to the Supreme (Primeval Lord -Adi Purusha) from whom all eternal activity streams out.

(5)
निर्मानमोहा जितसङ्गदोषा अध्यात्मनित्या विनिवृत्तकामाः।
द्वन्द्वैर्विमुक्ताः सुखदुःखसंज्ञै- र्गच्छन्त्यमूढाः पदमव्ययं तत्॥१५- ५॥

nirmana-moha jita-sanga-dosha
adhyatma-nitya vinivritta-kamah
dvandvair vimuktah sukha-duhkha-sanjnair
gachchhanty amudhah padam avyayam tat (15.5)

ni : free from | mana : (false) pride | moha : delusion | jita : conquered | sanga : attachment | disha : evil | adhyatma -nitya : always staying in the Self | vinivrtta-kama : free from sensory desires | sukh-dukha-samjnair : called pleasure and sorrow | gacchanti : reach | amudha : unfazed | padam : goal/objective | avyayam : imperishable/ultimate | tat : that

One who is free from false pride and delusion, has conquered all attachment to evil, always stays in the Self, has rid himself of sensory desires and effect of opposites like pleasure and sorrow, reaches unfazed the ultimate objective (of union with the Supreme Self).

(6)
न तद्भासयते सूर्यो न शशाङ्को न पावकः।
यद्गत्वा न निवर्तन्ते तद्धाम परमं मम॥१५- ६॥

na tad bhasayate suryo na shashanko na pavakah
yadgatva na nivartante tad dhama paramam mama (15.6)

na : not | tat : that | bhasayate : illumines | surya : sun | na : nor | shashanka : moon | na : nor | pavakah : fire | yat : where | gatva : having gone | na : never | nivartante : return | tat : that | dhama : abode | paramam : supreme | mama : my

Not illumined by the sun, nor by the moon, nor by fire, that is my supreme abode. Once having gone there, one never returns (to this material world).

(7)
ममैवांशो जीवलोके जीवभूतः सनातनः।
मनः षष्ठानीन्द्रियाणि प्रकृतिस्थानि कर्षति॥१५-७॥

mamaivansho jiva-loke jiva-bhutah sanatanah
manah-shashthanindriyani prakriti sthani karshati (15.7)

mama : my | eva : verily/only | ansha : fragment/part | jiva-loke : world of living beings | jiva-bhutah : the embodied soul | sanatanah : eternal | manah : mind | shashthani : sixth | indriyani : the senses | prakriti : nature | sthani : situated | karshati : attracts

The embodied soul which verily is an eternal part of myself attracts the five senses and the sixth mind situated in nature in this world of living beings.

(8)
शरीरं यदवाप्नोति यच्चाप्युत्क्रामतीश्वरः।
गृहित्वैतानि संयाति वायुर्गन्धानिवाशयात्॥१५-८॥

shariram yad avapnoti yach chapy utkramatishvarah
grihitvaitani sanyati vayur gandha nivashayat (15.8)

shriram : body | yat : as | avapnoti : receives | yat : as | cha : and | api : also | utkramati : gives up | ishvarah : the soul (jivatma) | grihitva : taking | etani : all these (the five senses and the mind) | sanyati : goes away | vayu : air | gandhan : smell | iva : like | ashayat : place (source)

When the soul receives a (new) body and also when it gives up (the old one), it goes away taking along all the five senses and the mind like air takes the smell away from its source.

(9)
श्रोत्रं चक्षुः स्पर्शनं च रसनं घ्राणमेव च।
अधिष्ठाय मनश्चायं विषयानुपसेवते॥१५-९॥
shrotram chakshuh sparshanam cha rasanam ghranam eva cha
adhisthaya manash chayam vishayan upasevate (15.9)

shrotram : ears | chakshuh : eyes | sparshanam : touch | cha : and | rasanam : tongue | ghranam : sense of smell | eva : also | cha : and | adhisthaya : placed | mana : mind | cha : also | ayam : he | vishayan : sense objects | upasevate : enjoys

The ears, eyes, tongue and sense of touch and also of smell placed with the mind, the embodied soul enjoys the sense objects.

(10)
उत्क्रामन्तं स्थितं वापि भुञ्जानं वा गुणान्वितम्।
विमूढा नानुपश्यन्ति पश्यन्ति ज्ञानचक्षुषः॥१५-१०॥
utkramantam sthitam vapi bhunjanam va gunanvitam
vimudha nanupashyanti pashyanti jnana-chakshushah (10.10)

utkramantam : while moving from one body to another | sthitam : staying | vapi : either | bhunjanam : experiencing | va : or | guna-anvitam : interacting with the modes of nature (the three gunas) | vimudha : fools | na : not | anupashyanti : see/understand | pashyanti : see/understand | jnana-chakshushah : eyes of knowledge

Fools cannot see how the soul is moving from one body to another or staying in the same body or experiencing interaction with the modes of nature (the three gunas). One needs special eyes of knowledge to see (understand) all this.

(11)
यतन्तो योगिनश्चैनं पश्यन्त्यात्मन्यवस्थितम्।
यतन्तोऽप्यकृतात्मानो नैनं पश्यन्त्यचेतसः॥१५-११॥
yatanto yoginash chainam pashyanty atmany avasthitam
yatanto 'py akritatmano nainam pashyanty achetasah (15.11)

yatanta : those trying | yogina : yogis | cha : also | enam : this | pashyanti : see | atmani : in the self | avasthita : residing | yatanta : attempting | api : even | akrita-atmanah : without self-realisation | na : not | enam : this | pashyanti : see | ache tasah : unintelligent

Yogis who try can also see this (Supreme) residing within their self. The unintelligent and those without self-realisation cannot see this even if they try.

(12)
यदादित्यगतं तेजो जगद्भासयतेऽखिलम्।
यच्चन्द्रमसि यच्चाग्नौ तत्तेजो विद्धि मामकम्॥१५-१२॥

yad aditya-gatam tejo jagad bhasayate 'khilam
yach chandramasi yach chagnau tat tejo viddhi mamakam (15.12)

yat : that/which | aditya-gatam : in the sun | teja : radiance | jagat : this world | bhasayate : illumines | akhilam : entire | yat : which | chandramasi : in the moon | yat : which | cha : also | agnau : in fire | tat : that | teja : radiance | viddhi : know this/understand | mamakam : from me

Know this that the radiance in the sun which illumines the entire world, that which is in the moon and which is also in fire, all come from me only.

(13)
गामाविश्य च भूतानि धारयाम्यहमोजसा।
पुष्णामि चौषधीः सर्वाः सोमो भूत्वा रसात्मकः॥१५-१३॥

gam avishya cha bhutani dharayamy aham ojasa
pushnami chaushadhih sarvah somo bhutva rasatmakah (15.13)

gam : planet earth | avishya : entering | cha : and | bhutani : living beings | dharayami : sustain/support | aham : I | ojasa : (my) energy | pushnami : nourish | cha : and | aushadhih : medicine/the herbs | sarvah : all | soma : moon | bhutva : becoming | rasa-atmakah : juice of life/nectar

And, entering planet earth with my own energy, only I sustain all living beings and myself becoming nectar-emitting moon I give power to all medicines.

(14)
अहं वैश्वानरो भूत्वा प्राणिनां देहमाश्रितः।
प्राणापानसमायुक्तः पचाम्यन्नं चतुर्विधम्॥१५-१४॥

aham vaishvanaro bhutva praninam deham ashritah
pranapana-samayuktah pachamy annam chatur-vidham (15.14)

aham : I | vaishvanara : fire in the stomach that helps digestion | bhutva : becoming | praninam : of all living beings | deham : bodies | ashritah : situated/existing | prana : outgoing breath | apana : ingoing breath | samayuktah : together | pachami : digest | annam : food | chatuh-vidham : four kinds

Becoming the fire of digestion existing in the bodies of all living beings, together with the outgoing and ingoing breath, I bring about digestion of four kinds of food.

(15)
सर्वस्य चाहं हृदि संनिविष्टो मत्तः स्मृतिर्ज्ञानमपोहनं च।
वेदैश्च सर्वैरहमेव वेद्यो वेदान्तकृद्वेदविदेव चाहम्॥१५-१५॥

sarvasya chaham hridi sannivishto
mattah smritir jnanam apohanam cha
vedaish cha sarvair aham eva vedyo
vedanta-krid veda-vid eva chaham (15.15)

sarvasya : all | cha : and | aham : I | hridi : in the heart | sannivishta : seated | mattah : from me | smriti : memory | jnanam : knowledge | apohanam : forgetting | cha : and | vedai : as per Vedas | cha : also | sarvai : all | aham : I | eva : verily | vedya : knowable | vedanta-krit : creator | ved-vit : one well-versed in the knowledge of Vedas/knower of the Vedas | eva : really | cha : and | aham : I

In the hearts of all, I am seated and from me (alone) memory, knowledge and forgetting (are caused) and as per Vedas also I am, verily, all that is worth knowing. I am the creator of Vedanta and really the knower of the Vedas.

(16)
द्वाविमौ पुरुषौ लोके क्षरश्चाक्षर एव च।
क्षरः सर्वाणि भूतानि कूटस्थोऽक्षर उच्यते॥१५- १६॥

dvavimau purushau loke ksharash chakshara eva cha
ksharah sarvani bhutani kuta-stho 'kshara uchyate (15.16)

dvau : two | imau : these | purushau : beings | loke : in this world | kshara : perishable | cha : and | akshara : imperishable | eva : also | cha : and | ksharah : perishable | sarvani : all | bhutani : living beings | kuta-stha : the Soul Consciousness | akshara : imperishable | uchyate : is spoken

Perishable and also imperishable - these are the two (kinds of) beings in this world. All the living beings (their material bodies) are perishable and only the soul consciousness is spoken of as being imperishable.

(17)
उत्तमः पुरुषस्त्वन्यः परमात्मेत्युदाहृतः।
यो लोकत्रयमाविश्य बिभर्त्यव्यय ईश्वरः॥१५- १७॥

uttamah purushas tv anyah paramatmety udahritah
yo loka-trayam avishya bibharty avyaya ishvarah (15.17)

uttamah : supreme | purusha : purush | tu : but | anyah : another | parama : the highest | atma : self (soul) | iti : thus | udahritah : is called | ya : who | loka : worlds | trayam : three | avishya : entering | bibharti : maintains/sustains | avyaya : inexhaustible/immutable | ishvarah : the Lord

But there is another supreme Purusha called the Highest Soul (Param-atma) who enters the three worlds and sustains them. He is the immutable Lord himself.

(As contradistinguished from individual embodied souls and shorn of its form attributes, Param-atma is actually the principle of the all-embracing collectivity of pure soul consciousness or the One Supreme Self Consciousness - Param-atma-chaitanya).

(18)
यस्मात्क्षरमतीतोऽहमक्षरादपि चोत्तमः।
अतोऽस्मि लोके वेदे च प्रथितः पुरुषोत्तमः॥१५-१८॥

yasmat ksharam atito 'ham aksharad api chottamah
ato 'smi loke vede cha prathitah purushottamah (15.18)

yasmat : because | ksharam : perishable | atita : transcend | aham : I | aksharat : to the imperishable | api : also | cha : and | uttamah : the best | ata : therefore | asmi : I am | loke : in this world | vede : in the Vedas | cha : and | prathita : celebrated/known as | purusha-uttamah : the Supreme

Because I transcend and am beyond both the perishable and the imperishable beings - the material bodies of beings and the souls, I am supreme and therefore both in the world and in the Vedas I am known as Purushottama or the Supreme Purusha. Purushottama is really a state of pure consciousness and may be called the Supreme Self Consciousness.

(19)
यो मामेवमसंमूढो जानाति पुरुषोत्तमम्।
स सर्वविद्भजति मां सर्वभावेन भारत॥१५-१९॥

yo mam evam asammudho janati purushottamam
sa sarva-vid bhajati mam sarva-bhavena bharata (15.19)

ya : who | mam : me | evam : thus | asammudha : free from delusion | janati : knows | purusha-uttamam : the Supreme Purusha | sa : he | sarva-vit : all knowing | bhajati : prays/worships | mam : to me | sarva-bhavana : with full devotion | bharata : O descendant of Bharata, Arjuna

O descendant of Bharata, Arjuna! Who knows me thus, free from delusion, as the Supreme Purusha - Supreme Self Consciousness - he knowing all, worships me with full faith.

(20)

इति गुह्यतमं शास्त्रमिदमुक्तं मयानघ।
एतद्बुद्ध्वा बुद्धिमान्स्यात्कृतकृत्यश्च भारत॥१५-२०॥

iti guhyatamam shastram idam uktam mayanagha
etad buddhva buddhiman syat krita-krityash cha bharata (15.20)

iti : thus | guhya-tamam : the most secret/mysterious | shastram : knowledge/teaching/science/doctrine | idam : this | uktam : spoken/imparted | maya : by me | anagha : free from sins, Arjuna | etat : this | buddhva : knowing/understanding | buddhi-man : wise/intelligent one | syat : becomes | krita-kritya : one who has fulfilled all his responsibilities | cha : and | bharata : descendant of the Great King Bharata, Arjuna

O sinless, Arjuna! Thus, this most secret knowledge has been imparted by me to you. One who understands this becomes wise and, O descendant of the great king Bharata, all his responsibilities stand fulfilled.

Thus ends the Fifteenth Canto titled 'Yoga of the Supreme'.

Sixteenth Canto

DEVASURSAMPAD VIBHAG YOGA
Yoga of the Divine and Demonic Attributes

(1)

श्रीभगवानुवाच
अभयं सत्त्वसंशुद्धिर्ज्ञानयोगव्यवस्थितिः।
दानं दमश्च यज्ञश्च स्वाध्यायस्तप आर्जवम्।।16.1।।

*Shribhagavan uvacha
abhayam sattva-samshuddhir jnana-yoga-vyavasthitih
danam damash cha yajnash cha svadhyayas tapa arjavam (16.1)*

Shribhagavan uvacha : Lord Krishna said | abhayam : fearlessness | sattva-samsuddhih : purity of heart | jnana : knowledge | yoga : yoga | vyavasthitih : getting established | danam : charity | dama : control over senses | cha : and | yajna : sacrifice | cha : and | svadhyaya : study of spiritual works | tapa : penance | arjavam : simplicity

Lord Krishna said: Fearlessness, purity of heart, getting established in yoga and knowledge, charity, control over the senses, sacrifice and study of spiritual works, penance and simplicity,

(2)

अहिंसा सत्यमक्रोधस्त्यागः शान्तिरपैशुनम्।
दया भूतेष्वलोलुप्त्वं मार्दवं ह्रीरचापलम्।।16.2।।

*ahinsa satyam akrodhas tyagah shantir apaishunam
daya bhuteshv aloluptvam mardavam hrir achapalam (15.2)*

ahinsa : non-violence | satyam : truth | akrodha : freedom from anger | tyagah : renunciation/sacrifice | shanti : peace of mind | apaishunam : not speaking ill of others | daya : compassion | bhuteshu : to all beings | aloluptvam : freedom from greed and attachment to sensory objects | mardavam : gentlemanliness | hrir : humility | achapalam : determination, absence of fickleness

Non-violence truth, freedom from anger, sacrifice, peace of mind, not speaking ill of others, compassion towards all beings, freedom from greed and attachment to sensory objects, gentlemanliness, humility, determination.

(3)
तेजः क्षमाधृतिः शौचमद्रोहो नातिमानिता।
भवन्ति सम्पदं दैवीमभिजातस्य भारत।।16.3।।

tejah kshama dhritih shaucham adroho nati-manita
bhavanti sampadam daivim abhijatasya bharata (16.3)

tejah : radiance | kshama : forgiveness | dhritih : courage/fortitude | shaucham : cleanliness | adroha : absence of envy | natimanita : not hankering for honour | bhavanti : happen to be | sampadam : the attributes | daivim : divine nature | abhijatasya : born of | bharata : O descendant of the great king Bharata, Arjuna

Radiance, forgiveness, fortitude, cleanliness, absence of envy, not hankering for honours - these happen to be the attributes of those born of divine nature, O descendant of the great king Bharata!

(4)
दम्भो दर्पोऽभिमानश्च क्रोधः पारुष्यमेव च।
अज्ञानं चाभिजातस्य पार्थ सम्पदमासुरीम्।।16.4।।

dambho darpo 'bhimanash cha krodhah parushyam eva cha
ajnanam chabhijatasya partha sampadam asurim (16.4)

dambha : ostentation | darpa : arrogance | abhimana : self-conceit | cha : and | krodhah : anger | paurushyam : rude behaviour | eva : verily | cha : and | ajnanam : ignorance | cha : and | abhijatasya : one born of | partha : son of Pratha, Arjuna | sampadam : attributes | asurim : demonic

O son of Pratha, Arjuna! Ostentation, arrogance, self-conceit, anger, rude behaviour and ignorance are attributes of those born of demonic nature.

(5)

दैवी सम्पद्विमोक्षाय निबन्धायासुरी मता।
मा शुचः सम्पदं दैवीमभिजातोऽसि पाण्डव।।16.5।।

daivi sampad vimokshaya nibandhayasuri mata
ma shuchah sampadam daivim abhijato 'si pandava (16.5)

daivi : divine/godly | sampat : quality | vimokshaya : to liberation/freedom | nibandhaya : to bondage | asuri : demonic | mata : deemed to be | ma : do not | shuchah : worry | sampadam : qualities | daivim : divine | abhijata : born of | asi : you are | Pandava : O son of Pandu, Arjuna

O son of Pandu, Arjuna! The divine quality leads to freedom and the demonic quality is deemed to lead to bondage. You need not worry because you are born of divine qualities.

(6)

द्वौ भूतसर्गौ लोकेऽस्मिन्दैव आसुर एव च।
दैवो विस्तरशः प्रोक्त आसुरं पार्थ मे श्रृणु।।16.6।।

dvau bhuta-sargau loke 'smin daiva asura eva cha
daivo vistarashah prokta asuram partha me shrnu (16.6)

dvau : two | bhuta-sargau : living beings created | loke : in the world | asmin : this | daivam : divine | asura : demonic | eva : only | cha : and | daivam : the divine | vistarasah : at length | prokta : spoken | asuram : demonic | partha : son of Pratha, Arjuna | me : to me | shrnu : listen

In this world, there are only two types of living beings created - the divine and the demonic. The divine have been spoken of at length, O Partha (Arjuna)! (now) Listen to me about the demonic.

(7)

प्रवृत्तिं च निवृत्तिं च जना न विदुरासुराः।
न शौचं नापि चाचारो न सत्यं तेषु विद्यते ।।16.7।।

pravrittim cha nivrittim cha jana na vidur asurah
na shaucham napi chacharo na satyam teshu vidyate (16.7)

pravrittim : coming forth/tendency (to do the right thing) | cha : and | nivrittim : retiring/not to do what is not right | cha : and | jana : persons | na : never | vidu : know | asurah : those with demonic attributes | na : neither | shaucham : cleanliness | na : nor | api : also | cha : and | achara : behavior | na : nor | satyam : truth | teshu : in them | vidyate : appears

Persons with demonic attributes do not know what to do and what to refrain from doing. Neither cleanliness, nor good behaviour nor truth is found in them.

(8)
असत्यमप्रतिष्ठं ते जगदाहुरनीश्वरम्।
अपरस्परसम्भूतं किमन्यत्कामहैतुकम् ॥16.8॥

*asatyam apratishtham te jagad ahur anishvaram
aparaspara-sambhutam kim anyat kama-haitukam (16.8)*

asatyam : unreal/without truth | apratishtham : without foundation | te : they | jagat : the universe | ahu : say | anishvaram : godless | aparaspara : by coming together (male-female union) | sambhutam : has arisen | kimanyat : what else | kama-haitukam : caused by lust only

They say that the universe is unreal, without foundation and godless and that it has arisen only from sex relationships and has no other cause.

(9)
एतां दृष्टिमवष्टभ्य नष्टात्मानोऽल्पबुद्धयः।
प्रभवन्त्युग्रकर्माणः क्षयाय जगतोऽहिताः॥16.9॥

*etam drishtim avashtabhya nashtatmano 'lpa-buddhayah
prabhavanty ugra-karmanah kshayaya jagato 'hitah (16.9)*

etam : this | drishtim : view | avashtabhya : holding | nashta-atmana : who have lost their soul (self-consciousness) | alp-buddhayah : persons of small intelligence | prabhavanti : appear | ugra-karmanah : engaged in extremist acts | kshayaya : destruction | jagata : of the world | ahitah : enemies

Holding this view, they have lost their consciousness of the Self (Soul). Persons of small intelligence, they appear as enemies of the world engaged in extremist acts of destruction.

(10)
कामामाश्रित्य दुष्पूरं दम्भमानमदान्विताः।
मोहाद्गृहीत्वासद्ग्राहान्प्रवर्तन्तेऽशुचिव्रताः ।।16.10।।

*kamam ashritya dushpuram dambha-mana-madanvitah
mohad grihitvasad-grahan pravartante 'shuchi-vratah (16.10)*

kamam : lust/desire | ashritya : taking shelter/depending on/possessed by | dushpuram : insatiable | dambha : arrogance | mana : false pride | mada-anvitah : self-conceit | mohat : by delusion | grihitva : taking | asatgrahan : evil thoughts | pravartante : function | ashuchi : impure | vratah : resolve

Possessed by insatiable lust, deluded by arrogance, false pride and self-conceit, they (persons with demonic attributes) are overtaken by evil thoughts and work for impure resolves.

(11)
चिन्तामपरिमेयां च प्रलयान्तामुपाश्रिताः।
कामोपभोगपरमा एतावदिति निश्चिताः ।।16.11।।

*chintam aparimeyam cha pralayantam upashritah
kamopabhoga-parama etavad iti nishchitah (16.11)*

chintam : anxiety | aparimeyam : innumerable | cha : and | pralaya-antam : unto the end of the world/until death | upashritah : having taken refuge | kama-upabhoga : gratification of senses | parama : the highest | etavat : that is all | iti : in this way | nishchitah : surely

Beset with innumerable anxieties unto the end of life, they come to regard gratification of the senses as the highest (aim of life) and believe that that is surely all to it.

(12)

आशापाशशतैर्बद्धाः कामक्रोधपरायणाः।
ईहन्ते कामभोगार्थमन्यायेनार्थसञ्चयान् ॥16.12॥

asha-pasha-shatair baddhah kama-krodha-parayanah
ihante kama-bhogartham anyayenartha-sanchayan (16.12)

asha-pasha : ties of hope | shatai : hundreds of | baddha : bound | kama : lust | krodha : anger | parayanah : given to | ihante : keep trying | kama : lust | bhog : sensory pleasure | artham : purpose | anyayena : through unjust means | artha : of wealth | sanchayan : accumulation

Bound by hundreds of ties of hope and given to lust and anger, they keep trying to accumulate wealth through unjust means for gratification of lust and sensory pleasure.

(13)

इदमद्य मया लब्धमिमं प्राप्स्ये मनोरथम्।
इदमस्तीदमपि मे भविष्यति पुनर्धनम्॥16.13॥

idam adya maya labdham imam prapsye manoratham
idam astidam api me bhavishyati punar dhanam (16.13)

idam : this | adya : today | maya : by me | labdham : gained | imam : this | prapsye : shall obtain | mana-ratham : desire | idam : this | asti : is | idam : this | api : also | me : mine | bhavishyati : will happen | punah : again | dhanam : wealth

This I have gained today, this I shall get as desired, this and this is mine also, again, all this wealth shall be mine.

(14)

असौ मया हतः शत्रुर्हनिष्ये चापरानपि।
ईश्वरोऽहमहं भोगी सिद्धोऽहं बलवान्सुखी॥16.14॥

asau maya hatah shatrur hanishye chaparan api
ishvaro 'ham aham bhogi siddho 'ham balavan sukhi (16.14)

asau : that | maya : by me | hatah : killed | shatru : enemy | hanishye : shall kill | cha : and | aparan : others | api : also | ishvara : the lord | aham : I am | aham : I am | bhogi : one given to sensory enjoyment | siddha : perfect | aham : I am | balavan : powerful | sukhi : happy

That enemy has been killed by me and I shall kill others also. I am the lord. I am the enjoyer. I am perfect, powerful and happy.

(15)
आढ्योऽभिजनवानस्मि कोऽन्योऽस्ति सदृशो मया।
यक्ष्ये दास्यामि मोदिष्य इत्यज्ञानविमोहिताः ॥16.15॥

adhyo 'bhijanavan asmi ko 'nyo 'sti sadrisho maya
yakshye dasyami modishya ity ajnana-vimohitah (16.15)

adhya : wealthy | abhijana-van : born in a high family | asmi : I am | ka : who | anya : other | asti : there is | sadrisha : like | maya : me | yakshye : shall sacrifice | dasyami : shall give | modishye : shall enjoy | iti : thus | ajnana : ignorance | vimohitah : deluded

I am wealthy, born in a high family. Who else is there like me? I shall sacrifice. I shall give. I shall enjoy. Deluded by ignorance, this is how the persons with demonic qualities talk.

(16)
अनेकचित्तविभ्रान्ता मोहजालसमावृताः।
प्रसक्ताः कामभोगेषु पतन्ति नरकेऽशुचौ ॥16.16॥

aneka-chitta-vibhranta moha-jala-samavritah
prasaktah kama-bhogeshu patanti narake 'shuchau (16.16)

aneka : many | chitta-vibhranta : perplexed minds | moha : illusion | jala : net | samavritah : surrounded | prasaktah : addicted to | kama-bhogeshu : sensual pleasures | patanti : fall down | narake : into hell | shuchau : dirty/foul

With minds perplexed in many ways, surrounded by a net of illusions and addicted to sensual pleasures, they fall down into foul hell.

(17)

आत्मसम्भाविताः स्तब्धा धनमानमदान्विताः।
यजन्ते नामयज्ञैस्ते दम्भेनाविधिपूर्वकम्॥16.17॥

atma-sambhavitah stabdha dhana-mana-madanvitah
yajante nama-yajnaiste dambhenavidhi-purvakam (16.17)

atma-sambhavitah : self-conceited | stabdha : arrogant/ haughty | dhana-mana : vanity of riches | mada : intoxication/delusion | anvitah : filled with | yajante : perform sacrifice | nama : only in name | yajnai : with sacrifices | te : they | dambhena : out of false pride | avidhi-purvakam : disregarding law and rules

They are self-conceited, arrogant and intoxicated with the vanity of riches. Their performing sacrifices (yajnah) is only for name sake and without following the law and rules.

(18)

अहङ्कारं बलं दर्पं कामं क्रोधं च संश्रिताः।
मामात्मपरदेहेषु प्रद्विषन्तोऽभ्यसूयकाः॥16.18॥

ahankaram balam darpam kamam krodham cha samshritah
mamatma-para-deheshu pradvishanto 'bhyasuyakah (16.18)

ahankaram : false pride/ego | balam : strength/power | darpam : insolence | kamam : lust | krodham : anger | cha : and | samshritah: possessed of | mam : me | atma : own | para : in the other | deheshu : bodies | pradvishanta : hate | abhya-suyakah : malignant/envious people

Possessed of false pride, power, insolence, lust and anger, the malignant persons hate me (the embodied soul/self) in their own and other bodies.

(19)

तानहं द्विषतः क्रूरान्संसारेषु नराधमान्।
क्षिपाम्यजस्रमशुभानासुरीष्वेव योनिषु॥16.19॥

tan aham dvishatah kruran sansareshu naradhaman
kshipamy ajasram ashubhan asurishv eva yonishu (16.19)

tan : those | aham : I | dvishatah : envious/ malicious | kruran : cruel | sansareshu : into these worlds | nara-adhaman : lowest among human beings | kshipami : throw | ajasram : perpetually/forever | ashubhan : evil-doers | asurishu : of demonic persons | eva : only | yonishu : into the wombs

Those who are envious and cruel evil-doers and the lowest kind of human beings, I throw them in these worlds forever into the wombs of demonic persons only.

(20)
असुरीं योनिमापन्ना मूढा जन्मनि जन्मनि।
मामप्राप्यैव कौन्तेय ततो यान्त्यधमां गतिम्।।16.20।।
asurim yonim apanna mudha janmani janmani
mam aprapyaiva kaunteya tato yanty adhamam gatim (16.20)

asurim : demonic | yonim : species/wombs | apanna : attaining | mudha : the fools | janmani janmani : birth after birth | mam : me | aprapya : not able to reach | eva : verily | kaunteya : O son of Kunti, Arjuna | tata : thereafter | yanti : go | adhamam : lower/worse | gatim : conditions

O son of Kunti, Arjuna! Being born again and again among the demonic species, not able to reach me, verily, the fools thereafter go down to worse conditions.

(21)
त्रिविधं नरकस्येदं द्वारं नाशनमात्मनः।
कामः क्रोधस्तथा लोभस्तस्मादेतत्त्रयं त्यजेत्।।16.21।।
tri-vidham narakasyedam dvaram nashanam atmanah
kamah krodhas tatha lobhas tasmad etat trayam tyajet (16.21)

tri-vidham : three kinds | narakasya : of hell | idam : this | dvaram : gate | nashanam : destructive | atmanah : of the self (soul) | kamah : lust | krodha : anger | tatha : and | lobha : greed | tasmat : therefore | etat : these | trayam : three | tyajet : should give up

Lust, anger and greed - these three kinds of gates leading to hell - are destructive of Self (soul), therefore these three ought to be given up.

(22)
एतैर्विमुक्तः कौन्तेय तमोद्वारैस्त्रिभिर्नरः।
आचरत्यात्मनः श्रेयस्ततो याति परां गतिम्।।16.22।।

etair vimuktah kaunteya tamo-dvarais tribhir narah
acharaty atmanah shreyas tato yati param gatim (16.22)

etai : from these | vimuktah : freed | kaunteya : son of Kunti, Arjuna | tama-dvarai : from the doors of ignorance | tribhi : of three kinds | narah : a man | acharati : acts | atmanah : for self | shreya : good | tata : thereafter | yati : goes | param : the supreme | gatim : state/condition

O son of Kunti, Arjuna! Once freed from these three kinds of doors of ignorance, a man acts for the good of the Self and thereafter reaches the supreme state (of self-consciousness).

(23)
यः शास्त्रविधिमुत्सृज्य वर्तते कामकारतः।
न स सिद्धिमवाप्नोति न सुखं न परां गतिम्।।16.23।।

yah shastra-vidhim utsrijya vartate kama-karatah
na sa siddhim avapnoti na sukham na param gatim (16.23)

yah : who | shastra-vidhim : rules laid down in sacred texts | utsrijya : giving up | vartate : continues | kama-karatah : engaged in acts of lust | na : never | sa : he | siddhim : perfection | avapnoti : attains | na : nor | sukham : happiness | na : never | param : supreme | gatim : destination

One who disregards rules laid down in scriptures and remains engaged in acts of lust can neither attain perfection nor happiness and can never reach the supreme destination (of union of the embodied Self with the Supreme Self).

(24)
तस्माच्छास्त्रं प्रमाणं ते कार्याकार्यव्यवस्थितौ।
ज्ञात्वा शास्त्रविधानोक्तं कर्म कर्तुमिहार्हसि।।16.24।।

tasmach chhastram pramanam te karyakarya-vyavasthitau
jnatva shastra-vidhanoktam karma kartum iharhasi (16.24)

tasmat : therefore | sastram : scriptures/sacred texts | pramanam : proof/evidence/sanction/authority | te : your | karya : work/duty | akarya : what is not to be done | vyavasthitau : in the system | jnatva : knowing | shastra : scripture | vidhana : rules and regulations | uktam : as stated | karma : action | kartum : to do | iha : here/ in this world | arhasi : should

One should, therefore, treat the rules and regulations stated in the scriptures as the final authority for understanding what acts to perform and what should not be done. Knowing the rules and regulations, one should act in this world accordingly.

Thus ends the Sixteenth Canto titled 'Yoga of the Divine and Demonic Attributes'.

Seventeenth Canto

SHRADDHATRAYA-VIBHAG-YOGA
Yoga of Three-fold Faith

(1)

अर्जुन उवाच
ये शास्त्रविधिमुत्सृज्य यजन्ते श्रद्धयान्विताः।
तेषां निष्ठा तु का कृष्ण सत्त्वमाहो रजस्तमः॥17.1॥

arjuna uvacha
ye shastra-vidhim utsrijya yajante shraddhayanvitah
tesham nishtha tu ka krishna sattvam aho rajas tamah (17.1)

arjuna uvacha : Arjuna said | ye : who | shastra-vidhim : rules laid down by the scriptures | utsrijya : giving up | yajante : worship/make sacrifices | shraddhaya : with devotion/reverence/faith | anvitah : full of | tesham : them | nishtha : position/faith | tu : but | ka : what | Krishna : O Lord Krishna | sattvam : goodness | aho : or else | rajas : passion | tamah : ignorance

Arjuna said: O Lord Krishna! What is the position of those who disregard the rules laid down in the scriptures but worship with full devotion? Is their conduct covered by qualities of goodness, passion or ignorance (sattoguna, rajoguna or tamoguna)?

(2)

श्रीभगवानुवाच
त्रिविधा भवति श्रद्धा देहिनां सा स्वभावजा।
सात्त्विकी राजसी चैव तामसी चेति तां शृणु॥17.2॥

Shribhagavan uvacha
tri-vidha bhavati shraddha dehinam sa svabhava-ja
sattviki rajasi chaiva tamasi cheti tam shrinu (17.2)

Shribhagavan uvacha: The Lord said | tri-vidha : of three kinds | bhavati : happens/becomes | shraddha : faith | dehinam : soul in the body | sa : that | sva-bhava-ja : born of ones nature | sattviki : goodness | rajasi : passion |

cha : and | eva : verily | tamasi : ignorance | cha : and | iti : thus | tam : that | shrinu : listen

Lord Krishna said: Faith happens to be of three kinds depending on the nature of the embodied. It may be in goodness (sattvika), in passion (rajasika) or in ignorance (tamasika). About that, listen.

(3)
सत्त्वानुरूपा सर्वस्य श्रद्धा भवति भारत।
श्रद्धामयोऽयं पुरुषो यो यच्छ्रद्धः स एव सः॥17.3॥
sattvanurupa sarvasya shraddha bhavati bharata
shraddha-mayo 'yam purusho yo yach-chraddhah sa eva sah (17.3)

sattva-anurupa : according to the nature | sarvasya : of each one | shraddha : faith | bhavati : becomes | bharata : O descendant of King Bharata, Arjuna | shraddha-maya : consists of faith | ayam : this | purusha : person | ya : who | yat : which | shraddhah : faith | sa : thus | eva : verily | sah : he

O descendant of King Bharata, Arjuna! The faith of everyone is dependent on ones nature. Each person is made of his/her faith. Thus, he/she verily is what his/her faith is.

(4)
यजन्ते सात्त्विका देवान्यक्षरक्षांसि राजसाः।
प्रेतान्भूतगणांश्चान्ये यजन्ते तामसा जनाः॥17.4॥
yajante sattvika devan yaksha-rakshamsi rajasah
pretan bhuta-gananash chanye yajante tamasa janah (17.4)

yajante : worship | sattvika : those in the quality of goodness | devan : gods | yaksha-rakshansi : demons | rajasah : those in the quality of passion | pretan : spirits | bhuta-ganan : ghosts | cha : and | anye : others | yajante : worship | tamasah : those in the quality of ignorance | janah : people

Those in the quality of goodness (sattvik persons) worship the gods, those in the quality of passion (rajasik persons) worship the demons and those in the quality of ignorance (tamasik persons) worship the spirits (pretatma), ghosts (bhut) and others.

(5-6)
अशास्त्रविहितं घोरं तप्यन्ते ये तपो जनाः।
दम्भाहङ्कारसंयुक्ताः कामरागबलान्विताः।।17.5।।
कर्शयन्तः शरीरस्थं भूतग्राममचेतसः।
मां चैवान्तःशरीरस्थं तान्विद्ध्यासुरनिश्चयान्।।17.6।।

ashastra-vihitam ghoram tapyante ye tapo janah
dambhahankara-sanyuktah kama-raga-balanvitah (17.5)
karshayantah sharira-stham bhuta-gramam achetasah
mam chaivantah sharira-stham tan viddhy asura-nishchayan (17.6)

ashastra-vihitam : not enjoined by scriptures | ghoram : severe | tapyante : undertake | ye : those who | tapa : penance | janah : persons | dambha : arrogance | ahankara : self-conceit/egoism | samyuktah : given to | kama : lust | raga : attachment | bala : power | anvitah : possessed of | | karshayantah : torturing | sharira-stham : situated in the body | bhuta-gramam : organs of the body | achetasah : devoid of sense/foolish | mam : me | cha : also | eva : verily | antah : within | sharira-stham : situated in the body | tan : them | viddhi : understand | asura : demons | nishchayena : certainly

Those persons who undertake severe penances not ordained by the scriptures, are given to lust and self-conceit. Possessed of lust, attachment and power, they also torture their body organs and verily, even Me (the embodied Soul/Self) within the body. They are certainly demons. Understand.

(7)
आहारस्त्वपि सर्वस्य त्रिविधो भवति प्रियः।
यज्ञस्तपस्तथा दानं तेषां भेदमिमं शृणु।।17.7।।

aharas tv api sarvasya tri-vidho bhavati priyah
yajnas tapas tatha danam tesham bhedam imam shrinu (17.7)

ahara : food | tu : indeed | api : also | sarvasya : of everyone | tri-vidha : of three kinds | bhavati : happens to be/is | priyah : dear | yajna : sacrifice |

tapa : penance | tatha : and | danam : charity | tesham : of them | bhedam : differences | imam : this | shrinu : listen

The food dear to everyone is also of three kinds indeed. This also applies to sacrifice, penance and charity. Now listen to the differences between them.

(8)

आयुः सत्त्वबलारोग्य-सुखप्रीतिविवर्धनाः।
रस्याः स्निग्धाः स्थिरा हृद्या-आहाराः सात्त्विकप्रियाः।।17.8।।

*ayuh-sattva-balarogya- sukha-pritivi-vardhanah
rasyah snigdhah sthira hridya aharah sattvika-priyah (17.8)*

ayuh : age/longevity | sattva : purity | bala : strength | arogya : good health | sukha : happiness/cheerfulness/joy | priti : appetite | vivardhanah : augmenting | rasyah : juicy/savoury | snigdhah : fatty | sthira : enduring | hridya : agreeable | aharah : foods | sattvika : those in the quality of goodness | priyah : pleasing/liked

Those persons who are in the quality of goodness (of sattvika nature) like foods which augment longevity, energy, strength, good health, happiness and appetite and which are juicy, fatty, enduring and agreeable.

(9)

कट्वम्ललवणात्युष्णतीक्ष्णरूक्षविदाहिनः।
आहारा राजसस्येष्टा दुःखशोकामयप्रदाः।।17.9।।

*katv-amla-lavanaty-ushna- tikshna-ruksha-vidahinah
ahara rajasasyesta duhkha-shokamaya-pradah (17.9)*

katu : bitter | amla : sour | lavana : salty | ati-ushna : very hot | tikshna : pungent | ruksha : dry | vidahinah : burning | ahara : food | rajasasya : one in the quality of passion | ishta : preference | duhkha : distress | shoka : sorrow | amaya : disease | pradah : causing

Foods that are bitter, sour, salty, very hot, pungent, dry and burning is the preference of those in the quality of passion (of rajasika nature). These cause distress, sorrow and disease.

(10)

यातयामं गतरसं पूति पर्युषितं च यत्।
उच्छिष्टमपि चामेध्यं भोजनं तामसप्रियम्।।17.10।।

yata-yamam gata-rasam puti paryushitam cha yat
uchchhistam api chamedhyam bhojanam tamasa-priyam (17.10)

yata-yamam : cold/cooked three hours (yama) earlier | gata-rasam : that has lost its essence/tasteless | puti : putrid/foul smelling | paryushitam : stale/cooked a day before | cha : and | yat : which | uchchhistam : left-over after eating by someone | api : also | cha : and | amedhyam : impure/filthy | bhojanam : food | tamasa : those in the quality of ignorance | priyam : dear

Food which is cold, tasteless, foul-smelling, stale and others' left-over as also filthy is dear to those in the quality of ignorance (of tamasika nature).

(11)

अफलाकाङ्क्षिभिर्यज्ञो विधिदृष्टो य इज्यते।
यष्टव्यमेवेति मनः समाधाय स सात्त्विकः।।17.11।।

aphalakankshibhir yajno vidhi-drishto ya ijyate
yashtavyam eveti manah samadhaya sa sattvikah (17.11)

aphala-akanksibhi : those not seeking any fruits of action | yajna : sacrifice | vidhi-drishta : as per the rules laid down in the scriptures | ya : which | ijyate : performed | yashtavyam : for its own sake | eva : only | iti : thus | manah : mind | samadhaya : fixed | sa : it | sattvikah : those in the quality of goodness

Those persons who perform yajna (offer sacrifice) for its own sake, with their mind fixed on it only, without seeking any fruit of their action, are in the quality of goodness (of sattvika nature).

(12)
अभिसंधाय तु फलं दम्भार्थमपि चैव यत्।
इज्यते भरतश्रेष्ठ तं यज्ञं विद्धि राजसम्।।17.12।।

*abhisandhaya tu phalam dambhartham api chaiva yat
ijyate bharata-shreshtha tam yajnam viddhi rajasam (17.12)*

abhisandhaya : keeping in view | tu : but | phalam : the fruit/the result | dambha : false pride | artham : for the sake of | api : even | cha : and | eva : only | yat : which | ijyate : performed/undertaken | bharata-shreshtha : O distinguished descendant of king Bharata | tam : that | yajnam : sacrifice | viddhi : know | rajasam : in the quality of passion (Rajasika Nature)

But, O distinguished descendant of King Bharata, Arjuna! Know that the sacrifice (yajna) which is performed only for the sake of false pride or even for the fruits thereof, belongs to the quality of passion (is rajasika in nature).

(13)
विधिहीनमसृष्टान्नं मन्त्रहीनमदक्षिणम्।
श्रद्धाविरहितं यज्ञं तामसं परिचक्षते।।17.13।।

*vidhi-hinam asrishtannam mantra-hinam adakshinam
shraddha-virahitam yajnam tamasam parichakshate (17.13)*

vidhi-hinam : without the sanction of the rules (laid down in the shastras) | asrishta-annam : without distribution of food | mantra-hinam : without chanting of hymns | adakshinam : without paying a fee to the priest | shraddha : faith | virahitam : without | yajnam : sacrifice | tamasam : nature of ignorance (tamasika) | parichakshate : is said to be

Any sacrifice (yajna) which is not performed in accordance with the rules (laid down in the shastras), where no food is distributed, no chanting of Vedic hymns takes place, priest is not paid and faith is missing, is said to be in the nature of ignorance (tamasika).

(14)
देवद्विजगुरुप्राज्ञपूजनं शौचमार्जवम्।
ब्रह्मचर्यमहिंसा च शारीरं तप उच्यते।।17.14।।

deva-dwija-guru-pragya- pujanam shaucham arjavam
brahmacharyam ahinsa cha shariram tapa uchyate (17.14)

deva : gods | dwija : the twice-born/the higher castes/the brahmanas | guru : the teacher/the spiritual master | pragya : the learned/the wise | pujanam : worship | shaucham : cleanliness/purity | arjavam : simplicity/straightforwardness | brahmacharyam : celibacy/continence | ahinsa : non-violence | cha : and | shariram : concerning the body | tapa : penance/austerity | uchyate : said to be

Worship of gods, brahmanas, teachers and the learned; purity, straight forwardness, celibacy and non-violence are said to be penance of the body.

(15)
अनुद्वेगकरं वाक्यं सत्यं प्रियहितं च यत्।
स्वाध्यायाभ्यसनं चैव वाङ्मयं तप उच्यते।।17.15।।

anudvega-karam vakyam satyam priya-hitam cha yat
svadhyayabhyasanam chaiva van-mayam tapa uchyate (17.15)

anudvega-karam : not causing annoyance | vakyam : words/speech | satyam : truthful | priya : dear/pleasing | hitam : beneficial | cha : and | yat : which | svadhyaya : learning of Vedas | abhyasanam : practice | cha : also | eva : verily | vak-mayam : concerning speech | tapa : penance | uchyate : said to be

Words which do not cause annoyance, are truthful, pleasing and beneficial as also the practice of regular study of Vedic literature, verily, are said to be penance of speech.

(16)
मनः प्रसादः सौम्यत्वं मौनमात्मविनिग्रहः।
भावसंशुद्धिरित्येतत्तपो मानसमुच्यते।।17.16।।

manah-prasadah saumyatvam maunam atma-vinigrahah
bhava-sanshuddhir ity etat tapo manasam uchyate (17.16)

manah : mind | prasadah : serenity | saumyatvam : kindliness | maunam : silence | atma : self | vinigrahah : control | bhava : purpose/motive/nature | samshuddhi : purity/purification | iti : thus | etat : this | tapa : penance | manasam : of the mind | uchyate : is said to be

Serenity of mind, kindliness, silence, self-control, purity of purpose are said to be (components of) penance of the mind.

(17)
श्रद्धया परया तप्तं तपस्तच्त्रिविधं नरैः।
अफलाकाङ्क्षिभिर्युक्तैःसात्त्विकंपरिचक्षते।।17.17।।
shraddhaya paraya taptam tapas tat tri-vidham naraih
aphalakankshibhir yuktaih sattvikam parichakshate (17.17)

shraddhaya : with faith | paraya : great | taptam : practiced | tapa : penance | tat : that | tri-vidham : three kinds | naraih : men | aphala-akankshibhi : not desiring any fruits (for action) | yuktaih : yogi/steadfast | sattvikam : (in the quality of) goodness | parichakshate : is called/is said to be

The three kinds of penance practised by yogi men with great faith (and) without desiring any fruits thereof are said to be in (the category/quality of) goodness.
(The reference being to the three qualities - sattvika, rajsika and tamsika).

(18)
सत्कारमानपूजार्थं तपो दम्भेन चैव यत्।
क्रियते तदिह प्रोक्तं राजसं चलमध्रुवम्।।17.18।।
satkara-mana-pujartham tapo dambhena chaiva yat
kriyate tad iha proktam rajasam chalam adhruvam (17.18)

satkara : respect | mana : honour | puja : worship | artham : for the purpose of | tapa : penance | dambhena : in arrogance | cha : and | eva : verily | yat : which | kriyate : done | tat : that | iha : here/in this world | proktam : is said to be | rajasam : in the quality of passion (rajas) | chalam : unstable | adhruvam : transient/temporary

Penance which is done here (in this world) in the spirit of arrogance and for the purpose of getting respect, honour and worship is verily said to be in the quality of passion (rajsik), unstable and transient.

(19)
मूढग्राहेणात्मनो यत्पीडया क्रियते तपः।
परस्योत्सादनार्थं वा तत्तामसमुदाहृतम्।।17.19।।

mudha-grahenatmano yat pidaya kriyate tapah
parasyotsadanartham va tat tamasam udahritam (17.19)

mudha-grahena : out of foolish insistence | atmana : self | yat : which | pidaya : torture | kriyate : is practiced | tapah : penance | parasya : others | utsadana-artham : for the purpose of destroying | va : or | tat : that | tamasam : in the quality of ignorance/darkness/tamsik | udahritam : is declared to be

That penance which is practised out of foolish insistence and involves torture of self or is aimed at destroying others is declared to be in the quality of ignorance (tamsik).

(20)
दातव्यमिति यद्दानं दीयतेऽनुपकारिणे।
देशे काले च पात्रे च तद्दानं सात्त्विकं स्मृतम्।।17.20।।

datavyam iti yad danam diyate 'nupakarine
deshe kale cha patre cha tad danam sattvikam smritam (17.20)

datavyam-iti : believing that it is good to be giving | yat : which | danam : charity | diyate : given | anupakarine : to one who is expected to do nothing in return | deshe : (at a proper) place | kale : (at the right) time | cha : and | patre : (deserving) person | cha : and | tat : that | danam : charity | sattvikam : in the quality of goodness | smritam : is held

Believing that it is good to be giving, to extend charity at a proper place and at the right time to a deserving person who is not required to do anything in return, is held to be in the quality of goodness (sattvika).

(21)
यत्तुप्रत्युपकारार्थं फलमुद्दिश्य वा पुनः।
दीयते च परिक्लिष्टं तद्दानं राजसं स्मृतम्।।17.21।।

yat tu pratyupakarartham phalam uddishya va punah
diyate cha pariklistam tad danam rajasam smritam (17.21)

yat : which | tu : but | prati-upakara-artham : for the purpose of getting something in return | phalam : a result | uddishya : keeping in view | va : or | punah : again | diyate : is given | cha : also | pariklishtam – grudgingly | tat : that | danam : charity | rajasam : in the quality of passion (rajasik) | smritam : is considered to be

But, that charity which is done for the purpose of getting something in return or keeping in view some result or done grudgingly is considered to be charity in the quality of passion (rajasik).

(22)
अदेशकाले यद्दानमपात्रेभ्यश्च दीयते।
असत्कृतमवज्ञातं तत्तामसमुदाहृतम्।।17.22।।

adesha-kale yad danam apatrebhyash cha diyate
asat-kritam avajnatam- tat tamasam udahritam (17.22)

adesha : at an inappropriate place | kale : time | yat : that which | danam : charity | apatrebhya : to undeserving person | cha : and | diyate : is given | asat-kriatam : without respect | avajnatam : disdainfully | tat : that | tamasam : in the quality of tamsik (ignorance/darkness) | udahritam : is said to be

That charity which is given to an undeserving person at an inappropriate place and at an inappropriate time without respect and is disdainfully said to be tamsik (in the quality of darkness/ignorance).

(23)
ॐ तत्सदिति निर्देशो ब्रह्मणस्त्रिविधः स्मृतः।
ब्राह्मणास्तेन वेदाश्च यज्ञाश्च विहिताः पुरा।।17.23।।

om tat sad iti nirdesho brahmanas tri-vidhah smritah
brahmanas tena vedash cha yajnash cha vihitah pura (17.23)

om : the Supreme Brahman/Om | tat : that | sat : reality | iti : thus | nirdesha : indicator/designation | brahman : the Supreme Soul/Self | tri-vidhah : three-fold | smritah : declared to be/said to be | brahmanas : the Brahmanas | tena : with that | veda : the Vedas | cha : also | yajna : sacrifice | cha : also | vihitah : were made | pura : old/from the earliest times

"Om tat sat" (Om is THA Trealty) is the three-fold indicator of the Supreme Self/Soul, the Brahman (the One encompassing all that is manifest or unmanifest). By THAT were created from the earliest times the Brahmanas, the Vedas and the Yajnas.

(24)
तस्माल्श ॐ इत्युदाहृत्य यज्ञदानतपः क्रियाः।
प्रवर्तन्ते विधानोक्ताः सततं ब्रह्मवादिनाम्।।17.24।।

tasmad om ity udahritya yajna-dana-tapah-kriyah
pravartante vidhanoktah satatam brahma-vadinam (17.24)

tasmat : therefore | om : Om | iti : thus | udahritya : uttering | yajna : sacrifice | dana : charity | tapah : penance | kriyah : acts | pravartante : begun | vidhana-uktah : As laid down by regulations in scriptures | satatam : always | brahma-vadina : the Vedic scholars

Therefore, as laid down by regulations in the scriptures, the followers of the Vedas always begin their acts of sacrifice, charity and penance by first uttering OM.

(25)
तदित्यनभिसन्धाय फलं यज्ञतपःक्रियाः।
दानक्रियाश्च विविधाः क्रियन्ते मोक्षकाङ्क्षिभिः।।17.25।।

tad ity anabhisandhaya phalam yajna-tapah-kriyah
dana-kriyash cha vividhah kriyante moksha-kankshibhih (17.25)

tat : that | iti : thus | anabhisandhaya : without seeking | phalam : fruit of action | yajna : sacrifice | tapah : penance | kriyah : acts | dana : charity | kriya : acts | cha : and | vividhah : miscellaneous | kriyante : done | mokshakankshibhi : those aspiring for supreme salvation from the cycle of death and birth

Thus, uttering that (OM), without seeking any fruit, various acts of sacrifice, penance and charity are done by those who aspire for ultimate salvation from the cycle of death and birth.

(26)
सद्भावे साधुभावे च सदित्येतत्प्रयुज्यते।
प्रशस्ते कर्मणि तथा सच्छब्दः पार्थ युज्यते।।17.26।।

sad-bhave sadhu-bhave cha sad ity etat prayujyate
prashaste karmani tatha sach-chhabdah partha yujyate (17.26)

sat-bhave : in the sense of truth | sadhu-bhave : in the sense of goodness | cha : and | sat : the word 'sat' | iti : thus | etat : this | prayujyate : is used | prashaste : auspicious | karmani : acts | tatha : also | sat-shabdah : the word sat | partha : son of Pratha (the other name of Kunti), O Arjuna | yujyate : is used

O Arjuna! Thus, this word 'sat' is used in the sense of truth and goodness. 'Sat' is also used for all auspicious acts.

(27)
यज्ञे तपसि दाने च स्थितिः सदिति चोच्यते।
कर्म चैव तदर्थीयं सदित्येवाभिधीयते।।17.27।।

yajne tapasi dane cha sthitih sad iti chochyate
karma chaiva tad-arthiyam sad ity evabhidhiyate (17.27)

yajne : in sacrifice | tapasi : in penance | dane : in charity | cha : and | sthitih : situation/engaged in/in the state of | sat : the true and the good/ultimate reality | iti : thus | cha : and | uchyate : is said | karma : action | cha : also | eva : verily | tat : that | arthiyam : purpose/meaning | sat : 'sat' | iti : thus | eva : certainly | abhidhiyate : is called

And, when one is in the state of performing acts of sacrifice, penance and charity, that state is verily said to be 'sat'. The acts done for that purpose are also certainly called 'sat'.

(28)
अश्रद्धया हुतं दत्तं तपस्तप्तं कृतं च यत्।
असदित्युच्यते पार्थ न च तत्प्रेत्य नो इह।।17.28।।

ashraddhaya hutam dattam tapas taptam kritam cha yat
asad ity uchyate partha na cha tat pretya no iha (17.28)

ashraddhaya : without faith | hutam : offering in sacrifice | dattam : given | tapa : penance | taptam : is practiced | krtam : performed | cha : and | yat : that | asat : false/meaningless | iti : thus | uchyate : called/said to be | partha : son of Pratha (Kunti), Arjuna | na : never | cha : also | tat : that | pretya : after death/hereafter | na : nor | iha : here/in this life

O Arjuna! Without faith, any offerings made in sacrifice, donations given in charity, penance practised or performed and good deeds done are said to be meaningless both here in this life and also hereafter on death.

Thus ends the Seventeenth Canto titled 'Yoga of Three-fold Faith'.

Eighteenth Canto

MOKSHA-SANYASA YOGA
Yoga of Salvation-Renunciation

(1)

अर्जुन उवाच
संन्यासस्य महाबाहो तत्त्वमिच्छामि वेदितुम्।
त्यागस्य च हृषीकेश पृथक्केशिनिषूदन।।18.1।।

arjuna uvacha
sannyasasya maha-baho tattvam ichchhami veditum
tyagasya cha hrishikesha prithak keshi-nishudana (18.1)

arjunah uvacha : Arjuna said | sanyasasya : of renouncing the worldly life | maha-baho : one of large arms | tattvam : the essential truth | ichchhami : I desire/am anxious | veditum : to know/understand | tyagasya : of sacrificing | cha : also | hrishikesha : master of the senses | prithak : separate | keshi-nishudana : destroyer of the demon Kesi

Arjuna said: O one with large arms, Lord Krishna! I am anxious to know the essential truth behind the act of renouncing the worldly life (of taking sanyasa). O master of the senses and destroyer of demon Kesi, also (tell me) separately (about the essence of) acts of sacrifice (tyaga).

(2)

श्रीभगवानुवाच
काम्यानां कर्मणां न्यासं संन्यासं कवयो विदुः।
सर्वकर्मफलत्यागं प्राहुस्त्यागं विचक्षणाः।।18.2।।

Shribhagavan uvacha
kamyanam karmanam nyasam sannyasam kavayo viduh
sarva-karma-phala-tyagam prahus tyagam vichakshanah (18.2)

Sribhagavan uvacha : Lord Krishna said | kamyanam : with desire for material fruits | karmanam : of action | nyasam : the renunciation | sanyasam

: renouncing worldly life | kavaya : the sages | viduh : know | sarva : all | karma : action | phala : fruits/results | tyagam : act of abandoning | prahu : is called | tyagam : act of abandoning | vichakshanah : the wise

Lord Krishna said: The sages know that renunciation of all action performed with a desire for material fruits is sanyasa (renouncing of worldly life) and all action to abandon the results thereof is called tyaga by the wise.

(3)
त्याज्यं दोषवदित्येके कर्म प्राहुर्मनीषिणः।
यज्ञदानतपःकर्म न त्याज्यमिति चापरे।।18.3।।

tyajyam dosha-vad ity eke karma prahur manishinah
yajna-dana-tapah-karma na tyajyam iti chapare (18.3)

tyajyam : deserving to be given up/renounced | dosha-vat : evil | iti : thus | eke : some | karma : action | prahu : say | manishinah : eminent thinkers | yajna : sacrifice | dana : charity | tapah : penance | karma : action | na : never | tyajyam : deserve to be given up | iti : thus | cha : and | apare : others

Some eminent thinkers say that all fruitive action being evil thus deserves to be renounced while others hold that action in matters involving sacrifice, charity and penance should never be given up.

(4)
निश्चयं शृणु मे तत्र त्यागे भरतसत्तम।
त्यागो हि पुरुषव्याघ्र त्रिविधः संप्रकीर्तितः।।18.4।।

nishchayam shrinu me tatra tyage bharata-sattama
tyago hi purusha-vyaghra tri-vidhah samprakirtitah (18.4).

nishchayam : for certain | shrinu : listen | me : to me | tatra : about that | tyage : giving-up/abandonment/renouncing | bharata-sat-tama : the best of the descendants of the great King Bharata, Arjuna | tyaga : renouncing | hi : verily | purusha-vyaghra : tiger among men | tri-vidhah : three-type | samprakirtitah : has been held to be

O the best among the descendants of the great King Bharata, O tiger among men, Arjuna! For certain, listen to me about that renouncing. Verily, renouncing has been held to be of three types.

(5)

यज्ञदानतपःकर्म न त्याज्यं कार्यमेव तत्।
यज्ञो दानं तपश्चैव पावनानि मनीषिणाम्।।18.5।।

yajna-dana-tapah-karma na tyajyam karyam eva tat
yajno danam tapash chaiva pavanani manishinam (18.5)

yajna : sacrifice | dana : charity | tapah : penance | karma : acts | na : never | tyajyam : deserving to be abandoned | karyam : acts that should be performed | eva : certainly | tat : that | yajna : sacrifice | danam : charity | tapa : penance | cha : and | eva : verily | pavanani : purifying | manishinam : great minds

One should never give up acts involving sacrifice, charity and penance. These certainly must continue to be performed because sacrifice, charity and penance verily purify great minds.

(6)

एतान्यपि तु कर्माणि सङ्गं त्यक्त्वा फलानि च।
कर्तव्यानीति मे पार्थ निश्चितं मतमुत्तमम्।।18.6।।

etany api tu karmani sangam tyaktva phalani cha
kartavyaniti me partha nishchitam matam uttamam (18.6)

etani : these | api : also | tu : and | karmani : acts | sangam : attachment/association | tyaktva : renouncing/giving up | phalani : fruits | cha : and | kartavyani : performed as duties | iti : thus | me : my | partha : son of Pratha (Kunti), Arjuna | nishchitam : definite/firm | matam : opinion/view | uttamam : best of all

O Arjuna! It is my firm opinion that renouncing all attachment to these acts and fruits of these (sacrifice, charity and penance) and also other acts, the best is to (continue to) perform ones duties.

(7)

नियतस्य तु संन्यासः कर्मणो नोपपद्यते।
मोहात्तस्य परित्यागस्तामसः परिकीर्तितः।।18.7।।

*niyatasya tu sannyasah karmano nopapadyate
mohat tasya parityagas tamasah parikirtitah (18.7)*

niyatasya : laid-down/prescribed/obligatory | tu : but | sannyasah : renunciation | karmana : of acts | na : never | upapadyate : proper | mohat : under delusion | tasya : of that | parityaga : abandonment | tamasah : tamasika/in the mode of ignorance | parikirtitah : is held to be

But, renunciation of obligatory action (non-performance of ones prescribed duties) is never proper. If done under delusion, it is held to be in the mode of ignorance (tamasika).

(8)

दुःखमित्येव यत्कर्म कायक्लेशभयात्त्यजेत्।
स कृत्वा राजसं त्यागं नैव त्यागफलं लभेत्।।18.8।।

*duhkham ity eva yat karma kaya-klesha-bhayat tyajet
sa kritva rajasam tyagam naiva tyaga-phalam labhet (18.8)*

duhkham : pain | iti : thus/because | eva : only | yat : which | karma : action | kaya : body | klesha : trouble/pain | bhayat : on account of fear | tyajet : abandons/relinquishes/gives up/renounces | sa : he | kritva : after doing | rajasam : in the quality of passion (rajo-guna) | tyagam : renunciation | na : not | eva : certainly | tyaga : renunciation | phalam : fruits/results | labhet : gains

Thinking that action brings only pain and afraid of bodily trouble, if one renounces action, it would come under the category of passion (rajas) and he would certainly not get the fruits of renunciation.

(9)

कार्यमित्येव यत्कर्म नियतं क्रियतेऽर्जुन।
सङ्गं त्यक्त्वा फलं चैव स त्यागः सात्त्विको मतः।।18.9।।

*karyam ity eva yat karma niyatam kriyate 'rjuna
sangam tyaktva phalam chaiva sa tyagah sattviko matah (18.9)*

karyam : ought to be done/obligatory action | iti : thus | eva : only | yat : which | karma : action/duty | niyatam : prescribed/assigned | kriyate : performed | arjuna : Arjuna | sangam : association/attachment | tyaktva : giving up | phalam : fruit/result | cha : and | eva : only | sah : that | tyagah : renunciation | sattvika : in the quality of goodness (sat) | matah : considered

O Arjuna! When one performs his assigned duty only as action that ought to be done renouncing all attachment and fruits, such renunciation alone is considered to be in the quality of goodness (sattvika).

(10)
न द्वेष्ट्यकुशलं कर्म कुशले नानुषज्जते।
त्यागी सत्त्वसमाविष्टो मेधावी छिन्नसंशयः॥18.10॥

*na dveshty akusalam karma kushale nanushajjate
tyagi sattva-samavishto medhavi chhinna-sanshayah (18.10)*

na : not/never | dveshti : hates/detests | akushalam : unpleasant/disagreeable | karma : action | kushale : pleasant/agreeable | na : nor | anushajjate : is attached | tyagi : renouncer | sattva : in goodness | samavishta : immersed | medhavi : intelligent | chhinna : resolved/dispelled/removed | sanshayah : doubts

One who does not hate disagreeable action nor gets attached to agreeable, is immersed in goodness, is intelligent and free from doubts is a true renouncer (tyagi).

(11)
न हि देहभृता शक्यं त्यक्तुं कर्माण्यशेषतः।
यस्तु कर्मफलत्यागी स त्यागीत्यभिधीयते॥18.11॥

*na hi deha-bhrita shakyam tyaktum karmany asheshatah
yas tu karma-phala-tyagi sa tyagity abhidhiyate (18.11)*

na : not/never | hi : indeed | deha-bhrita : the embodied being | shakyam : can | tyaktum : to renounce | karmani : actions | asheshatah : completely | ya : who | tu : but | karma : action | phala : fruit/result | tyagi : renouncer |

sa : he | tyagi : renouncer | iti : thus | abhidhiyate : is said to be

No embodied being can indeed completely renounce all action. Anyone who renounces the fruits of action is thus called a renouncer.

(12)
अनिष्टमिष्टं मिश्रं च त्रिविधं कर्मणः फलम्।
भवत्यत्यागिनां प्रेत्य न तु संन्यासिनां क्वचित्।।18.12।।
anishtam ishtam mishram cha tri-vidham karmanah phalam
bhavaty atyaginam pretya na tu sannyasinam kvachit (18.12)

anishtam : bad/undesirable/disagreeable/harmful | ishtam : good/desirable/agreeable/beneficial | mishram : mixed | cha : and | tri-vidham : of three kinds | karmanah : of action | phalam : fruit/result | bhavati : becomes | atyaginam : those who have not renounced | pretya : after death | na : not | tu : but | sanyasinam : those who have renounced all activities based on material desire | kvachit : at any time/ever

To those who have not renounced activities based on material desires, three kinds of results of action - bad, good and mixed - accrue after death but never to sanyasins.

(13)
पञ्चैतानि महाबाहो कारणानि निबोध मे।
सांख्ये कृतान्ते प्रोक्तानि सिद्धये सर्वकर्मणाम्।।18.13।।
panchaitani maha-baho karanani nibodha me
sankhye kritante proktani siddhaye sarva-karmanam (18.13)

pancha : five | etani : these | maha-baho : O large-armed one, Arjuna | karanani : causes | nibodha : learn from | me : Me | sankhye : in Vedanta | krita-ante : in conclusion/at the end of the act | proktani : said | siddhaye : for realisation | sarva : of all | karmanam : activities

O large-armed one, Arjuna! As has been said by way of conclusion in Vedanta, there are five causes for realisation of all activities. Learn from me about these five.

(14)
अधिष्ठानं तथा कर्ता करणं च पृथग्विधम्।
विविधाश्च पृथक्चेष्टा दैवं चैवात्र पञ्चमम्।।18.14।।

adhishthanam tatha karta karanam cha prithag-vidham
vividhash cha prithak cheshta daivam chaivatra panchamam (18.14)

adhishthanam : place of action (the body) | tatha : also | karta : the doer | karanam : the tools (the senses) | cha : and | prithak-vidham : of different kinds | vividhash : various | cha : and | prithak : different | cheshta : the functions | daivam : the supreme | cha : also | eva : certainly | atra : here | panchamam : the fifth

These five are the place of action (the body), the doer (the performer of action), the various senses, different functions of various kinds and the fifth being the Supreme (Soul Consciousness).

(15)
शरीरवाङ्मनोभिर्यत्कर्म प्रारभते नरः।
न्याय्यं वा विपरीतं वा पञ्चैते तस्य हेतवः।।18.15।।

sharira-van-manobhir yat karma prarabhate narah
nyayyam va viparitam va panchaite tasya hetavah (18.15)

sharira : the body | vak : speech | manobhi : mind | yat : whichever | karma : action | prarabhate : commences | narah : human person | nyayyam : right, just | va : or | viparitam : the opposite | va : or | pancha : five | ete : these | tasya : it's | hetavah : right/just

Whichever action a human person performs by body, speech or mind - whether it is right or it's opposite – its causes are these five.

(16)
तत्रैवं सति कर्तारमात्मानं केवलं तु यः।
पश्यत्यकृतबुद्धित्वान्न स पश्यति दुर्मतिः।।18.16।।

tatraivam sati kartaram atmanam kevalam tu yah
pashyaty akrita-buddhitvan na sa pashyati durmatih (18.16)

tatra : there | evam : thus | sati : being | kartaram : the doer | atmanam : the self | kevalam : the only | tu : but | yah : one who | pashyati : sees | akrita-buddhitvat : due to lack of intelligence | na : never/not | sa : he | pashyati : sees | durmatih : of perverted mind

But, (facts) being thus, one who, due to lack of intelligence, sees the self there as the only doer, sees not (and has) a perverted mind.

(17)
यस्य नाहंकृतो भावो बुद्धिर्यस्य न लिप्यते।
हत्वापि स इमाँल्लोकान्न हन्ति न निबध्यते।।18.17।।

yasya nahankrito bhavo buddhir yasya na lipyate
hatva pi sa imanl lokan na hanti na nibadhyate (18.17)

yasya : whose | na : not | ahankritah bhava : feeling of 'I' being the doer/false ego | buddhi : intellect | yasya : whose | na : never/not | lipyate : affected | hatva : killing | api : even | sa : he | iman : these | lokan : people | na : never | hanti : kills | na : never | nibadhyate : gets bound

One who is free from the egoistic notion of 'I' being the doer and whose mind is not besmeared, even if he kills these people, he never really kills and never gets bound to action or it's results.

(18)
ज्ञानं ज्ञेयं परिज्ञाता त्रिविधा कर्मचोदना।
करणं कर्म कर्तेति त्रिविधः कर्मसंग्रहः।।18.18।।

jnanam jneyam parijnata tri-vidha karma-chodana
karanam karma karteti tri-vidhah karma-sangrahah (18.18)

jnanam : superior knowledge/knowledge of the supreme | jneyam : what is known/what is knowable/what is the object of knowledge | parijnata : the knower | tri-vidha : three-fold | karma : action | chodana : cause/impulse | karanam : the senses | karma : action | karta : the doer | iti : thus | tri-vidhah : three-fold | karma : action | sangrahah : basis

The knower, the known and the knowledge are the three-fold impulses to action. The senses, the action and the doer constitute the three-fold basis of action.

(19)
ज्ञानं कर्म च कर्ता च त्रिधैव गुणभेदतः।
प्रोच्यते गुणसंख्याने यथावच्छृणु तान्यपि।।18.19।।

*jnanam karma cha karta cha tridhaiva guna-bhedatah
prochyate guna-sankhyane yathavach chhrinu tany api (18.19)*

jnanam : knowledge | karma : action | cha : and | karta : the doer | cha : also | tridha : of three kinds | eva : only | guna-bhedatah : distinctions in qualities/in modes of nature | prochyate : said to be | guna-sankhyane : in the number of different modes of nature | yatha-vat : as it is/duly | shrinu : listen | tani : them | api : also

Knowledge, action and the doer are also said to be of three kinds only based on the distinctions in different modes of nature. Listen duly to them also.

(20)
सर्वभूतेषु येनैकं भावमव्ययमीक्षते।
अविभक्तं विभक्तेषु तज्ज्ञानं विद्धि सात्त्विकम्।।18.20।।

*sarva-bhuteshu yenaikam bhavam avyayam ikshate
avibhaktam vibhakteshu taj jnanam viddhi sattvikam (18.20)*

sarva-bhuteshu : in all living beings | yena : by which | ekam : one | bhavam : principle/essence | avyayam : imperishable/indestructible | iksate : one sees | avibhaktam : undivided/inseparate | vibhakteshu : among the divided/separate | tat : that | jnanam : knowledge | viddhi : know | sattvikam : in the mode of goodness

Know that the knowledge by which one sees in all living beings the one indestructible essence of the undivided among the divided, is in the mode of goodness (sattvika).

(21)

पृथक्त्वेन तु यज्ज्ञानं नानाभावान्पृथग्विधान्।
वेत्ति सर्वेषु भूतेषु तज्ज्ञानं विद्धि राजसम्॥18.21॥

prithaktvena tu yaj jnanam nana-bhavan prithag-vidhan
vetti sarveshu bhuteshu taj jnanam viddhi rajasam (18.21)

prithaktvena : as distinct from each other | tu : but | yat : which | jnanam : knowledge | nana-bhavan : various entities | prithak-vidhan : of different kinds | vetti : knows/learns | sarveshu : all | bhuteshu : living beings | tat : that | jnanam : knowledge | viddhi : know | rajasam : in the mode of passion (rajo-guna)

But, know that the knowledge by which one learns to see in all living beings the distinction between various entities of different kinds is knowledge in the mode of passion (rajasik).

(22)

यत्तु कृत्स्नवदेकस्मिन्कार्ये सक्तमहैतुकम्।
अतत्त्वार्थवदल्पं च तत्तामसमुदाहृतम्॥18.22॥

yat tu kritsna-vad ekasmin karye saktam ahaitukam
atattvartha-vad alpam cha tat tamasam udahritam (18.22)

yat : which | tu : but | kritsna-vat : as if it were the whole | ekasmin : one single | karye : work | saktam : confined | ahaitukam : without any reason | attattva-artha-vat: without any basis in truth or substantial meaning | alpam : little/trivial | cha : and | tat : that | tamasam : in the nature of darkness (tamoguna) | udahritam : is said to be

But, knowledge which is confined to one single kind of work as if it were all, is without any purpose, devoid of any substantial meaning/ trivial and is said to be in the mode of darkness (tamasika).

(23)
नियतं सङ्गरहितमरागद्वेषतः कृतम्।
अफलप्रेप्सुना कर्म यत्तत्सात्त्विकमुच्यते॥18.23॥

niyatam sanga-rahitam araga-dveshatah kritam
aphala-prepsuna karma yat tat sattvikam uchyate (18.23)

niyatam : regulated | sanga-rahi tam : without attachment | aragadveshatah : without love or hatred | kritam : done | aphala-prepsuna : without desire for fruits of action | karma : action | yat : which | tat : that | sattvikam : in the mode of goodness | uchyate: is said to be

That action which is regulated, is without attachment, without love or hatred and which is done without any desire for fruits thereof, is said to be in the mode of goodness (sattvika).

(24)
यत्तु कामेप्सुना कर्म साहङ्कारेण वा पुनः।
क्रियते बहुलायासं तद्राजसमुदाहृतम्॥18.24॥

yat tu kamepsuna karma sahankarena va punah
kriyate bahulayasam tad rajasam udahritam (18.24)

yat : which | tu : but | kam-ipsuna : by one seeking desire/gratification | karma : action | sa-ahankarena : with self-conceit | va : or | punah : again | kriyate : is done | bahula-ayasam : with much effort | tat : that | rajasam : in the mode of passion (rajasik) | udahritam : is said to be

But action which is done with much effort or with self-conceit by one seeking desire or gratification is said to be in the mode of passion (rajasik).

(25)
अनुबन्धं क्षयं हिंसामनपेक्ष्य च पौरुषम्।
मोहादारभ्यतेकर्मयत्ततामसमुच्यते॥18.25॥

anubandham kshayam hinsam anapekshya cha paurusham
mohad arabhyate karma yat tat tamasam uchyate (18.25)

anubandham : consequences | kshayam : loss | hinsam : violence | anapekshya : without heeding | cha : and | paurusham : one's capability | mohat : by delusion | arabhyate : is begun/initiated | karma : action | yat : which | tat : that | tamasam : in the mode of ignorance (tamasik) | uchyate : is said to be

Action which is initiated out of delusion and without heeding the consequences of loss, violence and one's own capabilities, is said to be in the mode of ignorance (tamasik).

(26)
मुक्तसङ्गोऽनहंवादी धृत्युत्साहसमन्वितः।
सिद्ध्यसिद्ध्योर्निर्विकारः कर्ता सात्त्विक उच्यते।।18.26।।

mukta-sango 'naham-vadi dhrity-utsaha-samanvitah
siddhy-asiddhyor nirvikarah karta sattvika uchyate (18.26)

mukta-sanga : free from attachment to material things | anaham-vadi : non-egotistic | dhriti : determination | utsaha : enthusiasm | samanvitah : full of/endued with | siddhi : success | asiddhyo : failure | nirvikarah : unaffected/not subject to change | karta : doer | sattvika : in the mode of goodness (sattvika) | uchyate : is said to be

A doer free from attachment to material things, non-egotistic, full of determination and enthusiasm, unaffected by success and failure, is said to be in the mode of goodness (sattvika).

(27)
रागी कर्मफलप्रेप्सुर्लुब्धो हिंसात्मकोऽशुचिः।
हर्षशोकान्वितः कर्ता राजसः परिकीर्तितः।।18.27।।

ragi karma-phala-prepsur lubdho hinsatmako 'shuchih
harsha-shokanvitah karta rajasah parikirtitah (18.27)

ragi : full of attachment | karma-phala : fruits of action | prepsu : desirous | lubdha : greedy | hinsa-atmaka : prone to violence | asuchih : unclean/impure | harsh-shoka-anvitah : (easily) affected by joy and sorrows | karta : doer | rajasah : in the mode of passion | parikirtitah : is said to be

A doer who is full of attachment, desirous of fruits of action, greedy, prone to violence, unclean, easily affected by joys and sorrows, is said to be in the mode of passion (rajasik).

(28)
अयुक्तः प्राकृतः स्तब्धः शठो नैष्कृतिकोऽलसः।
विषादी दीर्घसूत्री च कर्ता तामस उच्यते।।18.28।।

*ayuktah prakritah stabdhah shatho naishkritiko 'lasah
vishadi dirgha-sutri cha karta tamasa uchyate (18.28)*

ayuktah : unsteady | prakritah : vulgar | stabdha : arrogant | satha : dishonest | naishkrtikah : malicious | alasah : lazy | vishadi : morose | dirgha sutri : procrastinating/always postponing action | cha : and | karta : doer | tamasa : in the mode of ignorance (tamasik) | uchyate : is said to be

A doer who is unsteady, vulgar, arrogant, dishonest, malicious, lazy, morose and procrastinating is said to be in the mode of ignorance (tamasik).

(29)
बुद्धेर्भेदं धृतेश्चैव गुणतस्त्रिविधं शृणु।
प्रोच्यमानमशेषेण पृथक्त्वेन धनञ्जय।।18.29।।

*buddher bhedam dhritesh chaiva gunatas tri-vidham shrinu
prochyamanam asheshena prithaktvena dhananjaya (18.29)*

buddhe : of intellect | bhedam : differences | dhrite : of steadiness | cha : and | eva : verily | gunata : according to modes of nature | tri-vidham : three-fold | shrinu : listen | prochyamanam : as described by me | asheshena : at length | prithaktvena : separately | dhananjaya : O conqueror of wealth, Arjuna

O conqueror of wealth, Arjuna! Now listen to the three-fold distinction of intellect and steadiness, verily, according to the three modes of nature as described separately by me at length.

(30)

प्रवृत्तिं च निवृत्तिं च कार्याकार्ये भयाभये।
बन्धं मोक्षं च या वेत्ति बुद्धिः सा पार्थ सात्त्विकी।।18.30।।

pravrittim cha nivrittim cha karyakarye bhayabhaye
bandham moksham cha ya vetti buddhih sa partha sattviki (18.30)

pravrittim : doing (path of action) | cha : and | nivrittim : not doing (path of renunciation) | cha : also | karya : what ought to be done | akarye : what ought not to be done | bhaya : fear | abhaye : fearlessness | bandham : bondage | moksham : salvation | cha : and | ya : which | vetti : knows | buddhih : intelligence | sa : that | partha : O son of Pratha (Kunti), Arjuna | sattviki : in the mode of goodness

O son of Partha (Kunti), Arjuna! That intellect is in the mode of goodness (sattvika) which knows the paths of action and renunciation, of what ought to be done as also of what ought not to be done, of fear and fearlessness, of bondage and salvation.

(31)

यया धर्মमधर्मं च कार्यं चाकार्यमेव च।
अयथावत्प्रजानाति बुद्धिः सा पार्थ राजसी।।18.31।।

yaya dharmam adharmam cha karyam chakaryam eva cha
ayathavat prajanati buddhih sa partha rajasi (18.31)

yaya : which | dharmam : righteous conduct (dharma) | adharmam : vicious action (adharma) | cha : and | karyam : what ought to be done/right action | cha : and | akaryam : what ought not to be done/wrong action | eva : verily | cha : also | ayatha-vat : a distorted picture | prajanati : apprehends | buddhih : intellect | sa : that | partha : O son of Pratha, Arjuna | rajasi : in the mode of passion (rajasik)

O son of Pratha (Kunti), Arjuna! An intellect which verily apprehends a distorted picture of righteous and vicious conduct - of what ought and what ought not to be done - is in the mode of passion (rajasik).

(32)
अधर्मं धर्ममिति या मन्यते तमसावृता।
सर्वार्थान्विपरीतांश्च बुद्धिः सा पार्थ तामसी।।18.32।।

adharmam dharmam iti ya manyate tamasavrita
sarvarthan viparitansh cha buddhih sa partha tamasi (18.32)

adharmam : vicious conduct | dharmam : virtuous conduct | iti : thus | ya : which | manyate : considers | tamasa : darkness | avrita : covered | sarvarthan : in every sense | viparitan : in the opposite direction | cha : and | buddhih : intellect | sa : that | partha : O son of Partha (Kunti), Arjuna! | tamasi : in the mode of ignorance

Thus, O Arjuna! The intellect which covered by darkness considers vicious conduct as virtuous and in every sense opposite, is in the mode of ignorance (tamasik).

(33)
धृत्या यया धारयते मनःप्राणेन्द्रियक्रियाः।
योगेनाव्यभिचारिण्या धृतिः सा पार्थ सात्त्विकी।।18.33।।

dhritya yaya dharayate manah-pranendriya-kriyah
yogenavyabhicharinya dhritih sa partha sattviki (18.33)

dhritya : holding power/firmness/will-power | yaya : which | dharayate : holds/regulates/restrains/sustains/controls | manah : mind | prana : life-breath | indriya : senses | kriyah : functioning | yogena : by practice of yoga | avyabhicharinya : without break/never-failing | dhirtih : firmness/holding power | sa : that | partha : O son of Pratha (Kunti), Arjuna | sattviki : in the mode of goodness (sattvika)

The holding-power which through the practice of yoga becomes never-failing, controls the functioning of the mind, life-breath and the senses, O son of Pratha (Kunti), Arjuna! That holding power is in the mode of goodness (sattvika).

(34)

यया तु धर्मकामार्थान्धृत्या धारयतेऽर्जुन।
प्रसङ्गेन फलाकाङ्क्षी धृतिः सा पार्थ राजसी।।18.34।।

yaya tu dharma-kamarthan dhritya dharayate 'rjuna
prasangena phalakankshi dhritih sa partha rajasi (18.34)

yaya : which | tu : but | dharma : righteousness | kama : sense gratification | arthan : economic goals/pursuit of wealth | dhritya : holding power/firm determination/will-power | dharayate : holds | arjuna : O Arjuna | prasangena : because of attachment | phala-akankshi : desire for fruits of action | dhrtih : holding power/firm determination | sa : that | partha : son of Pratha (Kunti), O Arjuna | rajasi : in the mode of passion (rajasik)

But, O Arjuna! The firm determination by which one holds on to righteousness (dharma), objects of sense gratification and pursuit of wealth because of the attachment to desire for fruits of action, that determination, Arjuna, is in the mode of passion (rajasik).

(35)

यया स्वप्नं भयं शोकं विषादं मदमेव च।
न विमुञ्चति दुर्मेधा धृतिः सा पार्थ तामसी।।18.35।।

yaya svapnam bhayam shokam vishadam madam eva cha
na vimunchati durmedha dhritih sa partha tamasi (18.35)

yaya : by which | svapnam : sleep | bhayam : fear | shokam : grief | vishadam : despondency | madam : conceit | eva : verily | cha : and | na : not/never | vimunchati : give up | durmedha : poor understanding | dhrti : determination/holding power | sa : that | partha : O son of Pratha, Arjuna | tamasi : in the mode of ignorance (tamasika)

O son of Pratha (Kunti), Arjuna! That determination by which a person of poor understanding, verily, does not give up sleep, fear, grief, despondency and conceit, is in the mode of ignorance (tamasika).

(36-37)

सुखं त्विदानीं त्रिविधं शृणु मे भरतर्षभ।
अभ्यासाद्रमते यत्र दुःखान्तं च निगच्छति।।18.36।।
यत्तदग्रे विषमिव परिणामेऽमृतोपमम्।
तत्सुखं सात्त्विकं प्रोक्तमात्मबुद्धिप्रसादजम्।।18.37।।

sukham tv idanim tri-vidham shrinu me bharatarshabha
abhyasad ramate yatra duhkhantam cha nigachchhati (18.36)
yat tad agre visham iva pariname 'mritopamam
tat sukham sattvikam proktam atma-buddhi-prasada-jam (18.37)

sukham : happiness | tu : but | idanim : now | tri-vidham : of three types | shrinu : listen | me : to me | bharata-rishabha : the best of King Bharatta's dynasty | abhyasat : by practice | ramate : enjoy | yatra : where | duhkha : of distress | antam : end | cha : and | nigachchhati : reaches | yat : which | tat : that | agre : to begin with | visham iva : like poison | pariname : as a result | amrita : nectar | upamam : example | tat : that | sukham : happiness | sattvikam : in the mode of goodness (sattvika) | proktam : it is said | atma : self | buddhi : intellect/understanding | prasada-jam : born of satisfaction

O the best from the dynasty of the great King Bharata, Arjuna! Now listen to me about the three types of happiness that one enjoys by practice and where one reaches the end of distress.

Which, to begin with, is like poison but results in nectar is an example of happiness that is said to be in the mode of goodness (sattvika) born of the understanding that concerns itself with the satisfaction of the self.

(38)

विषयेन्द्रियसंयोगाद्यत्तदग्रेऽमृतोपमम्।
परिणामे विषमिव तत्सुखं राजसं स्मृतम्।।18.38।।

vishayendriya-sanyogad yat tad agre 'mritopamam
pariname visham iva tat sukham rajasam smritam (18.38)

vishaya : sensory objects | indriya : the senses | sanyogat : coming together | yat : which | tat : that | agre : at the beginning | amrita-upamam : like the nectar | pariname : in the result/at the end | visham iva : like poison | tat : that | sukham : happiness | rajasam : in the mode of passion | smritam : is considered

The happiness that comes from the coming together of the senses with sensory objects and which at the beginning seems to be like nectar but at the end like poison, is considered to be in the mode of passion (rajasika).

(39)
यदग्रे चानुबन्धे च सुखं मोहनमात्मनः।
निद्रालस्यप्रमादोत्थं तत्तामसमुदाहृतम्।।18.39।।

yad agre chanubandhe cha sukham mohanam atmanah
nidralasya-pramadottham tat tamasam udahritam (18.39)

yat : that which | agre : at the beginning | cha : and | anubandhe : at the end | cha : also | sukham : happiness | mohanam : deluding | atmanah : of the self | nidra : sleep | alasya : laziness | pramada : illusion | uttham : born of | tat : that | tamasam : in the mode of ignorance | udahritam : is said to be

That happiness which at the beginning as also at the end is self-deluding and is born of sleep, laziness and illusion, that is said to be of the quality of ignorance (tamasika).

(40)
न तदस्ति पृथिव्यां वा दिवि देवेषु वा पुनः।
सत्त्वं प्रकृतिजैर्मुक्तं यदेभिः स्यात्त्रिभिर्गुणैः।।18.40।।

na tad asti prithivyam va divi deveshu va punah
sattvam prakriti-jair muktam yad ebhih syat tribhir gunaih (18.40)

na : not/nothing | tat : that | asti : exists/is there | prithivyam : on earth | va : or | divi : in higher planets/ in heaven | deveshu : in the midst of gods | va : or | punah : again | sattvam : reality/existence | prakriti-jai : born of nature | muktam : free | yat : that | ebhih : from these | syat : is | tribhi : three | gunaih : modes of nature - of goodness, passion and ignorance (sattoguna, rajoguna and tamoguna)

There is nothing that exists here on earth or in other higher planets in the midst of gods or again anything in nature that is free from these three modes - of goodness (sattoguna), passion (rajoguna) and ignorance (tamoguna).

(41)
ब्राह्मणक्षत्रियविशां शूद्राणां च परंतप।
कर्माणि प्रविभक्तानि स्वभावप्रभवैर्गुणैः।।18.41।।

brahmana-kshatriya-visham shudranam cha parantapa
karmani pravibhaktani svabhava-prabhavair gunaih (18.41)

brahmana : Brahmanas (the intellectual class) | kshatriya : Kshatriyas (the fighting/ruling class) | vihsam : Vaishyas (the business/trader class) | shudranam : Shudras (the service/workers' class) | cha : and | parantapa : O scorcher of enemies | karmani : activities/duties | pravibhaktani : are divided | svabhava : own nature | prabhavai : born of | gunaih : modes of nature

O scorcher of enemies, Arjuna! The activities of Brahmanas (the intellectual class), the Kshatriyas (the fighting/ruling class), the Vaishyas (the business/trader class) as also the Shudras (the service/workers' class) are all divided according to the qualities born of their own nature.

(42)
शमो दमस्तपः शौचं क्षान्तिरार्जवमेव च।
ज्ञानं विज्ञानमास्तिक्यं ब्रह्मकर्म स्वभावजम्।।18.42।।

shamo damas tapah shaucham kshantir arjavam eva cha
jnanam vijnanam astikyam brahma-karma svabhava-jam (18.42).

shama : serenity | dama : control of the senses | tapa : penance | shaucham : cleanliness | kshanti : forbearance | arjavam : integrity | eva : also | cha : and | jnanam : knowledge | vijnanam : realisation | astikyam : faith | brahma : Brahmana | karma : duties | svabhava-jam : born of his own nature

Serenity, control of the senses, penance, cleanliness, forbearance, integrity, knowledge, wisdom and also faith are the duties of a Brahmana, born of his own nature.

(43)

शौर्यं तेजो धृतिर्दाक्ष्यं युद्धे चाप्यपलायनम्।
दानमीश्वरभावश्च क्षात्रं कर्म स्वभावजम्।।18.43।।

shauryam tejo dhritir dakshyam yuddhe chapy apalayanam
danam ishvara-bhavash cha kshatram karma svabhava-jam (18.43)

shauryam : bravery | teja : boldness | dhriti : determination/firmness | dakshyam : dexterity | yuddhe : in the battle | cha : and | api : also | apalayanam : not running away | danam : generosity | ishvara-bhava : feeling of godliness | cha : and | kshatram : of a Ksatriya | karma : duty | svabhava-jam : born of his own nature

Bravery, boldness, determination, dexterity and also not running away from the battlefield generosity and feeling of godliness are the duties of a Kshatriya, born of his own nature.

(44)

कृषिगौरक्ष्यवाणिज्यं वैश्यकर्म स्वभावजम्।
परिचर्यात्मकं कर्म शूद्रस्यापि स्वभावजम्।।18.44।।

krishi-gau-rakshya-vanijyam vaishya-karma svabhava-jam
paricharyatmakam karma shudrasyapi svabhava-jam (18.44)

krishi : agriculture | gau-rakshya : protection of cows | vanijyam : trade | vaishya : of Vaishya | karma : duties | svabhava-jam : born of his own nature | paricharya-atmakam : consisting of service | karma : action | shudrasya : of the Shudra | api : also | svabhava-jam : born of his own nature

Agriculture, cow protection and trading are the duties of a Vaishya born of his own nature. Also, for a Shudra, action consisting of service is a duty born of his own nature.

(45)

स्वे स्वे कर्मण्यभिरतः संसिद्धिं लभते नरः।
स्वकर्मनिरतः सिद्धिं यथा विन्दति तच्छृणु॥18.45॥

sve sve karmany abhiratah sansiddhim labhate narah
sva-karma-niratah siddhim yatha vindati tach chhrinu (18.45)

sve sve : each to his own | karmani : action/duty | abhiratah : pursuing/following/doing/performing | sansiddhim : perfection/highest realisation | labhate : attain | narah : man | sva-karma : own duty | niratah : engaged | siddhim : perfection/realisation | yatha : as | vindati : achieves | tat : that | shrinu : listen

Each one engaged in performing his own duty can attain the highest realisation. Now, listen to me, how a man engaged in doing his own duty achieves that realisation.

(46)

यतः प्रवृत्तिर्भूतानां येन सर्वमिदं ततम्।
स्वकर्मणा तमभ्यर्च्य सिद्धिं विन्दति मानवः॥18.46॥

yatah pravrittir bhutanam yena sarvam idam tatam
sva-karmana tam abhyarchya siddhim vindati manavah (46).

yatah : where/from whom | pravritti : evolve/emanate | bhutanam : all living beings | yena : by whom | sarvam : all | idam : this | tatam : is pervaded | sva-karmana : by own actions/by performing his own duties well | tam : him | abhyarchya : by worshipping | siddhim : realisation | vindati : attains | manavah : man

From whom all living beings emerge and by whom all these are pervaded, man can attain realisation by worshipping Him through well performance of his own duties.

(47)

श्रेयान्स्वधर्मो विगुणः परधर्मात्स्वनुष्ठितात्।
स्वभावनियतं कर्म कुर्वन्नाप्नोति किल्बिषम्॥18.47॥

shreyan swa-dharmo vigunah para-dharmat sv-anushthitat

svabhava-niyatam karma kurvan napnoti kilbisham (18.47)

shreyan : better | swa-dharma : one's own duty | vigunah : with defects | para-dharmat : than others' duty | su-anushthitat : well-done | svabhava-niyatam : as settled by one's own nature | karma : duty | kurvan : doing | na : never | apnoti : incurs | kilbisham : sin

Performing one's own duty, even with defects, is better than other's duty well-done. Doing one's duty as settled by one's own nature never incurs sin.

(48)
सहजं कर्म कौन्तेय सदोषमपि न त्यजेत्।
सर्वारम्भा हि दोषेण धूमेनाग्निरिवावृताः।।18.48।।

*saha-jam karma kaunteya sa-dosham api na tyajet
sarvarambha hi doshena dhumenagnir ivavritah (18.48)*

saha-jam karma : duty one is born with/duty in accordance with one's own nature | kaunteya : O son of Kunti, Arjuna | sa-dosham : with defect | api : although | na : never | tyajet : give up | sarva-arambha : all undertakings | hi : for | doshena : with defects | dhumena : with smoke | agni : fire | iva : as | avritah : covered

O son of Kunti, Arjuna! One should not give up the duty one is born with even if it has defects, for all undertakings are covered by defects as fire is covered by smoke.

(49)
असक्तबुद्धिः सर्वत्र जितात्मा विगतस्पृहः।
नैष्कर्म्यसिद्धिं परमां संन्यासेनाधिगच्छति ।।18.49।।

*asakta-buddhih sarvatra jitatma vigata-sprihah
naishkarmya-siddhim paramam sannyasenadhigachchhati (18.49)*

asakta-buddhih : One whose mind is unattached | sarvatra : everywhere | jita-atma : one who has achieved control over self | vigata-sprihah : who has given up sensory desires | naishkarmya-siddhim : realisation of freedom from action | paramam : supreme | sanyasena : by renunciation | adhigachchhati : achieves

One whose mind is unattached every where, who has achieved control over self and has given up sensory desires, achieves supreme realisation of freedom from action through renunciation.

(50)

सिद्धिं प्राप्तो यथा ब्रह्म तथाप्नोति निबोध मे।
समासेनैव कौन्तेय निष्ठा ज्ञानस्य या परा।।18.50।।

siddhim prapto yatha brahma tathapnoti nibodha me
samasenaiva kaunteya nishtha jnanasya ya para (18.50)

siddhim : realisation/perfection | prapta : reaching | yatha : as | brahma : the Supreme | tatha : so | apnoti : reaches | nibodha : understand | me : from me | samasena : in brief | eva : verily | kaunteya : O son of Kunti, Arjuna | nishtha : consummation | jnanasya : of knowledge | ya : which | para : supreme/ultimate

O son of Kunti, Arjuna! Verily understand from me, in brief, how one who has achieved realisation reaches the Supreme (Brahaman) which is consummation of ultimate knowledge.

(51 - 53)

बुद्ध्या विशुद्धया युक्तो धृत्यात्मानं नियम्य च।
शब्दादीन्विषयांस्त्यक्त्वा रागद्वेषौ व्युदस्य च।।18.51।।
विविक्तसेवी लघ्वाशी यतवाक्कायमानसः।
ध्यानयोगपरो नित्यं वैराग्यं समुपाश्रितः।।18.52।।
अहङ्कारं बलं दर्पं कामं क्रोधं परिग्रहम्।
विमुच्य निर्ममः शान्तो ब्रह्मभूयाय कल्पते।।18.53।।

buddhya vishuddhaya yukto dhrityatmanam niyamya cha
shabdadin vishayans tyaktva raga-dveshau vyudasya cha (18.51)
vivikta-sevi laghv-ashi yata-vak-kaya-manasah
dhyana-yoga-paro nityam vairagyam samupashritah (18.52)
ahankaram balam darpam kamam krodham parigraham

vimuchya nirmamah shanto brahma-bhuyaya kalpate (18.53)

buddhya : with intellect | visuddhaya : pure | yukta : endowed | dhritya : determination | atmanam : the self | niyamya : regulating | cha : and | shabda-adin : sound etc. | vishayan : sensory objects | tyaktva : giving up | raga : attachment | dveshau : hatred | vyudasya : abandoning | cha : and | viviktasevi : living at a lonely spot | laghu-ashi : eating only a little | yata : controlled | vak : speech | kaya : body | manasah : mind | dhyana-yoga-para : yoga meditation | nityam : all the time | vairagyam : detachment | samupashritah : possessed of | ahankaram : arrogance/false ego | balam : false sense of power | darpam : pride | kamam : lust | krodham : anger | parigraham : proprietary feelings | vimuchya : freed from | nirmam : discarding the notion of me and mine | shanta : at peace | brahma-bhuyaya : for becoming Brahaman/reaching the Supreme Self | kalpate : is qualified/fit

Endowed with a pure intellect, regulating the self with determination, giving up sound and like sense objects, and abandoning attachment and hatred; living at a lonely spot, eating only a little, having controlled speech, body and mind, absorbed in yoga meditation all the time, possessed of complete detachment; freed from arrogance, false sense of power, pride, lust, anger, proprietary feelings, discarding the notion of me and mine and thus one at peace is fit for reaching the Supreme Self and becoming Brahaman.

(54)

ब्रह्मभूतः प्रसन्नात्मा न शोचति न काङ्क्षति।
समः सर्वेषु भूतेषु मद्भक्तिं लभते पराम्।।18.54।।

*brahma-bhutah prasannatma na shochati na kankshati
samah sarveshu bhuteshu mad-bhaktim labhate param (18.54)*

brahma-bhuta : becoming one with the Supreme Self (Brahaman) | prasanna-atma : self in a state of bliss and tranquility | na : never | shochati : laments/grieves | na : never | kankshati : desires | samah : same/equally disposed | sarveshu : towards all | bhuteshu : living beings | mat-bhaktim : devotion to me | labhate : gets | param : supreme

Once becoming one with the Supreme Self - Brahaman (Suprme Self Consciousness or Param-atma chaitanya) - the individual self gets into a state of bliss and tranquility, never grieving and never desiring anything, treating all living beings equally, as the same and thus has supreme devotion towards me.

(55)
भक्त्या मामभिजानाति यावान्यश्चास्मि तत्त्वतः।
ततो मां तत्त्वतो ज्ञात्वा विशते तदनन्तरम्॥18.55॥

bhaktya mam abhijanati yavan yash chasmi tattvatah
tato mam tattvato jnatva vishate tad-anantaram (18.55)

bhaktya : by devotion | mam : me | abhijanati : knows | yavan : as much as | ya cha asmi : as I am | tattvatah : actually/in fact | tata : then | mam : me | tattvata : in fact/actually | jnatva : knowing | vishate : enters | tat-anantaram : thereafter

By devotion, one gets to know me as I am in fact - who am I, what am I. Thereafter, thus knowing me, the devotee straightaway enters me, becomes one with Brahaman - the Supreme Soul.

(56)
सर्वकर्माण्यपि सदा कुर्वाणो मद्व्यपाश्रयः।
मत्प्रसादादवाप्नोति शाश्वतं पदमव्ययम्॥18.56॥

sarva-karmany api sada kurvano mad-vyapashrayah
mat-prasadad avapnoti shashvatam padam avyayam (18.56)

sarva : all | karmani : actions/duties/activities | api : though/even while | sada : always/all the time | kurvana : doing/performing/discharging | mat-vyapashrayah : one who takes shelter in me | mat-prasadat : at my pleasure/through my grace | avapnoti : achieves | shashvatam : eternal | padam : state | avyayam : indestructible/imperishable/immutable

Even while always engaged in performing all the actions, one who takes shelter in me achieves, at my pleasure, the eternal and immutable state (of bliss, of union with the Supreme Self Consciousness).

(57)
चेतसा सर्वकर्माणि मयि संन्यस्य मत्परः।
बुद्धियोगमुपाश्रित्य मच्चित्तः सततं भव।।18.57।।

chetasa sarva-karmani mayi sannyasya mat-parah
buddhi-yogam upashritya mach-chittah satatam bhava (18.57)

chetasa : mentally/consciously | sarva-karmani : all action | mayi : to me | sanyasya : renouncing/surrendering | mat-parah : regarding me as the supreme goal | buddhi-yogam : yoga through enlightened intellect | upashritya : resorting to | mat-chittah : with the mind fixed on me | satatam : all the time/constantly | bhava : be/have

Consciously renouncing (and surrendering) to me all action, regarding me as the supreme goal, resorting to yoga through enlightened intellect, have the mind constantly fixed on me.

(58)
मच्चित्तः सर्वदुर्गाणि मत्प्रसादात्तरिष्यसि।
अथ चेत्त्वमहङ्कारान्न श्रोष्यसि विनङ्क्ष्यसि।।18.58।।

mach-chittah sarva-durgani mat-prasadat tarishyasi
atha chet tvam ahankaran na shroshyasi vinanksyasi (18.58).

mat-chittah : with mind fixed on me | sarva : all | durgani : obstacles/difficulties | mat-prasadat : at my pleasure/through my grace | tarishyasi : you shall overcome | atha : so/but | chet : if | tvam : you | ahankarat : by arrogance/false ego/self-conceit | na shroshyasi : do not listen | vinankshyasi : shall be destroyed/shall perish

With mind fixed on me, you shall overcome all difficulties through my grace but if in your arrogance you do not listen you shall perish.

(59)
यदहङ्कारमाश्रित्य न योत्स्य इति मन्यसे।
मिथ्यैष व्यवसायस्ते प्रकृतिस्त्वां नियोक्ष्यति।।18.59।।

yad ahankaram ashritya na yotsya iti manyase
mithyaisha vyavasayas te prakritis tvam niyokshyati (18.59)

yat : if | ahankaram : self-conceit/arrogance/false-ego | ashritya : taking refuge/depending | na : not | yotsye : will fight | iti : thus | manyase : you believe/think | mithya : false | esa : this | vyavasaya : determination/resolve | te : your | prakriti : nature | tvam : you | niyokshyati : will compel/constrain (you to fight)

If depending on your self-conceit, you think you will not fight, this resolve will fail as your nature will compel you to fight.

(60)
स्वभावजेन कौन्तेय निबद्धः स्वेन कर्मणा।
कर्तुं नेच्छसि यन्मोहात्करिष्यस्यवशोऽपि तत्।।18.60।।

swabhava-jena kaunteya nibaddhah svena karmana
kartum nechchhasi yan mohat karishyasy avasho 'pi tat (18.60)

swabhava-jena : born of (your) own nature | kaunteya : son of Kunti, Arjuna | nibaddha : bound/fettered/conditioned | svena : by (your) own | karmana : actions | kartum : to do | na : not | ichchhasi : desire | yat : what | mohat : under illusion | karishyasi : will (have to) do | avashsa : helpless/beyond control | api : even | tat : that

O son of Kunti, Arjuna! Bound by your own nature and your own actions, you will feel helpless and against your desire, under illusion, you will have to do even that what you do not desire (and fight).

(61)
ईश्वरः सर्वभूतानां हृद्देशेऽर्जुन तिष्ठति।
भ्रामयन्सर्वभूतानि यन्त्रारूढानि मायया।।18.61।।

ishvarah sarva-bhutanam hrid-deshe 'rjuna tishthati
bhramayan sarva-bhutani yantrarudhani mayaya (18.61)

ishvarah : God | sarva-bhutanam : all living beings | hrit-deshe : at the spot of the heart | arjuna : O Arjuna | tishthati : resides | bhramayan : revolving/whirling around | sarva-bhutani : all living beings | yantra-arudhani : riding a machine | maya : maya/illusion

O Arjuna! God resides in the hearts of all living beings. It is Maya (illusion) that makes all beings whirl around as if riding a machine.

(62)
तमेव शरणं गच्छ सर्वभावेन भारत।
तत्प्रसादात्परां शान्तिं स्थानं प्राप्स्यसि शाश्वतम्।।18.62।।
tam eva sharanam gachchha sarva-bhavena bharata
tat-prasadat param shantim sthanam prapsyasi shashvatam (18.62)

tam : Him | eva : verily | sharanam gachchha : seek refuge/surrender | sarva-bhavena : in every sense | bharata : O descendant of Bharata | tat-prasadat : by his divine grace | param : supreme | shantim-sthanam : abode of peace | prapsyasi : thou shall reach | shashvatam : eternal

O descendant of king Bharata, Arjuna! Fully surrender to the Supreme in every sense. By His divine grace, thou shall reach the eternal abode of peace.

(63)
इति ते ज्ञानमाख्यातं गुह्याद्गुह्यतरं मया।
विमृश्यैतदशेषेण यथेच्छसि तथा कुरु।।18.63।।
iti te jnanam akhyatam guhyad guhyataram maya
vimrishyaitad asheshena yathechchhasi tatha kuru (18.63)

iti : thus | te : to you | jnanam : knowledge | akhyatam : described | guhyat : secret | guhya-taram : most secret | maya : by me | vimrishya : deliberate | etat : on this | asheshena : fully | yatha : as | ichchhasi : you wish | tatha : that | kuru : do

Thus, some of the secret and the most secret knowledge has been described to you by me (Lord Krishna). Deliberate on this fully and then do as you wish.

(64)

सर्वगुह्यतमं भूयः शृणु मे परमं वचः।
इष्टोऽसि मे दृढमिति ततो वक्ष्यामि ते हितम्॥18.64॥

sarva-guhyatamam bhuyah shrinu me paramam vachah
ishto 'si me dridham iti tato vakshyami te hitam (18.64)

sarva-guhya-tamam : the most secret of all | bhuyah : again | shrinu : listen | me : from me | paramam : supreme | vachah : words | ishta : dear | asi : you are | me : to me | dridham : very much | iti : thus | tata : therefore | vakshyami : saying | te : your | hitam : interest

Again, listen from me my supreme word which is the most secret of all. You are very much dear to me, therefore, I am saying this in your interest.

(65)

मन्मना भव मद्भक्तो मद्याजी मां नमस्कुरु।
मामेवैष्यसि सत्यं ते प्रतिजाने प्रियोऽसि मे॥18.65॥

man-mana bhava mad-bhakto mad-yaji mam namaskuru
mam evaishyasi satyam te pratijane priyo 'si me (18.65)

mat-mana : with mind full of my thoughts | bhava : become/be | mat-bhakta : my devotee | mat-yaji : my worshipper | mam : to me | namaskuru : offer respects/bow down | mam : to me | eva : only | eshyasi : you will reach | satyam : truly | te : to you | pratijane : I pledge | priya : dear | asi : thou art | me : to me

All the time thinking of me, be my devotee, my worshiper, bow down only to me, I promise you will reach me because you are dear to me.

(66)

सर्वधर्मान्परित्यज्य मामेकं शरणं व्रज।
अहं त्वां सर्वपापेभ्यो मोक्षयिष्यामि मा शुचः॥18.66॥

sarva-dharman parityajya mam ekam sharanam vraja
aham tvam sarva-papebhyo mokshayishyami ma shuchah (18.66)

sarva : all | dharman : doctrinaire actions/orders of righteous action/charters of duties/forms of rites and duties | parityajya : abandon | mam : to me | ekam : the One | sharanam : surrender/take refuge | vraja : go/come | aham : I | tvam : you | sarva : all | papebhya : from all sins | mokshayishyami : will liberate | ma : do not | shuchah : worry/grieve

Abandon all the different dharmas (righteous action orders), take refuge in me, the One. I will liberate you from all sins. Do not worry.

(67)

इदं ते नातपस्काय नाभक्ताय कदाचन।
न चाशुश्रूषवे वाच्यं न च मां योऽभ्यसूयति।।18.67।।

*idam te natapaskaya nabhaktaya kadachana
na chashushrushave vachyam na cha mam yo 'bhyasuyati (18.67)*

idam : this (knowledge given by Lord Krishna) | te : you | na : never | atapaskaya : one who is not used to austerity | na : nor | abhaktaya : non-devotee | kadachana : at any time | na : never | cha : and | ashushrushave : one who is not willing to listen | vachyam : should speak | na : not | cha : also | mam : of me | ya : who | abhyasuyati : one who is envious

This (knowledge being given to Arjuna) should never be spoken to anyone who is not used to austerity nor at anytime to one who is not a devotee, also not to anyone who is not willing to listen or to one who is envious of me.

(68)

य इमं परमं गुह्यं मद्भक्तेष्वभिधास्यति।
भक्तिं मयि परां कृत्वा मामेवैष्यत्यसंशयः।।18.68।।

*ya idam paramam guhyam mad-bhakteshv abhidhasyati
bhaktim mayi param kritva mam evaishyaty asanshayah (18.68)*

ya : who | idam : this | paramam : highly | guhyam : secret | mat : my | bhakteshu : devotees | abhidhasyati : explains | bhaktim : devotion | mayi : unto me | param : supreme | kritva : doing | mam : to me | eva : verily | eshyati : comes | asanshayah : undoubtedly

One who, with supreme devotion unto me, explains this highly secret knowledge to my devotees, undoubtedly comes to me.

(69)
न च तस्मान्मनुष्येषु कश्चिन्मे प्रियकृत्तमः।
भविता न च मे तस्मादन्यः प्रियतरो भुवि।।18.69।।

na cha tasman manushyeshu kashchin me priya-krittamah
bhavita na cha me tasmad anyah priyataro bhuvi (18.69)

na : no | cha : and | tasmat : than him | manushyeshu : among mankind | kashchit : anyone | me : to me | priya-krit-tamah : more dear | bhavita : will be | na : nor | cha : and | me : to me | tasmat : than him | anyah : any other | priya-tara : dearer | bhuvi : in this world

And, there is no one among mankind other than him who is more dear to me nor will there ever be in this world any other dearer to me than him.

(70)
अध्येष्यते च य इमं धर्म्यं संवादमावयोः।
ज्ञानयज्ञेन तेनाहमिष्टः स्यामिति मे मतिः।।18.70।।

adhyeshyate cha ya imam dharmyam samvadam avayoh
jnana-yajnena tenaham ishtah syam iti me matih (18.70)

adhyeshyate : will study | cha : and | ya : who | imam : this | dharmyam : pious/sacred | samvadam : dialogue | avayh : ours | jnana-yajnena : by yajna (sacrifice) of knowledge | tena : by him | aham : I | ishtah : worshipped | syam : shall be | iti : this/such | me : my | matih : opinion/belief

And, one who will study this pious dialogue between us will have worshipped me by yajna (sacrificial fire) of knowledge. Such is my belief.

(71)

श्रद्धावाननसूयश्च शृणुयादपि यो नरः।
सोऽपि मुक्तः शुभाँल्लोकान्प्राप्नुयात्पुण्यकर्मणाम्।।18.71।।

shraddhavan anasuyash cha shrinuyad api yo narah
so 'pi muktah shubhanl lokan prapnuyat punya-karmanam (18.71)

shraddha-van : full of faith | anasuya : free from envy | cha : and | shrinuyat : will hear/listen | api : even | ya : who | narah : man | sa : he | api : also | muktah : liberated | shubhan : auspicious | lokan : planets/celestial worlds | prapnuyat : achieves | punya-karmanam : people of virtuous deeds

A man who listens to this (knowledge in the dialogue) full of faith and free from envy, even he also can be liberated and achieve (reach) the auspicious celestial worlds like the people of virtuous deeds.

(72)

कच्चिदेतच्छ्रुतं पार्थ त्वयैकाग्रेण चेतसा।
कच्चिदज्ञानसंमोहः प्रनष्टस्ते धनञ्जय।।18.72।।

kachchid etach chhrutam partha tvayaikagrena chetasa
kachchid ajnana-sammohah pranashtas te dhananjaya (18.72)

kachchhit : whether | etat : this | shrutam : heard | partha : O son of Pratha (Kunti), Arjuna | tvaya : by you | eka-agrena : with full attention | chetasa : by the mind | kachchhit : whether | ajnana : ignorance | sammohah : delusion | pranashtah : destroyed | te : by you | dhananjaya : O victor of wealth, Arjuna

O son of Pratha (Kunti), Arjuna! Whether this has been heard by you with a fully attentive mind? Whether the ignorance and illusion have been destroyed by you, O victor of wealth, Arjuna!

Moksha-Sanyasa Yoga

(73)

अर्जुन उवाच
नष्टो मोहः स्मृतिर्लब्धा त्वत्प्रसादान्मयाच्युत।
स्थितोऽस्मि गतसन्देहः करिष्ये वचनं तव।।18.73।।

arjuna uvacha
nashto mohah smritir labdha tvat-prasadan mayachyuta
sthito 'smi gata-sandehah karishye vachanam tava (18.73)

arjuna : Arjuna | uvacha : said | nashta : destroyed | mohah : delusion | smriti : memory | labdha : got back | tvat-prasadat : by your mercy | maya : by me | achyuta : O infallible, Lord Krishna | sthita : stable | asmi : I am | gata-sandehah : with doubts gone | karishye : I shall do | vachanam : words | tava : your

Arjuna said: O infallible one, Lord Krishna! My delusion is destroyed and I have got my memory back by your mercy. I am now stable and with all doubts gone, I shall do as per your words.

(74)

सञ्जय उवाच
इत्यहं वासुदेवस्य पार्थस्य च महात्मनः।
संवादमिममश्रौषमद्भुतं रोमहर्षणम्।।18.74।।

sanjaya uvacha
ity aham vasudevasya parthasya cha mahatmanah
samvadam imam ashrausham adbhutam roma-harshanam (18.74)

sanjaya uvacha : Sanjaya said | iti : thus | aham : I | vasudevasya : of Lord Krishna | parthasya : of Partha (Arjuna) | cha : and | maha-atmanah : of the high soul | samvadam : dialogue | imam : this | ashrausham : have heard | adbhutam : wonderful | roma-harshanam : making the hair stand on end

Sanjaya said: Thus, I have heard this wonderful dialogue between the two high souls - Lord Krishna and Arjuna - making my hair stand on end.

(75)

व्यासप्रसादाच्छ्रुतवानेतद्गुह्यमहं परम्।
योगं योगेश्वरात्कृष्णात्साक्षात्कथयतः स्वयम्।।18.75।।

vyasa-prasadach chhrutavan etad guhyam aham param
yogam yogeshvarat krishnat sakshat kathayatah svayam (18.75)

vyasa-prasadat : through the grace of Vyasa | shrutavan : have heard | etat : this | guhyam : secret | aham : I | param : supreme | yogam : yoga | yoga-ishvara : master of yoga | krishnat : from Lord Krishna | sakshat : directly | kathayatah : describing it | svayam : himself

Through the grace of Vyasa, I have heard this supremely secret yoga with Lord Krishna - the master of yoga - himself describing it directly.

(76)

राजन्संस्मृत्य संस्मृत्य संवादमिममद्भुतम्।
केशवार्जुनयोः पुण्यं हृष्यामि च मुहुर्मुहुः।।18.76।।

rajan sansmritya sansmritya samvadam imam adbhutam
keshavarjunayoh punyam hrishyami cha muhur muhuh (18.76)

rajan : O King | sansmritya : recalling | sansmritya : recalling | samvadam : the dialogue | imam : this | adbhutam : wonderful | keshava : of Lord Krishna | arjunayoh : and Arjuna | punyam : holy | hrishyami : I am happy | cha : also | muhu muhuh : again and again

O King (Dhritarashtra)! Recalling and re-calling this wonderful and holy dialogue between Lord Krishna and Arjuna, I am happy again and again.

(77)

तच्च संस्मृत्य संस्मृत्य रूपमत्यद्भुतं हरेः।
विस्मयो मे महान् राजन्हृष्यामि च पुनः पुनः।।18.77।।

tach cha sansmritya sansmritya rupam aty-adbhutam hareh
vismayo ye mahan rajan hrishyami cha punah punah (18.77)

tat : that | cha : and | sansmritya : recalling | sansmritya : recalling | rupam : form | ati : extremely | adbhutam : wonderful | hareh : of Lord Krishna | vismaya : wonder | me : my | mahan : great | rajan : O King | hrishyami : I experience happiness | cha : also | punah punah : again and again

And, O King! As I recall and re-call the extremely wonderful form of Lord Krishna, my wonder is great, and I also experience happiness again and again.

(78)
यत्र योगेश्वरः कृष्णो यत्र पार्थो धनुर्धरः।
तत्र श्रीर्विजयो भूतिर्ध्रुवा नीतिर्मतिर्मम।।18.78।।

yatra yogeshvarah krishno yatra partho dhanur-dharah
tatra shrir vijayo bhutir dhruva nitir matir mama (18.78)

yatra : where | yoga-ishvara : the master of yoga | krishna : Lord Krishna | yatra : where | partha : son of Pratha (Kunti), Arjuna | dhanu-dharah : the holder of bow and arrow | tatra : there | shri : prosperity | vijaya : victory | bhuti : happiness | dhruva : firm | niti : policy | mati : conviction | mama : my

It is my conviction that where there is the master of yoga, Lord Krishna and the son of Pratha (Kunti), the holder of bow and arrow, Arjuna, there (there is surety of) prosperity, victory, happiness and firmness of policy.

Thus ends the Eighteenth Canto titled 'Yoga of Salvation-Renunciation'.